Black
Politics
in New Deal
Atlanta

The John Hope Franklin Series in
African American History and Culture

Waldo E. Martin Jr. and Patricia Sullivan, editors

Black Politics

in New Deal Atlanta

Karen Ferguson

The University of
North Carolina Press
Chapel Hill & London

© 2002 The University of
North Carolina Press
All rights reserved

Designed by Jacquline Johnson
Set in Charter
by Tseng Information Systems, Inc.

Manufactured in the United States
of America

The paper in this book meets the guidelines
for permanence and durability of the
Committee on Production Guidelines for
Book Longevity of the Council on Library
Resources.

This volume was published with the
generous assistance of the University
Publications Committee of Simon Fraser
University.

Chapter 9 was previously published as "The
Politics of Exclusion: Wartime Industrializa-
tion, Civil Rights Mobilization, and Black
Politics in Atlanta, Georgia, 1942–1946," in
*The Second Wave: Southern Industrialization
from the 1940s to the 1970s*, edited by Philip
Scranton (Athens: University of Georgia
Press, 2001), 43–80; reprinted with
permission.

Library of Congress Cataloging-in-
Publication Data
Ferguson, Karen (Karen Jane)
Black politics in New Deal Atlanta /
Karen Ferguson.
p. cm.—(The John Hope Franklin series
in African American history and culture)
Includes bibliographical references and
index.
ISBN 0-8078-2701-0 (alk. paper)—
ISBN 0-8078-5370-4 (pbk.: alk. paper)
1. African Americans—Georgia—Atlanta—
Politics and government—20th century.
2. African Americans—Georgia—Atlanta—
Social conditions—20th century.
3. African American social reformers—
Georgia—Atlanta—History—20th century.
4. Elite (Social sciences)—Georgia—
Atlanta—History—20th century.
5. Atlanta (Ga.)—Politics and
government—20th century.   6. Atlanta
(Ga.)—Social conditions—20th century.
7. Atlanta (Ga.)—Race relations.   8. New
Deal, 1933–1939—Georgia—Atlanta.
I. Title.   II. Series.
F294.A89 N438   2002
975.8′23100496073—dc21   2001059836

cloth   06 05 04 03 02   5 4 3 2 1
paper   06 05 04 03 02   5 4 3 2 1

For my parents,
Joan and David Ferguson,
and my sister,
Sandra Ferguson,
with love

Contents

Part IV Wartime Atlanta and the Struggle for Inclusion

Maps and Illustrations

Acknowledgments

Writing these acknowledgments and realizing my accumulated debts have been humbling experiences for someone whose self-identity has been, until now, I know, embarrassingly close to the myth of the self-made man or woman. I have benefited enormously from the generosity of family, friends, teachers, and institutions.

Most immediate to this project, I owe a great deal to the expertise and help of the archivists and librarians with whom I spent my days during a very happy year of research in Atlanta. I wish to thank the staff at the Special Collections departments of Clark-Atlanta and Emory Universities, the Atlanta History Center, the Auburn Avenue Research Library, the Georgia Department of Archives and History, and the National Archives Regional Office in East Point, Georgia. Outside of Atlanta, I am particularly appreciative of the extremely knowledgeable staff at the Roosevelt Library in Hyde Park, New York, whose expert navigation of its voluminous holdings led to a very productive research trip.

I also owe a great deal to those who supported me financially throughout graduate school. The history department of Duke University granted me a Sydnor Doctoral Fellowship for my first year of graduate school and the Richard Watson Instructorship for my last. In the interim, I received a Social Sciences and Humanities Research Council of Canada doctoral fellowship, which allowed me, among other benefits, to live for that year in Atlanta. A Franklin and Eleanor Roosevelt Institute Research Grant funded my visit to the Roosevelt Library. A postdoctoral fellowship at the sorely missed Frederick Douglass Institute for African and African American Studies at the University of Rochester gave me the opportunity to reconceptualize my doctoral dissertation and to work on turning it into a book. Finally, my parents provided emergency grants at several key junctures throughout my education without once asking me when I was going to get a real job.

I have been exceptionally lucky to encounter teachers throughout my schooling who have guided and inspired me. I was introduced to academic history by two extraordinary high school teachers, Helen Bell and Patricia Hall, who whetted my appetite for primary research and sharpened my critical thinking. They prepared me exceptionally well for honors history at McGill University, where John Herd Thompson's example and encouragement made me realize a career in history was both desirable and possible.

This book began as a dissertation at Duke University. There I lived and breathed African American history, thanks to a remarkable group of scholars and students. Foremost I wish thank two very different mentors, both models of intellectual generosity. First, I express my debt to my adviser, Raymond Gavins, a master graduate teacher who is a legend among a generation of Duke-trained African Americanists in awe of his quiet authority and encyclopedic knowledge. He provided me with a rock-solid foundation in African American history and then demonstrated tremendous discretion in supervising my project; always there to offer superb advice and support when I needed it, Ray showed extraordinary restraint in allowing me to find my own way. Second, I wish to thank Peter Wood, whose infinite intellectual curiosity, confidence, and charisma always inspired me and whose writing and teaching have greatly influenced my own. At Duke, I also treasure my experience as a field interviewer for the Center for Documentary Studies' "Behind the Veil: Documenting African American Life in the Jim Crow South" project. Thanks largely to the support of the project's principal investigators, William Chafe, Raymond Gavins, and Robert Korstad, and to the candor of the sixty remarkable women and men who spoke with me for the project, this was one of the seminal experiences of my life and the crucible of the central questions that inform this work. Equally important to my success were my fellow graduate students, especially Jonathan Abels, Alexander Byrd, Kirsten Delegard, Paul Husbands, Danna Kostroun, Deborah Montgomerie, Evelyn Sterne, and Anne Valk. I owe a great deal to Claudio Saunt, who helped me make it through graduate school through his love, example of perseverance, and intellectual companionship.

After graduate school, I was extremely fortunate to be hired by the history department of Simon Fraser University, where faculty research is encouraged and supported (in my case by a grant from University Publications Grants). In the history department I have been delighted and stimulated by my colleagues since the day of my interview, when chair Richard Boyer engaged me in an hour-long conversation about W. E. B. Du Bois's *Black Reconstruction* instead of filling me in on faculty benefits. William Cleveland, Michael Fellman, and Mary Lynn Stewart offered invaluable advice about the publishing process. My predecessor Don Kirschner's hard questions forced me to broaden my perspective and think more carefully about the national context of this study. Tina Loo offered a model of conceptual rigor, cheerful professionalism, and diligence that I have worked to adopt as my own. Tina, along with Paige Raibmon, Lawrin Armstrong, Chris Dummitt, Mark Leier, Michael Prokopow, and Leo Shin, read parts of this manuscript and helped me to polish it for final submission. I also owe a debt to my students of African American history, whose incredible engagement reminds me every day about the importance of this field to understanding American society.

Outside of my home institutions, many other scholars have contributed to this work. Sarah Judson has been my sounding board on all matters related to Atlanta history since we first met in the Clark-Atlanta University archives, and I look forward to reading her forthcoming book. As I worked on this manuscript, I benefited greatly from participating in two small conferences. The Black History Workshop at the University of Houston offered an extraordinary opportunity to share research and develop new ideas with junior and senior scholars in an extremely supportive and productive setting. I wish particularly to thank organizers Richard Blackett and Linda Reed and participants Alison Dorsey and Beth Bates. At the Georgia Institute of Technology, "The Second Wave: Southern Industrialization after World War II" conference proved an equally valuable experience and introduced me to Merl Reed, whose commentary on my paper helped me to refine my chapter on the Second World War, and Philip Scranton, whose extraordinary editing of the volume of essays that emerged from this conference greatly improved my writing. I also wish to thank participants and audience members in the sessions at which I presented my work at the North American Labor History conference, the Organization of American History conference, and the Southern Historical Association conference. Patricia Sullivan and the other, anonymous reader of this manuscript pushed me to refine my argument and to place this study in a broader context, both of which have resulted in a subtler, and more sophisticated and relevant, work. Despite the enormous contribution of all of these scholars, I remain responsible for any errors or omissions that remain.

My experience with the University of North Carolina Press has been felicitous from the beginning. I wish to thank Lewis Bateman for encouraging this project and his successor, Charles Grench, for shepherding my manuscript attentively and offering such savvy advice. Thanks also to Ruth Homrighaus for all of her patience and help and for answering all of my frantic emails so promptly. Suzanne Comer Bell copyedited the manuscript with meticulous care. I never expected the publication process to be as rewarding as it has proven to be.

Friends sustained me throughout the writing of this book. I wish particularly to thank my Vancouver circle, who have opened my world in so many ways. Native Vancouverites Paulina Chow, Susan Nance, and Paige Raibmon have constantly amazed and motivated me with their cultural sophistication, physical and emotional daring, and intense relationship with British Columbia's awesome mountainous terrain. Tina Loo and Meg Stanley have shown me, at last, how to play well with others. Jane Power and Jack O'Dell's extraordinary example and gentle encouragement have inspired me to edge toward political engagement and activism, despite my innate caution and cynicism. Chris Dummitt has guided me on my search for the middle way. Most important, Debby Meyer has shown me how close and supportive friendship can be.

My greatest debt is to my family. My parents, Joan and David Ferguson, have given me the priceless gift of unconditional love. I devote myself to integrating in my own life the yin and yang of my mother's loving compassion and my father's equally loving pragmatism. My sister Sandra has been a constant support and inspiration and has kept me laughing all the way. I dedicate this book to the three of you.

Abbreviations

ADW	*Atlanta Daily World*
AFL	American Federation of Labor
AFT	Atlanta Federation of Trades
ASSW	Atlanta (later Atlanta University) School of Social Work
ATA	Atlanta Tuberculosis Association
AU	Atlanta University
AUL	Atlanta Urban League
BTWHS	Booker T. Washington High School
CDT	Council of Defense Training
CIC	Commission on Interracial Cooperation
CIO	Congress of Industrial Organizations
CP	Communist Party
CWA	Civil Works Administration
FEPC	Fair Employment Practices Committee/Commission
FERA	Federal Emergency Relief Administration
FOL	Future Outlook League
GRA	Georgia Relief Administration
GRC	Georgia Relief Commission
ILD	International Labor Defense
NAACP	National Association for the Advancement of Colored People
NPHC	National Public Housing Conference
NRA	National Recovery Administration
NU	Neighborhood Union
NUL	National Urban League
NYA	National Youth Administration
PWA	Public Works Administration
RFC	Reconstruction Finance Corporation
SP	Socialist Party of America
TIC	To Improve Conditions
USES	United States Employment Service
USHA	United States Housing Authority

WLB	War Labor Board
WMC	War Manpower Commission
WPA	Works Progress Administration
YMCA	Young Men's Christian Association
YWCA	Young Women's Christian Association

Introduction

Today it makes little difference to Atlanta, to the South, what the Negro thinks or dreams or wills. In the soul-life of the land he is today, and naturally will long remain, unthought of, half forgotten; and yet when he does come to think and will and do for himself—and let no man dream that day will never come—then the part he plays will not be one of sudden learning, but words and thoughts he has been taught to lisp in his race-childhood. Today the ferment of his striving toward self-realization is to the strife of the white world like a wheel within a wheel: beyond the Veil are smaller but like problems of ideals, of leaders and the led, of serfdom, of poverty, of order and subordination, and, through all, the veil of race. Few know of these problems, few who know notice them; and yet there they are, awaiting student, artist, and seer—a field for somebody sometime to discover.
—W. E. B. Du Bois, The Souls of Black Folk

This book is about the fulfillment of Du Bois's prophecy. It is a study of a group of black Atlantans and their struggle to lift the veil of racial subordination and to move the city's African American community from the margins to the center of civic life. It is also an investigation of how that struggle and its achievements were inexorably shaped by the parallel society that Jim Crow forced black Atlantans to build behind the veil. For, while black Atlantans were bound together by their shared experience of race in a society that segregated and oppressed them according to their ancestry, within the inner wheel of the black community their lives were as various as white Atlantans', whose color united them in white supremacy. Given their diversity, African Americans in the city chose a variety of often conflicting paths to release themselves from the subjugation of Jim Crow. Struggles over the legitimacy and efficacy of these manifold strategies consumed the internal politics of the black community during the Jim Crow era. The resolution of these conflicts would help define the contours of the postwar black freedom struggle, its strategies and objectives, and its achievements. It would also set the stage for the widening gulf between those African Americans who have been able to take advantage of positive recognition from the state since the New Deal and those consigned to remain at the margins of civil society.

It was with a question about the origins of this gulf, so visible and remarked upon today, that I began this study. Why was it, I pondered, that some African Americans had done so well despite the continuing inequalities they and other black people faced in the United States, while others had been left behind, equally marginal in American society as they had been before civil rights achievements and Supreme Court victories? In order to answer this question, I took my cue from Du Bois, both by examining the internal dynamics of the "wheel within the wheel" of the black community and by studying Atlanta. As it was for Du Bois, Atlanta continues to be a bellwether. Even more a black middle-class mecca than at the turn of the last century, "Hotlanta" today is a national center of African American education, culture, and politics. It has been ruled by a black mayor since the election of Maynard Jackson in 1973, and since 1970 its population has been majority black. Nevertheless, it continues to be home to some of the poorest African American urban neighborhoods in the United States.

What I found as I began to seek to resolve this paradox was that the New Deal marked a crucial era by favoring the members and program of a group of black reformers who aimed to incorporate African Americans fully in American society through the vast social reordering promised by the Roosevelt administration. Professionally trained as social workers, sociologists, teachers, economists, and lawyers, and most of them under forty-five years of age, this group of "social engineers,"[1] as some of them described themselves, became a crucial element in the New Deal's progressive left wing, which sought to overturn the South's extreme racial and class exploitation. While members of the Washington, D.C., "black cabinet" were the best known of this group, in states and cities across the region, African American bureaucrats and activists worked on the ground to achieve this aim.[2]

No other city matched Atlanta, however, home to the South's largest population of college-educated African Americans and a crucial birthplace of the reform vision that drove the new generation of black elites. The city's numerous black postsecondary institutions, led by Atlanta University (AU), provided a base that acted as a nationwide magnet for social workers and social scientists. Students and graduates of W. E. B. Du Bois's department of sociology at AU and Forrester B. Washington's respected Atlanta School of Social Work (ASSW), members of Lugenia Burns Hope's settlement-house agency, the Neighborhood Union (NU), and black employees and volunteers of a full complement of black- and white-run social-work agencies, formed an unusually large and influential reform group unified in its devotion to uplifting black Atlantans.

Atlanta's environment of Jim Crow white supremacy inextricably shaped this group's perspective and program. In the year of Roosevelt's election, which marks the beginning of this study, black Atlantans were almost entirely excluded from public life. This exclusion was the product of a decades-long effort in Atlanta, in Georgia, in the South, and in the nation to oppress and marginalize black citizens by any means necessary. During this post-Reconstruction period, aptly called the "nadir" by one-time Atlanta University historian Rayford Logan, whites sought to circumscribe the meaning of black freedom to the narrowest of possible definitions. Officials disfranchised black Atlantans through the white primary and poll tax and separated them from whites through local statute and U.S. Supreme Court decree. This legal subjugation was reinforced by custom and by extralegal means. Racial "tradition" compelled social, economic, and residential segregation. White vigilantes regularly and effectively sought to maintain the racial order through antiblack intimidation and mob violence. As a result of these actions, black Atlantans lived beyond the pale of civil society. African Americans were largely unacknowledged except punitively by public officials who denied their citizenship and their contribution to city life.[3]

Elite black reformers shared this exclusion with all other African Americans during this period. Despite their superior schooling and credentials, white society lumped them with all other black people, meaning that their lives were circumscribed to the inner wheel of the black community, where they were forced to live, work, and conduct virtually all of their affairs among the penurious, unschooled, and overworked of their race. This shared exclusion was the basis of black reformers' efforts on the black community's behalf. Whether they liked it or not, they knew that their fate was intertwined with the majority of African Americans, and consequently, as one famous black reform slogan put it, they would have to lift if they wished to climb. Hence, for years before the New Deal, these leaders had worked to force local officials to acknowledge the citizenship of black Atlantans and to incorporate the black community into city affairs. Their frustrating, decades-long struggle for parks and schools, sewers and electricity for black neighborhoods, and black police and higher teachers' salaries, as well as efforts to prepare black Atlantans to assume full citizenship, attested to their confidence that the struggle would someday result in African Americans taking their rightful place at the center of civic life.[4]

However beneficial these efforts were, they were not democratic. Beginning with Jim Crow's effective disfranchisement of African Americans at the turn of the century, black politics were limited to brokerage by a tiny group of literate spokespeople who negotiated on behalf of the black community with white elites. This group's stranglehold on influence with the outer wheel meant that its particular ideology and program for liberation began to represent all African Americans to the outer wheel with little or no accountability to the rest of the black community and with disregard to or dismissal of other strategies for freedom.[5]

Atlanta is an ideal site to examine this elite's ideology and program, for in important ways the city was a well-spring for the "talented tenth." In fact, Atlanta was the birthplace of the term, coined by white Baptist educator Henry T. Morehouse in 1896 during the depths of the nadir. He believed that the masses of African Americans could best be controlled by liberally educated black "race managers" who would form a buffer between non-elite blacks and the white community. Eventually the school he helped found to achieve this aim, Atlanta Baptist College, would be renamed after him. Du Bois, who went on to found the NAACP, then subverted the accommodationism implied in Morehouse's meaning to refer to the group he believed would lead African Americans to full American citizenship through militant protest.[6]

The contradictions of these two definitions, and the racial custodianship essential to both, had enormous implications for black reform efforts in the Jim Crow period. The ambiguity of black reformers' self-defined position as both controllers and liberators was encapsulated in uplift ideology, the most pervasive elite social philosophy of the first half of the twentieth century. As Jim Crow shut African Americans out of the political, economic, and social life of the outer wheel, black reformers in Atlanta sought to prove the citizenship of black people through the only expression available to them—their behavior. By demonstrating that African Americans lived by and aspired to the same moral and behavioral codes as the white middle class, black reformers sought to show that black Atlantans were deserving of full citizenship.

This outward-looking behavioral code evolved into what Evelyn Brooks Higginbotham has called the "politics of respectability." By teaching African Americans to live lives of bourgeois respectability, black reformers sought to find "common ground on which to live as Americans with Americans of other racial and ethnic backgrounds." Through these shared moral and behavioral standards, black reformers fought to be seen as "both black and American," working against white rhetoric which would "deny this possibility by isolating the 'Negro's place' within physical and symbolic spaces of inferiority."[7] If African Americans were respectable in every way, they could refute the racist stereotypes that whites used to justify black subordination. The rhetoric of respectability, then, was a liberationist tactic to demonstrate African Americans' citizenship, deny white justifications for their imposed marginality, and move toward full inclusion in public life.

Yet by defining black citizenship in terms of behavior and morality, the politics of respectability was decidedly limited as an ideology of racial liberation. Most obvious, it excluded the legions of African Americans who did not and could not conform to the gender roles, public behavior, and economic activity deemed legitimate by bourgeois America but which the forces of Jim Crow white supremacy sought to prevent black people from achieving.

However, instead of simply excluding this group from their purview, black proponents of respectability asserted their citizenship in opposition to and at the expense of the black "masses," thus marginalizing the "unrespectable" even further. Identifying themselves as bourgeois missionaries of respectability, black elites claimed moral superiority and sought recognition of their citizenship by placing themselves above and as the natural leaders of what they considered the uncivilized and undeveloped majority of African Americans. Further, their efforts to uplift and liberate other black people would depend on their followers' adopting respectable behavior as a prerequisite for full citizenship.[8]

As a flowering of recent scholarship has shown us, the rhetoric of respectability infused the language of elite black reformers of every stripe during the first decades of the twentieth century. Its ubiquity pointed to the hegemonic power of the racial ideologies undergirding Jim Crow. However, during the nadir of the early twentieth century, the focus of most respectability literature, this ideology had few implications. Marginalized politically, economically, and socially, black reformers lacked the resources and power that would allow them to pursue their ambitious agenda. They found it impossible to develop large or influential constituencies for their program among whites or the black people they intended to serve. Instead they found themselves trapped within the accommodation of race management. Nor would the forces of Jim Crow allow them to distance themselves physically or symbolically from the poor. Born of futility, uplift ideology reflected the marginality of all African Americans to the polity in the early part of the twentieth century.

Only with the recognition of African Americans by the state during the New Deal did blacks begin to escape this marginality and uplift ideology begin to have material implications for African Americans. Atlanta's black reform elite immediately recognized the New Deal's potential as a tool to escape its borderline position and to advance black citizenship. Hired into federal agencies as social workers, adult education teachers, and "Negro Division" directors, these black bureaucrats worked from within the New Deal's social work meritocracies, manipulating them as much as they could to advance their long-held goals for the black community. Thus black reformers were not simply recipients of federal programs; rather, they shaped federal activity to help bring some black Atlantans from the social, economic, and political margins in ways never intended or dreamt of by white New Deal administrators. To borrow from historian Lizabeth Cohen, they made their own New Deal.[9]

Atlanta's black reformers were in a particularly good position to take advantage of these opportunities. Dominated by university-trained professionals eligible for work in federal bureaucracies, this group's position within the black community and the city strengthened during the 1930s. In other places in the South and the nation where entrepreneurs and professionals like physicians and lawyers figured prominently, the black elite's influence declined due to economic hardship during the Depression. These groups also had fewer opportunities to use the New Deal than Atlanta's social workers, teachers, and economists. Further, in industrial cities nationwide, elite African Americans faced an insurgent working class that threatened their claims to race leadership. While Atlanta's black workers certainly were not quiescent and supported radical movements such as Communism, the vast majority lacked the mobilizing opportunities of industrial work. Hence, the black reform elite's vision and program was unusually dominant in Atlanta.[10]

The relative security of Atlanta's educated elite meant that they responded positively to a shift in strategy among national black leaders away from Morehouse's accommodationism toward Du Bois's militance. Responding to working-class demands and the New Deal's interest-group politics, a new generation of reformers called for a program of assertive and independent action on the part of the black community, rejecting the conciliatory tactics of an earlier generation. This important turn was reflected in the pages of the NAACP's mouthpiece, *The Crisis*, the National Urban League's *Opportunity*, and much of the black press. As the NUL's Lester Granger put it, although the black intellectual class had lost touch with working-class issues and concerns, in the "state of confused despair and bitter disillusionment" that characterized the Depression, "lay the seeds of a new racial attitude and leadership."[11] George Streator, W. E. B. Du Bois's 1930s assistant, characterized this new spirit as one attuned to the concerns of the majority of black Americans and based on "mass initiative, mass organization, and mass pressure," including "more democracy, more local control, and wider participation by an ever-growing number of people in the affairs of any and every organization."[12] This strategy marked a sea change in elite reformers' perspective. Badly burned in the 1920s by coalition politics with whites, and suffering even greater exclusion from white-controlled society and economy during the privations of the Depression, many younger (and some older) black reformers turned inward in the 1930s, focusing on what Du Bois called the "internal self-organization"[13] of the black community. This strategy required educated black reformers to make common cause with all African Americans in order to achieve their citizenship aims. While they still would be engineered and led by the "talented tenth," the boycotts, protest meetings, civil court cases, and electoral strategies of this new program all relied upon mass support, both physical and financial.[14]

In Atlanta this new militancy was motivated largely by black reformers' hopes for the New Deal, best articulated by Du Bois. In his Depression-era articles and essays and in his 1935 masterwork on the subject, Du Bois hearkened back to the radical democratic experiment of Reconstruction, in which for the first and only time in the South, state power was subject to "wide democratic control" and exercised "for the benefit of the masses."[15] Du Bois saw the same potential in the New Deal, where federal programs fundamentally altered the function of the state in the South by expanding government's reach far beyond the protection of the interests of a tiny white elite to include the interests of the poorest southerners. Further, by recognizing the economic interests of the majority, the federal government demonstrated that in a truly representative democracy, political power would extend "over all manner of work and industry," thereby uplifting the "mudsills" on whose utter poverty and exploitation the region's economic system depended.[16] Thus, for Du Bois, racial uplift was only possible with a fundamental shift in the political and economic foundations of American society. This vision contrasted sharply with earlier black reformers who placed the burden of responsibility for racial uplift squarely on the shoulders of individual African Americans, rather than the polity. While Du Bois made moralistic statements about the lives and behavior of the masses of black people, he did not blame them for their condition; he condemned the political and economic system undergirding Jim Crow. For Du Bois, respectability and full citizenship could come to African Americans only with a second Reconstruction, in which the black "masses" were not only included as full participants in the polity but indeed were at its center. And while his vision still saw the black elite as guiding and directing the uplift that was to result, the main beneficiaries would be the poorest members of the black community, who had suffered the most from capitalist and racial exploitation. Thus, for Du Bois, the New Deal represented a fundamental democratizing shift in American society that would finally allow all African Americans to achieve racial uplift.

However great its promise, the New Deal was just as limited as the first Reconstruction in its definition of democracy and citizenship for African Americans. Black bureaucrats thus operated within a program that included African Americans and tried to ameliorate their condition but without effecting the fundamental social reordering that was required to recognize their citizenship fully. As George Lipsitz has pointed out, the New Deal represented the beginning of America's racialized social democracy through which powerful new forms of structural racial discrimination began to replace the overt segregation of the Jim Crow era. Atlanta, the city that was "too busy to hate," in the words of its long-time mayor William Hartsfield, was no exception.[17]

What this important history of racial exclusion and exploitation leaves out is the considerable support that even the most discriminatory federal programs, such as the slum-clearance and low-income-housing program, received from black reformers. In Atlanta, such support came from the fact that the New Deal permitted a group of black bureaucrats and lobbyists associated with AU unprecedented opportunities to influence and shape the African American community according to their uplift objectives. Their active participation in social welfare programs forces a reconsideration of the New Deal's impact on African Americans—one which takes into account black as well as white leaders' visions for African American urban communities, and black as well as white initiative in bringing those visions to fruition. More broadly, the black influence on Atlanta's New Deal refines our notions of America's social democracy and its beneficiaries. While the racialized exclusions and hierarchies of the welfare state undoubtedly continued and extended the marginalization of African Americans generally while elevating other ethnic groups to the privileges of "whiteness," it is also indisputable that beginning with the New Deal a tiny but growing minority of African Americans achieved upward mobility and fuller citizenship through federal initiatives. Exploring the varied consequences of the New Deal among black Americans is essential to a full understanding of the growing gulf *within* the African American community between haves and have-nots, which has grown progressively wider since the Second World War, and which complicates our understanding of the New Deal's "racial" impact.

One of the foundations of this division lay in the choices the New Deal's limits forced black reformers to make about the battles they would fight and the segments of the black community on whom they would focus their efforts for inclusion and citizenship. Given the black reform elite's dominance, it is not surprising that in Atlanta they chose to start their program from the high ground of the black-controlled campuses of Atlanta University and the city's four black colleges, where they felt safest. From there they worked their way down as far as they could, bringing many black Atlantans into their social and economic sphere but never reaching the majority living in the hollows and bottoms of Atlanta's hilly terrain. While this limitation was first a product of black reformers' circumscribed authority and resources, it was also a continuing legacy of uplift ideology. When they had the opportunity to determine the recipients of New Deal largesse, they did not choose the "mudsills" of the black working class but rather more prosperous elements who were most able to be respectable according to the reformers' vision. This triage had enormous implications in dividing the black community into those who conformed to the reformers' vision and thus benefited (and continued to benefit) from government programs and those who were left behind.

Uplift ideology continued to have legitimacy among black reformers because, despite appearances, they had not abandoned it. Historians have rightly noted a fundamental shift in black activism in the 1930s. Throughout the Depression and World War II, a younger generation of leaders urged a new model of inclusion and militancy even in elite-led organizations like the NAACP and NUL. This group asked educated African Americans to support the struggles of the "masses," reasoning that "since [the Negro's] is predominantly a race of workers, his interests are those of the working class."[18] Across the United States, local chapters of these organizations, including Atlanta's, became more assertive in their demands, shunning the accommodationist tactics of an older generation of leaders.

It is important, however, not to mistake this militancy for democracy; while this new generation sought to advocate for and mobilize black workers in its struggle for full citizenship, it also continued to presume that the educated would shape and lead this movement. For most of this group, "race determined class"[19] in relation to the "outer wheel" of white America, and thus educated African Americans would be the natural leaders of a united black community, all exploited, none exploiters. As Lester Granger put it, "Negroes are learning that we have common interests, not because our skins are tinged with the same dark hue, but because we are poor, exploited workers."[20] Thus even many spokespeople on the left continued to take it as a given that the learned elite would lead the black community, even in struggles unique to black workers, such as the fight for union representation. As socialist Bettie Parham wrote of the "Negro bourgeoisie's" need to support black workers' struggles: "The laissez faire attitude of the educated Negro toward the laborer can do no other than lead to racial deterioration. It is he who must teach the workers the best methods of handling their grievances and of organizing their unions."[21] In fact, black reformers' convictions as to their essential leadership role became even more powerful in the 1930s as they began to look to techniques of mass mobilization and group pressure to end Jim Crow.

Consequently, nationwide they responded with incredulity whenever their leadership was challenged, as it often was by black radicals during the 1930s. As W. E. B. Du Bois retorted in 1931 to Communist criticism of the "black bourgeoisie" and its supposed exploitation of the African American working class, the number of genuine black "capitalists" in the United States was infinitesimal, and in fact, he observed, "there is probably no group of 12 million persons in the modern world which exhibits smaller contrasts in personal income than the American Negro group." Furthermore, he wrote, "There is no group of leaders on earth who have so largely made common cause with the lowest of their race as educated American Negroes, and it is their foresight and sacrifice and theirs alone that has saved the American freedman from annihilation and degradation."[22] In other words, the new leadership of the 1930s made common cause with the masses with whom they shared a caste position imposed from the outer wheel. However, they continued to accept the social hierarchies of the inner wheel as natural, setting themselves apart as the group that would lead the race to full inclusion in American life. Their project as self-defined race leaders thus was not only to agitate for civil rights or economic opportunity, but also to continue to "lift" the majority of the black community to the perspective and behavior they considered necessary for inclusion and full citizenship. Therefore, while these leaders sought to democratize the South through mass action, theirs was not an egalitarian movement. They worked *for*, not *with*, black Atlantans.[23]

Black reformers' conflation of race and class and the persistence of uplift ideology meant that they saw individual gains for themselves, the natural leaders, as "race" victories that would eventually trickle down to all African Americans. Thus they provided rhetorical support for the 1930s workers' movement, and then reserved most of their energies for the Atlanta NAACP's campaign to equalize black teachers' salaries with white. For the reform elite, teachers were both oppressed workers and part of black Atlanta's educated leadership class, and thus the perfect group to support. On this basis they would also gauge the New Deal's recognition of African Americans on the basis of the number of white-collar and professional workers hired by the federal bureaucracy, rather than on the number of unemployed laborers or domestic workers employed by the WPA. Hiring black bureaucrats was more important to black reformers because, as federal welfare programs became more and more essential to their uplift program, so did their sense of their role as corporate representatives of the black community within the New Deal. The more of them hired into the New Deal bureaucracy the better. In other words, the formula had been significantly altered; in order to lift they had to climb—into government positions.

The black reform elite's dominance in Atlanta also had consequences for both those who joined its bandwagon and those who supported alternative strategies and freedom movements. Many black workers in Atlanta subscribed to the politics of respectability, signaling their frustration over, and protest against, the arbitrary constraints placed upon them in their quest for upward mobility. Federal initiatives like low-income housing or National Youth Administration scholarships, hallmarks of the New Deal's liberalism, tied these respectable Atlantans to the elite's uplift strategy when black bureaucrats rewarded them with the benefits of these programs. Building such a constituency was essential to black reformers' new mass strategy, and influence over New Deal largesse allowed them for the first time to demonstrate to black Atlantans the material benefits of their program and leadership. However, even if they wanted to, most of the poorest black Atlantans could not conform to an outward-looking bourgeois behavioral code. Their struggle for subsistence required a very different set of priorities and moral imperatives that diverged from those of the reform elite. Trapped in the most anachronistic and poorly paying work available, many domestic workers, laundresses, and unskilled laborers led lives that precluded participation in a struggle for inclusion. Rather than seeking recognition from an oppressive white society and state, these black Atlantans sought distance from them, looking inward to the black community for support or joining movements like the Communists' that sought to overturn or escape the prevailing order. In this conflict over strategy, the black reform elite's vision triumphed in important ways, a victory that would continue to reverberate in decades to come as America's black community was divided into those deemed deserving of the fruits of inclusion into the polity, including the enormous expansion of economic, educational, and political opportunities in the postwar decades, and those consigned to remain at the margins of civil society. Thus the most influential thinking among and about African Americans in the first half of the twentieth century had lasting material consequences in the second.

This book seeks to understand the implications of these crucial divisions within the black community during the New Deal era, as African Americans' inclusion in the polity began to impact the lives of all black Atlantans. The first six chapters trace the effect of the New Deal on the black reform elite and Atlanta's black community. After decades of nearly fruitless struggle for inclusion in civic life, the black reform elite's frustrations reached a pinnacle in the chaos of the early 1930s, when black suffering and white indifference exposed the depths of African American noncitizenship. Many black reformers joined the city's beleaguered black unemployed by refocusing their attentions inward toward the black community in this period, and some even chose to support the city's burgeoning Communist movement. The New Deal reversed this trend by recognizing African Americans as a vital constituency in its liberal-reformist crusade, and imposing a social-work meritocracy on the city's political culture. The black reform elite seized on this recognition and successfully inserted its members into the local administration of New Deal public welfare agencies. These reformer-bureaucrats used their new positions of authority within government as an opportunity to advance their citizenship goals for individual black Atlantans, and to build a constituency for their program through the power and resources they had garnered as New Deal insiders. Exercising their new muscle and responding to the evolving political climate in the city, they developed a strategy of interest-group politics, employing the collective power of their New Deal constituency to demonstrate to white officials their leadership of an organized and mobilized black community. By contrast, those black Atlantans whom the black reform elite could not or chose not to reach through their limited authority found themselves subject to white-controlled New Deal programs that sought to rationalize and entrench their Jim Crow caste position through the interventions of public relief and case work. For these black Atlantans the New Deal did not represent a welcome recognition of their citizenship, but rather unwanted attention by the state, which in some cases deepened their oppression.

The most dramatic example of this dynamic was in New Deal slum-clearance and public-housing efforts, the subject of chapters 7 and 8. In cities around the country, the New Deal housing program significantly and permanently altered residential and racial geography, ushering in the age of urban renewal. White officials interested in reshaping the city's racial landscape spearheaded this program in Atlanta with devastating consequences for many of the city's black neighborhoods. Despite these effects, black reformers participated willingly and actively in this program and had significant influence over the exact location of slum clearance in the black community, and the selection of tenants for the housing projects built to replace the "slums." As a result of the reformers' choices, the housing program uprooted thousands of black Atlantans from their homes and communities to be replaced in the projects by the "respectable" poor and middle class, desperate for, and deemed to be deserving of, modern, safe, and affordable federally funded housing. The reform elite embraced this unprecedented opportunity to participate in urban planning, with material and long-lasting implications for both those chosen to live in the first publicly legitimate black neighborhoods in the city, and those pushed farther to the margins by slum clearance. The ideological motivations that allowed black reformers' complicity in this racialized program highlighted the paradoxes and limits of their inclusion in Atlanta's New Deal order, and the divisions within the black community that called into question their claims of "race" leadership.

Chapter 9 examines the legacy of New Deal developments during wartime and the very beginnings of the postwar civil rights movement. By the beginning of the war, black reformers' experiences in building a constituency through New Deal programs and their struggles in local politics prompted them to imagine new, more democratic solutions to their struggles for full citizenship—solutions that required a mass constituency. The war's emancipatory possibilities also influenced this evolution. Positions in defense industries created a sizable autonomous and publicly visible African American industrial work force for the first time in Atlanta, free from the gross exploitation of traditional "Negro work," and ready to be mobilized for civil rights. The black reform elite, represented most prominently during the war by the ascendant Atlanta Urban League (AUL), recognized the potential of industrial employment, and sought to maximize black participation in war production. Its efforts made it the most important wartime broker between the black community and white officials, ultimately resulting in it becoming an essential partner in war manpower coordination in the city and giving it the power to choose those black workers who would receive the limited number of jobs available for black workers in defense plants.

The AUL's triage had enormous implications for the future of Atlanta's black community. Elitism and mistrust of the black working class continued to mark these reformers' vision of the path to full black citizenship, even as they broadened their outreach to the black community. The agency decided which black Atlantans deserved the best industrial positions on the basis of its leaders' conservative definition of black citizenship. These hand-picked workers became the critical core of postwar civil rights mobilization by the AUL, whose leaders from the beginning of the war had explicitly linked black incorporation into the South's modernizing society and economy to the attainment of civil rights. Those who were not chosen found themselves excluded from the upward mobility afforded by industrial employment and their concerns unrepresented by the emerging, narrowly defined movement for racial equality. The AUL's definition of black citizenship thus split Atlanta's black community for years to come into those who were determined to be deserving of the fruits of inclusion into the city's modernizing economy and polity and those who were consigned to remain at the margins of civic life.

As the epigraph from Du Bois suggests, the black reform elite merely represented one faction in Atlanta's African American community. But by breaking out beyond the veil and incorporating themselves within the polity of the "outer wheel" during the New Deal, black reformers bolstered their power and could impose their program for freedom on the rest of the black community. In Jim Crow Atlanta, they successfully represented themselves as "race" proxies to whites, the only legitimate representatives of the black community. The legacy of their triumphant incorporation continues to be felt today and is an important key to understanding the schisms that continue to split Atlanta's black community. This book traces the origins of this divide back to the Roosevelt era, when the politics of respectability began to have material consequences for black residents, as they were divided into those deserving and undeserving of full citizenship.

A note on terminology: Throughout this study, I refer to the "incorporative" strategies of black reformers and their goals for the full "incorporation" of the black community. I use this term to refer to the reform elite's belief that black Atlantans' full citizenship could be achieved only by their inclusion in every aspect of the public and economic life of the city. "Incorporation" is a better term for this goal than "integration" because black reformers neither worked for nor desired to meld into white society in the 1930s and early 1940s. For one, they knew that such a demand was anathema to white Atlantans. But more important, they knew the protective importance of black-controlled public and private institutions to Atlanta's African American community, especially as black Atlantans moved closer to their goal of full citizenship. The reform elite wanted to control how black Atlantans would finally be included in the public life of the city. The only way they could do that in the age of Jim Crow was through the parallel city behind the veil.

PART I

Life at
the
Margins

1

The Wheel within a Wheel

Black Atlanta and the Reform Elite

In 1933, at the very dawning of the New Deal, the Neighborhood Union (NU), black Atlanta's preeminent voluntary social-work agency, commemorated its twenty-fifth anniversary by looking back. Celebrating its founder, Lugenia Burns Hope, the NU produced a pageant highlighting the inspiration that led her to create the settlement-work organization. According to NU legend, in 1908 an invalid woman living on Atlanta's west side died needlessly after being neglected by her neighbors, who knew nothing of her or her illness. This woman lived in the shadow of Atlanta Baptist (later Morehouse) College, where Hope's husband, John, was then president. Hope, an experienced social worker who had trained at Hull House in Chicago and worked for years for the Young Women's Christian Association (YWCA), was appalled that this incident could take place in her neighborhood. Brooding, the pageant portrayed Hope looking down at the black neighborhoods that surrounded the hills of the campus, a broad cross-section of Atlanta's black community, including "large beautiful dwellings, humble cottages, rich and poor, learned and ignorant, block after block."[1] She wondered about these neighbors, asking, "How did they fare? Who suffered? What were their ambitions? What were their problems?"[2] From these questions a desire began to burn inside her "for a more neighborly understanding" in the black community, "to have the strong help hear the infirmities of the weak, to have the learned share their learning and culture in re-creating the environment of the unlearned, to have the rich share (at least in idea and ideals) their bounties with the poor."[3]

The NU's founding story perfectly evokes Du Bois's "wheel within a wheel," of a community united by the forces of segregation to which all its members were subjected, yet as socially, economically, and culturally diverse as the white city that confined black Atlanta from without. Hope's ability to see the full scope of the African American community from her lofty perch and her identification with all she observed attests to the common experiences of every African American in a Jim Crow city. However, her questions about the lives of her neighbors and the elitism of her reform vision suggest the social distances that needed to be breached in order to accomplish her vision of racial solidarity. Understanding Hope's perspective and black Atlanta's history in the quarter century leading up to the New Deal sets the stage for what would transpire in the decade to come.

The twenty-five years commemorated by the Neighborhood Union also represented the quarter century in which the Jim Crow system achieved its greatest institutionalization and stability in Atlanta. From the vicious riot of 1906, marking the triumph of white supremacy in the city, to the beginning of the New Deal, black Atlantans were trapped behind a white-imposed bulwark of segregation with few opportunities for escape. The "Gate City" that white boosters liked to promote as the South's most modern and progressive place, was also one of the region's most repressive cities for African Americans, whom whites managed to exclude from a burgeoning industrial economy and to consign to a paternalistic and exploitative order. In fact, as historian Tera Hunter has noted, "modernization and Jim Crow grew to maturity together" in Atlanta, where "each adoption of advanced technology or each articulation of platitudes of progress" strengthened a "commitment to keeping blacks subordinate and unequal."[4]

The Atlanta riot, a five-day orgy of white violence against the city's black community, marked Jim Crow's victory. Raised to fury by the gubernatorial campaigns of Hoke Smith and Clark Howell, both of whom raised the specter of "Negro domination" in their election speeches, white Atlantans sought to purge the city of black influence in a period when African American upward mobility, migration to the city, and potential political power threatened white supremacy. The targets of white violence during the riot pointed to these white fears. The assaults began on Decatur Street, the city's most infamous vice district, with the vigilantes in search of the black "rapists," whom Atlanta's pernicious yellow press and

Hoke Smith's campaign claimed roamed the city's streets seeking white victims. Then the mob moved the short distance to the central business district, where it first sought out prosperous black businesses catering to whites, destroying their property and attacking their employees, and then moved on indiscriminately to attack any African Americans they could find in the area, sometimes even dragging black passengers off of streetcars passing through. Finally the crowd moved into black neighborhoods, both poverty-stricken downtown neighborhoods and relatively prosperous enclaves such as Brownsville in south Atlanta, torching houses and vowing to "clean out the niggers."[5] At least twenty-five black Atlantans were killed in the riot, with hundreds seriously wounded or left homeless.[6]

The Atlanta riot attested to whites' determination to suppress or destroy any possibility of black equality with whites, whether "social" or economic, and to move African Americans once and for all beyond the pale of civic life, where white Atlantans believed they belonged. The riot was meant to show black residents that they had no claim on public space and no legitimate place in the city's economy except as the dependent employees of paternalistic and exploitative white employers. To entrench their position after the terror, white Atlantans enforced an increasingly rigid color line, threatening the resumption of violence against any African American who dared break it. This was the white-imposed order that bound together all black Atlantans on the eve of the New Deal.

By the early 1930s, Jim Crow's consolidation meant that black and white Atlantans lived more separately than ever before. Where the two groups had once lived in a checkerboard pattern throughout the city, now African Americans lived in solidly black enclaves behind a rigid color line. If these overcrowded black neighborhoods overflowed into white districts, racial violence always ensued, with residents defending the "whiteness" of their communities by attacking their new black neighbors or stoning the windows or dynamiting the porches of their homes. Where once the most prominent black-owned businesses catered to a white clientele in the city's central business district, now black entrepreneurs' only opportunities lay in serving the African American community. As this segregation suggests, African Americans were treated as unwelcome and temporary interlopers outside of their own neighborhoods. They could make no claim to the city's "white" public space.

The only truly legitimate place in the white city for black Atlantans was as workers under the protection and authority of a white employer. The root of black Atlantans' isolation from the social and political mainstream lay in their occupational and economic segregation. Like African

Americans around the country, black Atlantans faced extremely limited vocational opportunities. Outside of the black economy, they were only permitted to perform those jobs deemed "Negro work" by whites. The vast majority of these occupations were closely related to the work blacks had performed in slavery, and constituted the hardest, dirtiest, and most menial jobs. These occupations were so poorly paid that many families required more than one wage-earner to survive. Consequently, over 57 percent of black women and girls over the age of ten participated in the work force in Atlanta in 1930, almost twice the rate of white women.[7]

The occupational category that most exemplified "Negro work" was domestic and personal service. In 1930, 58 percent of all gainfully employed black Atlantans, and almost 90 percent of employed women served whites as maids, cooks, in-home and commercial laundry workers, janitors, bellmen, porters, and waiters. They worked in hotels, office buildings, railroad stations, commercial laundries, and in private homes. African Americans filled almost all service positions in the city. For example, of the 13,245 female house servants in Atlanta in 1930, only 265, or 2 percent, were white.[8]

While almost 80 percent of black women workers labored outside the commercial or industrial work place as domestic workers in private homes, only about 7 percent of black men did so. They had more choice when it came to their place of work, if not the kind of work they performed. Just fewer than three-quarters worked in manufacturing, in Atlanta's important transportation and communication industries, and in trade. Yet aside from constituting a significant minority of the total number of skilled construction workers, and a majority of tailors, locomotive firemen and mail carriers in the city, black men in these industries were consigned almost entirely to work as unskilled laborers. This labor category constituted the most physically demanding and dangerous work in the city, as well as the most insecure. Unlike black women, who could almost always find some kind of domestic work, black men often were part of the surplus industrial labor force, subject to frequent layoffs, and unable to find steady, let alone permanent, work.[9] (See Appendix, Table 2.)

Although Atlanta had a large population of high school or college-educated African Americans, this group was never considered for white-collar work in the white community. Similarly, black Atlantans were almost entirely excluded from any kind of modern mechanical work in the city's prosperous railroad yards, textile mills, and steel factories. Black men working in this sector were almost never permitted to operate machinery as operatives, machinists, or mechanics, work that was automatically defined as "white." The only skilled occupations that blacks were permitted to practice were the "trowel trades"—brickmasonry, plastering, painting, and carpentry—crafts with which African Americans had been associated historically and which did not involve mechanical work. Racial custom was entrenched into local labor relations by the politically powerful Atlanta Federation of Trades, most of whose craft union members banned blacks outright, making it impossible for African Americans to learn a craft through a union apprenticeship, let alone practice it, and making it difficult for skilled black tradesmen, such as brickmasons, to find work on construction sites.

Many black men and most black women did not participate in Atlanta's white commercial or industrial economy in any way. Instead, they worked in private homes, where their work most closely mimicked the premodern paternalism, coercion, and exploitation of slavery. Low wages made domestic work's ubiquity possible. In the 1930s, most female domestic workers in Atlanta earned six dollars or less for a seven-day work week in which they were expected to work twelve or more hours a day, except for an afternoon off on Thursday. Given that in 1930 almost a third of black households in Atlanta were headed by women, many of which included children, thousands of black women in Atlanta were forced to support their families on less than a dollar a day.[10]

Along with residential and occupational segregation, black Atlantans were subordinated through their exclusion from politics. The 1906 election that provoked the Atlanta riot was also the one that cemented black disfranchisement in Georgia. Like African Americans across the South, black Atlantans were barred from voting in the white Democratic primary, the crucial election for choosing all public officials in the region. And while they could cast ballots in general and "special" elections for municipal bond issues, the recall of public officials, and plebiscites on issues like Prohibition, voter registration was contingent on the payment of a one-dollar, cumulative poll tax, which kept all but a few hundred black Atlantans from registering by 1930. Without the power to participate in the electoral process, the black community could not extract support from local politicians or officials. Instead, these whites could ignore African Americans or turn against them to curry favor from their white constituencies, as Howell and Smith had, with brutal results, in 1906.[11]

The condition of the neighborhoods in which black Atlantans had to live was the most visible manifestation of their noncitizenship in the city. Black Atlantans lived in neighborhoods largely bereft of city services such as electricity or sewers. The city neglected to collect garbage in black neigh-

Working-class African American neighborhood, 1930s. (Charles Forrest Palmer Collection, Special Collections Department, Robert W. Woodruff Library, Emory University)

borhoods except sporadically yet located at least five municipal dumps in the African American community, including two adjacent to those most venerable of black Atlanta's institutions, the colleges. Many black Atlantans lived in neighborhoods tolerated by city officials as de facto vice districts where corrupt police allowed large-scale bootlegging operations and prostitution to prosper, for a cut of the profits. In all black neighborhoods the police acted with unchecked brutality, arresting people at will for no other reason than loitering. They often beat and even sometimes killed those who resisted such specious arrests. In short, black Atlantans, even if they resided in the middle-class enclaves of Auburn Avenue or on the west side or within the gates of the colleges, were reminded every day of their marginal position in the city by police harassment, their neighborhoods' lack of city services, or their homes' proximity to a city dump. Racial subordination and segregation consigned all black Atlantans to the same living conditions no matter their wealth or background.[12]

While the Atlanta riot marked the retrenchment of Jim Crow in Atlanta, it also produced a revitalization of black community life as African Americans fought back and sought to protect themselves from the white on-slaught. As soon as black Atlantans understood the fury and size of the white mobs involved in the riot, they began to organize for the defense of their own neighborhoods. In districts throughout the city, black men armed themselves through an underground network, creating informal militias to patrol their communities and fend off white attack. In working-class Dark Town, adjacent to the central business district, such a band of black men shot out the streetlights and at any intruders, successfully thwarting them. In south Atlanta's Brownsville, an ambush surprised a group of county police and white vigilantes intending to confiscate fire-arms in the neighborhood, resulting in the death of one of the police officers and injuries for many of the interlopers. Black institutions, in-cluding churches and the colleges, opened their doors to their neighbors, and this show of racial solidarity protected many African Americans from white attack. Indeed, the worse place for black Atlantans to be caught during the riot was outside their neighborhoods, and without community support.[13]

Black Atlanta's swift response reflected the ways in which African Ameri-cans had always responded to white supremacy and the expanding Jim Crow order. Defending themselves against the myriad ways in which white Atlantans actively and passively marginalized them from the political, social, and economic mainstream of city life, black Atlantans forged their own distinct, parallel city behind the veil of Jim Crow. In the words of his-torian Earl Lewis, they turned the negative white impulses of "segregation" into the constructive force of "congregation" by shifting their energies in-ward away from the white city to find support and sustenance within their own communities. In this way, they created an independent and autono-mous life outside the knowledge, experience, and understanding of the whites who would control them.[14]

After the riot, black Atlantans sought again to strengthen their institu-tions to protect themselves against the white city. While at one time they had lived scattered throughout the city in small enclaves near their em-ployment, after the riot African Americans intensified their concentration in black Atlanta's most established neighborhoods, such as those close to the Auburn Avenue business district or the west side, where Atlanta Uni-versity (AU), and Spelman, Morehouse, and Morris Brown Colleges were located. While the consolidation of Jim Crow residential segregation was partly responsible for this trend, black Atlantans made the move willingly; anchored by the black economy and the city's most powerful and indepen-

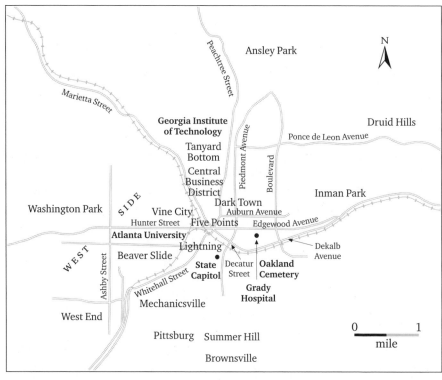

Map 1. Atlanta, 1930. (Adapted from map in Tera Hunter, *To 'Joy My Freedom: Southern Black Women's Lives and Labors after the Civil War* [Cambridge, Mass.: Harvard University Press, 1997])

dent black institutions, these neighborhoods provided the best insulation from the white city and its residents.

Within these enclaves, black Atlantans intensified efforts geared toward community self-help. Both formal and informal social service efforts in black neighborhoods mushroomed after the riot as their residents sought to cope with the hardening segregationist order. The Neighborhood Union, created in the months after the riot, brought women from Atlanta's west side together across class lines to provide many of the social services city officials denied to black neighborhoods. For example, the agency built a playground on the campus of Morehouse College to provide children with safe recreation. It also organized black neighborhoods block by block, enlisting a diverse group of women to represent their sections and the ills they faced. They sponsored clean-up and better-home campaigns to improve the conditions of their neighborhoods.[15]

The institutions that anchored these neighborhoods had their roots in the informal mutual aid that had built Atlanta's black community from its beginnings after the Civil War as an encampment of destitute freed people from Georgia's countryside. The interplay of poverty and rural roots that had shaped these pioneers' lives in the new city continued to mold Atlanta's black urban culture well into the twentieth century. Starting with freed people, the black community's growth had been spurred by many periodic waves of migration by rural folk to the city. In 1930, for example, a decade-long agricultural depression meant that Atlanta's black population had grown 43 percent from 1920, or by more than 27,000 (see Appendix, Table 1). These migrants, like the thousands who had preceded them, deeply influenced black urban culture, making the atmosphere of most black districts seemed closer to that of the rural South than that of a modern metropolis. In describing Summer Hill, a working-class neighborhood, one disapproving black commentator observed: "The inhabitants . . . sit on their porches crudely dressed, without shoes or stockings if they so desire; stand on their front porches and call their children who are at play several blocks away; and ask of their neighbors whatever they desire to know of their business, no matter how personal it may be." She continued to observe that "the men congregate on the corners of the main thoroughfare in their overalls on Saturday afternoons presenting the picture of a country town on Saturday between 3 and 7 o'clock."[16]

Like migrants and immigrants across the country, these new Atlantans used the customs and folkways of their birthplaces to ease their way into city life. Furthermore, the poverty and marginality of most of the city's black residents predicated a life of mutuality and interdependence between kith and kin very different from the privacy of modern bourgeois urban life. Poor black Atlantans demonstrated this mutual reliance in many ways. Not usually able to afford to pay a physician, they often employed the service of "root doctors," or folk herbalists, and midwives, who operated parallel to and almost entirely outside the purview of the established white or black medical establishment in Atlanta. Other poor residents provided goods and services specific to the needs of their communities and families' survival. Neighborhood women provided daycare to children whose mothers toiled in domestic work, and families opened their homes to boarders, offering their tenants inexpensive housing in the crowded city.[17]

Out of this informal self-help grew black institutions. Most African Americans in Atlanta belonged to some kind of mutual-aid organization, from neighborhood burial associations and social clubs to exclusive fraternal organizations like the all-black Prince Hall Masons. These self-help organizations provided financial insurance for a crisis, allowing black Atlantans some small measure of economic autonomy, despite their poverty. Furthermore, almost every black Atlantan had some kind of connection at some time to the most important institution in black Atlanta and black America—the church. Black churches in Atlanta in all their diversity—from the prestigious Friendship Baptist Church founded in the first years after the Civil War, to the enormous Auburn Avenue congregations of Wheat Street Baptist, Big Bethel AME, and Rev. Martin Luther King Sr.'s Ebenezer Baptist, to tiny storefront assemblies in poor black neighborhoods—offered much more than spiritual sustenance. The church was a social gathering place, a charitable welfare agency, and a black-controlled institution through which congregants could satisfy political and organizational aspirations otherwise unfulfilled by demeaning and unrewarding employment and exclusion from public life.

From these grassroots institutions grew the schools and businesses that made Atlanta's black community one of the most prosperous in the South. For example, Atlantans helped keep several national black-owned life insurance companies in business, among them the locally based and enormously successful Atlanta Life Insurance Company, founded by black barber Alonzo Herndon, who built it from a mutual-aid society. Atlanta's black colleges and the Atlanta University Center all had denominational affiliations and could trace their roots to specific black congregations founded in Reconstruction Atlanta and Georgia.

In the post-riot period, these businesses and schools sought to consolidate their strength for protection and community development, just as black neighborhoods had. As African American entrepreneurs were pushed entirely out of the white economy, they became fully dependent on their black clientele, a development that fueled the growth of the black economy. After the turn of the century, black businesses began to cluster on Auburn Avenue when the Odd Fellows, a fraternal organization, built a four-story headquarters there, with space for other black organizations and businesses. By the 1930s, "Sweet Auburn" had become the preeminent commercial, cultural, and social hub for black Atlantans of all classes, attracting over one hundred black-owned businesses and professional offices. The largest of these were the insurance companies that employed the bulk of black salespeople and clerks in the city; Citizens Trust Bank, the first black-owned bank to join the Federal Reserve (in 1936);

and the *Atlanta Daily World*, the only black daily newspaper in the country and flagship paper of the World Syndicate, which published papers across the South. Along with these businesses, which represented some of the nation's most profitable black-owned enterprises, were a full complement of retail and service operations, as well as important black social agencies, including the Butler Street Young Men's Christian Association (YMCA), located just off Auburn Avenue, and the only branch of the public library open to African Americans.[18]

As one of the oldest neighborhoods in Atlanta, the community surrounding Auburn Avenue was home to some of the most crowded living conditions in the city. Many of the very poorest black Atlantans lived in the neighborhood, in areas like Dark Town, or on blind alleys located behind commercial buildings or in rooms above stores on the avenue itself. The underground economy thrived on Auburn Avenue alongside legitimate business, with numbers runners, bootleggers, and prostitutes conducting their business with some openness on the sidewalks or in the many poolrooms and juke joints. Along with these illegal activities came the police, who felt free to facilitate "vice" and terrorize the neighborhood simultaneously.[19]

In search of better housing, many members of the black professional and white-collar group, along with more prosperous members of the black working class, sought to live away from the teeming east-side neighborhoods of which Auburn Avenue was the center. Their movement was blocked to the north and east by middle-class white neighborhoods such as Inman Park, Ansley Park, and Druid Hills, so they moved to the city's west side, where white officials had tacitly agreed to allow the residential expansion of a growing black population. In the early 1920s, Heman Perry, founder of the Citizens Trust Bank, purchased 300 acres of land on the west side, adjacent to the Atlanta University neighborhood. There he constructed bungalows for black homeowners and attracted them by lobbying local government for public facilities. On west-side land which Perry sold to the city, the city government established Booker T. Washington High School, the first public high school for African Americans, and Washington Park (after which the neighborhood was named), the city's only public park for blacks.[20]

Estelle Clemmons, whose family was among the migrants to Perry's development, remembered what it meant to move from the crowded conditions of the east side to this new spacious neighborhood, close to the park and the high school. The relocation provided her striving parents with a

tangible sense of upward mobility, a feeling that "we were going somewhere . . . having five rooms, with a bathroom on the inside and hot and
cold running water." Just being "able to get into a bathtub meant so much,"
Clemmons reminisced, in a period when most black neighborhoods and
homes lacked the sewers and plumbing required for indoor toilets and
bathing facilities.[21]

While west side migrants were attracted by the high school and park,
and Perry's neat suburban bungalows with their indoor plumbing and electricity, they also moved from the east side to be close to Atlanta's most
powerful, influential, and independent black institution, the Atlanta University Center, composed in 1933 of Spelman and Morehouse Colleges,
along with Atlanta University. The area surrounding the AU Center was the
home of Atlanta's most prominent black citizens. As an institution operating independent of local whites, the campus was the easiest place in black
Atlanta to forget the injustices and humiliations of Jim Crow. Located on
the highest land in the city, it was a self-contained community, with students and faculty living within its gates in a world all their own. W. E. B.
Du Bois described this world in the *Souls of Black Folk*: "The hundred hills
of Atlanta are not all crowned with factories. On one, toward the west,
the setting sun throws three buildings in bold relief against the sky. The
beauty of the group lies in its simple unity: a broad lawn of green rising
from the red street with mingled roses and peaches; north and south, two
plain and stately halls; and in the midst, half hidden in ivy, a larger building, boldly graceful, sparingly decorated, and with one low spire. It is a
restful group—one never looks for more; it is all here, all intelligible."[22]

The colleges and AU were restful not simply because of their geography and architecture. John Hope, the president of Atlanta University by
1930, along with his counterparts at Spelman and Morehouse, sought to
make the schools enclaves of order and respectability, where students and
faculty could lead sober and productive lives unfettered by reminders of
second-class citizenship. Students were encouraged to remain within the
confines of their institutions as much as possible, and most faculty lived
on campus. Visiting artists provided entertainment without the humilia-
tion of Jim Crow seating, and barbers came to the colleges to cut the
hair of faculty so they would not have to endure the sometimes disreputable surroundings of Auburn Avenue's public barber shops. AU librarian
Hallie Brooks remembered the university community as being deliberately
"pretty isolated," with a faculty that only "socialized within [their] own
group." Borrowing from W. E. B. Du Bois's words, she concluded that the
university was "really a wheel within a wheel"[23] in the city at large and

the black community. In short, by shielding AU's elite faculty and students from the indignities of Jim Crow and black poverty, the university's leadership sought to create a community in which African Americans would be permitted to live as respectable middle-class Americans, free from the marginal existence of most black Atlantans.

John Hope envisioned extending the borders of this enclave of respectability. He spearheaded a successful drive for the eventual relocation of all Atlanta's black postsecondary institutions on the west side and as part of the AU Center. He also worked with AU's trustees to develop the land surrounding the colleges and university into homes for middle-class and elite black homeowners, hoping to create for them and for the university community a black neighborhood protected from the ravages of Jim Crow.[24]

However, Hope had difficulty achieving his dream in the face of myriad public and private forces which sought to sustain the subjugation and marginalization of African Americans, whatever their background. While the west side may have offered better and less crowded housing conditions to many of its residents, they could not escape police harassment, overcrowded and underfunded public schools, municipal dumping, or white vigilantism in their new neighborhood. In fact, it was black Atlantans' westward migration that prompted the most violent white resistance to black infiltration of white neighborhoods, including bombings and at least one vigilante killing, that of Dennis Hubert in 1930, a Morehouse College student and son of a prominent black family of ministers and educators. Nor did west-siders entirely escape the blighted housing conditions of the east side. The AU neighborhood was dotted with unpaved, flood-prone, and ramshackle "slums," including Vine City and Beaver Slide, the latter of which lay literally in the shadow of Spelman College and some of the best housing for blacks in the city. Thus black Atlantans' efforts at community building combated the ills of Jim Crow but could not defeat them.[25]

In the days after the Atlanta riot, African American William H. Crogman, future president of Atlanta's Clark College, wrote a report of the carnage in a letter to northern white liberal Mary White Ovington. Crediting the militant defense of Dark Town by its residents for preventing an escalation of the violence, he commented on the irony of this situation: "Here we have worked and prayed and tried to make good men and women of our colored population, and at our very doorstep the whites kill these good men. But the lawless element in our population, the element we have condemned fights back, and it is to these people that we owe our lives."[26]

Crogman's comments about Dark Town's residents attest to the deep class and status divisions within Atlanta's black community. Although the African American community demonstrated remarkable solidarity against the white oppression that touched all of its members, its social and economic diversity meant that these periods of direct white assault were often the only times when black Atlantans experienced such unity. Paradoxically, the black community's very success in building formal institutions out of traditions of mutuality led to these divisions. As the city's black educational and business establishments developed and modernized, they moved away from their origins in the city's nineteenth-century community of penurious ex-slaves. The status distinctions that emerged ultimately resulted in the development of a black elite, whose members felt great alienation from the city's black "masses."[27]

These divisions had intensified in the quarter century after the riot. For example, by the 1930s the Neighborhood Union's membership had lost the class diversity that had been its hallmark in its founding years. Such diversity was victim to the union's success. As a pioneering social service agency in Atlanta, the NU's settlement-house work spurred a flowering of black social-work activities in the city, including the founding of the Atlanta School of Social Work (ASSW) in 1920. The institutionalization and professionalization of social work implicit in such developments dramatically changed the union's character. By 1930, the agency's leadership and membership was almost exclusively comprised of elite women, and it farmed out many of its activities to ASSW and Morehouse sociology instructors and students. Where once it had included and worked with the women of all the west side's diverse neighborhoods, now it worked for them, with all the implications of class division that such a shift suggests.[28]

This evolution was not surprising, considering the social hierarchies that already existed in Atlanta by the Neighborhood Union's founding. In Atlanta, home to AU, one of black America's most academically elite schools, along with four black colleges, these distinctions were based largely on education, rather than family pedigree. As early as 1894, a resident claimed membership in a distinct black elite in Atlanta based on "education, wealth and respectability,"[29] all of which could be obtained through association with one of the AU schools. These institutions employed or trained many of the twentieth century's most prominent African American leaders, including the sociologist and NAACP founder W. E. B. Du Bois; longtime national NAACP executive secretary Walter White; and civil rights leader Martin Luther King Jr. These institutions were the training ground for the relatively large educated black middle class of professionals, white-collar workers, and business owners who constituted just over 6 percent of Atlanta's black work force in 1930 (see Appendix, Table 2).

Virtually every black teacher, prominent minister, and professional in Atlanta was trained at one of these schools. In addition, the city's most successful black business people, including L. D. Milton, president of Citizens Trust Bank and co-owner of Yates and Milton Pharmacy; Jesse Blayton, vice president of Citizens Trust; and W. H. Aiken, a building contractor and real estate developer, worked on the faculty of one of the AU affiliated institutions.[30]

The strong and growing connection of the city's "talented tenth" with the colleges solidified this group's elitism and exclusivity. Due to the critical mass of educated African Americans in Atlanta, many members of the AU elite chose to limit their social group almost exclusively to college alumni. They did so by living in the vicinity of AU and by choosing their associates carefully. Some belonged to Friendship Baptist or First Congregational Church, whose members were culled almost entirely from the college-trained elite. They joined selective social clubs and maintained close lifelong ties to their college fraternities or sororities. They married within their own circle, or within similar circles in other cities whenever they could, creating a local and nationwide network of peers. Within their group, the black professional elite practiced the same level of interdependence and mutuality as the black working class; its members found each other jobs, patronized each other's businesses, and worked together to improve life in the black community.

This complicated and exclusive associational life pointed to the black elite's social distance from the majority of black Atlantans. Those who had been brought up in the AU milieu often spoke of their " 'Fair Street' standards,' "[31] referring to a street that ran past the AU Center and to their personal philosophy. Members of this exclusive group sought to carve out for themselves the respectable middle-class existence they believed was warranted by their education and position within the black community. However, as the experience of west-side migrants demonstrates, the white community's efforts at subjugating and marginalizing African Americans as a caste made this task an extremely difficult one. Black Atlantans of all occupations and backgrounds were subject to Jim Crow's inequities, indignities, and dangers. Like John Hope's efforts to isolate the AU community, the black elite engaged in a frustrating struggle to distinguish itself from the rest of the black community with whom it was lumped by whites into one, undifferentiated outcast group.

While Jim Crow residential segregation prevented geographic separation between the classes, black elites maintained their social distance. Teacher Pearlie Dove's experience is instructive, as it demonstrates the status consciousness of an ordinary member of black Atlanta's educated professional class. Like countless others, Dove achieved high status through education. Brought up by a single mother, Dove's immediate family was not elite. Both her aunts, however, were public school teachers, the predominant black profession, and they and their friends indoctrinated Dove in the importance of college and the respectability of a teaching career. Attending Clark College (the co-ed school that followed Morehouse and Spelman in prestige) in the 1930s, she obtained her MEd from AU in 1943.

While in graduate school, she worked for a YWCA summer program for working-class black children, an exceptionally challenging experience for Dove, who had "never had any work" with Atlanta's black poor. As she reflected on her experience in the early 1990s, "I had been reared in a so-called middle class family and saturated with middle class values. And the first day, to me, was a cultural shock." Her first instinct was to recoil from these "doorkey children" whose "parents had gone to work early in the morning . . . to take care of other people's kids, wash clothes and clean houses." Many of these children "arrived hungry . . ., needed baths, and they had many emotional hangups." Despite trying "very hard to establish rapport" and overcome her distaste, "[m]y verbal-non-verbal communication just said to these students . . . that I would rather be somewhere else. And I lost the kids."[32]

Dove's reminiscences demonstrated remarkable honesty and self-reflection, but her attitudes toward the poor were not exceptional among educated African Americans in the first decades of the twentieth century. Significantly, however, Dove overcame her estrangement from her working-class charges and committed herself to serving them, encouraged by Irene Harris, Dove's social-worker boss at the YWCA, and Dorothy Flemister, a public-health nurse who helped Dove instill the virtues of personal hygiene and good nutrition among the youth. These three women followed in the footsteps of Lugenia Burns Hope, William Crogman, and countless other elite blacks in early-twentieth-century Atlanta who were driven by an ideological commitment as members of "the talented tenth" to serve the "masses." Never abandoning their social distance from the poor, black reformers hoped nevertheless to uplift them to "middle class values." In fact, Dove capped off her tale by recounting an incident several years later where she met a young woman at Clark College who had attended that memorable YWCA program. Dove triumphantly recalled the freshman telling her, "I told you I would make it, and here I am."[33] Uplifted by her aunts, Dove's social work continued the tradition with a younger generation.

Dove and her predecessors' noblesse oblige represented the black elite's dilemma. While many fought against being associated with the poor, racial identities ascribed by Jim Crow prevented such differentiation in white eyes. Instead, just as Jim Crow had forced black-owned businesses to rely on black working-class support, so did the elite's struggle for public recognition as its members fought against the black community's marginality and public invisibility. As Jim Crow closed in, black reformers increasingly realized that their fate was tied to that of the entire black community. You could own one of the finest homes in the city, but how did that matter if the city dumped garbage behind your property, your neighbors lived in hovels, and the city police force offered you no protection, only harassment? Only by correcting these conditions for all black Atlantans could the elite improve its own lot.[34]

Black reformers needed to lift the black poor in order to develop a constituency for their reform ideology and agenda. Like Pearlie Dove's Clark College protégée, the reform elite hoped to lead working-class African Americans to join it in perspective, behavior, and ideology, and therefore in its struggle for recognition. In conformity with the outward-looking behavioral code of respectability, black reformers eschewed much that was distinctive about black urban culture. They did not shoot craps, play the numbers, moan and holler in church, take in boarders, sit on the porch in an apron and kerchief, socialize on street corners, or patronize juke joints—all of which had or could be construed by middle-class whites as evidence of a delinquent culture. Black elites condemned such behavior in other African Americans. But as great as their concern over white perceptions was their belief that working-class black behavior was emblematic or symptomatic of the parochialism of the masses of black Atlantans and their acceptance of their marginal place in society.

The same Atlanta University sociology graduate student who wrote disparagingly of the countrified street life in Summer Hill articulated the frustration of the reform elite with the black working class. She wrote of the indifference of Summer Hill's inhabitants toward "a program of community advancement," including the reform elite's efforts to obtain a public playground for the neighborhood, citing residents' "affection for the laissez-faire method of social adjustment." She blamed this attitude on the community's inward-looking parochialism, in which residents lived their entire lives on the street or district in which they were born, associating only with other residents of their neighborhoods, and finding their only social outlet in the church, never coming under the influence of "progressive" members of the black reform elite. She noted with frustration Summer Hill residents' ignorance of the "mass movements that have concerned the city at large in which this area was only slightly concerned and active." She knew that without the cooperation of Summer Hill's residents in its campaign and strategy to join the political, economic, and social mainstream, the black elite would never achieve its goals.[35]

This aspirant to the reform elite shared her mentors' interpretation of the attitudes and activities of the "masses," which were so different from her own. The forms of racial oppression faced by working-class black Atlantans often prompted them to adopt separatist strategies to further their distance from the white community and its oppressive structures, not to seek out white recognition. To these ends, many poor black Atlantans, living in close-knit neighborhoods like Tanyard Bottom, Lightning, and Mechanicsville, used their marginality from the mainstream to their advantage, even sometimes seeking to increase their public invisibility to further insulate themselves from the insidious control and prying eyes of whites. For example, knowing they had virtually no vocational option but the exploitation of domestic work, black women used the position's anachronisms to carve out a degree of personal autonomy unheard of by more modern service or industrial workers. Subject to their white employers' paternalistic control, they nevertheless avoided the sometimes brutal and more arbitrary oppression of white public officials, workers, bystanders, and bosses on the streets and in the more public work places of Atlanta, scattered as they were throughout the city in private homes. Domestic workers moved to increase this independence early in the twentieth century by refusing to dwell with their employers, choosing instead to live in the black community, where they could safely let down their guard among their friends and family. Furthermore, in 1930, almost one-quarter of Atlanta's female domestics worked out of their own homes by taking in laundry to their homes in the black community, thereby distancing themselves almost entirely from white scrutiny. Living and working in the black community was so important to these women precisely because of its marginality. Black neighborhoods' irrelevance to all that was deemed legitimate or important by middle-class white Atlanta was a double-edged sword. While leaving streets unpaved and unlit, white official neglect meant that black residents had some control of their own communities.

Black reformers rejected this response to Jim Crow as ignorant disinterest in self-improvement, community uplift, and the politics of respectability. Consequently, the reform elite launched a myriad of efforts to reach the masses of working-class blacks and to bring them into the social, economic, and political mainstream. Thus for this group, social work in the black community was an essential preliminary step in the black freedom struggle.

By 1930, Atlanta had a well-established network of elite African Americans imbued with this reform ethos. In 1930, the leaders of this group comprised some of the best-educated and most influential African Americans in the city, and indeed the nation. They formed the interchangeable executives of Atlanta's most prominent black social work and civil rights agencies. Leading the black reform elite were a number of key figures, including: Lugenia Burns Hope, who was also a local NAACP leader; Forrester B. Washington, ASSW president and future NAACP branch president; Jesse O. Thomas and Reginald Johnson, respectively Southern and Atlanta Urban League secretaries; A. T. Walden, lawyer and president of the Atlanta branch of the NAACP, as well as national committeeman for that civil rights organization; J. Raymond Henderson, the militant pastor of Wheat Street Baptist Church, the largest black church in Atlanta; and W. E. B. Du Bois, soon to be chair of AU's sociology department and NAACP founder.

While many older members of this group, like Thomas and Walden, were southerners with long histories in the city, by 1930 a new cadre of leaders had eclipsed them, one with few or no ties to Atlanta. Predominantly northern- or western-born, members of this new group were characterized by their high educational attainment and professional affiliations. They had moved to Atlanta to pursue their education or to take posts at one of the colleges or social-service agencies as part of career paths that would as often as not lead them to move away from the city for other opportunities. They belonged to national networks of black professionals and educators, and had close contacts with prominent white peers in their fields. In short, their horizons stretched far beyond Atlanta. Forrester B. Washington was a typical example of this group's leadership. The president of the ASSW was born in Massachusetts and attended Tufts University and the New York School of Social Work before pursuing graduate studies at Harvard University and the University of Michigan. Along with belonging to national black organizations, including the Alpha Phi Alpha fraternity, he served on the executive of the National Conference of Social Work, and was an active member of the American and Southern Sociological Associations.[36]

This cosmopolitan group was frustrated by local custom and tradition, and indefatigable in its quest to destroy the veil of segregation. Its members worked tirelessly to force white officials simply to recognize that they had some responsibility to black citizens and their communities. For example, in 1932, the Atlanta Urban League (AUL) lobbied the city to build drainage canals on Phoenix Alley, where a natural spring perpetually flooded the street. Once the work was finally begun, AUL officers monitored it carefully, ensuring its promised completion. Similarly, Forrester B. Washington and John Hope worked in vain in 1932 to protect the job of the sole black probation officer in Fulton County's juvenile court, whose job was created after intense lobbying by the black reform elite in the late 1920s, and who was laid off in 1932 in a cost-cutting measure made easy by the public invisibility of African Americans. In fact, every meager gesture made by public officials—in the form of schools, libraries, public health services, recreation facilities, and electricity, pavement, sewers, and street lights for black neighborhoods—testified to the refusal by the black reform elite to allow the city to ignore totally its black citizenry.[37]

According to their uplift ideology, this group also sought to reform nonelite black Atlantans. In the early 1930s the Neighborhood Union, the AUL, and the black branches of the YMCA, YWCA, and the Atlanta Tuberculosis Association all "organized" poor blacks by sex and occupation into a variety of clubs and programs like Pearlie Dove's summer class a decade later. These efforts attempted to instill in their participants notions of respectability and citizenship, teaching them "how to lead a happier home life through home and self improvement," and fostering "activities in the fields of education and recreation . . . to develop community leadership."[38]

These efforts were almost never greeted with enthusiastic support by the groups they were meant to serve, demonstrating the ineffectiveness of the social-work approach to constituency building. An examination of the AUL's efforts to organize unskilled black workers provides an ideal example. The programs, which the AUL sometimes described as being part of the agency's drive to gain union recognition for black workers, almost always condemned the individual work and leisure behavior of black workers, and played to the interests of white employers. Thus a group of special-delivery messengers were "encouraged to make the best use of their leisure time by engaging in wholesome recreation" and were "made

W. E. B. Du Bois, the pioneering African American sociologist and preeminent black intellectual, 1938. (Special Collections and Archives, W. E. B. Du Bois Library, University of Massachusetts, Amherst)

Lugenia Burns Hope, founder and president of the Neighborhood Union settlement house organization. (Emma and Lloyd Lewis Family Papers [ELL neg. 9], Special Collections, The University Library, University of Illinois at Chicago)

Forrester B. Washington, president of the Atlanta School of Social Work.
(Photographs and Prints Division, Schomburg Center for Research in Black
Culture, The New York Public Library, Astor, Lenox and Tilden Foundations)

to realize that their security of employment rests upon their efficiency, observation of rules and regulations, and their general attitude towards the public."[39] The "Janitors Training School" went even further, inviting white employers to deliver the message of efficiency and clean living to the students. The AUL's Neighborhood Clubs sought to teach "better house-keeping" practices to black women, thus providing, in the hopes of club organizers, a more respectable home life to participants and instilling do-mestic workers with better work habits to serve their white employers. No wonder that the AUL "lost" at least one of these groups, the Southside Neighborhood Club, including women from Pittsburg, Summer Hill, and Brownsville. According to one commentator, members failed to "sympa-thize wholeheartedly with the [AUL's] Neighborhood Club Council's entire program" and would "accept the Urban League's service in part only."[40] Such activities held little appeal for Atlanta's black workers since they did not result in better employment conditions or better wages, only greater scrutiny by both whites and condemnatory blacks. In fact, the black reform elite, in its powerlessness, had nothing to offer the workers it supposedly led in exchange for their respectability.

As these elite efforts suggest, the politics of respectability often led re-formers into complicity with the city's white power structure. Their com-promised position was a product of both powerlessness and ideology. In its quest for public recognition for the black community, the reform elite worked hard to find independent strategies for victory, but with very lim-ited success. For example, it mobilized black Atlanta's limited electoral power whenever it could to force whites to acknowledge the black com-munity. The most notable example of this tactic was the school bond elec-tion in 1921, which resulted in the building of Booker T. Washington High School, Atlanta's first public high school for African Americans. While black Atlantans were not permitted to vote in the white primary elections that elected all public officials, they could cast ballots in other elections, such as those for school bonds. The reform elite took advantage of this opportunity in 1919 by helping to defeat two school bond issues, demon-strating its anger toward local officials who had time and again failed to deliver on promises of better accommodations for black schoolchildren. After demonstrating their electoral power in this way, even the very small number of black registered voters were able to extract a commitment from Atlanta's mayor James Key that their support in the 1921 election would re-sult in concrete improvements for black schools, including the building of BTWHS, which opened in 1924 as one of Atlanta's finest school structures.[41]

While such victories were impressive, they were also rare. Very seldom did circumstances come together to make the thousand or fewer black voters in Atlanta a powerful political force. More commonly the black reform elite was forced to pursue its objectives for the black community in closed-door meetings with white officials, petitions to city council, and alliances with the few local whites sympathetic to its causes. These were the default strategies of black reformers in their campaigns to increase black teachers' salaries, end overcrowding in black schools, secure parks and recreational facilities for African Americans, and obtain black police for black neighborhoods, among other efforts.[42]

Black reformers seeking public recognition for the black community sought white support by framing their objectives in terms that would appeal to the self-interest of whites with whom they hoped to create alliances. They found their warmest welcome within the liberal and charitable communities centered around the Commission on Interracial Cooperation (CIC) and its local Fulton-DeKalb Committee, and the Atlanta Community Chest, which provided funding to the Atlanta Urban League, the Atlanta School of Social Work, and the Neighborhood Union. The Fulton-DeKalb Committee included the tiny number of white liberals willing to work with black Atlantans for improvements in public accommodations and against police brutality and racist vigilantism. Its leadership represented an impressive list of some of the most historically important southern white liberals, including Will W. Alexander, Jessie Daniel Ames, Arthur Raper, Clark Foreman, and the young C. Vann Woodward. These figures were almost as marginal as African Americans in terms of their influence over city affairs. They were reviled by most whites as "nigger lovers," and their campaigns against police brutality and for black police, for example, had virtually no impact on city politics. In addition, the committee and its members, partly because of their tenuous position in Atlanta, were extremely conservative in their tactics and outlook. Many members' actions on behalf of blacks were motivated by paternalism, and they often saw their work only in terms of preventing racial violence, refusing to consider any fundamental societal reforms as one of their goals. In a report most telling of the CIC's gradualist approach, the chairman of the 1930 meeting of the Georgia CIC found that it "seemed to be the consensus of opinion among those present that more Negroes should be afforded the privilege of voting."[43]

The only other white leaders in Atlanta who acknowledged African Americans belonged to the city's social work and charitable community organized under the Community Chest. This diverse group comprised both the professional social workers who led Atlanta's private charitable agencies like the Family Welfare Society and the Atlanta Tuberculosis Association, and business and society leaders who were these organizations' major donors and the chairpeople of the Community Chest funding drives. Black Chest agencies found that their funding came at a price; they had to conform to the wishes of chest leaders, sometimes even relinquishing the definition of their mission and role to white outsiders.[44]

Further, the only way in which black reformers could successfully make the black community visible to white charity workers was through an appeal to white self-interest and by playing to white racial assumptions about black "criminality" and "immorality," a distasteful but relatively easy step for them to take, given their own preconceptions about the majority in the black community. As the Atlanta School of Social Work explained to whites in its promotional literature, "[d]isease and crime can no longer be segregated." Exploiting white employers' desire for "steady, sober employees," the ASSW advanced its campaign for public recreation in the black community by claiming that the "degrading pool rooms, low dance halls and bootleg joints" patronized by black workers with no other place in which to spend their leisure time, prompted them to "carouse all night long." Consequently, these workers' "regularity and efficiency on the job is affected."[45] By invoking stereotypes about black workers and connecting them to the woeful conditions of the black community, black reformers hoped to spur the white charitable community to support black welfare agencies, and to work for more and better black schools, recreational facilities, and public health care through which black "criminality," "immorality," and "inefficiency" could be combated.

Thus at the eve of the New Deal, Atlanta's black reform elite found its aspirations and goals for the black community thwarted at every turn. White officials who were committed to maintain the racial and social order of the city had no interest in helping to advance the cause of black reformers who wanted to end the black community's public invisibility. Black elites could only attract potential white allies to their cause by appealing to racial preconceptions and fears of black disease and criminality. These appeals often led to oppressive crackdowns on the black community.

When reformers turned their focus inward to the black community for support, their own elitism and rigid behavioral codes alienated them from the majority of black Atlantans whom they hoped to develop as a constituency. Their social distance from even those members of the black working class who conformed to their notions of respectability and their reluctance to see the masses of black Atlantans as active partners in their fight for public recognition meant that elite black reformers who saw themselves as the natural leadership class of the black community largely worked without a following.

The black elite's effort to "organize" black Atlantans into a malleable constituency was largely fruitless both because it often condemned black working-class culture and it exposed black workers to the white scrutiny they spent their lives trying to minimize. The black working class was not parochial and passive, contrary to its portrayal by the reform elite. As we shall see, its members worked vigilantly, publicly, and militantly on behalf of their distinct and specific community interests. But its members did not share the black elite's interest in public recognition from the white Atlantans who were responsible for their ongoing exploitation. They knew from experience that such recognition could very well result in deepened oppression. Instead, they worked and continued to work within their own communities for the support with which they would resist their condition and seek to change it.

CHAPTER

A Road
Not Taken

*The Radical Response
to the Great Depression*

In the early 1920s, Mary Beale[1] and her family
moved from Rockmart, Georgia, to Atlanta. Along with thousands of other
rural Georgians, her parents hoped to find a better life for their family in
the city. The Beales found more success than most in this quest. Thanks
to Mr. Beale's income as a bricklayer, the family could purchase a family
car, Mrs. Beale could remain at home to raise a growing family, and Mary
could complete high school. The Beales quickly established themselves in
Atlanta as members of the respected and respectable artisanal class.

However, in 1929 or 1930 Mr. Beale began to come into increasing conflict with white workers infiltrating traditionally black construction crafts,
including bricklaying, as white unemployment rose in the city. Black artisans in these trades had gained a reputation in Atlanta for skill and pride
in craftsmanship and in the black community for labor and racial militance. Mary Beale's father lived up to this reputation. Not only had his skill
earned him some of the most challenging bricklaying jobs in the city, but
he also followed a long family tradition of racial pride and fearlessness.
"My Daddy was not afraid of a white man that walked,"[2] Mary Beale recalled. Such fearlessness would prove essential to resisting growing white
aggression and violence against black workers.

At first, Mr. Beale's skill and willingness to defend the place of black
craftsmen on construction sites kept him in work despite white intimidation. Mary vividly remembered one work-place incident, which her
family found out about upon her father's return from work one day. He

emerged from the family car with his white overalls covered with blood. The family rushed from the house, certain that somebody had hurt this "quick-tempered" man. But, as Mary Beale recalled, he "didn't have a scratch on him." Instead, he explained that "one of [the] crackers . . . infiltrating the bricklayers" had called him "that no-no word." In response, Mary recounted, "Daddy come down across his head with a brick hammer." Instead of Mr. Beale's own, "it was the cracker's blood that was all over him." Ten minutes later, two white men drove up to the Beales's home. They were foremen from the construction site, begging Mr. Beale to return to work; they assured him that the offending white man had been fired. As Mary Beale explained it, the foremen were so anxious to have her father return to their worksite because of his superior abilities as a bricklayer: "Daddy could raise the corner. He could raise the corner, and that was an art."[3]

Despite Mr. Beale's recognized skill, his victory was short lived. The depression in the construction industry and white pressure for skilled construction work soon drove him out of bricklaying. His unimpeachable reputation meant nothing as the exigencies of white supremacy took over the labor market, making black workers expendable in the campaign to provide white men with employment. Mr. Beale could not find any worthwhile replacement work in Atlanta. Consequently Mary's mother was forced to turn to domestic work to support the family until her father found a New Deal job on a Tennessee Valley Authority dam project that required him to move to Alabama, leaving the rest of the family behind. Later, he faced an even greater separation from his wife and children when he moved to Cleveland in the 1940s to find industrial work in the wartime economy.[4]

Stories like the Beale family's, of economic hardship and family dislocation, were played out across the United States in all communities during the capitalist crisis of the 1930s. What compounded African Americans' situation, however, was their deliberate, often violent, economic and political displacement as soon as the effects of the Depression began to be felt. Whites felt no compunction in shutting African Americans out so that all available economic and political resources could be used to ease the suffering of white workers. Consensus among white Atlantans allowed the purge that pushed black Atlantans even further beyond the margins of civic life.

In Atlanta, whites worked to displace black workers even from the menial positions that in prosperous times represented their caste position.

White bellmen replaced black at all but one downtown hotel. Members of the Board of Education attempted to remove black janitors from white schools. White-controlled construction unions imported white workers from outside the city to fill skilled bricklaying and plastering positions, shutting out local black craftsmen like Mr. Beale.[5] White citizens developed schemes in which they envisioned African Americans retreating altogether from the city's labor market, either toiling toward self-sufficiency in community garden plots or, in a plan cooked up by the Chamber of Commerce, moving back to the countryside and farm tenantry.[6] A short-lived white vigilante group, the Black Shirts, mushroomed in 1930 to thousands of members in its quest to rid the city entirely of black workers through violent intimidation and forcible evictions of black Atlantans back to the farm. White resentment of black workers ran so high that it resulted in a rash of white civilian and police terrorism, which left black homes on the racial borders of residential segregation torched or bombed and several black men shot dead.[7]

This displacement was not new to Atlanta. White efforts to remove black artisans from their trades, for example, had been ongoing since the late nineteenth century. Often black workers like Mr. Beale successfully fought back these offenses. However, in times of white economic or political insecurity, such as the early 1930s or the race riot of 1906, white displacement efforts became systematic and violent, making an effective defense nearly impossible. These attacks constituted ritual reassertions of the racial order on the part of the white population, as it sought to topple an "uppity" black community from its tenuous economic and political foothold in the "white" city, and return it to its place outside the parameters of civic life and citizenship. The black community always fought back militantly to preserve its stake, but in the face of such a united attack its members had few options but to leave the city or to retreat behind the veil and regroup within the strength and safe confines of the black community.

In the early 1930s, many black Atlantans turned this crisis into a positive assertion of community autonomy. As white Atlanta continued its hostile and exclusionary campaigns against African Americans, black Atlantans sought to strengthen their "race" institutions and sever their ties to the white community. Black elite reform organizations, like the NAACP, which had lain virtually dormant through the 1920s, or like the Atlanta Urban League (AUL), which had served as the agent of white interests, sprung to life or switched gears to serve as militant defenders of black community interests. This spirit of independence and renewed racial assertiveness set the stage for black Atlanta's response to the radical challenge of Communism.

In December 1931, Lugenia Burns Hope visited Fulton County's Relief Center, established by city government to distribute relief to the destitute in Atlanta. She made her visit on behalf of the Neighborhood Union (NU), after receiving complaints that city relief officials were refusing to distribute Christmas gifts to African American children. At the center, she witnessed the manager, a Mr. Nix, telling a black father that the toys were only meant for white youngsters. When Hope confronted Nix and presented him with a requisition obtained from the city council's Relief Committee for 200 toys, he reluctantly relinquished the gifts to Hope, but not without gratuitously adding, "The trouble of it is that you people do not contribute to these things." Hope responded that black Atlantans were tax-paying citizens fully entitled to municipal relief. Nix then complained that the African American community did not care for its own, citing an instance one week before when he had chased off a black minister seeking fuel from the municipal wood yard for his family's stove. Hope responded again by asserting African Americans' citizenship and their equal entitlement to publicly funded aid.[8]

Hope captured this confrontation in an uncharacteristically angry, defiant, and dramatically written memorandum. Its mood encapsulated a growing frustration among the reform elite during the early years of the Depression. A decade-long quest for legitimacy and inclusion in the city's white charitable establishment had led to nothing but frustration. In fact, by the early 1930s, black reformers could see that their lack of progress might even result in greater marginalization for the black community, as relief work moved from private efforts to an institutionalized public responsibility. Unless the black community could secure a legitimate place at the center of civic life, and thus establish its members' citizenship, its entitlement to public aid would always be in question. However, by the eve of the New Deal, many members of the reform elite had turned away from this Sisyphean task in frustration, looking elsewhere for strategies and solutions. As for African American artisans, the Depression reminded the black reform elite how very marginal and expendable they were to the white establishment in a Jim Crow city.

For Lugenia Burns Hope and the Neighborhood Union, this reckoning came through bitter experience. In the 1920s union leaders, like other forward-looking settlement house workers around the country, sought to move from their voluntarist roots and to transform their organization into a professional social work agency. NU leaders recognized the growing civic influence of social workers and their institutions, and felt that the union's professionalization could serve as a conduit to white acceptance and public legitimacy, both for black reformers and for the black community as a welfare constituency. To these ends, the Neighborhood Union helped found the Atlanta School of Social Work (ASSW) in 1920, and it encouraged its members and young volunteers to earn training and credentials in the profession. As the decade progressed, the union relied more and more on faculty and students from the ASSW and the Morehouse College sociology department to run its programs according to the latest in social-work theory. Union leaders aimed to establish the Neighborhood Union as an all-black version of Atlanta's largest social work agency, the Family Welfare Society, with a professional staff charged to serve the welfare needs of the black community. Poised to assume that responsibility, the Neighborhood Union joined the Community Chest in 1925, confident that membership in the white charitable establishment would ultimately lead to the funding and legitimacy necessary for such expansion.[9]

Almost immediately, union leaders regretted their action. As a condition for joining its ranks, the Community Chest required that the Neighborhood Union confine its work to a pediatric clinic, ostensibly to avoid duplication of the charitable services of the Family Welfare Society. This Faustian bargain was the first of many. Chest membership did not bring civic recognition to the union and equal partnership with the white charitable and social-work community, but, rather, resulted in a steady onslaught of criticism and diminution of the union's work. Through the 1920s and early 1930s, chest leaders complained constantly that the union's program was too limited and its personnel too slow to professionalize in order to deserve chest funds. Yet the chest itself impeded the NU's growth. Despite constant requests and petitions by the Neighborhood Union, it refused to expand the black agency's mandate or funding, even ejecting the union in 1926 for overstepping the bounds imposed by the chest without permission.[10] As one anonymous union member put it, the chest crippled the union. It gave union leaders "far too little capital to finance their work on a professional basis, [while] at the same time robbed them of their independence and stripped them of their most useful functions." In short, she concluded, joining the chest was "one of the most serious mistakes which this organization has made."[11]

Just how serious a mistake became clear in the Depression when

Atlanta's city government took its first tentative steps into public relief, a move unprecedented in Atlanta. Besides running a city soup kitchen and the municipal Relief Center, and appropriating tens of thousands of dollars for direct relief, the city began to fund the Family Welfare Society to provide case work for public relief recipients. The society became a quasi-public agency, providing help with lodging, health care, employment, and dealing with angry creditors for 800 families, or about 4,000 public-relief recipients in Atlanta.[12]

This step further entrenched the marginal position of the black community in relation to white-controlled relief efforts. Although public funding of relief represented a desperately needed infusion, it only served as a drop in the bucket, so great was the need of the city's 20,000 or more unemployed. In the triage that ensued, white welfare officials made African Americans their last priority. Neighborhood Union leaders seethed in anger as the Family Welfare Society, charged by the city with responsibility for the African American poor, neglected the black community. White social workers appeared indifferent to African Americans in need, failing to keep appointments for home visits or to intervene on behalf of black clients. This inattention persisted and intensified as these workers assumed their new public mandate with the city.[13]

Furthermore, racist assumptions about African Americans became the foundation of public policy as the city became involved in relief. Black relief recipients received less aid than their white counterparts, on the belief that blacks could survive on less. Local relief for whites, inadequate by any standard, meant that black families were required to subsist on a pittance. Even those families with six or more children were rarely offered more than $2.50 in weekly grocery orders, and the black poor were sometimes barred entirely from receiving the flour, greens, and coal distributed daily at the Relief Center. Furthermore, municipal relief officials distributed what relief was available to African Americans in a slipshod and random manner, taking no time to ascertain family size or specific need. The assumptions of white superiority and black deference that prompted these policies meant that many unemployed African Americans returned to their families from the Relief Center empty handed. One observer estimated that of the 8,000 to 9,000 families receiving municipal relief before the New Deal, only 1,800 of those were black, even though blacks comprised one-third of Atlanta's population, and a much greater proportion of the unemployed poor.[14]

The Neighborhood Union and other reform organizations protested this publicly sanctioned inequality and abuse, both in petitions and official delegations, and in individual confrontations such as Lugenia Hope's with Mr. Nix. However these efforts resulted in half measures at best. For example, the city only granted black citizens relief jobs at the municipal soup kitchen when the Neighborhood Union offered to pay their wages.

Seeing the gross inequalities of municipal relief, the Atlanta Urban League stepped into the fray. Despite having done relatively little relief work prior to 1932, the AUL, whose "professional" staff met with approval from the Community Chest, was in a better position than the NU to exert authority and influence over white officials. Still, even it could not induce city officials to reverse their racist policies. After the AUL protested to city council, Relief Center employees began distributing groceries to black recipients, but only in the afternoons, and only if the white unemployed had not cleared out the supply in the morning. The AUL also managed to reduce the gap between municipal cash relief offered to white and black families, but it could not prevail upon white officials to eliminate it. AUL leaders persuaded the city council to pay black workers at the Relief Center out of its regular funds and to allow the AUL's secretary, Charles Washington, to convene a committee to supervise black personnel at the center. Despite these improvements, most of the abuses of the local relief system remained.[15]

The Neighborhood Union responded to white officialdom's neglect of the black community by abandoning its long and fruitless quest for white acceptance. In defiance of the Community Chest, the Neighborhood Union sought to provide the black community with the relief services the Family Welfare Society and city would not provide. In early 1931, just as Atlanta made its first forays into public relief, the Union formed the West Side Unemployment Relief Committee. It brought together the individual efforts of churches, parent-teacher associations, and black charities to launch a systematic program of aid for black Atlantans living in a large district surrounding Atlanta University (AU). Likening the seriousness of the Depression to wartime, the committee combined the most modern social-work methodology with old-fashioned private charity to attack the economic crisis head on. To gauge the extent of need on the west side, the committee enlisted Morehouse sociology students to compile and report upon a door-to-door survey of the needs of more than 7,000 residents. To bankroll its relief efforts, the committee organized a carnival which raised $500, arranged a benefit film screening at a black cinema which allowed the purchase of 14 tons of coal, and held a charity concert at D. T. Howard Junior High School at which the audience contributed $100. The committee spent these funds on groceries and clothing for the poor, all of which were systematically distributed through the neighborhood by ASSW students who "organized" west side neighborhoods for relief. The committee also interceded on behalf of individual families in crisis, finding shelter for the homeless and fending off repossession of homes and furniture. By March of 1932, the committee could boast of helping 1,100 west side families in some way. In the face of public neglect, the Neighborhood Union worked, in effect, for the west side community to help its own.[16]

In the face of the Depression's devastating impact on the black community, the Neighborhood Union rejected the great cost of inclusion in the public life of the city. The public-relief crisis provided the ultimate demonstration to union leaders that the white charitable establishment never shared its public welfare goals or recognized its legitimacy, and indeed wished to prevent its evolution into a modern social-work agency. Consequently, the union broke out of its Community Chest–imposed shackles and looked inward to the resources of the black community to achieve its ambitious welfare scheme.

Yet, although NU leaders memorialized the West Side Committee as an important strike for independence, its program of private, voluntary charity work proved inadequate and anachronistic in the dawning age of public welfare. The committee's work, which consumed the lives of its members for more than one year, fell far short of the union's ambitious goals. The relief committee had to devote most of its time to fund-raising rather than relief work. Furthermore, the pittance raised by the committee could not possibly achieve Lugenia Hope's dream of not only "help[ing] the unemployed today" but also of "making a sufficiently strong organization to stand for at least two years in order to hold the family together."[17] In addition, the Neighborhood Union's lack of mandate to help the black poor kept it from the systematic coordination of black relief. For example, the Relief Committee hoped to control panhandling and the duplication of relief by having all indigent black Atlantans report to its offices. But it had neither the resources, such as a hostel for the black homeless, nor the jurisdiction to have such control in the black community or in greater Atlanta.[18]

The enormous gap between the committee's goals and its achievements points to the futility of private welfare work in the face of the tremendous needs of the black community in the Great Depression. To be achieved, the committee's schemes required broad public authority and municipal financing. However, such authority would never be forthcoming from a city government and white welfare establishment that had worked to marginalize African Americans just as the city moved from private to public welfare. The Depression crisis intensified the invisibility of African Americans in civic life, despite the best efforts of the most visible and elite black leaders in Atlanta to bring the plight of the black unemployed and the work of black relief agencies to public attention. The bitterness and disillusionment that accompanied the black elite's failure to achieve white recognition for the black community or public legitimacy for its institutions made it unusually receptive to the radical challenge of Communist organizers who moved into Atlanta in the early 1930s with promises of an alternative route to black freedom and full citizenship.

In the 1930s Atlanta gained national notoriety as the site of two of the most infamous Communist "show trials" of the decade. The court cases of the "Atlanta Six" and of Angelo Herndon became causes célèbres, eliciting publicity for the Communist Party (CP) and its legal wing, the International Labor Defense (ILD), and financial support from around the country for the defendants. In both cases, local officials arrested the suspected radicals under the state's antebellum "anti-insurrection" statute, passed by white Georgians after the Nat Turner rebellion to prosecute rebellious slave leaders and abolitionists, but now invoked to arrest radicals believed by whites to have been sent south to overturn the region's social order. Demonstrating remarkable historical continuity, the white descendants of the statute's authors were spurred to action, not so much by the Communists' economic theories, but by how and for what purpose the radicals intended to mobilize the descendants of the enslaved African Americans, against whom the law was originally passed.[19]

The CP made its first tentative forays into Atlanta in 1929. Concentrating its southern organizing efforts in industrial cities like Birmingham, Alabama, and Chattanooga, Tennessee, and rural areas of the Deep South, the party only gave scant and sporadic attention to Atlanta. In late 1929, the CP launched a limited drive for African American support in Atlanta by distributing Communist literature in black neighborhoods and holding organizational meetings there. The CP made targeted appeals to skilled black artisans—men like Mr. Beale who had lost the most from labor displacement. Organizers held meetings in the black community to which both blacks and whites were invited, but African Americans always constituted most of the audience. Police arrested the "Atlanta Six" at two of these meetings in 1930, a group that contained only one Atlantan, black printer Henry Story.[20]

These arrests and the publicity they garnered only intensified the party's organizing efforts in Atlanta. By the time police arrested Angelo Herndon in June 1932, Atlanta's Communist organization had established an Unemployed Council through which it gained a solid foothold among the city's poor and unemployed, both black and white. Herndon, a young black CP organizer from Birmingham, led a mass demonstration to protest the county commission's refusal to institute a tax increase to deal with a financial crisis that had recently shut down the Relief Center. The protest attracted nearly one thousand black and white protesters—a show of interracial working-class unity that badly frightened local officials. Not willing to acknowledge or recognize the protests of poor blacks but wanting to quell the unrest as quickly as possible, county commissioners agreed to meet with a small group of white demonstrators at the protest, and the next day approved a $6,000 appropriation for relief grocery orders. Further, in an effort to stop the potentially revolutionary interracial organization of poor whites and blacks, police arrested Herndon eleven days later as he picked up his mail from a local post office, thus beginning one of the most notorious legal cases of the 1930s.[21]

Herndon's arrest prompted the arrival of the ILD in Atlanta and the most protracted Communist-led activism in the city. Run from its Harlem headquarters by Communist black lawyer William Patterson, the ILD had already become an important player in the fight against the racial inequality of Jim Crow by the time of Herndon's arrest. The ILD first captured the nation's attention through its participation in the Scottsboro case, in which the organization led the legal defense for nine black adolescent boys in Alabama who were wrongly convicted and, save one, sentenced to death in 1931 for the rape of two white women. Approaching the case from the conviction that the courts were a capitalist tool, the ILD based its Scottsboro appeals not only on the basis of the youths' innocence but also, importantly, on a direct attack against the southern justice system, in this instance the region's all-white juries. Furthermore, believing the justice system to be fundamentally biased against the working class, the ILD combined legal defense with aggressive tactics of mass protest in order to bring public attention to legal inequities and to put political pressure on the courts. As Patterson summarized this two-pronged strategy, "The ILD believes that only mass pressure can bring about the release of a class war prisoner; that pressure must be supplemented by legal defense . . . of the most expert character."[22] In the Scottsboro case, these tactics achieved important victories. The Supreme Court's 1935 decision, *Norris v. Alabama*, a direct result of the ILD's Scottsboro defense strategy, created an important precedent which found the all-white jury system to be unjust. Meanwhile, the ILD's mass protest strategy resulted in a worldwide campaign in support of the Scottsboro defendants and against the racism of the southern courts.[23]

The ILD intended to extend this strategy to Angelo Herndon's case. His defense was based on the unconstitutionality of the insurrection statute and the exclusion of African Americans from juries. The ILD also used the case to assert the rights of citizens to assemble and demonstrate, especially against capitalism and white supremacy. Thus the organization sought not only to defend Herndon but also to confront the Jim Crow system. It reinforced this point by retaining two local black attorneys, Benjamin Davis Jr. and John Geer, for Herndon's defense in a jurisdiction that had rarely seen all-black legal teams in court.[24]

The ILD's strategy and Communist activism generally presented an unprecedented threat to national black leadership. The CP, with its identity bound explicitly to its class and outsider status, challenged the elite's uplift strategy and ideology, along with its incorporative aims. The party rejected the need for white approval to achieve its goals, looking inward instead for the support of black and white workers whom it believed were actors and catalysts, not simply victims or ciphers awaiting uplift. By distancing themselves from and indeed declaring war on the white establishment, the Communists broke from the hegemonic power of the racial ideologies underpinning Jim Crow. Hence their vision of black citizenship and freedom was more universal and less conditional than the black reform elite's, which was based on bourgeois behavioral standards dictated by the politics of respectability.

Scottsboro quickly revealed this fundamental conflict. While the ILD jumped in rapidly to defend the youths, the NAACP hesitated, concerned about being perceived as supporting alleged rapists. Once the NAACP did join the struggle, it disavowed the ILD's mass protest tactic, averring that it did more harm than good to the defendants in the vicious antiblack atmosphere of Deep South Alabama. Instead, the NAACP's approach stressed gradualism and rationalism, confirming its belief in American institutions, if not their Jim Crow–distorted form. Further, the ILD included the youths' mothers as a central part of their protest strategy, offering, in the words of historian Mark Solomon, "hitherto anonymous southern black women the opportunity to become active players in the battle for their sons' freedom."[25] Such respectful treatment contrasted sharply to that of national NAACP executive secretary Walter White, who patronized the women, assuming that they were ignorant and uncouth victims led to slaughter by dangerously bold radicals. White's antiradicalism was more than matched by the ILD in the early 1930s; following the CP's "Third Period" strategy, Patterson and his fellow activists rejected any cooperation with "social fascists," or non-Communist reformers, and in fact viciously denounced reform groups like the NAACP as vigorously as it did capitalist bosses. Ideological differences and the ILD's inflexibility led to the NAACP's exit from the Scottsboro case in January 1932.[26]

Paradoxically, however, despite their extreme ideological and strategic differences, black reformers and the CP shared many of the same goals both nationally and at the local level. Indeed, Angelo Herndon's arrest resulted from his activism against the same local relief establishment that the Neighborhood Union fought in its struggles to equalize local relief. In fact, one of the Unemployed Council's key demands to the city commission was to bring an end to racial disparities in relief distribution. Further, like the NU's West Side Committee, the Unemployed Council worked to stop evictions of black tenants who could not pay their rent. However the CP's strategy to achieve these goals was directly antithetical to the reform elite's. Instead of employing a gradualist reform program, the Communists used direct action and mass protest to achieve their goals. For example, while a few select members of the reform elite quietly and politely petitioned city council for black police to combat the rampant and often deadly police brutality of the early 1930s, the CP organized a very public and publicized "mass protest funeral" for Glover Davis, a blind man shot by police in his home.[27]

Such antagonistic mass actions jeopardized the foundation of black reformers' strategic appeals to the paternalism or self-interest of white officials. As in the Scottsboro case, the CP in Atlanta mobilized black workers as leaders and active participants in its protest efforts, rather than seeing them as the passive objects of noblesse oblige. Its success in mobilizing the black "masses" in Atlanta belied the reform elite's characterization of the black poor as passive and parochial, revealing instead ordinary black Atlantans' deeply felt frustrations and willingness to organize in their own self-interest. For example, Hosea Hudson, a Communist organizer in Atlanta, noted the particularly welcome reception he and his comrades received in People's Town, an appropriately named black neighborhood settled largely by recent migrants to the city. These new Atlantans comprised the very group that elite black reformers claimed to be most in need of racial uplift, characterizing them as set in their backward, rural

ways, unaware of the possibility or desirability of community improvement, and desperately needing the counsel of the black elite to bring them
to self-awareness. By mobilizing the residents of People's Town and other
"backward" districts, the CP called into question the reform elite's self-
proclaimed leadership of the black community and its assumed authority
over the lives of the black poor. For the Communists, black workers would
be the agents of their own deliverance.[28]

Ideologically, the CP presented an even more fundamental attack on the
reform elite by rejecting the very basis of uplift ideology. The party repudiated black reformers' connection of black oppression to the social pathol-
ogy of the black poor, and disavowed any definition of citizenship based
on morality or behavior. Approaching the task of black self-determination
from the ground up, the CP and its supporters interpreted black oppression
and noncitizenship purely as matters of economic and racial exploitation.
As one Communist pamphlet distributed in black Atlanta proclaimed: "By
first setting off the . . . Negroes of this country into a special racial group . . .
they make it all the easier . . . to persecute the Negro workers even more
in industry. . . . This double exploitation of the Negro workers and their
families has forced the Negro masses, both North and South, into the most
miserable living conditions, forced them into old dilapidated houses in the
cities, for which they pay high rents; forced husband, wife, and child to
work; has denied their children even elementary education."[29]

The scales did not fall from the eyes of black workers when they heard
or read such messages; they were fully aware of the nature and causes
of their oppression. What was important was that the Communists fearlessly articulated this stark message which the forces of white supremacy
had silenced and made taboo. Further, they used their message to mobilize black workers, whom the forces of white supremacy had marginalized
in the public life of the city. By refusing to accommodate or internalize
the racial ideologies of white supremacy, the Communists broke out of the
corner in which black reformers had trapped themselves.

No wonder, then, that one black Atlantan observed to a congressional
committee investigating CP activities in Atlanta that "mighty near every
colored man you met was a [CP] sympathizer when he read those pam-
phlets."[30] Black workers had a history of being receptive to radicalism and
enthusiastic about programs that linked their lived experience of the Jim
Crow South's pernicious mix of capitalist and racial exploitation to broader
political movements. For example, in the midst of the labor displacement
of the early Great Depression, an outburst of African American interest re-

vived the nearly moribund Atlanta chapter of the Socialist Party (SP) until national and local white leaders' racial supremacy and capitulation to Jim Crow led them to reject the new recruits. The SP's initial foray into the black community came at the invitation of E. W. Pearlstein, described by white SP organizer Edith Washburn as a "colored man who is well read and a thinker," to address a group at an unidentified Baptist church in the black community. Washburn went reluctantly, but realized that "there is a much more receptive field among the colored" than among whites for the party's message.[31] Pearlstein was "a fairly well-to-do Negro" who owned a "chain of stores here in the colored sections." Among others who approached Washburn were a "union brick mason" from Savannah interested in organizing a SP local there, and the Church Mother, who also belonged to the "Women's Aux[iliary] of the colored Masons," a group within which, she promised Washburn, she hoped to tap great potential interest in socialism.[32]

After this initial meeting, Washburn received a steady stream of invitations to address a variety of groups within the black community. Although her correspondence reveals little or nothing about the attraction of socialism for African Americans, it is easy to surmise how a brick mason or other members of the upper echelons of black workers belonging to the Masons might be interested in joining a party which made a colorblind appeal to the working class at a time when black workers like Mr. Beale were being displaced from their trades and shunted to the margins of the labor market. As Robin Kelley has observed about local black Communist leadership in Birmingham, the core group emerged from "respected, upwardly mobile, working-class families" like the Beales, and even sometimes by non-elite bourgeois like Pearlstein. Indeed, from the scanty evidence about the CP in Atlanta, it appears that the dominant group of indigenous black leaders were craftsmen, including printers like Henry Story, stonemasons, and painters. For this group of strivers, "the Party merely constituted an alternative stepping stone toward respectability within the confines of their world."[33] The SP's stated willingness and the CP's practice to include black workers as equal members, along with their distance from the white establishment, raised black Atlantans' hopes that they had found an "outsider" organization that would support their battles for inclusion and citizenship. However, Atlanta's white Socialists' desire to move inside from the cold, especially among white voters and conservative white trade union circles, meant that they largely ignored this potential black constituency which was "ready" for socialism's message, effectively leaving the city for the CP.

Despite the challenges Socialism and Communism presented to their leadership, strategy, and ideology, Atlanta's black elites were remarkably ambivalent in their reactions to the interlopers. When the Communists arrived in Atlanta, they found a frustrated reform elite. Rejected by the white charitable community, and marginalized from the public life of the city, black reformers were discouraged, even disillusioned, by their own strategies. Licking their wounds from the battle for white acceptance, Atlanta's black reformers were perhaps as receptive as they ever could be to the Communist appeal. Accordingly, Atlanta's black reformers reserved judgment on the CP, waiting to see what it could offer black Atlanta to revitalize the spent forces of the struggle.[34]

This receptivity resulted in unexpected and unprecedented behavior by the black middle class and reform elite. Hosea Hudson remembered speaking in the early 1930s to a group of schoolteachers at a secret meeting arranged by one of Angelo Herndon's lawyers, Benjamin Davis Jr. Hudson was reluctant to make the speech, but once he warmed up he "forgot they was schoolteachers," and proceeded to instruct them on "the conditions of the world and the danger of fascist war, and . . . how the economy itself would automatically breed war." After the meeting, many of the teachers told Davis that although Herndon's "English is very bad . . . he knows a lot. . . . He knows things I never thought of."[35]

Both Hudson's reluctance to address the teachers and their surprise at his intelligence and sophistication point to the novelty of this incident. In the rigid social hierarchy of the black community, unschooled laborers could not possibly enlighten teachers. Yet the Communists and their working-class black leaders clearly carried a message that also had pertinence for the black middle class—a message so pertinent that some members were willing to risk detection and transcend social norms to hear it. Teachers in particular had reason to be receptive to the Communist appeal. They were city and county employees, dependent on the white-controlled Board of Education for their employment. Earning only two-thirds the salary of their already poorly paid white peers, they were subject to the most egregious public discrimination suffered by black Atlanta's college-educated minority. Further, they experienced the same kind of displacement and instability as other black workers in the Depression when Atlanta proposed closing black night schools and laying off black teachers to keep its white schools afloat. Unsheltered by the black economy or black-controlled institutions like the colleges, public school teachers shared many of the experiences of discrimination and marginalization suffered by other black workers forced to toil in the white world.[36]

Many younger members of the reform elite were also open to the Communist appeal, drawn especially to the new activist strategies and economic critiques Party members offered. Observing the Neighborhood Union's struggles and the teachers' layoffs, these young men and women saw firsthand the fruitlessness of the older generation's strategy of gradual incorporation into the white establishment. With less investment in the status quo than their parents, and many having formal understanding of Marxist theory through their studies, they entertained the notion that Communism could help them achieve the reform elite's goals through more direct and less accommodating means. They were greatly influenced by W. E. B. Du Bois who, in the face of massive black Depression-era displacement, abandoned his integrationist philosophy and called for the "internal self-organization" of the black community along socialist lines, in order to overcome racism and capitalism's impediments on black progress.[37] Thus they shared the perspective of many black workers in Atlanta attracted by Communist ideology, although almost none of them joined either the CP or the Socialist Party.[38]

For example, AU historian Rayford Logan was openly sympathetic to the aims of the ILD and sought to organize faculty to protest police repression of Communism. His support stemmed in part from his frustrations with the timidity of the local branch of the NAACP in fighting the rash of racial terrorism and police killings in and around Atlanta in the early 1930s.[39]

Joining Logan was Rev. J. Raymond Henderson, outspoken young pastor of Wheat Street Baptist Church, who wrote in the ADW of his "sympathies . . . with the Communists" and his frustration with the two major parties and their "adher[ence] to the capitalistic system, which has broken down the world over and brought untold suffering to millions of people."[40] He was one of the few members of Atlanta's reform elite to criticize openly the hypocrisies of the white establishment. In the early 1930s, he, too, wrote of his impatience with the reform elite's futile petitions and meaningless committee resolutions to deal with the police brutality, vocational displacement, and economic privation facing the black community. Like Logan, he called for voter registration drives and a revitalized and community-supported NAACP to fight for black Atlantans' interests at the polls and in the courts. His support for the radicals also probably stemmed in part from leading the city's largest black congregation, representing the full spectrum of Atlanta's black community, including hundreds who had been displaced by the Depression and many striving and respectable members of the working class who likely supported the CP.

Probably Atlanta's most prominent elite Communist was Angelo Herndon's lawyer, Benjamin Davis Jr. Educated at Amherst College and Harvard Law School, Davis became an important party leader after moving to New York City in 1934, where he won a seat on city council as a Communist in 1944. Davis's political activism was likely prompted by his family history. His father had a long history in politics and for decades had been actively involved with the Republican Party, valiantly if futilely fighting against the "lily white" faction seeking to eject black party faithful. Further, Davis's father had a reputation for militancy as the owner-editor of the Atlanta *Independent*, a black newspaper predating the ADW.[41]

Ready for a new activist strategy to achieve their goals, and recognizing the dangers of the anti-insurrection statute in stifling any black activism on behalf of African Americans, many young black reformers forged an alliance with the Communists to support the ILD's efforts on behalf of Angelo Herndon. In 1933, Davis established a remarkably nonpartisan, interracial, and class-diverse defense committee to support the young Communist's case, despite the protests from the ILD's national office warning of the dangers of a "united front" with liberals. It included closeted black and white Party members such as Davis; Clarence Weaver, a black painter and local Party leader; and Walter Washburn, a prominent white member. Notable non-Communist black reformers and white liberals also joined, including Reverend Henderson; Jesse Blayton, a banker, AU faculty member, and chairman of the Negro Chamber of Commerce; Sadie Mays, a faculty member at the ASSW; and C. Vann Woodward, the future historian and white CIC leader.[42]

The committee had wide, if not universal, support in black reform circles, in part because it presented frustrated black reformers with opportunities to challenge the racial status quo head on. For example, in December 1933, Reverend Henderson addressed an ILD fund-raiser for the Scottsboro defendants at Holsey Temple, an AME church. When participants arrived at the meeting, they found the church surrounded by Ku Klux Klan members distributing anti-Communist and antiblack leaflets. The scene turned ugly after an ADW photographer pointed his camera at the vigilantes, and Klan leaders physically prevented ILD organizers from entering the church to make their speeches. When the police arrived, they arrested an Emory University student, Nathan Yagol, for inciting to riot by attending the meeting, a charge that was dropped the next day. The rally received wide, negative publicity in the virulently anti-Communist white press, which praised the KKK for its vigilance against Communism. Henderson understood the violent potential of the meeting and the negative publicity that would surely result from it, especially after a white college student had been arrested while "mixing" with blacks at a Communist-sponsored rally. Further, as a longtime NAACP member, Henderson's support for the ILD was remarkable considering the association's bitter conflict with the Communist organization over the Scottsboro defendants' legal representation. Yet he delivered an address on behalf of the ILD speakers who were stuck outside the church. No doubt he relished this opportunity to challenge openly and militantly the southern racial code he and his congregation so despised. By directly and fearlessly challenging the status quo, Communists offered liberation to the reform elite from the straitjacket of gradualism and accommodation.[43]

Still, even if many members of the black reform elite found the Communists' direct-action techniques and their economic and racial critiques to be the antidote to the intensified marginalization they faced in the early years of the Depression, fundamental differences prevented Party membership or even a long-term alliance with the radicals. The Communists, especially in the rigidly sectarian early 1930s, required an ideological acceptance that class, not race, ultimately lay at the root of black oppression. If that were the case, the black middle class had to accept responsibility for participating in the exploitation of the black "masses" and renounce any prior assumptions of class chauvinism. Also on this basis, Communists denied the possibility of any form of unity between the black elite and working class based on their shared experience of racism. To add insult to injury, the Communists did not keep their beliefs about the black bourgeoisie to themselves. Instead, as in the case of their attacks on the NAACP in the Scottsboro case, they viciously denounced the black middle class, leaving no room for compromise or common ground.

Yet beyond their maddening tactics and crude denial of the racial oppression of all African Americans, Communism's ideological emphasis on class exploitation was what ultimately made it impossible for even the most militant black reformer to accept the doctrine. Communism required a total repudiation of the foundation of elitism upon which uplift ideology rested, along with the reform activism accomplished in its name. In the end, even those members of the black reform elite who engaged in radical critiques of capitalism could not envision relinquishing their "leadership" of the black community to men like Mr. Beale, Hosea Hudson, or Clarence Weaver of the Herndon Defense Committee, no matter their demonstrated militancy or political sophistication. They could not let go of the notion, as J. Raymond Henderson put it, that the key to black salvation was an educated leadership class whom "the great body of workers . . . would gladly follow" because they unquestionably "need guidance."[44] As W. E. B. Du Bois wrote in 1933 of his own endeavors to adapt socialist ideology to the black struggle, he found much good in the Communist message but had to reject it outright when it claimed that "the natural leaders of the colored people, the educated and trained classes have . . . goals and interests different from the mass of Negroes."[45] For black reformers to reject their hierarchical understanding of the African American community and black citizenship would indeed be akin to renouncing "nature."

This difference crystallized when the national ILD shattered the Herndon Defense Committee's carefully constructed coalition of radicals and reformers by suggesting openly that self-preservation rather than selfless noblesse oblige governed the black reform elite's actions. It was one thing for Logan and Henderson to call from within Atlanta's reform community for the regeneration of the NAACP's program or for greater commitment from white liberals for the black struggle. It was another for Communist "outsiders" to condemn all reformers' efforts outright as a treacherous betrayal of the black masses. A few months after the Holsey Temple incident, black reformers closed ranks against the ILD after it issued a national bulletin openly criticizing Atlanta's NAACP president, lawyer A. T. Walden, for betraying his clients and the black community in order to curry favor with the white legal establishment in his legal defense work for the association. Black reformers found it intolerable that the ILD would criticize one of their own leaders and organizations, especially since the NAACP was in the midst of its crucial annual fund-raising drive. Responding to the ILD's charge of apparent collusion between the Atlanta NAACP and white liberals, and the "bosses'" court in the execution of John Downer (convicted of raping a white woman in a highly publicized case), black ministers and leaders from the AUL and Butler Street YMCA joined in barring the ILD from meeting in their institutions. Henderson, soon followed by other non-Communist members, resigned from the Herndon Defense Committee with the following statement: "I shall not, nor do I believe the citizens of Atlanta will stand by supinely and see the good attempted by the NAACP and its president, and the noble work of the interracial committee [CIC] . . . repudiated by a group of people more rash with words than with sense."[46]

Henderson's reference to CIC leadership was instructive, for black reformers also feared that association with the Communists would threaten a cordial relationship with white liberals, their only white allies in Atlanta. Members of this group, like the CIC's Will Alexander, were uncompromising in their anti-Communism, blaming the radicals for undoing years of gradualist, nonconfrontational interracial work by rejecting all of the racial mores of the South in their revolutionary quest to bring justice to workers. The ILD's handling of the Angelo Herndon case illustrated the problem for CIC leaders. Will Alexander believed Herndon was "lending himself quite willingly" to impossible causes in his trial. In Alexander's view, Herndon was defended in the most inflammatory and quixotic manner by Communist black lawyers who elected to challenge the all-white jury system and argue "the merits and demerits of communism" in front of an "ignorant, fanatical" prosecutor and an all-white jury. In white liberals' minds, Herndon's trial was a nightmare come true.[47]

The CIC believed the actions of the ILD kindled white vigilantism and threatened racial peace, the attainment of which was a primary motivating goal of the organization. Herndon was eventually freed, and the insistent work of the ILD in the South ultimately led to an important blow against the all-white jury system through *Norris v. Alabama*. Nevertheless, white liberals believed ILD tactics and goals to be impossible, and they fought the incursion of radical "outsiders" in Atlanta with the same vehemence of Georgia's states' rights governor, Eugene Talmadge, or the Ku Klux Klan.[48]

While most members of Atlanta's black reform elite did not subscribe to Alexander's visceral anti-Communism, many shared his resentment of the ILD and the CP and their criticisms of the traditional leadership. Beyond this grudge, black reformers, like white liberals, feared that the Communism issue would result in their further marginalization from the white establishment. Alexander wanted the Herndon case to be tried by white southerners like himself because he dreaded the ramifications of Communist involvement in local affairs in Atlanta for the CIC and other liberal organizations. He fought for the Herndon trial to be tried purely as a free-speech case because he knew that if the anti-insurrection statute were not overturned that all liberal reform work would be in jeopardy, as indeed it was. After Herndon was tried and his appeal rejected by the Georgia Supreme Court, local authorities initiated a red scare in Atlanta and in the process were able to implicate white organizations like the CIC as Communist, thus cutting them off from Community Chest funding or shutting them down altogether.[49]

The red scare started in September 1934, during the general strike against the virtually all-white cotton industry that spread throughout the South that fall. Police in Atlanta used the anti-insurrection statute to arrest two white Communist women for distributing Party literature at a picket set up outside a local textile mill. The strike, which at its height had the support of 400,000 workers nationwide, was unprecedented in its scope, militancy, and violence. It terrified southern public officials and business leaders fearful of class warfare, leading to an intensified crackdown against "radicals" throughout the region, including in Georgia the largest peacetime mobilization of the National Guard and the establishment of barbed-wire "concentration camps" for arrested strikers. Although the white press in Atlanta publicized the arrest and trial of the two accused women, it characterized the strike in Atlanta as being relatively quiet and peaceful compared to the radicalism and violence of the walkout in Georgia's mill villages. In an approach to labor "agitators" common to places where the strike was less confrontational, the *Constitution* characterized the radical women as non-Atlantan outsiders who did not represent the interests or goals of "loyal" local workers, emphasizing that picketers themselves had detained the women and held them until police arrived.[50]

This example to demonstrate white Atlantans' staunch antiradicalism stood in stark contrast to local officials' beliefs about the loyalty of African Americans. The real crackdown on Communism in Atlanta came after the strike in October 1934, when two spectacular raids showed that, for Atlanta's political establishment, a red scare was most valuable as a way to whip up frenzy in the white community by linking Communism to African Americans and to an ideology of racial equality and "mongrelization." On 16 October, police raided two Communist meetings held in private homes—one in a middle-class white neighborhood on the eastern edge of Atlanta in DeKalb County, and another in the heart of the black west-side district. The host at the DeKalb County gathering was Mrs. R. W. Alling, a white widow who had taught in the Atlanta public schools for fourteen years. Police arrested six people at her home, including Nathan Yagol, the Emory graduate student who had been arrested at the Holsey Temple ILD fund-raiser. At the other meeting on Lindsay Street, police arrested seven African Americans, and in the home of one of those detained, Julia Weaver, they found lists, apparently of black CP members. The only direct link between the two meetings was Clarence Weaver, a painter who was the only African American arrested for attending Mrs. Alling's meeting. He was the husband of Julia Weaver.

These two raids, with their common denominator of the Weavers, set the stage for an anti-Communist witch hunt in Atlanta in which "red" became a synonym for black. Since the Angelo Herndon trial, the anti-Communist white press had emphasized the CP's goal to establish "self determination in the black belt" and to break down the barriers of Jim Crow. The result, in the fearful minds of white southerners, would be an age of miscegenation. Weaver's arrest demonstrated concretely the link between black and white Communists and thus in the fecund imaginations of the white press and Atlanta police force showed that the Communists were putting their ideology into practice.

These first two raids established the foundation for a series of others in which African Americans and some whites were arrested, although never again in a white neighborhood. Even more troubling was how this red scare allowed white officials to conflate the moderate reform efforts of the black elite with the revolutionary thrust of the Communist agenda, and the police to extend their harassment to respected and established black charitable organizations. Police raided the AUL's offices after DeKalb County officials found Clarence Weaver carrying an advertisement for a "Workers' Council" to be held at the league. The police also searched the Butler Street YMCA after they found that Alex Racholin, a white lawyer from New York arrested in the DeKalb raid, had lodged there.[51]

Concurrent with these police scare tactics aimed at the black community and especially black reform organizations, the solicitor general, John Boykin, and the Fulton County grand jury initiated an all-out judicial war on Communism. They called one hundred African Americans to testify in the grand jury investigation. Among this group, Fulton County officials questioned Rev. J. A. Martin, who had been active in the Angelo Herndon Defense Committee, and John Hope II (son of the Atlanta University president), who had connections to the National Students' League, an association with Communist ties.[52]

Furthermore, Solicitor General Boykin used the raids and the grand jury hearings to showcase his proposal for an anti-Communist law which would make it a crime simply to possess "insurrectionary" literature. Boykin sent his proposal to prosecutors throughout the South, urging them to join him in the fight. Just what he was fighting against became clear when the Fulton County grand jury made its presentment regarding the October hearings. Such a law was overdue, according to Boykin, because the Communist literature seized by the police was "designed to encourage social and racial equality" in violation of "the best traditions of our country." This literature of "racial amalgamation" would in his mind "inflame racial prejudice" and "stir up strife," leading to "riots, civil strife, and a general break down of our law." Both blacks and whites would be better served, he claimed, by concentrating on the preservation of "racial integrity and racial purity than in any movement to weaken or destroy either race."[53] The Ku Klux Klan commented positively on Boykin's speech and actions, noting that he finally understood the "danger to the southern social order and the peace of the territory" posed by Communism.[54]

The black reform elite in Atlanta responded quickly to the Red Scare targeted at the black community, especially since it affected not only the "humble poor" but also the "intelligentsia" and some of its most cherished institutions.[55] It understood the power of the Red Scare to squelch all attempts at racial progress and its potential to unleash a police reign of terror in the black community. While reformers disavowed Communism, they reviled the scare tactics of local authorities and came to the defense of those accused, understanding the repercussions if they did not fight back. Rev. J. Raymond Henderson told white readers in a letter to the *Constitution* that although most black Atlantans were not Communist but God-fearing, law-abiding citizens, they would defend those African Americans accused of Communism, because, as African Americans suffering "more by infraction of the law than anyone else," they knew "how costly a thing it is" to be black and "to come within the grip of the law." They also knew that to be black and labeled Communist was a double sentence in a red-scare atmosphere where it was "too easy . . . to interpret everything and everyone as communistic." "Within the present mental frame of Atlanta," he concluded, "our citizens . . . may easily be arrested and given 20 years in prison for absolutely no crime whatever."[56]

Realizing the vulnerability faced by all black reform organizations, the local NAACP branch, despite the national office's public disputes with the Communist Party, established a special defense committee to defend Clarence and Julia Weaver. The Weavers were well-respected and respectable members of the artisanal class in Atlanta, and they had been active in the Atlanta Urban League's efforts to obtain union charters for skilled black workers in the construction trades. The reform elite found it easy to support the Weavers, who represented the highest echelon of the black working class and, despite their Communism, supported the uplift agenda through their participation in AUL-led programs. Furthermore, the red scare had shown black reformers once again how intertwined their fate was with that of black workers, a shared caste position that had led in the first place to black reformers' flirtation with radicalism.

The mass meetings and fund-raisers that resulted from the NAACP's defense efforts rejuvenated the organization, which for years had not found or chosen to promote a popular cause around which the community could rally. The group of young militants led by Reverend Henderson who had called for opening up the NAACP spearheaded the campaign, which resulted in 800 paid-up members for the organization and active community support for its legal defense efforts. The NAACP's efforts resulted in Clarence Weaver's release from DeKalb County jail and the reduction of Julia Weaver's jail bond, allowing her to leave Fulton Tower, Atlanta's county jail. Ultimately, no black Communists went to trial, since Angelo Herndon's successful appeal to the U.S. Supreme Court in 1937 rendered unconstitutional the anti-insurrection law under which they had been arrested.[57]

While the 1934 arrests did not result in convictions, they had a profound effect on the black reform community in Atlanta. Some reformers had welcomed the CP and the ILD to Atlanta, seeing them as potentially powerful allies in the struggle for recognition and retribution for the black community. But this alternative path was effectively blocked by the anti-Communist and antiblack campaigns of white vigilantes and the white justice system, which effectively marginalized and repudiated the legitimacy of the Communist cause. Recoiling from this association, the black reform elite as a whole began to consider other, less confrontational tactics. By being branded as Communists by local officials, however, black leaders had to represent and defend their community militantly and systematically against a witch hunt, and the experience gained in this effort would become more and more important as the era of interest-group politics took hold. Indeed, developments like the NAACP's defense of the Weavers demonstrated the reform elite's growing sympathy and interaction with upwardly mobile and politically mobilized skilled members of Atlanta's black working class. Although the black elite was not ready to concede leadership to them, it was increasingly ready to support and represent these black Atlantans' interests.[58]

The Communists offered an activist agenda and ideology that found its strength in being fundamentally outside the economic and social restrictions of southern society. Most black elites, who had always worked for black inclusion into the mainstream of public life, shared little in common with an ideology militant in its outsider identity, despite many reformers' sympathies with socialist interpretations of African Americans' marginal economic position. Furthermore, the Communists' mobilization techniques could not be further from the elitist strategies of black reformers, who heretofore had shunned developing a mass constituency to support their reform efforts. The coming of the New Deal offered the elite another alternative—one of greater participation in the affairs of the state. In addition, the inclusive thrust of the New Deal and the exigencies of the electoral goals of black reformers made them realize that some kind of mobilization of the black "masses" would be indispensable to their efforts. Struggles to determine just what form that involvement would take, and a determination of what their relationship would be to the New Deal, preoccupied the minds of black reformers for the remainder of the decade.

II

The New Deal

3

Carpetbaggers and Scalawags

*The New Politics of
the New Deal*

When President Franklin Roosevelt took office in
1933, so did Eugene Talmadge, Georgia's infamous populist governor. The
governor's inflammatory political style, in which he placed himself in direct opposition to the New Deal and its liberal forces, represented powerful interests in Georgia that sought to protect politics and society as usual
in relation to states' rights, economic life, and race relations. Talmadge's
opposition to change and his populist posturing provoked one of the most
protracted political battles in the country over the New Deal "revolution."
At the center of these ongoing struggles was Georgia's black citizenry on
whose dismal economic and social position so many powerful white Georgians depended for their continued prosperity. Now liberal social workers,
economists, and activists, intent upon modernizing the state's economy
and social relations, saw these same black citizens as central to the New
Deal's public-welfare agenda.

Because of almost universal support from Georgia's white voters for
Roosevelt and his program, the state's New Deal forces won the battle
against the governor. Talmadge's stubborn opposition to federal programs
allowed officials in Washington to wrench control of New Deal programs
from the governor and his local patronage appointees and hand it to the
"progressive" forces of Georgia's small but flourishing social-work community. In so doing, federal officials created a "parallel government"[1] in
Georgia that rivaled the state government in resources, power, and prestige among the state's voters. The social workers who controlled this new

government apparatus ran the New Deal in Georgia from top to bottom, and in the process dramatically altered the way in which the state operated. Where once personal friendships and political patronage determined political power, now professionals and trained experts controlled it. This social-work meritocracy sought to modernize Georgia's economy and society, and saw the inclusion of African Americans in the New Deal as an essential part of its mandate.

Understanding the vicious political battles that accompanied Georgia's entry into the New Deal requires an acknowledgment of the threat federal money and intervention posed to the state's political order. Limited in its regulatory and taxation powers, sustained by a spoils system based on political patronage, and ultimately defined by its exclusion and subjugation of the state's poor, both black and white, Georgia's political system served the interests of the plantation and mill owners who dominated the state's economy. The New Deal threatened the political status quo fundamentally by vastly expanding the federal government's mandate to include responsibilities like public welfare that had always been state prerogatives. Further, the Roosevelt administration approached this new mandate with political and policy goals directly antithetical to those of Georgia's political elite, resulting, for example, in an unprecedented recognition of the state's disfranchised and impoverished majority. Before the New Deal, Georgia, like other southern states, eschewed support for the poor. Public relief threatened to disrupt the state's low-wage economy and the labor system of paternalism and dependency on which most employers relied. The state's constitution enshrined this proscription. It barred Georgia from public spending for public welfare and only permitted counties to provide a tiny amount of tax-based relief to fund almshouses—the last destination of the utterly destitute. Georgia resisted any move to reform this system; as other states began to move in the 1910s and 1920s toward the expansive public-welfare model promoted by professional social workers, it remained unreconstructed. On the eve of the New Deal, Georgia and South Carolina remained the only states without a mother's aid program, the vital precursor to government-sponsored welfare.[2]

Federal relief therefore represented a fundamental threat to Georgia's political establishment. At first Eugene Talmadge believed he could limit the disruption by controlling the distribution of the federal funds and using them to bolster his political machine. In January 1933, when both Roosevelt and Talmadge took office, federal relief was confined to the Recon-

struction Finance Corporation (RFC). (The RFC was a federal agency created by Herbert Hoover that provided the states with low-income loans
and grants for self-liquidating public works projects to help them deal
with the Depression crisis.) Talmadge sought to expand and control the
RFC program in Georgia by establishing the Georgia Relief Administration
(GRA), a state oversight committee with counterparts in every county responsible for the administration of the federal program in the state. He
appointed one of his political cronies, Herman P. De La Perriere, to head
the GRA, and he in turn named Talmadge's stepson to be his assistant field
visitor. The three men, along with the politically appointed GRA staff and
executive committee, distributed direct and work relief to the counties according to the rules of patronage, not according to need.[3]

At the county level, ad hoc determinations of eligibility for relief and
the amount and kind of aid distributed reflected the economic and political priorities of the local committees, usually comprised of representatives
of business and plantation interests. In Fulton County, where Atlanta is
located, committee members betrayed their continued reluctance to take
even the smallest responsibility for Atlanta's poor or to acknowledge the
depth of the crisis faced by these residents. They administered relief according to the minimal provisions of the poor law, for example, distributing grocery orders rather than cash. Officials worked to keep government
aid to a minimum, fearing that its expansion might begin a slippery slide
toward higher taxes and disruption of wage scales. In a meeting with a federal official about the unemployment situation in Atlanta, W. E. Mitchell,
chairperson of the Georgia Power Company and of Fulton County's Relief
Committee, revealed his attitude toward Atlanta's poor: "I don't want to
see them, don't let me see them. There will be casualties of this movement
[the Depression] and we must steel our hearts against them all as we did
against wounds and death in the war."[4]

Mitchell and his ilk particularly did not wish to "see" African Americans, lest it result in the disruption of the low-wage, low-tax economy on
which the state's businesses depended. White officials conveniently used
the notion that black families could get by on less than whites to deny
or limit relief to African Americans. Being nonvoters, black Atlantans did
not have the political leverage that some white relief recipients may have
had. Even more important, in a city where most voting whites depended
on cheap, unskilled black labor to work in their homes and businesses,
municipal officials did not welcome unemployed African Americans to the
dole.[5]

The state's small white social-work community vociferously opposed the GRA's administration. For years, social workers, both within Georgia's tiny, purely advisory and supervisory Department of Public Welfare, and outside of government had fought a long and lonely battle against Georgia's political establishment to expand the state's jurisdiction over social welfare and to eliminate the "archaic" county almshouse system. They expected such a development to usher in a new era in which they and their professional, administrative social-work vision would triumph over the forces of politics as usual. When, in effect, the RFC achieved the social workers' goal, they felt a powerful sense of entitlement to run the program. To them, Talmadge's assumption of control over the federal funds constituted an outrageous usurpation of their power by an enemy who represented all they hoped to eliminate through a public-welfare program. As Gay Shepperson, director of the Department of Public Welfare, wrote in 1933 to Frank Bane, director of the American Public Welfare Association, the RFC's "defect" was that it failed "to give proper supervision to the expenditure of these funds to see that the money is used wisely for those who are destitute."[6] She was responding directly to political and patronage considerations that had governed Talmadge's distribution of federal relief. In her definition, wise use of RFC funds meant their administration by professional social workers under the Department of Public Welfare's authority.

In response to her frustration at having to administer the GRA's policies, Shepperson, Georgia's most influential state-employed social worker, led the attack against her employer. Born in Richmond, Virginia, to an elite family, Shepperson's career followed the pattern of many white professional social-work pioneers nationwide. She began her working life as a schoolteacher but moved on to social work when she began to volunteer through the Presbyterian church to help that city's poor. Finding her vocation, she pursued her new career before World War I through apprenticeships—virtually the only kind of social-work training then available—first with the Associated Charities in Washington, D.C., and then the Red Cross in Alabama. In 1923 she attended the New York School of Social Work, the nation's first professional social-work program, and then returned to the South to work for Georgia's Department of Public Welfare, founded only a few years before in 1920. Once in Atlanta, she quickly became a prominent member of the South's and nation's female-dominated social work network, even living with another member of the profession, Louisa Fitzsimmons.[7]

Shepperson used her contacts within the national social work and wel-

Gay Shepperson, Georgia's federal relief administrator, flanked by unidentified New Deal bureaucrats. (Gay Shepperson Collection, Atlanta History Center)

fare reform communities to complain about the practices of Talmadge's GRA to her newly powerful counterparts in Washington who now controlled the disbursement of millions of dollars of New Deal relief money for the states. Most important among these contacts was Shepperson's longtime friend and fellow social worker, Harry Hopkins, who administered the national relief program throughout the 1930s as head of the Federal

Emergency Relief Administration (FERA) and later the Works Progress Administration (WPA).[8]

Shepperson's influential ties to powerful federal officials who shared her vision led to the ascendancy of the social-work model for the relief program in Georgia. Watching Talmadge's machinations, federal representatives believed, in the words of regional FERA field representative Allen Johnstone, that for the New Deal to take effect in Georgia it was "literally necessary to take the State of Georgia away from Talmadge on the question of relief and the whole relief program."[9] Shepperson worked with Hopkins and his staff to these ends, all the while skillfully manipulating the situation to downplay federal interference in Georgia's affairs or the undermining of Talmadge's political cronies. When Roosevelt announced the creation of FERA in May 1933, Shepperson convinced Harry Hopkins that if the "Department of Public Welfare could be designated as the administrative unit for the distribution of federal relief that it would considerably lessen the tension,"[10] between Georgia and Washington, while also putting those responsibilities for once in the hands of professional social workers. They worked on this scheme long distance and not in Washington or Atlanta, since Shepperson was afraid that Talmadge's forces would learn of her maneuvering and of labeling her what she was—a staunch New Dealer with direct ties to federal authorities. Hopkins agreed to her scheme and named Shepperson the state's FERA administrator, making her one of the few women in the country appointed to this position. In a sop to Talmadge for this abrogation of his authority, Hopkins permitted the governor to appoint a Georgia Relief Commission (GRC) to oversee FERA in Georgia. However, Hopkins had final approval over the composition of the commission and named Shepperson its executive secretary, in effect giving her full authority to hire and direct personnel, and to decide on appropriations on the state and county levels.[11]

Hopkins's move transformed government in Georgia by shifting authority from Talmadge the politician to Shepperson the social worker and, in important ways, from Atlanta to Washington, D.C. Upon taking her post, Shepperson fired the staff of the GRA, began hiring professional social workers to replace them, and sought other trained workers to staff the county relief administrations. Talmadge vehemently opposed these moves to subvert state authority and used all his political capital to stop them, but the importance of the federal funds to an impoverished state and the resulting popularity of the New Deal were too great. As Allen Johnstone wrote to Harry Hopkins: "To mention Mr. Roosevelt's name in any county in Georgia produces great enthusiasm and when this whole program is explained as an effort on his part and his associates to redeem the south from economic slavery it creates an enthusiasm comparable to that in war times."[12] While many county politicians continued to oppose Shepperson's takeover of relief distribution, they could not refuse the federal money she disbursed, which represented more outside public funding than they had ever before received, and which even exceeded some counties' annual budgets. Realizing the leverage FERA's popularity gave them, federal administrators consolidated Shepperson's power by making her the Georgia Emergency Relief Administrator, independent of the GRC's and Talmadge's control. In this capacity she resisted all attempts to infuse the relief administration with personnel or executives out of sync with the social-work ideology, even when Georgia Democrats appealed directly to the president.[13]

Unlike other initially resistant governors who found a political logic in embracing the New Deal, Talmadge remained unreconstructed in the face of the federal juggernaut. His continued opposition to the New Deal, including his various actions to subvert Shepperson's authority, and his opposition to mandatory state contributions to federal relief programs and the newly enacted Social Security program led Hopkins finally to dissolve the GRC in 1935. He then named Shepperson the relief administrator of Georgia, making her responsible only to officials in Washington. Talmadge continued his attacks on Shepperson and her overwhelmingly female staff, referring to the New Deal's "wet nursing"[14] in one particularly egregious comment. On a broader front, he stepped up his political fight with Roosevelt, even attempting an abortive third-party presidential bid in 1936, but his tactics failed. He lost his race for the U.S. Senate in 1936, and the Roosevelt booster who replaced him in the governor's office, Eurith D. Rivers, removed all barriers to Social Security in Georgia and enacted his own "Little New Deal" in the state. Talmadge was silenced for a time, but political battles over states' rights and federal intervention continued, and in 1940 he rose like a phoenix to recapture the governorship, running on the same anti–New Deal platform.[15]

Talmadge's defeat at the hands of Gay Shepperson and Harry Hopkins drew the political battle lines between the mainly rural forces of the political status quo in Georgia led by Talmadge, and the mainly urban, social-worker meritocracy led by Shepperson. By "federalizing" relief in Georgia, Harry Hopkins established a powerful New Deal administration in Georgia dominated by social workers and their interests. These included the establishment of a permanent public-welfare apparatus to handle the needs of Georgia's poor, the consolidation of a professional social-work bureaucracy to administer public welfare in Georgia, and the economic and social modernization of the state. These three goals intermeshed and had dramatic implications for African Americans in Georgia and particularly in Atlanta.

Gay Shepperson marked each successive move toward federal control of the New Deal in Georgia by professionalizing the administration and the personnel of the relief set-up, both at the state and local levels, and ridding it of patronage appointees. When she assumed the administration of FERA in January 1934, for example, she purged the staff of the Fulton County Relief Commission and replaced it with hand-picked allies from the social-work field who rationalized its management and eliminated abuses in relief distribution, such as racial differentials. Soon every county in the state had a "trained" administrator in charge of relief, usually a social worker but sometimes a teacher or nurse, often from outside the county, and in all but one case a woman. In Fulton County, Wilma Van Dusseldorp and then Ada M. Barker, both prominent Atlanta social workers and friends of Shepperson, headed the Relief Commission. These workers and the county relief set-ups they managed, though meant to be temporary, ultimately established the local social-service departments that exist today across the state administering public-welfare programs.[16]

Shepperson's quick action pointed to the eagerness and preparedness of the state's white social workers to assume their new public authority. On the eve of the New Deal, Georgia's white social-work leadership was dominated by women, mainly northern-trained transplants from other parts of the South. This group had struggled for fifteen or twenty years through private agencies or the virtually powerless state Department of Public Welfare to effect the kind of changes undertaken by the New Deal and to modernize both public and private charity in the state. For example, social workers in Georgia had long worked to eliminate the "archaic" constitutional restriction in Georgia that prohibited the enactment of mother's aid or any other kind of large-scale public relief. They believed the extension of the state's responsibility to its citizens through public welfare to be necessary for the modernization of Georgia. In 1929, Rhoda Kaufman, the former secretary of the Georgia Department of Public Welfare, expressed a hopeful prediction shared by many in the state's social-work community: "Just as public education was the outstanding development of democracy in the last generation . . . so is development of public welfare in government the outstanding development of government of this generation."[17]

In their efforts to involve the state in public welfare and to expand the mission of poor relief, Georgia's social workers not only intended to provide cash relief to the poor but also to intervene directly in their lives, to help them overcome their "social handicap." Social workers in the 1920s and 1930s found the "social disorganization" of the poor to be extremely distressing. Unlike earlier reformers, they did not blame the poor for their condition, but rather understood the economic necessity that forced mothers to work long hours outside the home, fathers to be absent from their families, and children to attend school sporadically. Nevertheless, they believed that these environmental social conditions resulted in moral delinquency and criminality and sought to organize the disorganized poor into socializing activities such as supervised recreation or, more important, to place them under the protective wing of a case worker who would show them "right living."

Rhoda Kaufman articulated the mission of public welfare. Defining democracy as "that state of society in which every human being has the chance of full normal development," she found Americans "very glib" in their claims that their society provided "equal opportunity for all." After all, she continued, "[t]he child who lives in a normally functioning family within reach of the public school has the opportunity of what schooling he needs, but the child whose father is out of a job, whose mother is ill, and has no books or clothes with which to make school attendance possible, cannot be said to have equal opportunity with the other child." Only if society made "that opportunity available," in Kaufman's view, did the poor child have "the chance to develop into a full normal human being; then democracy is in effect for him."[18] Thus Kaufman articulated Georgia's white social workers' New Deal liberalism. They sought to intervene in the lives of the poor, providing them with a minimum standard of living and, with the guidance of caseworkers or teachers, guiding them to the "normalcy" of middle-class social standards.[19]

While Georgia's white social workers had long desired to have this kind of control over the state's poor, only the New Deal gave them the power and the constituency to truly touch the lives of the majority of Georgians. For example, white charity workers made few inroads into settlement work among poor whites in Progressive-era Atlanta, a vital development in the evolution of professional social work in northern cities. By contrast, the New Deal, which touched the life of virtually every poor Atlantan, gave white social workers the constituency in which to implement their schemes and the power and money of the state through which to achieve their goals. As Arnold J. Todd, dean of sociology at Northwestern University, told the annual convention of the Georgia Conference of Social Work in 1934: "For the first time in the history of the country, the long arm of the law is reaching down into each home and herein social workers have unparalleled opportunity. They are the long arm of the law and must rescue the homes while economic machinery is being repaired."[20]

Government social workers' reach into the homes of black Atlantans marked a new era of state relations with its African American citizens. Where once virtually all agents of the state ignored them, now federal officials considered them an important New Deal constituency to be rehabilitated both economically and socially. Where once all but the most liberal white social workers considered African Americans to be beyond redemption or reform, more and more whites now considered their "rehabilitation" to be essential to the economic and social "rescue" that the New Deal hoped to engender.

A sudden racial enlightenment on the part of the social-work community, however, did not produce this shift to include African Americans. Georgia's white social workers were not revolutionaries, and their social vision was limited. For instance, Gay Shepperson followed the lead of other Southern New Deal administrators and upheld Georgia's plantation economy by insisting that rural relief recipients pick cotton or else lose their benefits. Rather, Georgia's white social workers' incorporative plans marked a growing consensus among New Deal supporters that in order for the South to recover from the Great Depression, the region had to modernize by bringing the poor into the economic and social mainstream. White New Dealers in the South believed that the dire poverty of the majority would ultimately drag down the prosperous minority. They did not intend a social transformation, but wanted instead to improve the living conditions, wages, and education of the domestic worker, the common laborer, the mill hand—and the cotton picker—so that these workers could participate fully in the modern consumer economy and lift the region from being "the sweatshop of the nation" to economic equality with the rest of the United States. But despite the conservatism of their thinking, it nevertheless marked a fundamental ideological turning point concerning the function of the state and the citizenship of the poor generally, and African Americans more specifically. As such, the New Deal represented a second Reconstruction of sorts, with all of the original potential and ultimate limitations of the federal government's foray into the South after the Civil War.[21]

The New Deal's potential fueled the dreams of many members of Atlanta's black reform elite. Most basic, Georgia's New Deal administrators included African Americans at the center of their public welfare program, something that state and local officials had steadfastly refused to do. Such recognition freed private black agencies from the burden of providing emergency relief, sponsored long-term black welfare goals such as the creation of public nursery schools, and, as we shall see in future chapters, even provided funds and lent federal prestige to projects sponsored by the black community. For most in Atlanta's black reform community, such acknowledgment of the black community's needs, let alone its existence, was a long overdue step in the road to full citizenship. Adequate income, housing, food, health care, and recreation were African Americans' due, and the New Deal's implicit recognition of these rights provided an extraordinary boost to the long struggle for black civil rights. Organizations and reformers had long struggled privately for such basic recognition for black neighborhoods and citizens, but the New Deal brought these services to African Americans at a level only before dreamed of by black leaders.

From the beginning, black reformers supported the New Deal enthusiastically, even though it threatened the autonomy and influence of Atlanta's voluntary black social-work community. The Neighborhood Union had already experienced in its unhappy dealings with the Community Chest the dangers of ceding control to white agencies in an effort to integrate into the larger reform community in the city. This threat certainly existed with federal intervention in Georgia and the different foci and emphases of the white social workers heading the federal machinery. Yet black reformers did not complain or voice concerns over these developments. For them, the potential threat posed by the New Deal was more than counterbalanced by the fact that federal relief agencies in Georgia hired black experts and included them in the administration of federal programs, within a social-work framework that matched their own ideology and program. These pioneer black bureaucrats, social workers, public-health nurses, adult education teachers, and black advisers became an integral part of the New Deal relief program in Georgia and brought the black reform elite in from the cold, thus fulfilling their decades-long dreams of incorporation.

The African American reform elite in Atlanta actually found itself in a better position than its white counterpart to embrace a new government of social worker "experts," given its long tradition of private social work in the black community. Since at least the turn of the century, black leaders had shown their commitment to the uplift of the black poor through the pioneering settlement work of the Neighborhood Union, among other charitable organizations, along with the research efforts of AU's sociology department, led by W. E. B. Du Bois. Growing out of this tradition, Atlanta had an established social-work community by the advent of the New Deal, centered at the Atlanta School of Social Work (ASSW) founded in 1920. The school was respected within the national social-work community, and its graduates found jobs in welfare agencies throughout the country. By contrast, white students had to leave the state for social-work training until 1934, when the University of Georgia finally inaugurated a training program in response to New Deal demands for professional workers.[22]

The expansion of social services, especially to African Americans, fueled the ASSW's growth and burnished its national reputation. The school's enrollment grew tremendously during the 1930s, making it one of the ten largest social-work programs in the country, and its graduates had their pick of jobs in the ever-expanding federal public-welfare field. In 1934, federal officials chose the school as a regional training site for 142 black FERA workers in the South, all of whom did their fieldwork in the agency's Fulton County offices. The ASSW's growing reputation allowed it to professionalize further. In 1935, it raised its admission standards from a high school certificate to a college degree, and in 1938 it affiliated with Atlanta University (AU) to become the Atlanta University School of Social Work and began to offer a master's of social work.[23]

ASSW graduates who chose to remain in Atlanta found jobs easily with the New Deal. Every federal relief agency in Atlanta had segregated black programs, all of which needed black personnel. Graduates from each college and from the black nursing program at Grady Hospital filled these positions as adult education teachers, recreation leaders, caseworkers, and public-health nurses. These government positions paid more than many college-educated African Americans had ever before earned, and many left their jobs to join the federal bureaucracy. These new civil servants, some of whom first joined the payroll as unemployed FERA work-relief recipients, found unparalleled opportunities for professional advancement and upward mobility in government, and many spent their entire career rising in the ranks of various government welfare agencies.[24]

The men and women who had taught these new black professionals in Atlanta's black colleges became sought-after experts in the federal bureaucracy. New Deal administrators summoned several ASSW and AU faculty members to Washington as consultants or "Negro advisers" on various projects. For example, Ira De A. Reid, a prominent sociologist on the faculty of Atlanta University, spent the Roosevelt era shuttling between Atlanta and Washington, when he was hired by federal officials in both cities to supervise statistical studies about African American life for numerous agencies, including FERA, the WPA, and the Social Security Board.

While some black Atlantans worked for the federal government before the New Deal, the nature and scale of government employment changed fundamentally in the 1930s. Historically, African Americans attained government posts through political patronage. In particular, black Republicans in the solidly Democratic South benefited from their loyalty to the GOP when their candidate won the presidency. Republican administrations rewarded black party loyalists with minor patronage positions. In the limited sphere of vocational opportunities and low wages available to African Americans, membership in the party could translate into upward mobility and expanded occupational opportunities for these "post office" Republicans. With the New Deal, however, government employment for African Americans largely became a matter of professional credentials, not politics.[25]

This did not mean, however, that influence peddling ended with the New Deal. Instead, power largely shifted from white politicians to white welfare bureaucrats, who cut off government employment to all but the most "expert" African Americans. The Commission on Interracial Cooperation's (CIC) Will Alexander made explicit this shift from patronage to professionalism when he lobbied for black advisers in New Deal agencies, both in Washington and at the state level. In pursuing this goal, Alexander worked closely with Clark Foreman, white adviser on Minority Affairs to Harold Ickes in the Interior Department, and a prominent ex-Atlantan and former secretary of the Georgia branch of the CIC.[26] Alexander wanted black advisers not only to raise the visibility of African Americans within government but also to act as a bulwark against Communist radicals and, more important, reactionary state New Deal administrators, who, in his estimation, were "men of only average ability and training" who always "think politically," and who he feared would deprive blacks of federal relief in favor of whites. To combat this inequity, Alexander felt it was important to place as government advisers "well-trained Negroes in such positions." However, he counseled vigilance against those who were already "seeking such appointments through political influence. . . . It seems to me that instead of appointing Negroes who are proposed to them by politicians, the authorities in Washington should set out to find the very best men available for the jobs."[27]

Just what he meant by the "best men" became evident a few months later when Washington officials consulted Alexander on the appointment of a Negro adviser to Harry Hopkins, then head of FERA. Two Atlanta residents were up for the job: Jesse O. Thomas, southern field secretary for the National Urban League, and Forrester B. Washington, president of the ASSW. Since 1918, Thomas had been a militant activist for black Atlantans in his work for the Urban League. He helped initiate the idea of the School of Social Work and had, more recently, courageously voiced black Atlantans' demands for equitable distribution of city resources for black schools, recreation, and hospitalization in a weekly Urban League column in the white *Atlanta Constitution*.[28] To Alexander, however, Thomas did not represent the ideal of professional nonpartisanship promoted by New Deal agencies. For one thing, Alexander wrote, Thomas had only a "limited education" and no credentials as a professional social worker. More critical, Alexander expressed doubts about Thomas's ability to bring "constructive leadership" to the government position, calling him a "political manipulator" who would "undoubtedly bring to bear on this situation the manipulations of an amateur politician."[29]

On the other hand, Alexander considered Washington an excellent candidate. Unlike Thomas, with his merely "casual relations" with national social-work leaders, blacks and whites in the field respected Forrester B. Washington and his school. In addition, Washington's success in attracting white foundations to fund the ASSW was one of the "best indications" of the high quality of his work and his school. In fact, Washington's ability to get along with whites and his connections to white institutions, along with his cool professionalism, were key to Alexander's praise of him. As he explained to Aubrey Williams, "the whole situation in America makes it almost impossible for a Negro, however well educated, not to 'think black.' To a surprising degree, Washington seems to me to be able to view the problems of the Negro with the minimum of racial feeling."[30] That perception, true or not, demonstrated to Alexander that Washington was no racial demagogue. Alexander believed that Washington's appointment would be viewed as being "based on merit alone and as due to no political manipulation whatever, for he belongs to no clique and has not depended upon political methods to establish himself in the position of leadership which he occupies."[31]

Forrester B. Washington was no accommodationist. In fact, he left his job at FERA fewer than six months after his appointment, disgusted by the racial inequalities he found in the New Deal's administration. Returning to Atlanta, he became one of the city's most passionate defenders of poor African Americans. However, Alexander was right in asserting Washington's nonpartisanship. Throughout the 1930s Washington insisted that African Americans should remain independent, only throwing their support behind political candidates who represented black interests. He and other members of the new generation of black reformers rejected the divisiveness and paltry, even destructive, returns of party politics in a region where African Americans were disfranchised, and where pandering to white party leaders only resulted in individual benefits, never racial uplift.

Older black leaders, such as Masonic leader John Wesley Dobbs, Atlanta NAACP president A. T. Walden, and militant newspaper editor and father of Angelo Herndon's black lawyer, Benjamin Davis Sr., had joined the Republican Party in the days when the "party of Lincoln" still would occasionally fight for black rights. By the 1930s that time was long over, and black Republicans found themselves in the discreditable position of supporting a state GOP machine dominated by a "lily-white" faction just as committed as southern Democrats to the maintenance of Jim Crow. While Benjamin Davis Sr. defended his continued membership in the Republican Party during the 1930s as an opportunity to effect reform from within the white establishment and decried black reformers' new independent political strategies as ineffective "hot air speeches in churches, by radicals,"[32] the tide had turned both in terms of government employment and black politics.[33]

Despite black bureaucrats' nonpartisanship, Will Alexander's correspondence demonstrates that their power continued to rely on whites. Forrester B. Washington's authority rested not only on the respect of the black community but also on his recognition outside that circle by the state and national ranks of professional, and largely white, social workers. Washington and other leaders skillfully presented themselves to whites as educated messengers bridging the gap between the black and white communities. They and they only could solve the problems of the black community because only they could understand the problems of the unincorporated, inarticulate masses and successfully convey these problems to white leaders. This is how Atlanta University promoted its "leadership" training in the early 1930s in the midst of white Atlantans' Depression-era anxieties and the beginning of their concerns about black radicalism: "The racial situation is often difficult . . . but there are always a few leaders who counsel moderation . . .—the educated Negro businessman, the colored physician, the school teacher, and the preacher. The Negro college has made these leaders who sprinkle themselves among the mass leavening its ignorance and hopelessness, and they patrol with success where sheriffs fail."[34] With the New Deal, social workers joined this leavening mix of elites.

The black elite's longstanding offer to the white community to control the behavior of the black community in return for the role of racial intermediary and power broker finally found receptive white ears with the New Deal. Now that the state recognized African Americans, they became an important, even preeminent, welfare constituency. Consequently, white government social workers saw the value of hiring black social workers and administrators to run the black divisions of New Deal programs or to act as case workers for black clients. The vast majority of government employees in Atlanta working with African Americans in New Deal social-welfare programs were black, a practice never questioned in a city and region defined by racial segregation.[35]

The hiring of black bureaucrats spurred white social workers' acceptance of their black peers. Before the 1930s, some of the city's most liberal whites knew nothing of the educated black middle class in Atlanta, and had only the haziest notion, if any, of the city's black colleges and reputation as a national center of black intellectual life. The most enlightened white attitude toward African Americans was tainted by paternalism: as one white liberal remembered, "that you were good to blacks, but that blacks weren't equal to whites." In the words of one white reformer, her peers perceived the domestic workers, janitors, and elevator operators with whom they came into contact daily as "just a bunch of pickaninnies and yassuh boss, Uncle Tom characters."[36]

With the New Deal, white liberals' perceptions of the black community were transformed as more and more of them worked with African Americans who were their peers in terms of education, profession, and class. Augusta Dunbar, a white administrator with the Fulton County Department of Public Welfare, had her world turned upside down in the 1930s "when I went out to Atlanta University and saw the buildings for the first time . . . and these cultivated people, and people like the people at [Atlanta's white] Emory [University]." Countless other whites had similar experiences in which their first interactions with educated African Americans radically altered their view of the black community. The awkward first meetings at which whites refused to shake hands or to speak to their

African American colleagues as equals soon gave way to frequent dialogue. To be sure, whites did not experience a similar revelation in their attitudes toward the black working class. And the way for the black elite was never smooth or paved by equality, with black social workers always under the close and critical supervision of whites and housed in inferior "Negro quarters." However, once white New Dealers in Atlanta found that their black counterparts shared with them, at least on the surface, education, a reform ideology, and a class, they became collegial allies in their New Deal advocacy.[37]

While liberal southerners began to talk about the possible economic benefits to be derived from raising the standard of living in the South for blacks and whites, national New Deal leaders were far more explicit in their aims. In a notorious instance, Frances Perkins, secretary of labor, explained to a 1933 meeting of white business leaders in Atlanta the philosophy behind federal relief legislation. Telling them that increasing the purchasing power of the masses was key to the nation's recovery, she used a regional example to illustrate her point: "When you realize the whole southern section of this country is an untapped market for shoes, you realize we have not yet reached the end of the social benefits and social goods [to be gained] from the further development of the mass production system on a basis of consuming power in the South which will make possible the universal use of shoes in the South."[38]

White political, business, and labor leaders in Georgia reacted to this statement with outrage, believing that Perkins had impugned the culture and civilization of their South by implying that they and their peers did not wear shoes. So politically invisible and irrelevant was the majority of poor Georgians to the state's public life that these white leaders did not even consider that Perkins could be talking, not about them, but about the destitution of the thousands of state residents who could not afford the most basic consumer goods. In fact, when Perkins attempted to smooth the Georgian white elite's ruffled feathers, she reassured its members that she was not referring to them but to the state's poor whites and "large colored population."[39] Thus Georgia's social-work community was at the vanguard in a state where the white leadership was only beginning to reluctantly acknowledge some connection to and responsibility for its poor citizens, and especially its poor black citizenry.

Given the white elite's difficulty in imagining or accepting the New Deal's recognition of the state's poor, it is not surprising that many other white

Georgians and Atlantans were alarmed and outraged when federal officials included African Americans in their relief programs. At first, white Atlanta did not protest the New Deal, assuming that, like municipal relief efforts, it would concentrate on getting them back on their feet and ignore African American suffering. In fact, some white Atlantans believed that federal authority could work on their behalf and directly against African Americans by forcibly shipping the black unemployed back to the farm.[40]

Instead, the New Deal recognized African Americans by including them in relief rolls in unprecedented numbers and paying them equally to whites. For whites not used to any positive state acknowledgment of African Americans, it did not matter that the New Deal consigned African Americans to unskilled, lower-paid work relief or that emergency measures did not include black Atlantans in numbers commensurate with black unemployment rates. Ever-vigilant white Atlantans only saw in federal intervention an attack on the bulwark of the South's society and economy, and they fought fiercely against the threat of a second Reconstruction.

White protest against the New Deal in Atlanta occurred against a backdrop of increased white paranoia about African Americans. Growing economic competition and mushrooming black migration from rural Georgia to Atlanta spurred vigilante groups like the quasi-fascist Blackshirts. White paranoia about black criminality and antiwhite terrorism intensified with the economic uncertainty of the Depression. Whites worried about the potential breakdown of the paternalistic order of race relations and that African Americans might be at the point of rebellion or revolution. Whisper campaigns in white districts spread rumors of black youths parading through the streets brandishing ice picks and threatening to "take the neighborhood."[41] Eugene Talmadge made political hay out of white fears in the 1934 gubernatorial campaign that he won partly on the basis of his inflammatory rhetoric concerning African Americans. His refusal to adopt the National Recovery Administration code provisions for highway laborers cemented his victory, justifying his obstruction of federal policy on the grounds that he did not think "that negroes [sic] should get 40 cents an hour out of state tax money when good white men and white women are working in [sic] the same roads get barely 40 cents a day."[42] Recognizing the political power of racist rhetoric, state and local politicians joined Talmadge in bringing race into criticisms of New Deal programs by invoking inflammatory images of Reconstruction after the Civil War, the last time a strong federal presence in the region had antagonized white southerners. For example, complaints about the disruption of traditional patronage practices abounded in the state legislature in early 1935.

While these complaints began with criticism of the number of New Deal "outsiders" taking jobs away from native Georgians, state representatives soon began to target these "carpetbaggers" for espousing racial equality in federal offices. Responding to such criticisms by Kenneth Murrell, head of American Legion Post I in Atlanta, state legislators accused federal bureaucrats in Atlanta of insisting upon "equality of races."[43] They charged that white federal employees were being "instructed to address negro [*sic*] employees as 'Mr., Miss or Mrs.' "[44] and that "in many instances white girls are serving under negro [*sic*] executives—the negroes not being Georgians."[45] Ellis Arnall, a future liberal governor of Georgia, was one of many who compared the current situation with the Reconstruction era. "It's nothing more nor less than carpetbagging," he exclaimed in the state legislature, "except that the old carpetbaggers drove the South around with bayonets while the present ones are using federal money in an effort to undermine the South." Even Virginian Gay Shepperson was accused of being a carpetbagger, demonstrating that the term had strong ideological as well as geographic associations for many white Southerners.[46]

As the "carpetbagger" controversy attests, white Georgians distrusted particularly any moves toward public recognition of African Americans in the state's New Deal administration. In Atlanta, they leveled complaints against FERA social workers. The American Legion, for example, claimed that whites and blacks worked together in the same offices at FERA and that they shared drinking fountains, having erased the "white" and "colored" signs over the fountains. The complaints of the legion and the United Spanish American War Veterans marked the first action by a "Community Americanism Committee" made up of several organizations working to preserve "color lines and defeat moves for racial equality" in response to the actions of the New Deal. The committee not only protested the workings of the local office but also charged that the black and white reform elites working for federal agencies were "spending our money purchasing race equality." Thus the legion and its allies betrayed their anxiety about the alternative "Americanism" promoted by the New Deal, which, while not advocating social equality or an end to racial segregation, did recognize African Americans as citizens and an important constituency. Local forces sponsoring these protests reacted to the "outsiders" running federal programs who promoted this inclusive vision. These bureaucrats represented a biracial professional class answering to federal authority and protected from local forces in its efforts to undermine local patronage and to bring African Americans under the federal umbrella.[47]

The attacks had some impact. As Will Alexander complained to fellow white liberal Howard Odum about the unequal distribution of FERA relief and education money in Georgia, the Roosevelt administration in its sensitivity to the South "accepts [discrimination] as inevitable and necessary." However, he noted that Georgia was better in recognizing African Americans than any other deep South state thanks to Shepperson's vigilance. For example, while white backlash against black white-collar workers initially resulted in layoffs, most were quietly rehired, and Georgia's New Deal agencies continued to hire black bureaucrats in ever-increasing numbers throughout the 1930s. Such leverage was only possible because of the independence that came from federal authority.[48]

White and black liberals who supported racial justice without such federal protection faced a harder struggle against local forces. Unlike the New Deal, which enjoyed firm support among its white beneficiaries who associated it with a very popular president, private liberal organizations did not enjoy such endorsement or protection. In their advocacy of the hiring of black administrators, for example, liberals found themselves subject to unrelenting criticism, especially by organizations like the American Legion, which successfully conflated racial liberalism with Communism in its rhetorical protests. In the midst of the Angelo Herndon appeals and "anti-insurrection" raids on local Communist cells in the mid-thirties, organizations like the American Legion accused the CIC of being a Communist front, despite its antiradical stance. In 1937, the Community Chest finally excluded the commission from funding due to complaints of "encouraging communism and social equality."[49]

In a similar case, the American Legion accused a peace organization, the Southern Institute of International Relations, of Communist ties when it held its convention at St. Luke's Episcopal Church in 1935. Funded by the Quakers and other religious groups, the institute counted among its sponsors such distinguished African Americans as John Hope, Forrester B. Washington, poet James Weldon Johnson, and Tuskegee Institute principal Robert Russa Moton, along with such well-known white liberals as Will Alexander, philanthropist George Foster Peabody, and educator Frank Porter Graham. The interracial nature of the meeting, which had white and black speakers such as A. Steve Nance, Atlanta's white labor leader, and AU professor Rayford Logan speaking on topics like "Race and Peace" and "Labor's Stake in World Peace," raised the ire of the legion. Legion members disrupted the institute's conference, and the action had a chilling effect on the organization, which lost sponsorship due to the charges.[50]

The American Legion's red-baiting of the cic and the Southern Institute of International Relations exemplified white anger against the New Deal reform elite. When white reactionaries could not successfully lash out at the New Deal or its administrators, they found surrogates in private liberal organizations that represented the same group from which New Deal administrators emerged. The legion's action was the legacy of a long history of disrupting private interracial efforts in Atlanta, leading Forrester B. Washington to criticize the city's liberals in 1938 as "timorous" and easily bullied. As he put it, "the more you shy away, the more these articulate minorities go after you."[51]

However, while the legion may have restrained many black and white liberals, these reformers regrouped under the New Deal's protective umbrella. The social-work meritocracy that ran Georgia's federal programs welcomed these groups who shared its desire to reform the political and economic status quo. This welcome fulfilled one of the reform community's most cherished dreams. By turning the state's political culture on its head, Georgia's federal bureaucracy brought black and white reformers into the political mainstream, into positions from which they could effect the changes for which they had worked fruitlessly to achieve through private efforts. The effects of these changes would have enormous implications for Atlanta's black community.

4

Lifting the Taboo

The Black New Deal
in Atlanta

In 1932 Jacob Henderson, a recent graduate of South Carolina State College, moved to Atlanta to pursue a master's degree in economics at Atlanta University (AU). Henderson, a native of Hartsville, South Carolina, had distinguished himself as an undergraduate, and his professors groomed him to move on to prestigious Atlanta University, helping him secure a scholarship essential to his progress during the Great Depression. This move represented a step up for the son of a waiter and a poorly paid county teacher. At AU, Henderson became a student leader, excelling in his classes and throwing himself into the social life and reform efforts of the university community. After graduation in 1934, the university hired him as a bookstore manager and assistant purchasing agent. This job, for which today we would consider Henderson overqualified, was then considered a plum position at AU, reserved for its favorite sons and daughters. For in 1934, an African American with a graduate economics degree had very few options. Henderson might have been able to find work teaching at a black college, but beyond education there would have been few options for him in the black community, and no opportunities in white Atlanta. Jim Crow prevented this ambitious young man from reaching any further.

In 1936, however, an opportunity for advancement presented itself. The twenty-five-year-old Henderson decided to expand his options by seeking administrative work in one of the New Deal agencies that were opening their doors to black professionals. He enrolled in a summer course at Columbia University on public housing management sponsored by the Public Works Administration. Soon after his successful completion of the course, Henderson was appointed bookkeeper for University Homes, the newly opened, 600-unit, $2 million federal housing project for African Americans in Atlanta.

While Henderson's new position still did not test his abilities, he made the most of his job and was promoted quickly, first to assistant manager of University Homes in 1939, and then in 1941, when he was only thirty, to manager of John Eagan Homes, one of seven new projects built by the recently created Atlanta Housing Authority. Henderson continued working for the Housing Authority until 1963, when he was hired by the United States Economic Development Corporation, where he worked until his retirement from the public sector in 1983.[1]

While Jacob Henderson certainly profited personally from his move into the civil service, he did not simply pursue individual gain through his position. Instead, he demonstrated the "socially responsible individualism" that Stephanie J. Shaw has shown to be the foundation of black professionals' ideology in the Jim Crow period.[2] As a housing manager, he took on the mission of using his government position to raise the political, economic, and social consciousness of the black tenants he served. While he understood the structural impact of Jim Crow, like other AU reformers he attributed the black community's marginality to behavioral factors as well. An unidentified speaker represented the tenor of this perspective during a 1932 meeting on voting at which Henderson was one of the speechmakers: "We cannot become citizens in the full sense of the word until we register and vote for those who are to run our government." Despite the overwhelming burden of the cumulative poll tax for many black Atlantans, this speaker complained that for "[t]oo long . . . the Negro refused to register," and warned that "it will bankrupt the state and community morally to have people vote for us while we lag behind, whine, beg for things for which we should vote, and grumble about things that lie within our power to correct through the ballot box."[3]

Consequently, Henderson labored indefatigably, both at University Homes and John Eagan Homes, to transform his tenants into voting citizens interested in self-improvement, racial advancement, and community action. He urged tenants to save so that they could purchase their own homes, promoted "citizenship training" at John Eagan Homes by holding elaborate elections for the tenants' council, and organized voter registration drives for the projects' residents. In fact in 1946 his tenants delivered the key votes in the upset victory of Helen Mankin over favorite Thomas Camp in the first congressional election in Atlanta after the end of the white primary, thus providing a potent demonstration of the black electoral strength that would shape the city's political future.[4]

Henderson's government work represented the intertwined goals that Atlanta's black reform leaders hoped would be achieved through black participation in the administration of federal programs. New Deal agencies enormously expanded the vocational options of educated black Atlantans by employing hundreds of them for professional and white-collar positions. Like Henderson, many of these workers turned their first work-relief job for Federal Emergency Relief Administration (FERA) into a lifelong career in federal public service. However, these workers, most of whom had close ties to Atlanta's reform elite, did not see their jobs merely as means to individual ends. Instead, they used their government work as a unique opportunity to achieve their long-held goals for racial advancement, opportunities that they had found difficult to create through private voluntary efforts in a city whose white leaders denied black residents participation in civic life. They used their federal positions to further their goal of leading African Americans to take their rightful place as citizens.

New Deal agencies hired African Americans as white-collar workers and professionals from the very beginning of the Emergency Relief program in 1933. Under FERA, about 25,000 unemployed Atlantans received relief, with African Americans comprising approximately two-thirds of that number. Most of the 16,000 or so black relief recipients were domestic workers or unskilled laborers, but some 200 black professionals, mainly laid-off teachers, joined this majority. Although they comprised a tiny segment of federal relief recipients, the assignment and treatment of these black professionals became the single most important gauge used by Atlanta's African American reformers in assessing the New Deal's treatment of the black community. Consequently, the activism of the black reform elite began to focus on protecting the occupational gains of these federal workers.[5]

Self-interest and ideology motivated black reformers' inordinate attention to this small group of educated black relief recipients. By opening professional and white-collar positions in public service, federal relief employment represented an unprecedented opportunity for educated black Atlantans to escape the vocational and wage ghettos to which they had previously been consigned by the local economy. These constraints affected all African Americans, uniting black Atlantans in their relation to the "outer wheel" and allowing black reformers to see their efforts as benefiting the whole community when they often only aided a privileged few. The experience of teachers under FERA best illustrates how this perspective could develop. As the largest group of black professionals, teachers enjoyed a respect and status within the black community that was not reflected in their pay scale. Often earning less than janitors in their own schools, Georgia's black teachers took home paychecks equaling only 40 percent of those of their already poorly paid white peers. This wage differential meant that black county teachers in Georgia with two years of college training typically received only $45 a month, and then only during the school year. During the Depression, these teachers' situation worsened when the counties cut their pay by as much as $30 a month. Black teachers hired by the Atlanta Board of Education generally earned more than their county counterparts, but during the Depression they suffered months without pay. Once teachers were laid off and taken on by FERA as emergency adult-education instructors, their situation improved measurably. The federal government erased racial wage differentials, paying both black and white workers equally. And by offering $50 to $60 a month year round, FERA jobs paid many black teachers more than they had ever earned. Unemployed black clerical and social workers had similar experiences under FERA, finding unprecedented opportunity in and pay from federal employment.[6]

Beyond their desire to preserve and expand these excellent job opportunities for their educated peers, black reformers genuinely believed that black needs would not be served without African Americans within government administration. Time and again racial discrimination or indifference of white administrators or social workers devastated black families seeking support from government agencies. Augusta Dunbar, a white supervisor of the local FERA offices, admitted as much: white case workers in the black section of her office either displayed callous indifference toward their black clients or treated them "more harshly"[7] than white relief applicants, applying federal regulations stringently to their cases, and consigning them to the bottom tier of relief jobs.

Black administrators and supervisors undoubtedly treated black relief recipients with more respect, concern, and equity than whites. Increasingly, however, black reformers conflated their concern for the black poor with their professional self- interest by concentrating single-mindedly on New Deal welfare agencies' policies and practices in hiring and retaining black professionals, rather than on racial equity for relief recipients. Almost without exception, black reformers expressed the belief that the only way that ordinary African Americans could achieve any progress through New Deal programs was with the appointment of black bureaucrats and white-collar workers who would work within government to improve the lot of the black poor. As the Neighborhood Union petitioned Gay Shepperson, black bureaucrats would "help the Negro masses to adjust themselves to the type of world in which they must live."[8] According to the Union, the "masses" could only adjust to New Deal programs if an African American "qualified by training, experience, emotional balance and residence is employed . . . as advisor . . . on Negro Problems"[9] within each local, state, and national office of New Deal agencies.

The explicit elitism of these statements had its roots in the "lifting as we climb" ideology of private black uplift agencies nationwide. In the past, this ideology supported concerted efforts by black reformers on behalf of the poorest African Americans. With the New Deal's usurpation of social-welfare responsibilities from private agencies, reformers concentrated less on the poor and spent more and more of their energy agitating for the appointment of black bureaucrats. As a result, for many members of the black educated class, the issue of racial inequities in relief distribution became subsidiary to the issue of black representation within New Deal bureaucracies.

This shift in focus became apparent in 1935 and 1936 during the administrative shift from the emergency relief of FERA to the work relief of the Works Progress Administration (WPA). The end of FERA struck fear in the hearts of African American reformers. They predicted that white-collar positions for African Americans would be eliminated with the transfer from FERA, with its emphasis on public welfare projects, to the WPA, which was to concentrate on large-scale public works. These fears led to an outcry from black leaders to preserve these jobs and a new focus of black reform activism to work toward the appointment and retention of black white-collar workers and permanent black advisers to federal agencies. Although the agency shift from FERA to WPA was an uncertain time for all black workers, and had a particularly deleterious effect on skilled artisans such as stonemasons, black leaders reserved their most concerted protests for the preservation of the gains made by black professionals on relief.[10]

As the protesters' thinking went, there had always been black laborers, and even artisans, but an African American stenographer working in a government office represented real progress for the race, and even warranted an announcement in the *Atlanta Daily World*. Therefore, they could not allow her dismissal to pass without a fight. In a letter to the president, Rev. Evan Hurley reflected the sentiments of many educated black Atlantans when he protested the imminent layoff of the "creditable number" of black white-collar FERA workers. Hurley demanded that some provision be made for this group which had "been trained in some of our finest educational institutions." Otherwise, he warned, mixing the language of the pulpit with that of the social scientist, "the Devil begins to wreak his evil," as the "energy of this young group would normally expend through participation in the processes of production finds no outlet."[11] Letters poured into WPA from black individuals and organizations, like the Neighborhood Union, demanding an adviser on African American issues in the local WPA office to promote the "strengthening and perpetuation"[12] of gains made by black professionals during FERA. Otherwise, these groups believed, "[m]ost jobs for Negroes would be unskilled labor and domestic."[13]

Black Atlantans' letters to federal agencies were part of a growing national movement to ensure that the federal government did not forget the interests of educated blacks or the growing political clout of this group. In Washington, the Democratic National Committee responded to these efforts through the Good Neighbor League, an election organization formed to campaign for Roosevelt among African Americans. In a memorandum in preparation for the 1936 election, the League outlined the Roosevelt Administration's achievements and suggested further action it could take on behalf of African Americans; with remarkable frankness suggestions emphasized the concerns of the black educated class. In articulating this bias, the league wrote: "One feature kept in mind in these suggestions is that public opinion among Negroes is made by the White Collar Class. Therefore the measures suggested are intended to serve that class as well as the basic population."[14] In other words, educated blacks were the ones who voted, and New Deal leaders should consider their concerns above all others. Black appointments to government posts impressed black voters more than any other gesture the Roosevelt administration could make to African Americans.

National political pressures forced federal officials in Atlanta to respond to this increasingly powerful constituency. From the beginning of the Roosevelt administration, national Democratic Party leaders and New Deal boosters were aware that the middle-class constituency represented by the Good Neighbor League carefully monitored the progress of African Americans in the New Deal, not only in their own communities, but also nationwide, and particularly in the South. Party officials recognized that a few highly publicized black appointments in Washington and the states could be the best strategy to counteract negative impressions of racial discrimination in the New Deal. "It would be a very great advantage if we could get Negroes scattered about in the administrative machinery of these relief measures," wrote Will Alexander in 1933 to fellow white liberal Lucy Randolph Mason. Responding to her scheme to counteract black anger over the various racial biases built into the National Recovery Administration, he wrote that black appointments would "have a fine effect on Negroes generally across the country and would do much to clear up pessimism and doubt with which they view the whole development."[15]

By 1935, when talk had begun about the transfer from FERA to WPA in Georgia, Alexander and Randolph's concerns about black support for the New Deal had become more critical. While black reformers clamored for the expansion of white-collar opportunities for African Americans in Georgia and fretted over the implications of the agency transfer, local supporters of Georgia's virulently anti–New Deal and antiblack governor Eugene Talmadge worked to wrench control of federal programs from officials in Washington, D.C. The Democratic Party recognized that FDR's reelection might hinge upon black voters and their perceptions of the administration's support of black interests against southern demagogues like Talmadge. In the summer of 1935, George Foster Peabody, counselor to FDR, wrote to Gay Shepperson that the conflict over states' rights and the New Deal in Georgia should be handled by "avoiding any development of feeling by the Negroes that they are being ignored." He explained that "the Negro vote in our Northern States may prove to be decisive in the Election of 1936. Therefore there is but little time to make sure of a positive consideration of the Negro in the South where his interests are so directly related to Federal assistance."[16] Shepperson's response to Peabody was instructive: in assuring him of her support of black interests she wrote not of the thousands of unskilled black workers who had been given work or relief by FERA, but rather boasted that "we have been able to give some teacher training courses at Georgia University and at the Negro College at Forsyth for those teachers who have been in our Emergency Education Program teaching adult education. Among these were included more than 250 negro [sic] teachers."[17] New Deal supporters and Democratic Party leaders understood that white-collar appointments of African Americans held more weight with black voters than other actions they might have made toward African Americans.

In the end, federal officials resisted local forces that would have turned back the progress made by educated African Americans during FERA in the transfer to the WPA. While concentrating on large-scale projects like sewer construction, the WPA in Atlanta also initiated a social-work program dwarfing the FERA program. It included nursery schools, workers' and adult education, sewing rooms, and a citywide supervised playground program that brought organized recreation to most Atlantans for the first time. As the federal government expanded its social welfare mission, so it expanded its recognition and inclusion of African Americans as a welfare clientele. Each of these new social-work projects served black Atlantans in segregated divisions staffed by African American supervisors, managers, and workers. Furthermore, after FERA, some agencies, most notably the National Youth Administration (NYA), hired "Negro advisers" to head administrative staffs that ran black programs from top to bottom.[18]

This expanded welfare mandate resulted in a mushrooming of professional employment opportunities, particularly for black social workers. All but 7 of the 259 graduates of the Atlanta School of Social Work (ASSW) found employment in their chosen field from 1934 to 1943. These professionals entered the job market at a fortuitous time. Nearly 60 percent of them first found work in the new federal public welfare agencies or local and state agencies patterned on New Deal models, instead of private agencies (typically local Urban League or YWCA and YMCA chapters) that heretofore had supplied their only employment options. Given these opportunities, it is not surprising that enrollments at the ASSW mushroomed in the 1930s: its graduating class grew by more than threefold between 1934 and 1943, despite ever more strenuous eligibility qualifications for matriculation.[19]

Thus the shift to WPA consolidated the gains of educated black government workers, thereby fulfilling the activist goals of black reformers. These WPA-era New Deal workers were the first in a long line of educated black professionals and white-collar workers to flock to federal employment, especially to welfare agencies. Their reasons were not surprising: nowhere else but in federal work could these workers find the same job security, employment commensurate with their skills and education, and explicit (if not always enforced) nondiscrimination policies. Having opened the doors of government employment to educated African Americans, black reformers within and outside the New Deal could now turn their efforts elsewhere. They now sought to work from under the protective umbrella of the New Deal and to use the vast resources of the federal government to further their long-held objectives for the uplift of Atlanta's African American community.

While whites supervised the new black government workers, they took their most important direction from local sponsors and mentors within

Atlanta's black reform community. Black bureaucrats worked with their counterparts outside government to use New Deal programs—in ways never intended by local white administrators—to advance the reform agenda for which they and their peers had been working for so long through private means. Mutual support toward common goals allowed these two groups of black professionals to use their access to federal funding and resources to best effect. This approach achieved unprecedented success achieving black incorporation and uplift, and bolstered the security and strength of both black government administrators and private black agencies. Nowhere were the results of this strategy more apparent than in the functioning in Georgia of the NYA and the civic education program, the Public Forum.

Aubrey Williams, the southern white liberal who headed the national NYA, was uncommonly attuned to the black reform elite and its goals. Influenced by prominent black leaders in the social-work field such as Eugene Kinckle Jones of the National Urban League, and Mary McLeod Bethune, who was to direct the NYA's national Division of Negro Affairs, Williams promised at the NYA's inception that his agency would address many of the incorporative goals black reformers had been working for privately. In a 1935 meeting with national black leaders, he told his audience that he wanted the NYA to help sponsor the youth programs of local African American agencies and thus bring "the prestige and power of the President's office" to their work. Furthermore, he hoped that NYA money would help these agencies expand their work by building libraries and recreation centers for African American youth, and sponsoring leadership training courses which would "employ as many Negro youth as possible." He also planned that the NYA would provide opportunities for vocational training for African Americans even though "there seems to be no immediate outlets" for that training in a segregated labor market. In addition, he told the assembly he wanted the NYA to provide opportunities to get "Negroes in the actual functioning organizations of government"[20] by getting a black bureaucrat appointed to the staff of every state NYA office. Williams's speech exactly articulated black reformers' hopes and dreams for African Americans' inclusion in federal programs.[21]

While the NYA *was* the most liberal of all New Deal relief programs, in most of the country Williams's promises did not come to fruition. By 1937, only nineteen state NYAs had black administrative assistants, including one each for New York City and Washington, D.C. The agency's programs never neared racial equity, excluding blacks almost completely in some states and cities. There was one notable exception, however; Georgia was the only state in which the NYA program neared the potential for African Americans envisioned by Williams and in which a fully staffed office of black administrators, supervisors, and clerks supervised black participation in the program.[22]

The Georgia program's success lay mainly in the support it received from the private black reform community, which both bolstered the work of black administrators and provided them with the ideological underpinning for their work. First, the black reform elite had trained and influenced the city's surplus of social-work professionals who could administer the black components of the agency's program. This talent pool led the white administrator of the Georgia NYA to comment that the staff of the "Colored Division" had "superior . . . training and preparation for their work"[23] than the administrators of the white program. Under the leadership of Ralph Bullock, an administrator for the National Council of YMCA, and then of William Shell, a graduate of Morehouse College, Atlanta University, and the ASSW, the Colored Division grew to an expanded "Division of Negro Affairs" with a staff of eleven, the largest in the country. This staff oversaw the activities of a larger group of black supervisors of individual NYA projects.[24]

The reform elite also aided the Colored Division by providing it with valuable connections to the vast network of local and national black social work activists and private welfare agencies. In fact, the Colored Division owed its existence to the Interracial Committee of the National Committee of the YMCA, which paid up to two-thirds of Bullock's salary during his time at the NYA, and provided the segregated Colored Division with office space in the Butler Street YMCA. In Atlanta, black organizations made NYA work projects possible by providing the local sponsorship they required. For example, the Prince Hall Masons and the local Phyllis Wheatley YWCA donated rent and space, respectively, so that black women, like their white counterparts, could have two NYA sewing-room projects. These sewing rooms comprised the only work relief available to young women in Atlanta, and provided emergency employment for hundreds of black girls in Atlanta during the 1930s.[25]

In return for their aid, black reformers and the private agencies and local institutions they represented benefited from their connection to the NYA and its access to federal funds and resources. Specifically, the Colored Division worked with African American leaders to use black NYA workers in projects that would benefit Atlanta's private black institutions. NYA workers built a recreation center for unemployed youth in South Atlanta sponsored by the ASSW, gutted and entirely refurbished the Butler Street YMCA, provided clerical work to the Phyllis Wheatley YWCA, and graded and landscaped the grounds of Booker T. Washington High School, among other projects. These were much needed and much appreciated improvements which would have been impossible without federal funding.[26]

The unity of mission between the NYA's Colored Division and its local supporters extended to their ideological goals for the black youth who became the agency's clients. In working to assume as much control as they could over the NYA's program for black youth, Atlanta's black reformers sought to use the agency's program to further their incorporative goals for the black community. They wanted both to push the limits of Jim Crow in expanding black opportunity, and to infuse black participants with their uplift ideology. There were two fundamental goals for both of the NYA's programs—a work-study scholarship program for students from high school to graduate school, and a lesser-known work-relief program for out-of-school youths from 16 to 25 years of age.

In the out-of-school program, Atlanta's black agencies sponsored and used work relief projects, like the sewing rooms, to ensure that at least some of the legions of poor, unemployed youth in the city did not sink into total destitution and social marginality due to the Depression. Yet no mere palliative, black reformers believed the NYA's work program could have the potential to circumvent or even correct the discrimination faced by black youth in the labor marketplace. Black reformers believed that the NYA could promote their incorporative schemes for black Atlantans by providing the training, equipment, and opportunities for skilled trades that white industry and organized labor would not, and black industry and agencies could not, offer to African Americans. Any progress made in these areas was considered a real breakthrough by black reformers, who had been constantly thwarted in their efforts to overcome southern custom in labor practices.[27]

White NYA administrators in Georgia did not share this vision for the agency. They had no desire to disturb the South's vocational apartheid, so while they offered white boys training in skilled construction work, they limited opportunities for African American youth to unskilled work. Furthermore, white administrators in Georgia revealed their commitment to the racial status quo by laying off black NYA workers seasonally in rural areas so that they would be forced to pick cotton, and by insisting that black girls, if they were to be afforded any work relief at all, be trained in domestic service. They sought to use the state's expanding welfare responsibilities to institutionalize the "Negro's place." These practices resulted in protest to the National NYA by the Colored Division and black activists around the country, but to no avail.[28]

In order to combat these inequities, the Colored Division worked with private black agencies for the sponsorship of projects, such as sewing rooms or the renovation of the Butler Street YMCA, which would offer work opportunities to black youth outside the typical venues. The YMCA project was especially important because it offered experience in skilled work to relief recipients. NYA workers renovated the five-story Butler Street building "from basement to top story."[29] They installed window frames, fitted new plumbing, and rebuilt the indoor swimming pool, among other specialized tasks. In effect this project offered a few black boys the taste of a trade apprenticeship, an opportunity barred to most black workers by white-controlled unions. By providing this project and others with sponsorship, black reformers inside and outside government shaped the Colored Division's program to their own ends of racial advancement, even in resistance to the aims of white NYA officials for black youth.

The Colored Division's achievement in expanding opportunities for out-of-school youth lent credence to the importance placed by the reform elite on the employment of black bureaucrats. Clearly they had reason to believe that only black administrators could transform federal welfare programs into an instrument of racial progress. However, the expansion of vocational opportunities only comprised part of the Colored Division's work. The other half of its mission consisted of preparing black working-class youth to take on these expanded opportunities. For in the minds of the black reform elite, only through careful behavior modification and training could these young people take advantage of these new opportunities and be prepared to take their place in the economic mainstream.

Every one of the Colored Division's work relief, job training, and recreation projects included activities intended to socialize out-of-work youth for productive citizenry. For example, the NYA-funded Atlanta Center for Negro Youth, a YMCA recreation center located at the Butler Street branch, offered participants, "constructive leisure time activities," including "psychological guidance," "character building," and "other activities as are calculated to contribute to their general social and civic well being."[30] Sewing-room workers were offered similar training on the job through etiquette and civic education classes to fill the need "for knowledge of better health, better home conditions, personality development, in short, better living."[31] The NYA's South Atlanta Center for youth who "have not been able to obtain employment or opportunities of attending school" offered vocational and psychological guidance, along with "supervised leisure time activities"[32] all led by ASSW faculty or students. These programs matched efforts by the Atlanta Urban League (AUL) and other private organizations to reform black working-class behavior and to indoctrinate the black poor to the importance and validity of uplift ideology. Given past difficulties in finding or maintaining a working-class constituency for these efforts, black reformers jumped on the potential of New Deal welfare programs and their captive clientele to create a mass constituency for the continuation and expansion of these efforts. Only black administrators knew the importance of this component of the uplift strategy and could advance it from within the federal government. In this way as well, the NYA proved a ground-breaking success for Atlanta's black reform elite.

Like NYA work relief, the Colored Division used the scholarship program to expand black opportunity and to extend the influence of black uplift ideology. Despite sharing the same ultimate goals, the Colored Division placed an impermeable barrier between these two programs, targeting them at entirely different groups of black youth. This separation points to the elitism embedded in this strategy for racial advancement. On the surface, however, the scholarship program appeared decidedly egalitarian. In its five-year existence, it benefited some 9,000 black Georgians, including at least 5,000 high school students. African American students needed this aid so desperately that college presidents in Atlanta reported that they were only able to make grants to about 45 percent of those students who applied for them. In fact, school enrollments declined significantly when the eligibility standard for the college and university program was tightened for the 1937–38 school year.[33]

NYA scholarships had far-reaching and long-lasting implications for their recipients, many of whom would not otherwise have been able to stay in school due to lack of funds during the Depression. NYA scholarships had the potential to shake up the South's almost static social structure. They could allow poor southerners, both black and white to dare to believe that, in the words of CIC leader Arthur Raper, "they could ever be anything except a sharecropper's son or a sharecropper's daughter,"[34] or, in the urban context, a domestic worker's son or a millworker's daughter. Despite the achievements and radical potential of the scholarship program, however, ample evidence demonstrates that the NYA's student-aid program eluded the reach of a majority of black students. Left-wing critics of the New Deal, like John Davis of the National Negro Congress, recognized this shortcoming from the beginning of the program. Davis pointed out that scholarships of fifteen dollars a month for college students and of three to six dollars for high school students would only help those who received some kind of supplement from their families, meaning that "the poorer child has no chance to go back to school."[35] Davis was right; while the NYA helped thousands of black students achieve a high school education, it did little for the countless others who had no resources or whose families' survival depended on their employment.

While these inequities originated in Washington, elitism in NYA student aid ran even deeper in Atlanta. The Colored Division censured college presidents and school principals who denied NYA aid to commuting students in favor of boarders, and based the scholarships on academic achievement instead of financial need. One year after critics exposed these abuses to the Colored Division, Mary McLeod Bethune reported to the Georgia NYA that she had received complaints that the agency granted scholarships to students whose families' monthly income was as much as $100 to $200, "while others whose parents earn only $40 are denied the aid."[36] This inequality was striking for a "relief" program, when thousands of black families in Atlanta earned less than even the $40 paid monthly to unskilled WPA workers.[37]

While Ralph Bullock was clearly concerned about the most extreme examples of abuse of the scholarship program, and admitted that all NYA scholarship students "ought really to be from a relief family," he considered this to be an "impossible" goal.[38] Bullock's comments point to the difficult choices the black elite had to make when choosing the recipients of this limited program. College presidents did not hope to effect social transformation for the working class through the scholarships, but to secure the expansion and advancement of the educated class. Black Atlantans suffered from lack of opportunity, whatever their income. Even students whose parents earned $1,000 dollars a year were not rich compared to whites of similar social and educational status, and they faced a constricted future that offered few vocational options. Why should these students, who had never had the privilege of government funding, be denied the opportunity of a NYA scholarship, while poorer and less prepared students be given a chance to complete high school or college? Why not use the NYA program to fund many Jacob Hendersons, gifted students from upwardly mobile families who were sure to reach the ranks of the middle class, rather than dubious scholars or very poor students facing difficult barriers to success even with a government scholarship?

The inequities of the scholarship program extended beyond its eligibility standards. The NYA in Georgia institutionalized the social distance between scholarship recipients and the out-of-school group by establishing a direct hierarchy between these two groups of black youth. The scholarship program, in effect, trained its recipients to assume leadership over the NYA's poorer, less educated, out-of-school clients. Black colleges sent NYA students, who were required to work for their stipends, into the community to serve as recreation or social work leaders for their poorer brothers or sisters who did not share their opportunities. This work requirement reinforced the existing mission of black colleges that already saw social-service leadership as an essential goal for their graduates and as an important institutional role. "The community uses us not only as a school for the training of Negroes . . . but also as an agency for the promotion of welfare work among Negroes," Forrester B. Washington wrote of the ASSW. Before the NYA, "the coordination of our training functions and our promotional functions was a real problem and one not faced by many, if any, nonracial schools of social work."[39] The NYA provided some temporary support to this mission by allowing scholarship recipients to be paid to fulfill the "promotional functions" of black institutions in their assumption of responsibility for the welfare of the black community.

In this capacity, the scholarship recipients were to lead their less educated brothers or sisters toward the uplift goals of the reform elite. NYA administrators never questioned the elitism of this move; after all, in sending college students to lead their poorer peers the Colored Division merely applied the same rationale as black reformers did in their quest for white-collar opportunities for black workers. Black New Dealers in Atlanta believed that the black poor needed to be prepared for social and economic incorporation. In this scheme, the traditional black elite clearly conceived and led the move for racial advancement while the "masses" of African Americans followed. The scholarship program allowed the expansion of this leadership cadre and its employment through the welfare programs of the New Deal.[40]

Although black reformers professed their commitment to the uplift of the "masses" as a means toward racial incorporation, they often had real difficulty in translating their rhetoric into action. Even when the New Deal provided their efforts with the backing and larger legitimacy they heretofore lacked, ideological and practical barriers blocked cross-class intraracial communication. Nowhere was this limitation more apparent than with the Public Forum, a program with the potential to implement the reform elite's uplift agenda for the black poor. Initiated as a civic education program in 1937 by the U.S. Office of Education, the Department of Interior, and the NYA, the Public Forum was locally administered by the Atlanta Board of Education. Soon after its inception in Atlanta, local Public Forum administrators appointed an African American committee made up of Atlanta's black reformers to administer the "colored" project, and a black director, Atlanta University history professor Rayford Logan, to run it.

The forums were public discussions led by a local expert on topics pertinent to the city's residents. National forum advocates grandly envisioned the Public Forum bringing back the spirit of the New England town meeting, the chatauqua, or even the Forum of ancient Rome, as all citizens pondered and discussed issues important to the city. The program was inspired by the antifascist impulse of the 1930s to include and involve all people in government in order to enrich American democracy. For white forum leaders, this democratizing impulse remained an abstraction; it was enough that the forums would take place at all. But for African American leaders fighting against Jim Crow for full citizenship, the forums provided a unique opportunity to bring the black community together in preparation for the struggle for true democracy.[41]

The Public Forum provided the "citizenship training" that black leaders considered vitally important for African Americans if they were to become full-fledged Americans. Such a requirement, black reformers believed, would require black Atlantans to think of themselves as Americans and to understand the rights and duties of citizenship. The black reform elite claimed that most African Americans lacked such civic consciousness, victimized as they were by the parochialism imposed on them through exclusion from the political, economic, and social life of the city. The black "masses," in reformers' minds, had to be taught to see themselves as part of the processes that affected their lives.

For black forum leaders, the program could begin the course of civic awakening necessary for the black community to join the fight for full citizenship. As Rayford Logan wrote, inclusion in the Public Forum "promoted a realization" for the first time among "the underprivileged colored citizens of Atlanta" that they were "inescapably Americans, that everything affecting other Americans also influences their life. The vital significance of such an awakening," Logan continued, "can be appreciated only by those who know that the almost complete exclusion of this group from non-religious activities has meant to many of them that happenings in [public] spheres of life were mysteries of another world, incomprehensible, inscrutable and taboo."[42] Logan used the Public Forum to lift the "taboo" and to prepare African Americans to take their place at the center of Atlanta's public life.

Forum leaders reflected their interest in education for citizenship in the theme "The Meaning of Democracy," which they chose for the first year of the Public Forum in 1937. Prominent black Atlantans, including W. E. B. Du Bois, led forums in schools and churches across the city on topics such as "The Press in a Democracy," "Industrial Democracy," "The Church in a Democracy," and "The Supreme Court and the Constitution," as well as "The Meaning of Democracy." Forums in the 1938–39 season extended this theme to address African Americans' place in American democracy and black citizenship.[43]

Forum leaders urged black Atlantans to act on their civil rights. For example, a 1938 forum on "The Negro and Citizenship" did not dwell on abstract notions of civic duty, but instead comprised a workshop on voting rights which covered the poll tax, how to qualify to vote, city elections in which African Americans could vote, and Georgia voting laws. A 1939 forum for 700 high school students stressed the importance of black youth to accept their "civic responsibility"—in other words, to register to vote—"as early as possible."[44]

Remarkably, black leaders delivered these militant messages without censure or harassment from white program administrators, the police, or vigilantes. Black leaders clearly attributed this achievement to the Public Forum's Washington funding and origins. Rayford Logan, no stranger to political repression after the shutdown of the Southern Institute of International Relations during Atlanta's red scare, pointed out that the greatest achievement of the Public Forum "has been the affording, under the protection of the Federal Government, of an opportunity for the unmolested discussion of vital controversial topics." In a period in Atlanta when all dissenting voices were branded as Communist, the "Federal Forum . . . definitely promoted freedom of speech among the colored people."[45] The protective federal umbrella opened even further after 1937 when most black forums were held at the black federal housing project, University Homes, the site of the city's only public auditorium for African Americans. The police rarely entered the complex unless called upon by the black project manager.[46]

Despite the opportunities afforded by the Public Forum afforded to incorporate African Americans into the political and social mainstream and to mobilize them to accept their civic responsibilities, the program attracted relatively few African Americans beyond the educated classes. For example, although Logan claimed to be reaching "underprivileged persons" and transforming their "community thought and behavior," his only evidence was the creation of a political science club and an "open forum" at Atlanta's most prestigious black colleges, Spelman and Morehouse. According to Logan, part of the reason for the limited appeal of the program was that all forum sessions were led by members of "the university and professional groups," only a few of whom were able to "bring the discussion down to the level of the audience" or be "successful in speaking to the working class."

Logan admitted this limitation, but justified it on the grounds that "there is no real labor organization and leadership in Atlanta" that could have provided forum leadership, "because of fear of interference by police." Furthermore, he believed that many poor black Atlantans would never be attracted to the Public Forum, citing in particular domestic workers, whose wages were "so lamentably low that the large number of persons in this class . . . hardly have the minimum interest which could be aroused by even intensive propaganda."[47]

Logan's justification for ignoring black workers was not born out in fact. While the red scare had significantly quieted Communist activities in the city, black workers were not silent in the 1930s. The Communist-influenced WPA union, the Workers' Alliance, formed a militant and black-dominated local in Atlanta, skilled artisans continued to work with the Urban League for union recognition, commercial laundry workers had begun a decade-long organizing struggle, and FERA's Workers' Education program (whose mandate was very similar to the Public Forum's) had found a constituency among a wide spectrum of Atlanta's black workers.[48] Rather, working-class nonparticipation in the Public Forum likely had more to do with the program's focus on the educated elite's ideals and aspirations. The focus on voter registration held little appeal for black workers daunted by the prospect of paying a cumulative poll tax so that they could vote in the few local elections in which they could participate. These black Atlantans may have been more interested in forums that addressed the reasons their wages were "so lamentably low," but such a focus would most assuredly have brought complaint from local whites. Rather, the assemblies appealed to the educated and upwardly mobile, by offering a rare "opportunity of participating, under capable leadership, in the discussion of public affairs."[49] The Public Forum further aided this group in its class-based incorporative goals by offering work-relief positions to blacks to administer the program, and by inviting whites to lead African American forums so that the outsiders could be impressed with "our universities and the interest of our students in the discussion of public affairs."[50]

When black reformers lobbied for the hiring of African American administrators and white-collar workers, they did so with the firmly held belief that this approach would ultimately provide the most good to the most black Atlantans. They believed that African American bureaucrats could focus their work on the aims that had driven black reform for many years. But this goal was extremely difficult to achieve; most black white-collar workers did not share the autonomy or authority of the black administrators of the NYA or Public Forum. Instead, they worked under the direct supervision of white superiors who did not share their aims for the black community. In fact, many programs that brought blacks into the state did so in ways that had intrusive or repressive repercussions for African American participants and clients. Therefore black government administrators and employees often found themselves in an ambiguous position in which even the actions they were able to take to further their reform agenda occurred within the context of white-led programs which sought to control African Americans' lives.

One such example was the antisyphilis campaign launched in 1936 by the U.S. surgeon general, Thomas Parran. Parran's ambitious testing and treatment program sought to remove the stigma attached to venereal disease and to bring medical attention to the countless poor who had previously lived outside the health-care system. He brought the New Deal's inclusive sensibility to the U.S. Public Health Service by applying his belief that "[e]very citizen, North and South, colored and white, rich and poor, has an inalienable right to his citizen's share of health protection."[51]

Unfortunately, while state and local officials accepted syphilis control money from the federal government, they did not accept the idea of impartial testing and treatment: instead, white paranoia and racist assumptions about African Americans and syphilis colored the program. Even the most liberal white New Dealers in Georgia shared the view that syphilis was an African American disease caused by black sexual promiscuity and general lack of hygiene. They seized on Parran's syphilis control program as an opportunity to create a "clean" black work force. African American workers on federal programs were examined for sexually transmitted diseases. Local white politicians applauded this policy and called for legislation requiring black service workers in the private sector to be tested for syphilis, even though the disease was well known to be spread only by sexual contact. It was within this repressive context that black physicians, nurses, and bureaucrats attempted to achieve their own public-health goals for African Americans.[52]

Black reaction to the antisyphilis campaign against service workers was mixed. On the national level, NAACP leaders vigorously protested the compulsory testing of domestic workers as racist paranoia. The organization lobbied the U.S. Health Department to issue statements regarding the "false assumption[s]" that guided whites to demand that their servants be tested for syphilis. While the black press reported these developments in Atlanta, African American reformers there chose not to protest the crackdown on domestic workers. Instead, they used the new white attention on blacks and venereal disease to promote health-care programs for African Americans and to further their inclusive aims for the black community.[53]

African American reformers' participation in the antisyphilis campaign stemmed partly from their recognition that venereal disease posed a serious health risk in the black community. Although syphilis rates for the 1930s are difficult to determine because of the racist assumptions surrounding the disease and the extreme unreliability of syphilis testing at that time, it does appear that black Atlantans suffered from syphilis in great disproportion to whites. Like other contagious diseases, syphilis ravaged the black community because of African Americans' limited access to health care. Black reformers responded wholeheartedly to the Public Health Service's antisyphilis message and sought to deal with the disease through a dispassionate public health campaign like the one advocated by Thomas Parran. Local black physicians led a Public Forum on "social diseases." In the 1930s Negro Health Week organizers added syphilis to a list of other communicable diseases such as tuberculosis which they attacked in their health education campaign. Moreover, black social-service agencies, like Spelman College's Leonard Street Orphans' Home, administered syphilis tests to its clients. In other words, black leaders saw Thomas Parran's antisyphilis programs as yet another opportunity to benefit African Americans through inclusion in federal programs.[54]

Parran's campaign also appealed to African American reformers because he explicitly promoted the use of black physicians and nurses in the fight against syphilis among African Americans. As he wrote in *Survey Graphic* in 1938, "the well-qualified Negro nurse and physician are much more successful in caring for their own people than are the well-qualified and well-intentioned white nurse and physician. . . . That is why we need more good ones helping on this public health job, and we need them now."[55] This kind of talk warmed the cockles of black physicians' hearts, who had employed just this rationale in their efforts to force open the doors of Jim Crow clinics and hospitals closed to them in Atlanta. The federal government's reinvigorated public-health efforts offered a fruitful new pathway into full citizenship for the black medical community. Black physicians hoped they could use their race to promote themselves as the brokers of health education between the white public-health establishment and the black people it hoped to serve. As Dr. Herman Nash wrote of public-health efforts against tuberculosis: "Health education would teach Negroes to cooperate with those who are trying to help them. This information can be most effectively disseminated by the Negro health education workers. They move in every phase of Negro life, from the front door to the kitchen—from the boulevard to the alley."[56]

Black physicians participated in all aspects of syphilis control efforts in the black community. They even used the funds made available by the Public Health Service to create their own opportunities and to shield black Atlantans from the repression of the white antisyphilis campaign. They established a clinic at which black patients could avoid abusive treatment from white physicians and the prison-like atmosphere of the city's venereal disease clinic at Grady Hospital. Probably using federal dollars for drugs, and employing donations of money, personnel, and equipment from the Atlanta School of Social Work, Medical Women's Auxiliary, and NYA sewing rooms, four black physicians led by Dr. Georgia Dwelle founded a free syphilis clinic on Auburn Avenue. This facility would finally provide a facility at which "needy persons of the race in the city" could "receive expert and courteous service from physicians and nurses of their own race."[57]

But while the Auburn Avenue syphilis clinic protected some African Americans from white scrutiny, other aspects of the syphilis control program in Atlanta in which black medical personnel participated played on the racist paranoia which fueled white support for syphilis control for blacks. In the fall of 1936, two white administrators of the Georgia NYA contacted the Atlanta Tuberculosis Association (ATA) to conduct tuberculosis and syphilis tests on black women working in the administration's sewing rooms. The ATA agreed to conduct the tests as long as the state and city health departments, their budgets newly enriched by antisyphilis federal funding, would analyze and follow up the tests. Black physicians and nurses who worked with the "colored" branch of the ATA were hired to conduct the tests.[58]

On the surface, these examinations appeared to further the goals of black reformers by using federal programs and black medical personnel to bring some rudimentary preventive health care to a population that was notoriously underserved. But the white motivations behind the testing programs sullied this seemingly purely beneficial program. White administrators only intended the physical examination program for black women, except for a small group of black men. In fact, the supervisors of white sewing rooms who "coveted" similar services for their workers had to specially request a similar program from their NYA superiors and the ATA, making tuberculosis and syphilis testing perhaps the only New Deal program in Atlanta available to blacks and not to whites.[59]

Racial preconceptions clearly motivated the special attention afforded black women. The testing program was carried out in the midst of white hysteria about blacks and syphilis, most notably a city council debate over an ordinance requiring the testing of black domestic workers for the disease. White administrators perceived black sewing-room workers, all of whom were subjected to mandatory training in domestic work, as future servants in white homes who needed to be "cleaned" up before they could take their place in society. So while black physicians and nurses brought black NYA sewing-room workers under the purview of the health-care system, they did so in the context of a program initiated by paranoid whites seeking to control the bodies of black workers under their supervision. Through their participation in this program, black nurses and physicians forged a Faustian bargain in their promise to local white public-health officials that they were the best ones to conduct public-health programs in the black community.[60]

The NYA's syphilis control program demonstrates how difficult it was for black government employees to work on behalf of African Americans within the context of the racialist assumptions that governed most New Deal programs. The results of efforts to bring black Atlantans into full citizenship could at best be ambiguous, given that they occurred within the larger framework of efforts to control and repress African Americans.

Even in programs run largely by African Americans, black bureaucrat-reformers faced enormous difficulties challenging the limits of Jim Crow. Programs like the NYA's vocational-training effort met white resistance at every turn, lest African Americans leave their preordained place at the bottom of southern society. Nevertheless, these Herculean black efforts represented an important first step in the active effort to bring African Americans into the mainstream and a new pathway by which the reform elite could achieve its incorporative objectives.

Notwithstanding the importance of the involvement of black administrators in New Deal programs, their efforts did not touch the majority of black Atlantans' lives. Limited authority and funding within a racist framework meant that these programs could only reach a minority of the black community. Consequently black bureaucrats most often concentrated their efforts on the educated and upwardly mobile. Their programs showed them to be out of touch with the concerns of the majority of working black Atlantans and frankly elitist in many of their aims. This was so despite their convictions that they were serving the entire African American community and its interests against whites, who would block all black progress. In the end, the black New Deal in Atlanta achieved most for those who were hired into the federal bureaucracy and little or nothing for the "masses." The New Deal helped hundreds of Jacob Hendersons on their way to the American Dream; its legacy was more uncertain for the thousands of other African Americans who did not possess the wherewithal to open the door, or to shut it, when the New Deal came calling.

5

Unwanted Attention

*Black Workers and
the New Deal*

In 1934 or 1935, white social worker Lucy McIntire
wrote a short play to train administrators and supervisors of the Georgia
Civil Works Administration (CWA), the New Deal work relief program that
preceded the Works Progress Administration (WPA). Called "The Confused
Worker," the skit comprised an interview between a CWA Women's Division administrator named Miss Felton and a black relief recipient named
Mrs. Green who worked at a CWA sewing room. Mrs. Green's supervisor
sent her to Felton because of her inability to follow the instructions for
making "stepins," the simple undergarments that sewing-room workers
made in their workshops. In the course of the interview, the audience
learned that Mrs. Green was illiterate and that she was the sole bread-
winner for a family that included her husband, recently released from
prison and physically incapacitated, and her unmarried daughter, who had
recently given birth. Presumably, McIntire meant this scenario to be representative of situations faced by New Deal agency employees as they encountered Georgia's relief population.[1]

Miss Felton was the ideal social-work professional. She treated Mrs.
Green with sympathy. She recognized that Mrs. Green was a hardworking
person who meant well and that her lack of education and very stress-
ful home situation understandably affected her work from time to time.
Felton's careful interview techniques, which elicited her environmentalist
understanding of Mrs. Green's particular situation, represented the cutting
edge of casework practice and theory in the 1930s. And by addressing her
as "Mrs. Green," Felton demonstrated an uncommon amount of respect
for her African American client, whose real-life counterparts were used to

being addressed by whites by their first name or a variety of other disrespectful and insulting monikers.

Yet despite McIntire's sensitivity, this skit was a product of its author's own environment of Jim Crow white supremacy. McIntire wrote Mrs. Green's dialogue in the dialect of minstrelsy and made her a clown, portraying her as a laughable simpleton. Furthermore, the situations in which McIntire placed Green conformed to white stereotypes of black behavior, including having a criminal husband and sexually promiscuous daughter. In McIntire's evocation, Mrs. Green could not even adequately perform the kind of domestic tasks traditionally assigned to black women workers, or at least not according to the modern standards of the New Deal. For example, she did not understand why she was thrown off the CWA's school-lunch work relief program after being caught chewing tobacco while preparing food. McIntire ended her skit with a joke highlighting Green's ignorance. When Green's sewing room problems seemed to have been solved, she reassured Felton by declaring: "All right, ma'am . . . I'll get them stepins right effen somebody'll jess tell me what a stepin is en how it orter look."

McIntire's skit exposes the paradoxes of New Deal relief programs in their relationship with their black recipients in Atlanta. White social workers in the 1930s rejected the biological determinism of previous generations, and understood that an environment borne of poverty, not race, caused the hardships that plagued the city's African American community. This understanding prompted the New Deal's unprecedented rehabilitative program for black Georgians. However, as McIntire's stereotypical rendering of Mrs. Green suggests, this program was also shaped by paternalism and traditional white assumptions about African Americans' caste position. White New Deal administrators in Georgia sought to rehabilitate black relief recipients within the structures of racial exploitation, not release them from Jim Crow.

This mix of ideologies had a pernicious impact on black relief recipients. While the New Deal's recognition and incorporation of African Americans in its welfare programs brought much-needed services to a population used to being virtually invisible to any but the most repressive agents of the state, the New Deal's relief agencies' scrutiny of African Americans constituted unwelcome attention for many black Atlantans. They soon realized that the "rehabilitation" intended by Georgia's white New Deal social workers sought to modernize and rationalize, indeed to institutionalize, their caste position. Thus their incorporation into the state came at a very heavy price.

The depth of alienation between poor black Atlantans and any level of government before the New Deal is difficult to grasp in this age of state involvement in every facet of the lives of citizens, and particularly of the poor. Before the New Deal, governments dealt with African Americans by ignoring or repressing them. Black Atlantans had virtually no contact with the state except for the police and justice systems, and the woefully inadequate black public schools. Their neighborhoods enjoyed few of the municipal services of white neighborhoods such as garbage collection, sewers, and electricity, giving added meaning to the racial designation "Darktown" for one of the poorest black neighborhoods in Atlanta. City officials denied existence to some of the streets and alleys in black neighborhoods, making even mail delivery impossible. In fact, the New Deal gave many black Atlantans their first and most basic connection with the federal state, a postal address, so that they could receive their relief checks.[2]

Given this historic exclusion, poor African Americans had little reason to believe that federal relief would offer them much succor. Their more recent experience of discrimination at the hands of municipal emergency relief officials gave them even less reason to expect anything more from the federal government. Yet in fact, to a surprising degree, when Gay Shepperson and Harry Hopkins "federalized" relief in Atlanta and Georgia, administrators worked to distribute it according to need rather than race.

Wilma Van Dusseldorp, a white social worker who helped establish the Atlanta Relief Commission, estimated that before federal intervention in 1933, of 8,000 or 9,000 families receiving emergency relief in Atlanta, only around 1,800 were black, despite unemployment levels of up to 75 percent in some black neighborhoods. Within three and a half months of the federal takeover, 29,000 families had qualified for relief, over one-half of them black. Of course, all federal relief was supposed to be colorblind in its eligibility standards and level of financial support. But local officials across the country used many methods to deny relief to eligible African Americans, making Atlanta's relative evenhandedness still more surprising.[3]

This more equal distribution of emergency relief marked the ascendancy of the philosophy and practice of professional social work in Atlanta. When federal officials took over the local relief setup they found it, in the words of Van Dusseldorp, "dominated by local politics that were not in harmony with . . . the New Deal aims."[4] Along with race-based abuses, relief was also often dependent on the pull that recipients had with city politicians who controlled the available funds. The federally appointed social workers who took over local relief were committed to bringing relief up to a modern, rational standard. Their first step was to apply Washington's single eligibility and payment standard for blacks and whites based on their real needs.

This nonracial standard not only modernized the administration of relief; it also began the process of modernizing the South by dealing with its enormous poverty problem. White social workers in government and their liberal counterparts in other spheres of life were coming to an understanding that in order for the entire South to progress economically the poverty of the South's workers had to be tackled. The underpayment of black Atlantans, who sometimes earned as little as two or three dollars for a seventy-hour week, depressed the wages of all southerners, black or white, and kept the region from escaping poverty. White social workers, although they were very tentative in their efforts, wanted to "break right across"[5] prevailing wage patterns through federal relief. In fact, federal relief payments disrupted the status quo enough to prompt some of the poorest-paid domestic workers to quit their work in favor of the Federal Emergency Relief Administration (FERA) dole.[6]

Modernization through relief programs consisted of more than higher wages in the minds of white administrators. They also hoped to improve the living environment of the state and city's poor according to modern scientific, medical, and social-work standards. This rehabilitation took on many forms. Civil Works Administration work relief projects in Fulton County included rodent control to prevent typhus outbreaks, school renovations, and a lunch program for poor children, all of which touched the lives of black Atlantans. In Georgia, 52 percent of white and black "white-collar" relief workers for FERA were directly involved in education to combat illiteracy and medical work to halt the spread of preventable illnesses. CWA nurses attended to all phases of public health by providing thousands of Atlantans with tests for communicable diseases, handing out sickness prevention information, and offering pre- and postnatal care to all mothers on relief. With these projects, the government spotlit poverty for the first time in Georgia and tackled its most glaring effects.

Relief administrators believed that if they could ameliorate the environment of their clientele they could improve the lives of the poor and prevent diseases and criminal tendencies that they believed were connected to poverty. However, they also more directly attacked the perceived social pathologies of the poor. For example, CWA sewing rooms, which, beginning in 1934, took able-bodied FERA recipients and put them to work in government workshops, always included the socialization of recipients in their program. Jane Van de Vrede, director of women's and professional work for the CWA, described the sewing rooms as "miniature community centers" at which workers were "given talks and demonstrations on the need for personal cleanliness, sanitation, home hygiene, and nourishing, well-balanced meals." These activities, Van de Vrede believed, worked "to re-establish the morale of the individual woman and to encourage rehabilitation of home and community life."[7]

Yet despite their efforts to combat poverty, these first federal relief programs in Atlanta did little to overturn the existing economic rules that governed the lives of the city's poorest group, African Americans. Social proscription and powerful southern economic interests meant that New Deal work relief programs offered all but a handful of black workers nothing but unskilled labor, and National Recovery Administration codes with their regional differentials and exclusions kept black wages low. Even the white social workers running Georgia's rehabilitative New Deal programs never envisioned a social transformation to accompany the individual improvements they hoped to accomplish. While Georgia's CWA administrators might have wanted to benefit poor blacks by providing daycare, recreation, and public-health services, they did not attempt to bring black workers out of poverty by offering them vocational training and skilled jobs. Instead, they sought to advance the "social adjustment" of the poor, improving their situation, not changing it. Rhoda Kaufman, doyenne of Georgia's social-work community, talked in 1928 about society's "problem" children, including juvenile delinquents, "feeble-minded" children, and, by implication, white southerners' biggest "problem," African Americans. She remarked that these groups only became a social ill when they "failed to fit into society." The responsibility for this failure rested not on the groups themselves but on the case worker "who has not" helped them "fit into the social scheme of things."[8] The idea that the poor had to be rehabilitated by social workers to "fit into the social scheme of things" and to accept their social position governed much New Deal thinking in Atlanta. This was particularly true for white social workers in relation to the "Negro problem" in Atlanta and Georgia. Their interventionist, rehabilitative approach, while a novel one for southerners, nevertheless sought to preserve the status quo.

While the white social workers who ran the New Deal's relief and training programs in Georgia always described themselves as following the most modern social-work practice, most of their efforts directed at African

Americans evolved from entrenched notions of race and race relations in the South. As Lucy McIntire's skit attests, programs for poor blacks were often shaped by a paternalistic noblesse oblige which middle-class whites felt for the unfortunate black race. Their charitable impulses dictated that blacks had to be cared for by state relief, but not that African Americans should improve their social or economic position in Atlanta relative to whites.

Furthermore, white officials imbued with this paternalistic ideology sought to use the inclusion of black Atlantans in New Deal programs as an opportunity to control black behavior in ways that before had been impossible. The repressive results of these efforts weighed most heavily on Atlanta's black women, 80 percent of whom were employed in domestic work. The Depression hit these women particularly hard, making them the largest group of FERA relief recipients in the city. According to a May 1934 survey, 43 percent, or about 11,000 of all FERA recipients in Atlanta, were domestic workers, meaning that unemployment had affected more than 50 percent of the approximately 20,000 counted by the federal census in 1930. And considering that almost one-third of black women were the primary breadwinners for their families, this crisis in domestic work had deep implications for the black community.[9]

Black women may have made up the largest group of unemployed workers in Atlanta, but the New Deal work relief agencies that followed FERA severely restricted their programs for women of all races, both in numbers of recipients and the work options available to them. In 1938, for example, women comprised only 10,220 (or about 15 percent) of the 71,000 WPA workers in Georgia. While large public-works projects, like sewer construction, employed thousands of black and white men at a time in Atlanta, the largest women's relief project in Atlanta supported only around 1,000 women. New Deal administrators limited work relief opportunities for women because they did not want the New Deal's programs to disturb the roles that blacks and whites, and women and men, played in the state's economy. The status quo was to be preserved until the emergency of economic depression was over. Thus the CWA and WPA in Atlanta restricted unskilled, unemployed women mainly to such traditional projects as sewing rooms because they wanted to preserve public-works projects for working-class men. Federally sponsored work for women beyond the parameters of that which was traditionally woman's work would confuse both gender and race relations by calling into question the patriarchal premise of white men's primacy as family breadwinners for white women and would disturb the vocational restrictions that virtually limited African American women to low-paid domestic work. As Jan Van De Vrede assured a radio audience, work relief projects for black and white women breadwinners would "not lose sight . . . of normal home work for this great number of women who cannot and should not be absorbed in the industrial system."[10] As always for black women, however, the "home" was not their own—it was their employer's.

New Dealers' concerns about women's work relief were dictated by white community concerns. Local government and agencies concentrated on large-scale projects for men, such as the massive city sewer project, or smaller projects in "traditional" fields for white-collar women, such as training in library cataloging. Programs for working-class women were limited and conformed to race and gender stereotypes. For example, Atlanta's only outdoor work relief program for women was for "strong and able-bodied" African Americans who performed heavy manual labor in Washington Park. As one black Atlantan astutely observed, these women were metaphorically "put to work in the fields."[11] This program was meant to be a stopgap measure, as was the main women's work program, CWA and WPA sewing rooms sponsored by the Fulton County Department of Public Welfare. These projects provided unemployed working-class women with a paycheck but nothing in the way of meaningful work or training.

Equipped at best with old-fashioned hand treadle machines, sewing rooms more often provided relief workers with little more than needle and thread. One worker at the Morris Brown College sewing project remembered how tedious and meaningless the work was: "We sewed everything by hand. You'd sew a litle piece about an inch long, and if every stitch wasn't perfect that teacher would pull it [sic] every bit out."[12] In a desperate move to obtain more equipment, WPA sewing-room supervisors at a 1938 meeting decided to take advantage of a recent promotional offer by the Octagon Soap Company. They would begin a campaign among women relief recipients to collect soap wrappers; for every seventy-five collected, a sewing room would receive one free pair of scissors.[13]

While underfunding plagued all of Georgia's sewing-room projects, racial conventions also kept black workers from learning anything vaguely resembling modern, industrial sewing. The Jim Crow caste system largely barred African Americans from the industrial economy, and racial stereotypes assumed black ineptitude or unpreparedness for modern, rationalized work. According to Lucy McIntire's skit, Mrs. Green worked well at the beginning of the CWA's sewing-room project when women pieced quilts, a traditional folk skill. Her trouble came when asked to manufacture stepins according to government specifications and the quotas the CWA set for each worker. Even these unproductive make-work projects faced criticism for disturbing community conventions. For example, when the WPA moved a black sewing room to Edgewood Avenue, a street of white-owned businesses catering to a mainly black clientele, merchants signed a petition opposing the move. They considered the project to be a "factory" and a black business, and therefore a threat to their economic control of the district.[14]

Much white community concern focused around black women abandoning domestic work for better-paid work relief, a complaint voiced throughout the New Deal.[15] This concern was well founded. While there are no reliable statistics on the number of women who left private employment for federal work relief, a study of 140 domestic workers in Atlanta conducted by the Phyllis Wheatley YWCA in Atlanta found that on average household servants earned twelve cents an hour compared to thirty cents on WPA work projects. Work relief administrators limited the number of positions available to black women partly in response to this threat to the labor supply. Furthermore, administrators always cut women's relief projects first when the WPA periodically reduced its appropriation to the states. For example, during 1935 the WPA cut its women's program in Georgia from 18,000 workers to 12,000. Subsequently, 2,000 of those laid off found "private employment," most likely in domestic service. In another instance in July 1937, the WPA removed 1,500 black and white sewing-room workers in Atlanta and placed them on local relief, putatively for being "marginal" workers who should receive newly enacted Social Security. While Social Security legislation mandated that only those unable to work due to age, disability, or child support should be laid off from work relief, black women were forced off these projects more than white women, and for reasons other than their incapacity to work. Lucy McIntire, appointed head of the Women's and Professional Division of the WPA, alluded to one of these reasons in a talk to WPA administrators. Regarding "Personnel Handling" on unskilled projects, McIntire told her audience that "special group[s], i.e. colored women, should either be cared for in special work which the community will sponsor, or [be] turn[ed] back to the D[epartment] of P[ublic] W[elfare] as no assignment is available which they can fill."[16] In disqualifying these women for work relief, the WPA consigned them to inadequate and irregular local relief, which sometimes offered recipients only two or three dollars a month. This level of support forced black women back into domestic service. In fact, one woman remembered that "the government . . . would help folks get jobs in private homes and vouch for us"[17] after the WPA closed her sewing room. When Social Security was finally enacted in Georgia in 1937, these workers were ineligible for its major benefit, the old-age pension program, because it excluded domestic workers from its purview.[18]

While black women in Atlanta found limited opportunities for work relief due to white efforts to protect the labor market for domestic service, those women who did qualify for WPA positions found themselves subject to the repressive impulses of the white social workers who ran women's projects. These administrators had a particular interest in bringing black women under the New Deal umbrella because black women, as domestic workers, represented one of the largest impoverished groups in the state. Many black domestic workers in Atlanta worked independently, either out of their own homes by taking in laundry, or changing employers frequently when working in white people's homes. This independence was part of a long-term trend away from the paternalism of slavery and the postemancipation period; very few black domestic workers lived with their employers in the 1930s, and more and more of them did not even work in a single family's home, but rather did day work for several employers. From one perspective this independence demonstrated how domestic workers managed to avoid scrutiny and social control by whites, a freedom cherished by black women whose abysmal pay and long hours forced them to make so many other sacrifices. However, from another it showed how the Depression forced domestic workers to move from position to position, or to hold several jobs at once in order to feed their families. In any case, the breakdown of the bonds of paternalism and the growing independence of domestic servants caused extreme anxiety among whites. This concern manifested itself in calls for training in domestic service for black women, ostensibly to improve their efficiency and skill, but also to subdue them through subservience.

White New Dealers responded to widespread white concerns by creating several programs to train black women in domestic service. For example, black CWA, WPA, and National Youth Administration sewing rooms, while supplying little or no training in industrial or even machine sewing, always included some type of training for domestic work in their segregated black projects. Similarly, FERA, the CWA, and the WPA provided courses to black women in domestic service. These programs sought to "establish standards of household employment"[19] for students in occupations noted for their lack of modern, rationalized standards and indeed the informality of their work arrangements. For an "elite" group of black women trained in these programs, the state created a corps of roving domestic workers through the Housekeeping Aide project, a wpa program that sought to teach black women household management and practical nursing so that they could provide temporary household help to relief families where the mother was incapacitated by illness or disability. And in a related project, Grady Hospital sponsored a wpa "hospital auxiliary worker" program starting in 1939, which provided formal training to black women and men to become service workers as maids, cafeteria cooks, and waiters, janitors, and orderlies. These training programs, which comprised the only vocational education provided to black women in the New Deal, demonstrate clearly what white New Dealers sought from black women in bringing them under the wing of the state as domestic workers.[20]

Domestic training programs originated during the cwa under the leadership of Jane Van De Vrede. She found her job difficult because gender bias and the large number of unskilled and unschooled workers in the South greatly restricted the possibilities of work relief for women. A project to train domestic workers was one such possibility, made even more attractive by the "demand for trained household workers in the South."[21] In these courses the cwa taught women "the use of modern kitchen equipment as well as the preparation of food and the care of the home."[22] Administrators hoped that relief recipients could find domestic work based on the skills obtained through training. National cwa officials applauded Van De Vrede's plan as a pragmatic solution to the national problem of providing women, and particularly black women, with relief.[23]

While "scientific" training in domestic work might have been a practical work relief option for black women, it also reflected growing white concerns about the future of domestic work in an era where household workers could, in some instances, earn more on federal relief than in private employment. During the New Deal, white Georgians persisted in their perennial complaints over the "servant problem," comparing their current domestic help unfavorably to that of a mythical antebellum past where servants favored their employers with servility, a lifetime of loyalty, and a willingness to work practically around the clock for nothing. These complaints intensified during the 1930s because whites believed that the Depression should force black workers back to the paternalism of the past through loyal domestic service. Instead, to their consternation, domestic workers became more independent than ever, moving from job to job, or from private employment to work relief to laundry work and back, in an attempt to maximize scarce wages and improve their families' situations. For example, one domestic worker, Mary Morton, worked as a sick nurse taking care of mothers and babies and also did some day work during the Depression. When the WPA disqualified her husband from work relief, she took in laundry, which she did not like to do, "but if I got in a tight, I would. I'd have to . . . take care of my children during the Depression."[24]

Even white liberals shared this nostalgia for the golden age of domestic service and criticism of the modern, peripatetic servant. For example, Rev. John Moore Walker of St. Luke's Episcopal Church in Atlanta made the charge to black members at a Commission of Interracial Cooperation (CIC) meeting that "the type of domestic servant seems to have changed. It was once held by responsible colored people." He complained that in one short period of time, his family had gone through a succession of twenty-one cooks, when one after another had quit. His solution to this problem was instructive: "I should say that one of the features of any effort to meet the unemployment situation would be an effort to train young Negro girls in domestic service."[25] Walker's complaints suggest that such training would likely concentrate on servant behavior and loyalty, rather than on instruction in modern nutrition theory, food preparation, and household management.

New Dealers responded to these concerns with various domestic-training programs which they hoped would restore the *status quo ante* by expediting the "transfer [of] Negro women from relief rolls to pay rolls."[26] Furthermore, the women who moved back to private employment would have the proper skills and attitude for loyal domestic service. Lorena Hickok, one of Harry Hopkins's itinerant national relief reporters, placed a telling spin on the purpose of domestic training for black women in her description of an early CWA program in Georgia. While the project was meant to train "Negresses," as Hickok put it, Jane Van de Vrede also told Hickok that she hoped that it would provide relief employment to "Southern gentlewomen, last survivors of the old aristocracy." According to Hickok, Van De Vrede told her in a meeting that she wanted to have "the gentlewomen train the Negresses for domestic service. 'The only trouble,' she said, 'is that the Negresses won't go in for it. They don't want to learn how to be servants.'"[27] Hickok's racist terminology and description showed this project to be a peculiar mix of the modern and the retrograde; it attempted to reinforce customary social and race relations in the South by encoding them in state programs.

These intentions become even clearer when examining the actual content of the training courses which attempted to instill their students with respect for racial and social hierarchies. The Grady Hospital's training program made this point explicitly. A lecturer told black female hospital trainees that "An aide has to meekly accept, as right and necessary much that she cannot understand," and that she should "see every situation from the view point of those in authority." Furthermore, she told the trainees that "[l]ack of respect for authority is a distinctive mark of bad breeding," and gave them the following instruction in respectful behavior: "When going in elevators or wards, always stand back for the physician and nurse to go first. If sitting, stand when approached. Be orderly in all parts of the hospital, not forgetting to be quiet in halls and corridors; in walking always go to the right. Never speak in a loud tone of voice. Be orderly at all times."[28]

Black nurse's aide Mary Beale[29] remembered the anger she felt at a similar discipline imposed at Battle Hill sanitarium near Atlanta. When Battle Hill hired a "green" white nurse with similar training but less experience than Beale, Beale had to demonstrate basic procedures to the new hire, all the while having to call her "Miss" while she called her "Mary," and to stand when the novice entered the room "just 'cause she was white." "But," as Beale concluded, "I worked under those conditions because I needed a job so badly."[30]

Along with attempting to control the behavior of black domestic and service workers, New Deal programs also worked to control their bodies. Another symptom of Depression-era white anxiety over the growing independence of black domestic workers was the obsessive concern with black women bringing contagious disease, and particularly venereal disease, into the white homes in which they worked. In this case, the New Deal's intervention into the lives of the poor actually helped spawn this paranoia, when the U.S. Public Health Service's antisyphilis campaign subjected black relief clients to physical examinations. White New Deal administrators intended that this program would provide much needed health care to an underserved population, but their intervention also sought to create a "clean" and "disease free" black work force. In fact, many relief workers, such as housekeeping aides and school lunch workers, found that the first and only qualifications for inclusion in these programs were a physical examination for syphilis and other communicable diseases and a "personal examination" insuring "cleanliness."[31]

Historically, African Americans had been seen by the public health community and the white public to be a "notoriously syphilis-soaked race."[32] Over the years, black proclivity to venereal diseases had been attributed to a presumed biological sensitivity and, more common, to black sexual promiscuity. Usually based on pseudo-scientific research, these assertions about African Americans and syphilis gained widespread acceptance around the country as fact.

Notions about African Americans and syphilis reinforced perceptions of innate black inferiority by whites, who did little to control the disease among African Americans before the New Deal. Moreover, the organizations that did want to tackle syphilis among blacks could make few inroads into the problem as they perceived it, given that they had no organized constituency with whom to work. For example, in 1927, the American Social Hygiene Association came to Atlanta to make a report on syphilis in the city. While the association found appalling incidence of "sex delinquency" in Atlanta, it found no political will among local officials to tackle the problem. Furthermore, it saw the goal of attacking the problem as an almost insurmountable one, since black workers were not employed and organized in industry but, rather, were scattered throughout the city doing laundry and domestic work, thus hidden from the sight of anti–venereal disease crusaders.[33]

Both community indifference and black invisibility to whites disappeared with the appointment of Thomas Parran as U.S. surgeon general in 1936. Parran, a longtime antisyphilis crusader, wished to remove the social stigma of syphilis by turning the fight against the disease into a public-health campaign like any other. He advocated widespread testing and free treatment for syphilis and backed up his wishes with money. Public-health appropriations to the states attached to the Social Security Bill contained a rider that 10 percent of the disbursed money had to go to syphilis control. Although Parran's motives may have been pure, as we have already seen, intrusion into people's lives through government sanctioned social or, in this case, public-health work often had repressive implications for the recipients.

In Georgia, federal appropriations for syphilis testing meant that the State Board of Health could test all suspected cases of the disease at no cost to the patient. In 1937, the board tested 120,000 Georgians, most of them in Atlanta. D. T. F. Abercrombie, director of the Health Department, attributed the large number to a public awakening to the dangers of syphilis, which he claimed affected more than 300,000 individuals in the state. The free testing service would go a long way toward eliminating the problem, because more than 50 percent of all of those suffering from the disease were too poor to obtain medical treatment.[34]

While Abercrombie talked of a public awakening, he did not mean one of the affected African Americans. He referred instead to fearful white Georgians' awakening to the threat (manufactured by the antisyphilis campaign) that their servants might bring sexually transmitted diseases into their homes. With the advent of public testing, an irrational fear of the nonsexual transmission of syphilis grew as more and more white Georgians made a negative test for syphilis a condition for their domestic employees. Officials like Abercrombie fanned these fears of contamination, pointing out explicitly that of all those tested by the state for syphilis, 20 percent tested positive, while among blacks the rate grew to nearly 60 percent. Furthermore, he pointed out that 35 percent of domestic workers and 41 percent of cooks tested positive.[35]

These statistics, while scientifically suspect, nevertheless caused great consternation among white Atlantans. In 1937, Atlanta considered an ordinance requiring all domestic workers and food handlers to obtain a syphilis test prior to employment. While it enacted the law only for food handlers, increasingly employers of domestic workers required a physical examination before employing any household servants.[36]

New Deal programs to subdue African American domestic workers and service employees marked a new era in state intervention both to improve black life expectancy and, perniciously, to control black behavior. In marked contrast to the corrupt and violent workings of the local justice system, white government administrators worked to control black workers through the apparently benevolent intervention of modern social work. The intrusive methods of social work and public health, which probed the most intimate and personal affairs of its clients, were well suited to controlling black lives and black bodies. But it was not until the New Deal, and its reach deep into the poorest black neighborhoods, that social workers through the state had the clientele for such work.[37]

African Americans were not only incorporated into the New Deal through their relief checks. They were also brought into the state in more profound ways by the New Deal's attempts to teach relief recipients how to become citizens. FERA used unemployed white-collar workers, and particularly teachers, to bring ordinary workers into the mainstream of American life. This was done in a variety of ways, including literacy training. One of the more radical examples of this impulse was FERA's national worker-education program. This program taught both black and white workers in Atlanta about the New Deal and, more radically, preached the gospel of the benefits of organized labor and spread the word about the rights of workers to join unions and to use collective bargaining.[38] Like all of FERA's adult-education programs, workers' education was intended to teach its participants how to become "well-informed, responsible and self-supporting citizens." Workers' education, however, had a more specific goal of informing workers "who are confused by changing industrial conditions, and seek to understand their own responsibilities as workers and as citizens." Workers' education classes gave these workers in "industry, commerce, domestic service and other occupations an opportunity to train themselves in clear thinking through the study of those questions closely related to their daily lives as workers and citizens." After being instructed in an atmosphere of "scientific inquiry in light of all the facts," and one of "complete freedom of teaching and discussion," newly enlightened workers would develop "an active and continued interest in the economic problems of our times and . . . develop a sense of responsibility for their solution."[39]

The idea of bringing southern workers together to "train themselves in clear thinking" in order to talk about "economic problems" and how they themselves could solve them was directly inimical to the repressive workings of southern labor relations, especially among unskilled and unorganized black workers. Needless to say, given the taboo-like proscription against worker organization, let alone unionization in the South, the program was not sponsored by the local Relief Commission but instead by the education division of FERA on direct instructions from Washington, D.C. The program was also linked to the Affiliated Schools for Workers, a private regional organization that held summer schools in worker education for whites, and that hired and paid the director of the FERA program in Atlanta.[40]

Workers' education was initiated in Atlanta in the spring of 1934 under the leadership of Tom Tippett, a New York–based author and labor activist. Guided by his direction, five black and two white teachers, all unemployed relief recipients, taught labor issues to ten black and six white classes. The white classes were held in the Atlanta Federation of Trades' Labor Temple, mainly for already unionized white workers. The black classes were held at the Atlanta Urban League and the Phyllis Wheatley YWCA for nonunionized groups—such as brickmasons and workers from the local Scripto pencil factory—that these agencies had already organized into social groups and quasi-unions. Black instructors also held independent classes in their homes for workers in their neighborhoods and for an interested group of nurses.[41]

None of the teachers hired for the project had any special knowledge of workers' issues, and their only preparation consisted of a one-week training period prior to the beginning of their classes. Consequently they remained dependent on Tom Tippett's expertise and, by extension, his ideological preoccupations in teaching their classes.[42] Unfortunately, Tippett's naive idealism diluted the effectiveness of the classes. Tippett, like many white labor organizers of his day, was convinced that salvation for all workers lay in organized labor. Furthermore, his understanding of the struggles faced by black workers was based on a single-minded belief that the "way out of the Negro problem is through the trade union movement,"[43] and a brand of determinism that reduced the plight of African American workers to merely economic factors shared with white workers. This belief led him, for example, to take at face value bland assurances from Georgia's American Federation of Labor leaders that a new day had dawned in southern race relations, where Atlanta's trade-union establishment would welcome black workers with open arms, an absurd assertion for anyone familiar with the history of race and labor relations in Atlanta or the United States. His ideological convictions also led Tippett to dismiss black charges of racism among local white unions as being a thing of the past, and to condemn black scabs as class traitors while discounting the exclusion of blacks from white unions as the cause of such action by black workers.[44]

In fact, Tippett saw black workers' organization through the Atlanta Federation of Trades as a panacea to all their complaints, and encouraged them to organize through the "labor temple and ask the labor people to help them. That is the way for them to get the protection they need."[45] He also believed that by virtue of black workers soliciting help in organizing from white unions, the "race problem" in Atlanta would be solved through the cooperation of the "working masses."[46] Although he was able to achieve a few interracial meetings of garment and laundry workers through the AFL union locals in Atlanta, the Federation of Trades unions continued to be closed to virtually all African Americans until the Second World War.

Tippett's race blindness drove away many black students, including an entire class of messengers that met at the Atlanta Urban League and a group of women workers from a local overall factory.[47] Though many workers, both black and white, were intimidated by their employers from attending due to the "radical" content of the course, others were skeptical about the message they were receiving from their teachers. Those who attended the meetings scoffed at the notion of making common cause with Atlanta's union establishment, given the fact that white workers knew that they benefited from the subordination of black labor. They rejected Tippett's formulations and retorted that they "were justified in scabbing because they have been barred from unions."[48] Others, like women workers from Scripto, complained that "they had a definite program" of their own liking at the YWCA and that when the workers' education teachers came in they "monopolized the time"[49] with their heavy-handed ideology and sometimes condemnatory comments. For example, Tippett wanted his teachers to get their students to stop singing spirituals that talked of a "promised land," and instead to sing labor songs that preached making a better life on earth. As he told his teachers: "There are other ways by which people can get peace on earth. That is the purpose of labor songs. Songs that express something else can be done besides prayer."[50] Teachers also fought against other "reactionary" African American folkways such as "superstitions" and fortune telling, which Tippett and his teachers believed impeded enlightenment to the rational message of organized labor.[51]

Tippett's ignorance placed definite limits on his programs' influence on black workers. On the other hand, his belief in the labor movement and his ignorance of local racial customs meant that the classes were often the first opportunities black workers had to talk openly, except among themselves, about the workplace frustrations and economic issues which affected them. The teachers also discussed matters of politics and government with their classes, concentrating especially on New Deal legislation, and got their students involved with the political process by urging them to write letters to their congressmen about pending unemployment insurance and antilynching legislation. This kind of open participation in public debates was virtually prohibited to disfranchised African Americans, who by custom and law were denied entry into the public sphere by whites. Many black workers feared reprisals from their bosses if they openly asserted their opinions openly. Even white-collar workers for black businesses were apprehensive, so entrenched was the white-imposed proscription against involvement in public issues. For example, a group of clerical workers from Atlanta's black insurance companies balked at signing their names to a letter they wrote to Senators Walter George and Richard Russell urging passage of the Costigan-Wagner antilynching bill, insisting instead that only their teacher sign it.[52] When teachers expressed frustrations over this attitude, Tom Tippett told them: "Negroes who felt they could not remain in a room when such questions as 'Does the Code operate in your factory?' was being discussed must be gotten over that fear. The Codes, Hours and Wages and Union, Strikes, etc. have become popular subjects of our day. You can't pick up a newspaper anywhere that isn't half full of such news."[53]

Tippett's crusade was to bring black workers into these debates, to feel a part of the New Deal, and to use that new involvement to work toward the organization of black workers into unions. While his ultimate goal of mass mobilization for labor organization may not have been achieved, worker education did help mobilize some black workers. Hilton Hanna, one of the worker education teachers, told of how some workers attending his classes had dropped out because of their fear of discussing economic issues. But "by working through the members of the class who remained we were enabled to get back some of the deserters and before the project closed some of those persons had been liberated to the extent that they actually joined unions."[54] Ultimately, however, the project's modest efforts were too great a contravention of southern labor relations, which tolerated no challenge, however small. The Atlanta Relief Commission received anonymous complaints about the project, against which the Affiliated Schools for Workers tried to defend itself, but to no avail. Workers' education ended in Atlanta in June of 1934, not to reappear again until 1938, when the WPA instituted a much less controversial and less challenging project.[55] Even leaders of the Affiliated Schools for Workers were fearful and disapproving of Tippett's maverick stance. When the New Yorker proposed writing an article about his Atlanta experience called "Zig Zagging across the Jim Crow Line" for *Harper's* magazine, Mary Barker, the Affiliated Schools director, warned him:

> Frankly, you do not realize with what dynamite you are dealing. You had no opportunity in the few weeks that you were here to get acquainted with the Atlanta which makes the conditions about which you write. . . . Rewrite it in a much more objective style . . . and make the place anonymous. Otherwise emotional reaction will absolutely destroy any possibility of appreciation of values, which you must desire. . . . It would not be fair for me not to say to you that I am alarmed for . . . the safety and welfare of particular interests with which you were associated here if this story is published as written.[56]

Barker may have been right, and the article was never published, but Tippett's egalitarian vision of black incorporation into the state provides an intriguing counterpoint to white social workers' conservative programs.

Like the Communist program in Atlanta, Tippett's project promoted the disruption of the racial status quo even if, as in the case of the Communists, his constituency did not fully share his ideological convictions. Unlike the Communists and their defiant outsider status, Tippett worked from within promoting government programs to black workers through his black teachers, thus bringing African Americans into the New Deal and affirming their membership in the American body politic.

Still, the vast majority of white Atlantans, even within the liberal or social-work communities, were afraid of or unprepared for the kind of inclusion of African Americans, and particularly of black workers, which Tippett proposed. They sought to transform southern society not through a radical reordering of power relations between workers and bosses, blacks and whites, but rather through improving living conditions for poor southerners within their proscribed roles of inferiority.

6

The New Face of
Black Activism

On 4 October 1933, the city of Atlanta sponsored a massive parade under a banner of support for the National Recovery Administration (NRA) and its emblem the Blue Eagle, both important symbols of Franklin Roosevelt's emerging New Deal. More than 50,000 Atlantans participated in patriotic support of the president and his program, including a group of enthusiastic black residents marching in the eighteenth and final division of the parade.[1] This public celebration was symbolic of the perils of African Americans' involvement in the New Deal. Participation in the parade affirmed their inclusion and participation in the recovery program, but their consignment to the end of the parade also officially and publicly entrenched their second-class citizenship.

It was fitting that the parade commemorated the NRA, a pioneer New Deal program that taught black Atlantans just how pernicious putatively positive state intervention could be, and pushed them to adopt new strategies in order to protect their interests in the new political environment. While loyalty to the Blue Eagle became the preeminent test of patriotic support of the New Deal in Atlanta as around the country, the NRA's policies represented the New Deal's most blatant racial discrimination. Regional codes for industries that employed many African Americans, such as commercial laundries, set extremely meager hourly pay rates in the South so as not to disrupt the region's low-wage economy, and other mainly black occupations such as domestic work were not regulated at all. Furthermore in Atlanta, like other cities, black workers were fired and replaced with whites in occupations where NRA codes raised wages or their employers forced them to repay the "surplus" wages imposed by federal codes or risk losing their jobs. Such policies and actions precipitated nationwide protest by black leaders against the "Negro Removal Act."[2]

Such were the paradoxes of the New Deal for black reformers. By recognizing and including African Americans, it achieved one of their most cherished dreams. However, as the NRA demonstrates, the terms of this inclusion often had negative implications when African Americans were included in ways that officially entrenched their exploitation and caste status through government policy. Such ambiguities lent a new urgency to the reform elite's incorporative goals as it sought to ensure that the New Deal helped rather than hindered black Atlantans. In the new atmosphere of federal activism, state recognition became utterly crucial to the future of the African American community in Atlanta and around the country. In the New Deal era, such recognition came about only through corporate pressure by organized, mobilized interest groups that could find a legitimate place in the political arena. As we have seen, the federal government granted educated African Americans such legitimacy, but it was still a contested point at the local level where most New Deal money was disbursed and spent. Thus the New Deal dramatically altered the terms of engagement for black activists. The battle for inclusion was no longer primary as the newly activist federal government recognized African Americans as an important constituency in the New Deal's social welfare program. Rather, as black Americans were incorporated into New Deal programs and ushered into the political mainstream they had to employ new strategies and tactics to insure that their inclusion happened on their own terms.

As the black reform elite struggled to determine the best way to achieve its goals, its members learned the hard way that they alone could not wage this battle. In the new political environment, black reformers had to adopt the tactics of interest-group politics by showing the collective strength of the black community. Such strength could only be demonstrated through the public organization and mobilization of black Atlanta, making it a significant public presence through the ballot box, protests, and strikes. Thus, black reformers had to build a mass constituency for their goals, something in the past they had attempted only sporadically and with mixed results. In the 1930s, however, they realized that mass mobilization formed the center, not simply an auxiliary part, of their struggle for inclusion. As the resolution passed at a mass rally protesting NRA discrimination in Atlanta proclaimed, black Atlantans had to fight collectively to ensure that the New Deal fulfilled its promise "to realize the greatest measure of economic security for all of the people."[3] However, as the black reformers who organized the rally would discover, not all black Atlantans shared their notion of security or of the best path to attain it, nor was the elite willing and able to make the community connections necessary for mass mobilization. The creation of a constituency for their goals, then, was a very difficult task indeed.

The transition to interest-group politics was a gradual process in the 1930s as the black reform elite reworked its strategies to fit the altered political terrain of New Deal Atlanta. Black reformers learned the hard way the importance of an independent political voice as federal funds began streaming into the city. Like most cities nationwide, the first massive infusion of federal money came with the creation of the Works Progress Administration (WPA) in 1935. That year, Atlanta City Council announced a bond issue intended to fund WPA sewer construction and major school renovations. This bond represented one of the most important and extensive works projects in Atlanta during the New Deal era. Tens of thousands of men were employed in New Deal–financed improvements and extensions of the city's sewer system, which had not been overhauled since 1911. The sewer project brought Atlanta's waterworks into the modern era, finally making possible indoor plumbing in many black and white neighborhoods, and eliminating the seasonal floods that swamped the city's low-lying, mostly black-occupied areas every year.[4]

Along with the $2.35 million to fund sewers, the $4 million bond also earmarked $1.65 million for school construction and renovation, representing the first school bond for the city since the early 1920s. While the school projects, like the sewers, marked a long-overdue upgrade of city services, the city's plans for spending these funds were decidedly one-sided, with only around $100,000 slotted for the improvement of overcrowded and underfunded black schools. Thus the opportunities for modernization presented by the New Deal through the sewer bond were not extended to black children through the proposed school budget. Black students would continue to confront double and triple sessions in their schools, along with the shabby, overcrowded, even primitive facilities that the city provided them.

Black leaders at first responded to this inequality with an open and militant opposition that had important precedents in the black community's history. Bond elections were among the exceptional ones when African Americans were permitted to vote, and black reformers had used this power in the past with mixed results. Their most notable victory was the 1924 one, when the power of the black vote in a school bond election forced the city to build Booker T. Washington High School (BTWHS). When the city announced the 1935 bond and its proposed distribution of school funds, black leaders again responded with outrage and promises for mobilization against the issue unless a more equal distribution of school funds was written into the proposal. Militant pastor Rev. J. Raymond Henderson exhorted black Atlantans to attend a public meeting to discuss the bond, issuing this prescient warning: "If Negroes do not bestir themselves they will wake up to discover that the white man, who cannot be trusted, will use almost all of this money for white schools, while our overcrowded conditions and double sessions continue."[5] Both he and Jesse O. Thomas, Southern regional secretary of the National Urban League (NUL), urged black Atlantans to mobilize under the leadership of the local NAACP and to register to vote against the bond, believing that African Americans must "develop a collective mind in order that they might bargain collectively in the interest of protection of themselves and [their] children."[6]

These dissenting voices urging mobilization through a strategy of militant interest group politics marked the early days of the bond campaign. Accordingly, the NAACP played a prominent role in urging voter registration in order to produce an electoral constituency that would force local politicians to allocate more money for black schools. Behind the scenes, however, another African American group worked toward a very different goal. Reginald Johnson, executive secretary of the Atlanta Urban League (AUL), saw the bond issue as a unique opportunity for African American leaders to participate as insiders in local political affairs. Capitalizing on black voters' potential as an important constituency in the election, he launched a lobbying initiative to get African Americans included in the citywide campaign committee supporting the bond issue. Reminding James Key of African Americans' potential power, Johnson wrote Atlanta's mayor of his "regret that no representative for the Negro population" had been consulted regarding the bond campaign, especially considering that "the City of Atlanta is one third Negro, the population of the first ward is 95% Negro, and the population of the fourth ward is 61% Negro."[7] In a response respectful of black Atlantans' potential electoral power, and reflecting his concern over the success of the bond election given the gathering of anti-New Deal forces in white Atlanta, Key responded to Johnson's veiled threat by appointing all of the leaders the Urban League secretary had suggested for a black bond committee.[8]

This committee, with its superior resources, publicity, and prestige, overshadowed the NAACP's efforts. The city-sponsored group which included Johnson, Lugenia Burns Hope, NAACP president A. T. Walden, Parent-Teacher Association leaders like Mrs. H. R. Butler and Willie Daniels, along with prominent ministers and business men and women, abruptly changed the attitude of many black leaders toward the proposed bond issue. Where Henderson and Thomas saw the bond election as an opportunity to mobilize a dissenting black community, Reginald Johnson saw it as an opportunity to incorporate black voices into the mainstream of city politics, replicating black professionals' success in infiltrating New Deal bureaucracies. Where the NAACP organized a voter registration drive in order to defeat the bond unless the city met black demands for better schools, the new committee worked unequivocally with its white counterpart to support the bond and to mobilize black voters to secure its passage. Consequently, where Henderson and Thomas concentrated on the inequality of proposed school funding, the new committee concentrated on the equal distribution of sewers in the bond issue. Unfortunately, such cooperation with local officials did not result in the same constructive dividends that had cooperation with the New Deal social welfare agenda.

The Citizens Committee, as it was known, organized an impressive voter registration campaign. It assigned workers to all parts of the city and organized neighborhood rallies in every black section. Black voters also received uncommon attention from white leaders, with the Mayor and white campaign leaders addressing black rallies in person or through the ADW, urging passage of the bond. City officials courted the black vote as never before and made black Atlantans an integral part of the campaign for the bonds.[9]

Yet while the appointment of the black committee was an important achievement, it was a pyrrhic victory, coming with the loss of an independent voice for the black community. The black bond committee found that by joining the city's white probond forces it lost its independence and the ability to assert the black community's specific demands. Although they might have thought they could work from inside official white structures to provide more funding for black schools, black leaders found they could no longer criticize the unfairness of the school bond or, more importantly, bargain for more equal treatment of black schools if they wanted to retain the support of the mayor and his allies. Nor could they agitate for written assurances of equal treatment of black workers in sewer construction, which would to be the largest WPA project in Atlanta. Consequently, white campaign leaders could easily ignore the issues most important to the well-being of the black community and, according to the ADW, failed to be "forthcoming with those assurances as how we will fare if and when the bond issue becomes operative."[10]

Nonetheless, black leaders rallied around the committee and supported the bond, keeping their reservations to themselves. Even Jesse O. Thomas granted his grudging support, writing that despite the inequalities of the school bond, that black voters were "justified" in supporting the bond issue "in order to remove the present health menace" through the sewer project.[11] However, despite this almost universal support from the ministers, teachers, social workers, and businessmen, and the indisputable benefits the sewers would bring, only 958 of 90,000 black Atlantans registered for the bond election. The Citizens Committee's experience and the low voter turnout attested to black leaders' logistical problems in using the ballot as a tool in the age of Jim Crow. Atlanta's black reformers would look for ways to overcome these difficulties through the rest of the decade.[12]

The 1935 election reinforced lessons Atlanta's black leaders had learned throughout the 1920s and early 1930s—that instead of courting white leaders they had to work independently for their own interests and in their own defense through concerted community-wide efforts that would bolster African Americans' independent political and economic strength. Organizations like the NAACP and the AUL abandoned their elitist, back-room strategies and began to act publicly against corporate ills like police brutality, salary and wage inequities, and discrimination in New Deal relief. They learned these lessons personally during the red scare or the Neighborhood Union's unhappy dealings with the Family Welfare Society. These local experiences echoed those of black organizations nationwide, which, in response to the Great Depression's displacement and New Deal political realities, began to look to to achieve their aims through militant mass mobilization and communal self-help rather than dependence on dubious white beneficence.

Black leaders adopted this new strategy of community organization during a period of growth for black Atlanta. The decade marked a period of expansion and strengthening of the black community; a constantly growing black population meant that housing-hungry African Americans continued testing and expanding the borders of black neighborhoods on the west side of the city, and institutions such as Atlanta University moved to strengthen their position through consolidation. Black reformers sought to reinforce these advances and to spur organized action in the black community. Jesse O. Thomas, for example, urged African Americans to patronize black businesses and to boycott shops in the black community that refused to hire black clerks. He rationalized his position by stating that "we have finally . . . arrived at the point in our economic culture where we recognize the very definite relationship between organized buying power and employment opportunity." He urged black Atlantans to use this growing awareness to "demonstrate by mass conduct that it does make some difference finally, as to how people treat us and what consideration is given us as to how we react."[13] W. E. B. Du Bois advocated the establishment of an all-black economy in the national black press, and in Atlanta inspired Morehouse economics students to establish economic cooperatives that linked black farmers with urban black consumers.[14]

The black community's vitality and independence in the 1930s led to an intensification of the fight against Jim Crow by Atlantans from all walks of life. Ministers in large numbers began to join iconoclasts like J. Raymond Henderson in speaking out on the secular issues affecting their flocks. After a decade or more of relative quiescence, many ministers moved into the vanguard of the battle against Jim Crow. Baptist, African Methodist Episcopal, and other ministers and their ministerial unions protested the white primary, police brutality, and unequal teachers' salaries, and urged their congregations to register for the vote. They admonished their fellow ministers to do the same, deploring the passive "attitude of the Negro preacher toward civic affairs."[15] As civic leader John Wesley Dobbs chided a minister who refused to let him speak of the "worldly matter" of voter registration to his congregation: "This work is being done for our people of Atlanta and I think ministers who refuse to espouse the righteous cause of their neglected followers immediately stamp themselves as being out of tune and harmony with the times."[16] The ministers of Atlanta's largest black churches, including Henderson at Wheat Street and his 1937 replacement, William Holmes Borders, and Martin Luther King Sr. at Ebenezer Baptist Church, along with John C. Wright of the upper-crust First Congregational Church, became important and militant members of the reform elite. They belonged to the executive committees of organizations like the NAACP and participated openly in the fight for teachers' salaries and against police brutality.[17]

In 1939, activist ministers joined together across denominational lines under the leadership of Martin Luther King Sr. in the Atlanta Ministerial Council "for the purpose of doing something about the status of the Negro."[18] The ministers in the council took their lead from their forefathers of the Reconstruction era, ministers like the black nationalist Henry McNeal Turner who, as they memorialized, "gave their lives for the Negro people."[19] They remembered a time when the church was the single most important institution in the black community, providing its followers with their educational, social, and political leadership.

African American workers also showed their readiness to meet the challenge of an open fight against Jim Crow. Black support of Communist demonstrations against local relief authorities demonstrated disfranchised African Americans' willingness to fight for their rights. While the Atlanta University reform elite urged cooperatives and don't-buy-where-you-can't-work campaigns, in the streets black Atlantans established their own boycotts of white businesses that discriminated against African Americans. No doubt inspired by the movement sweeping black urban communities nationwide in the 1930s, neighborhood leaders in the city's west side organized a boycott of a neighborhood A&P grocery where in November 1935 a white clerk beat a black customer, an unemployed father of three, for allegedly stealing a pound of sugar. The community rallied immediately, with demonstrators forming a picket around the store and urging black customers to stay out until the company hired black clerks and assured better treatment of African American customers. Despite visits from the Ku Klux Klan and a menacing police cordon which "protected" the store from vandalism with sawed-off shotguns, the picketers persisted, albeit a prudent few hundred feet removed from the grocery. The boycott received wide community support, especially after schoolboys distributed handbills in the surrounding black neighborhood urging black consumers to stop patronizing A&P. In retaliation, the company forced all of its black warehouse drivers, truck drivers, and porters to buy at the store. While at the time A&P did nothing but fire the offending clerk, ultimately a long-term unofficial boycott of the outlet led to its closing in the 1940s.[20]

The A&P boycott and other similar actions point to a growing fearlessness in the black community and its members' own recognition of their collective strength. In the flourishing heart of the black economy, Auburn Avenue, African Americans felt secure enough in 1937 to taunt and jeer a Ku Klux Klan parade, even dehooding marchers, an unthinkable action earlier in the century when the memory of the 1906 race riot was still fresh in many Atlantans' memories. These actions demonstrated a growing spirit among all segments of black society in Atlanta to fight openly against the inequity they faced in their day-to-day lives.[21]

Despite the widespread willingness of black Atlantans to fight for their rights and new strategies of mass activism, the black reform elite tightened its grip on interest-group politics in the 1930s, dominating black activism and shutting out "upstart" leaders and organizations from below.

Atlanta's black reformers' growing influence as New Deal powerbrokers and their absolute domination of black Atlanta's reinvigorated welfare and civil rights agencies, the AUL and the NAACP, meant that black reformers would work for the black "masses" but not with them.

Atlanta's black reformers even excluded the labor elite and educated African Americans outside Atlanta University circles from participation in setting the activist agenda, and their stranglehold on "legitimate" protest successfully shut out rival leaders or organizations in the city. The reform elite's inordinate power distinguished Atlanta from more industrial cities nationwide where in the 1930s insurgent working-class politics presented a serious challenge to elite claims to community "leadership." In Cleveland, for example, a militant working-class organization, the Future Outlook League (FOL), engaged in confrontational mass-action boycotts and strikes, ultimately "swamping" the nearly dormant NAACP chapter and seriously undermining that city's Depression-weakened elite's legitimacy. In Atlanta, organizations like the FOL did not rise to such prominence. By the mid-1930s, Red Scare tactics had forced the Communists underground, and renewed working-class organization was difficult because most African Americans workers dispersed through the city in nonindustrial employment. Further, because Atlanta's elite was dominated by university-associated professionals and not entrepreneurs, instead of faltering in the 1930s it grew larger and more secure and assertive in pursuing its goals, thanks to the New Deal. Gone were the days of the Angelo Herndon Defense Committee when black reformers felt compelled to work as peers with radicals and workers like painter Clarence Weaver. Now they felt such collaboration was unnecessary and probably unwise, given their newfound New Deal legitimacy.[22]

Consequently, the brickmason, the minister of a neighborhood church, and the local merchant who led the very successful A&P boycott never reappeared in the public record as protest leaders, nor did their protest strategy take wing.[23] Instead, the NAACP and AUL grew to such prestige during the 1930s that it became uncommon for even other elite figures or organizations to broker between black Atlantans and white officials in any capacity. Ministers, despite their history of leadership and their growing militance and organization in the 1930s, only met with white officials in their capacity as members of delegations organized by the NAACP or AUL. Similarly, the NAACP and the AUL subsumed the role of other organizations prominent in the past, such as the Neighborhood Union, largely because their emphasis on "professional" legal or social work gave their representatives more legitimacy than ministers or women volunteers with the emerging New Deal meritocracy.

The Neighborhood Union and the Ministerial Council did not openly dispute the ascendancy of the AUL and NAACP because their members were often invited to serve in executive capacity for these revitalized organizations. However, the exclusion from the newly powerful brokerage leadership of even skilled workers or non-AU-affiliated professionals fundamentally shaped these agencies' agendas in the 1930s. While the Communist challenge, New Deal interest-group politics, and Depression-era displacement reoriented the reform elite toward the black community, its successful incorporation into the New Deal's social welfare apparatus reinforced its sense of rightful race leadership. This crucial persistence meant that black Atlanta's increasingly powerful brokerage agencies continued to be shaped by uplift ideology in fundamentally important ways.

In the 1930s, the AUL underwent a transformation in keeping with black reformers' new interest-group politics and the labor movement's national resurgence. While the agency maintained its accommodationist relationships with white employers through the continuation of programs like the Janitors' Training School, it began to chart a new, more independent course of labor organization in pursuit of protecting and expanding opportunities for black workers devastated by white displacement during the Depression. Construction workers, for example, unprotected by trade unions that barred them by charter, were the first to be excluded from dwindling work sites as construction drew to a near halt in the early 1930s. New Deal agencies, allied closely to organized labor, hindered black craftsmen further by favoring union tradesmen to the exclusion of other skilled workers on federal work sites. Clearly, black workers had to respond vocally and collectively to these developments if they were to protect themselves.

In response, the NUL developed a nationwide program of "Workers' Councils" to spur labor organization among African Americans. The Urban League hoped the councils would provide a crash course in labor organization so that African Americans could survive and protect themselves in a new labor environment of collective bargaining and interest group politics. NUL leaders worried about the future of black workers, that unless they "exert determined, constant and insistent pressure through a united organization, they will find themselves when the depression lifts far behind where they were when it began."[24] Thus the agency moved away from "appeals to employers," and instead looked at ways in which it could use "the pressure device, now more influential in government than the Constitution . . . to rally Negroes in defense of their economic rights,"[25] and especially in relationship to white organized labor and the federal government.

The AUL organized Workers' Councils in Atlanta in 1934 for brickmasons, house painters, post office special-delivery messengers, carpenters, railroad firemen, cleaners and dyers, roofers, janitors, and drugstore messengers and porters. Some of the targeted workers, like the janitors, messengers, and porters, were new to labor organization of any kind and showed only "sporadic" participation in the program. However, workers from the construction trades, especially the brickmasons and painters, responded enthusiastically to the program. These craftsmen had been interested in union organization and workers' issues long before the Workers' Councils and, as their support of the Socialists and Communists demonstrated, represented some of the most militant working-class activists in Atlanta. In 1932 the brickmasons launched an unsuccessful effort with the AUL to obtain a union charter. Tom Tippett and his Federal Emergency Relief Administration (FERA) workers' education teachers, who worked with the AUL's Workers' Councils, commented on the enthusiasm of the brickmasons for workers' education and their militant rhetoric. Clarence Weaver, the Communist arrested in the 1934 raid in DeKalb County, was a member of the Painters' Council, and had brought the police to the AUL in an anti-Communist raid after he was found to be carrying a leaflet announcing the organization's next meeting when he was arrested.[26]

Unsurprisingly then, the painters and brickmasons were the two groups that managed to unionize and affiliate with the American Federation of Labor's Atlanta Federation of Trades while working with the AUL through the Workers' Council. The brickmasons received a union charter in 1934 after two years working with the Urban League. The painters followed in 1937 after a four-year struggle in which they had been red-baited, denied admission from the white local, rejected for an international charter by the AFL, and become one of the subjects of a nationally publicized and NUL-prompted AFL investigation of discrimination against black workers. Their victory helped black painters in Cincinnati and St. Louis in their organizing quest. These victories granted these craftsmen hefty pay increases to meet union scale and allowed them an even chance, in theory at least, to work on large-scale government construction projects, such as public housing, from which they had been excluded in the past by virtue of being unrecognized by the Atlanta Federation of Trades.[27]

The success of the Painters' and Brickmasons' Councils is instructive on two counts. First, it demonstrates the growing importance of "race" organizations such as the AUL or the NAACP in their role as powerbrokers for the black community. Despite their longtime interest in union organization, the brickmasons and painters only succeeded after they obtained the aid and protection of the AUL. It is difficult to imagine that the painters could have successfully withstood the onslaught of anti-Communist forces had they not been meeting under the auspices of the AUL, a respected Community Chest agency with strong ties to white charitable and social-work circles in Atlanta. The AUL had become an indispensable channel for the voices of black workers to be heard by the white community. Like the New Deal's recognition of black professionals, the AUL provided crucial help in ending the marginalization of black craftsmen. Incorporated into the ranks of organized labor, this success marked an important victory in black reformers' uplift agenda.

Second, the success of the painters' and brickmasons' organizing efforts, while pathbreaking, masked the fact that the workers' council effort failed for all but the most elite groups the AUL attempted to organize. The NUL's program emphasized black workers' "self-determination."[28] In fact, Lester Granger, who ran the NUL's program, believed that it was "utter hopelessness" to expect "the intellectuals and professionals of the race to plan the way for Negro labor." Instead, he insisted that black workers "assume their own leadership" in the Workers' Councils, an "organization in which workers, without the interference of outsiders, may meet to discuss their mutual problems and learn ways of facing them."[29] He believed black workers' problems "can be solved only by leaders produced from their own ranks, which can be met only on the ground of intelligent self-interest."[30] Skilled construction workers had certainly used the Workers' Council to these ends, but they were hardly typical. Instead, they constituted the pride of black labor in Atlanta, even dominating some trades like brickmasonry. Their relatively high pay and recognized skills gave these tradesmen an enviable and unique status among male workers in the black community, and many of them were married to teachers and other white-collar and professional women. Like Communist Clarence Weaver's association with the AUL and the NAACP's defense of him and his wife during the Red Scare, black craftsmen and reformers found it relatively easy to collaborate, given their social ties and shared commitment to uplift and respectability.

But what about the more typical black workers that the AUL organized through the Workers' Council? Here, the shibboleths of respectability re-emerged in full force, denying the democracy implied in the NUL's program except for the top echelon of black labor. The agency blamed these groups' "sporadic rather than well-defined cooperation" for the Workers' Councils on the average black worker who, according to one AUL spokesperson, "still doesn't appreciate the value of organization," never considering that the craft-union model might be an inappropriate organizing unit for all but skilled workers.[31] Furthermore, the councils did not touch the largest group of black workers in Atlanta, domestic workers. This omission highlighted again the difficulty in organizing or incorporating black workers who dispersed throughout the city in private homes in personal service or unskilled day labor, outside of the industrial or commercial sector. Although the reform elite made sporadic attempts or promises to organize these workers in Atlanta, they continued to treat them according to archaic models of paternalism which defined programs like the Janitors' Training School, which continued through the 1930s, and dismissed them in efforts like the Workers' Councils. Indeed, one of the greatest hurdles faced by the FERA workers' education program was the widespread belief among black Atlantans that labor organization and by extension the Urban League's incorporative aims were only for "brickmasons or plasterers,"[32] not the entire African American work force.

The Atlanta NAACP, like the AUL, underwent significant changes in its mission during the 1930s as it became a brokerage organization for the black community. At the eve of the New Deal, the agency was in the doldrums. Although it had 750 members thanks to the annual membership drive, only a handful were active, and even those rarely met. The branch's work consisted almost exclusively of legal defense on behalf of individuals wronged by the police or justice systems, often from outside of Atlanta in rural areas where, without the Atlanta NAACP's help, they would have no legal recourse. Given the sensitivity of this work, the branch's president since 1920, lawyer A. T. Walden, worked alone on these cases, often taking action without consulting the membership or publicizing his work, and only reporting on the outcome after the cases were resolved. Thus the Atlanta NAACP in no way represented a mass organization.[33]

With the New Deal, the NAACP began to branch out. Its legal work for accused black Communists struck a responsive chord in black Atlanta, and appeals for donations for a special defense fund and mass meetings against the Red Scare received enthusiastic support. Further, as a complaint organization for black Atlantans discriminated against by New Deal programs, the NAACP expanded its brokerage work beyond legal defense. Ultimately, this changing orientation and the black community's growing need for corporate representation from black reform organizations resulted in a changing of the guard at the Atlanta NAACP. Younger supporters like J. Raymond Henderson were frustrated by Walden's dictatorial ways and his inaction on causes and cases they felt were important. As Henderson wrote to the NAACP's executive secretary, Walter White, "Our branch of the Association here is inactive. We haven't met but once since the [membership] campaign. I want action but can't go ahead of Mr. Walden."[34]

Leaders like Roy Wilkins at the national office in New York City also were distressed by Walden and worked with reformers in Atlanta to ease him out in favor of the younger and more militant leadership that was taking over branches nationwide. In 1936, Forrester B. Washington replaced A. T. Walden as president of the Atlanta NAACP. Washington's leadership represented a new era in the chapter's history, signaling the ascension of a new generation of black social-work reformers. His activist mindset pleased those who had, from the onset of the Great Depression and the Communist challenge, been clamoring for a more militant and mass-based reorientation of Atlanta's most venerable civil rights organization.[35]

Washington reinvigorated the NAACP by ending the back-room strategies employed by A. T. Walden in his work for black defendants and plaintiffs. Washington's NAACP continued to focus on legal work and to use Walden as counsel, but now it publicized its cases in the *ADW* as part of a strategy to mobilize Atlanta's black citizenry against police brutality, New Deal discrimination, and egregious segregation. The Atlanta NAACP used the cases it took on to challenge and publicize the inequities faced by the entire black community and not just to benefit the individuals involved.[36]

For example, the agency took on the case of Ruth King, a young invalid who had been kicked in the stomach by Atlanta police officers when they came to her home in the middle of the night to arrest her brother for allegedly stealing a bicycle. After an internal police investigation exonerated the officers responsible for the assault, the NAACP helped King's mother bring a suit of gross misconduct against the policemen. Although this unprecedented action resulted predictably in failure for the prosecution, the NAACP saw the case to be successful in exposing police brutality in the black community and furthering its campaign for black police for black neighborhoods. The NAACP's secretary exulted that because of the case, "[p]olice brutality in Atlanta was hit," and "the pitiless light of publicity has been turned on"[37] to the issue as police officers were forced to account for their renegade actions to the court.[38]

The NAACP's open handling of the King case also had democratic implications for poor black Atlantans. In the past, local officials intimidated black plaintiffs in these kinds of cases into dropping their charges. While police tried to silence the King family, the NAACP's vocal support prompted them to go ahead with their charges against the department. Washington encouraged black Atlantans to come to the NAACP with their complaints, even opening an office in the Herndon building on Auburn Avenue as "a community headquarters for complaints" of all kinds.[39]

Atlanta's revived NAACP program was part of a nationwide rethinking of civil rights strategy on the part of liberal black reformers—an impulse that inspired figures like Howard Law School dean Charles Hamilton Houston and his team, architects of the national NAACP's celebrated legal strategy against segregation. Influenced by the International Labor Defense's (ILD) tactics, Houston believed that court challenges would only be successful if they also mobilized the black "masses" to assert their rights. After witnessing the national protest movement resulting from the Scottsboro case, Houston believed that antisegregation court cases could be an effective instrument to agitate ordinary African Americans to fight on their own behalf. Thus the NAACP helped branches across the South to launch legal battles against segregation, seeking not only to win precedents against the "separate but equal" doctrine but also to mobilize local communities against discrimination. While Houston was impressed by the Communists' strategy of broad community protest, he was also convinced of the overarching importance to develop, in his words, "professional cadres" (in this case lawyers) to direct and lead the fight against Jim Crow. Unlike the Communists' more egalitarian vision, the mobilization of the black "masses" in Houston's mind would simply be one element of the battle against Jim Crow, masterminded and led by the professionally trained social engineer.[40]

Of course, such appeals to professional leadership had particular resonance in Atlanta, and Forrester B. Washington's NAACP program reflected Houston's vision. The NAACP's new leadership tried to expand membership to the black working class through neighborhood recruitment meetings, brought in representatives from the CIO to encourage black unionism, and complained to the WPA about the treatment of black women sent to do hard outdoor labor at Washington Park, Atlanta's only public park for African Americans. In the words of one of Washington's protégés, public school teacher Helen Gray, these actions sought to create "a more democratic organization in the Atlanta branch which would draw heavily upon the masses from the humblest citizen to the highest." At an organizational meeting, she received enthusiastic approval for her vision of "a local organization with a membership so large that each meeting would take the form of a mass meeting and forum; an organization having numerous committees for as many problems."[41] Such was the spirit of optimism that the chapter briefly moved its meetings from the cramped assembly rooms of the Butler Street YMCA to Atlanta's biggest church, Wheat Street Baptist.

The move was short-lived, however, because, while the NAACP reached out to black workers and their interests, its leadership remained firmly elite. Unlike chapters in more industrial cities with fewer black professionals like New Orleans, Norfolk, Cleveland, and Mobile, the changeover in the Atlanta branch's leadership did not represent a fundamental reordering by bringing black workers into the association's leadership. The fact that Atlanta's power shift lacked the convulsive conflicts of these other cities is likely testament to the chapter's executive committee's lack of working-class representation, even from the labor elite of unionized bricklayers or painters, despite the fact that Washington expanded the body to thirty-five members.[42] Instead, this reform broadened the agency only enough to bring in the greatly expanded number of young, educated black Atlantans, like Helen Gray, whose uplift strategies, like Charles Hamilton Houston's, had been reoriented by the Depression crisis, the influence of radical political ideology, and the New Deal. The committee comprised black reformers' new generation—college-educated ministers, teachers, journalists, and business people well versed in the social-work and social-engineering activism espoused at the Atlanta School of Social Work (ASSW). While Washington infused the association with "young blood" ready for open, independent protest and rejected the compromised coalition politics of the past, he had not moved beyond the college gates in reviving the agency's leadership. The "masses" toward whom he directed Helen Gray were decidedly elite; she worked to organize the chapter's new Youth Council—comprised entirely of college students.[43]

Such selective broadening shaped the NAACP's program in fundamental ways. While its activities became more militant and its programs sought to serve the black community writ large, its adherence to the national NAACP's program, and its conflation of race and class, meant it once again found it had limited appeal in the black community. While Washington implemented such programs as the Herndon Building complaint office, they were overshadowed by the fight for equal teachers' salaries, an initiative that increasingly consumed the branch's energies from its beginnings in 1934 through the 1940s. This struggle was part of the national NAACP's long-term legal strategy against segregation and inequality in the South's public education system.[44]

Despite teachers' professional status, Atlanta's NAACP leadership considered the salary campaign to be its first effort to organize the "masses" and to attack the "fundamental problems of education [and] labor" in Atlanta. In fact, in launching the campaign, the NAACP distinguished between this effort and past work which dealt with wholly disfranchised sharecroppers and domestic workers victimized by the justice system. In its 1934 annual report, the NAACP's secretary marked the teachers' issue as the beginning of a new chapter in the branch's history. In a telling passage, she distinguished this focus from the NAACP's "earlier years," when its efforts "involved cases which . . . pertained to the illiterate classes of people." While she reasoned that this past work "was of great importance at that time" in building the branch, it had limited impact because "it was done for individuals more than for any particular group as a whole." By contrast, now the NAACP took on cases "of a more serious nature; cases which involved the masses more," including ones like the salary issue, connected to the national office's and involving broader issues of political and economic rights.[45] However, by doing so through the teachers' salary issue, educated professionals once again conflated their interests with that of the entire black community, a limitation forged by the narrow perspective of the NAACP's leadership, which itself was a product of black reformers' persistent elitism.

Although the NAACP continued to include the "illiterate classes" in the legal defense work it had always done, they had no place in the organization's proactive and militant new legal activism which paradoxically sought to mobilize and obtain corporate gains for the black community through teachers, a high status group. Given this elitism, it is no wonder that the organization continued to have serious difficulties attracting a mass membership. Thurgood Marshall criticized this failing when he was sent down from NAACP headquarters in New York to help with the teachers' salary fight in 1940. He complained to branch leaders that "not too much persuasion has been used to convince the majority of Atlantans, who are apparently more subject to the cruelties imposed under a Jim-Crow society"[46] to support the NAACP. But a legal strategy on behalf of the highest echelon of black society was no way to mobilize the multitudes, no matter how worthy the fight.

As both the AUL and NAACP's reorientation demonstrate, the reform elite began increasingly to consider the importance of mobilizing the "masses" during the 1930s. The most obvious sign of this strategic change was the growing attention black reformers gave to voter registration and voting. They knew the potential power of the black electorate from past victories, such as the 1924 bond election that led to the erection of BTWHS. In the repressive environment of the early 1930s, black reformers began to see such voter mobilization as the best possible strategy to end police brutality in the black community, antiblack campaigns such as that of the Red Scare of 1934, and exclusion from a full array of city services, including public schools—in short to end their public invisibility. However, in order for the black community to show its political muscle for collective gain black reformers had to involve themselves in sustained mass mobilization, moving beyond the sporadic efforts of the past.

As a result of their elitist perspective, reformers' first efforts at voter mobilization concentrated not on the activism of voter registration but, rather, on the potential of "citizenship education" that would prepare black Atlantans to vote. By citizenship education, reformers meant an effort to overcome what they perceived as the ignorance and parochialism of the majority of black Atlantans. In the words of one reformer, this was training "for the purpose of helping the masses of our people to become more effective and better citizens by becoming better informed concerning our civic life and more active in promoting the general welfare of all people in the community."[47] In effect, the reformers wished to reorient the focus of ordinary black Atlantans from their own tightly knit neighborhoods so that they could become visible participants in the larger world of city government and civic affairs.

The NAACP initiated citizenship training in Atlanta with its "Citizenship School" program, which found support from the Alpha Phi Alpha fraternity, and leadership from the Neighborhood Union's Lugenia Burns Hope (who was also the Atlanta NAACP's vice president) and Rayford Logan and Clarence Bacote of Atlanta University's history department. The citizenship school held its first term in April 1933 at the Butler Street YMCA and sought to teach its students, in the words of the NAACP's branch secretary, "a feeling of race consciousness with reference to the ballot" through a civics course "so simple, direct, and plain that any one of our group with even a most rudimentary education shall be able to grasp it."[48]

In its second year, the school expanded to two venues, prominent churches in the city's West Side and Summerhill neighborhoods. In 1934, the students purchased a simple civics primer written by A. T. Walden. This primer and the course received widespread attention from black organizations around the country that ordered copies to use in their own citizenship efforts. Along with its focus on civics, the program also brought up other issues including public health, education, and the rights of labor.[49]

In 1934, the Citizenship School attempted to make its course "more practical" by conducting an election among its students conforming to standard electoral procedure. This effort matched those of Booker T. Washington High School, David T. Howard Junior High School, and the various night schools around the city that also held annual elections as a practical application of civics lessons. These elections became an important and popular part of the school calendar. They were "modeled closely as possible after regular governmental procedures"[50] for presidential elections, including poll taxes, voter registration, party conventions, primaries, election rallies, and inaugural ceremonies. As the 1930s progressed, these campaigns became more and more elaborate, especially at Washington High School, with parades flanked by motorcycle police, inaugural ceremonies attended by thousands of black Atlantans, and even radio broadcasts of candidates' speeches. All of these efforts were part of an ongoing campaign on the part of black reformers to show black youth, in the words of one leader, that the only difference between them and young whites "was the color of the skin." Consequently, they must "think and believe that they are young Americans." One way to do that was through citizenship training which "encourage[s] citizenship among the thousands of youth who may otherwise be denied a chance to obtain the information which will make him [sic] a law-abiding citizen of his school, city and country."[51]

While the school election campaigns were enormously successful, the NAACP's Citizenship School limped along and eventually petered out. Unlike public schools, which had a built-in constituency for their citizenship programs, the NAACP did not have the community connections which would draw great numbers of people to the school. Furthermore, the school's organizers had no rallying issue around which rank-and-file black Atlantans could be motivated to learn about voter registration and voting, no concrete issue for which they could be mobilized to vote. Instead, the school asked black Atlantans to respond to a fundamentally elitist appeal: to be taught by the race's best and brightest to participate in a system for which they had to pay through the cumulative poll tax, and in which they could only participate partially. In the school's first two years, its most successful, it only granted 225 citizenship certificates to those who had met the attendance requirements of the school, and it is not even clear that these participants represented the unschooled "masses" whom the program's directors hoped to attract.[52]

Nevertheless, the Citizenship School represented an important reorientation of the black reform elite's strategy for change. Citizenship training inaugurated a new era in which reformers began to concentrate their efforts on voter registration, seeing a demonstration of black political power as the solution to many of the problems confronting black Atlantans. The achievement of this goal meant an uphill battle for the elite—which claimed to represent the "black community" in its power brokerage with federal and local officials—for it required that it establish a mass constituency. Furthermore, this constituency had to be made to believe that the vote was the best strategy for change.[53]

A first attempt to build a mass electoral base came in 1936, around the same time that Forrester B. Washington expanded the activist mission of the NAACP. John Wesley Dobbs, a prominent Masonic leader and Republican, set out to register 10,000 black voters in Atlanta through a new organization, the Civic and Political League. As Dobbs wrote in inaugurating the league, it sought to develop a "simple, strong, separate voting organization" that would bring the entire black community "together one time when no one will be thinking about making a dollar; when no one will be running for office, but when the high and low, the rich and the poor, the big and the small can meet upon one common level of honest patriotism and citizenship." These groups would join together to create a powerful and independent voting bloc. "The immortal Lincoln started us on our way to freedom," Dobbs wrote in an appeal for support for the Civic League; "[t]he rest of the journey we must travel alone and depend very largely upon the wise use of the ballot."[54]

Dobbs received wide support from the new black social-worker elite, as well as from the older "political" powerbrokers whom he represented. Both groups recognized that Atlanta lagged behind in voter registration compared to other southern cities. For example, while 27,000 of 110,000 African Americans in Memphis had registered to vote, fewer than 2,000 black Atlantans were eligible out of a population of 100,000. Dallas, Chattanooga, and Daytona Beach, Florida, each with total black population less than Atlanta's, had more black registrants than the Gate City. Dobbs brought in black leaders from elsewhere, such as his son-in-law and father of Atlanta's first black mayor, Maynard Jackson Sr. from Dallas, and Adam Clayton Powell Jr. from New York, to address black Atlantans about their successful voter-mobilization campaigns and what they had achieved in local politics.[55]

The men and women who attended these speeches and who came to support the Civic League represented the same class of business people, journalists, activist ministers, teachers, and social workers who controlled the AUL and the NAACP. They saw the Civic League as the electoral branch of a three-pronged strategy, with the NAACP pursuing legal goals and the AUL working to expand the vocational and economic opportunities of African Americans. The Civic and Political League represented their recognition that, in the words of Forrester B. Washington, "this is the age of pressure groups, that we have to learn the value of them."[56]

Reformers envisioned a day when the league, in control of a massive black electorate, would achieve its goals for the black community, "[dictating] policies of the city administration as to jobs of teachers, firemen, playgrounds, hospitals, etc."[57] In pursuing that dream, Dobbs distilled the reform elite's activist objectives to four civic goals: more and improved black parks; better hospital facilities for African Americans, including black physicians and interns for Grady Hospital; better schools, including auditoria, more classrooms, and especially higher teacher salaries; and black police and firemen for black neighborhoods. These would remain the reform elite's political goals for the black community for the coming years.

Dobbs and the Civic League demonstrated the same contradictions as other reform organizations in relating to the black community at large. Although the group needed a mass constituency to achieve its registration goals and boasted of its appeal to "every colored citizen in Atlanta," not just the "doctors, ministers and teachers,"[58] its registration efforts carried the same elitist taint of other organizations. It singled out teachers and ministers in its registration efforts, believing that they, having the most contact with ordinary black Atlantans, must register as a "preface to the movement" of mass mobilization for the vote. Thereby, they would set an example of "fearless intelligent action" to parents and parishioners. For, as Dobbs believed, if the vanguard to the movement "comes not from . . . the intelligentsia, whence will it come?"[59]

Furthermore, by choosing the vote as its weapon, the league was fundamentally elitist, given Georgia's draconian poll tax laws. Only the minority of property owners in the state did not have to make a special effort to pay the levy since it was automatically part of their property taxes. More important, unlike most other southern states where the poll tax was, at most, only cumulative to the previous two or three years, Georgia required eligible voters to pay back taxes of one dollar per year plus interest to the last year they had paid or, if they had never voted, for the previous seven years.[60] Despite this onerous burden, the Civic and Political League used payment of the tax as proof of "citizenship" and a prerequisite for membership. As Dobbs put it in a promotional essay for the league, "good citizenship" first included "the duty of paying all taxes due the City, County, State, and Federal government." After that, the citizen's second duty was voter registration, since the "ballot is the one weapon left for a citizen to use as a buckle of defense in a modern Democracy like ours here in America."[61] Civic League leaders never questioned the fairness of having to pay to vote, even in the 1940s when the anti–poll tax movement was in full swing, although they surely knew that most black Atlantans were prevented from registering to vote because they could not afford to. And while they encouraged African Americans to pay the tax, they reserved the fight for those who had done so, limiting their constituency to a solvent minority.

Despite the selectivity of the league and its small regular membership, it organized itself for mass mobilization. It divided the city into twelve districts, with a neighborhood leader to coordinate a door-to-door registration and get-out-the-vote campaign for every election in which African Americans could vote. At election time, it decided on the candidate or slate of candidates it would support and made it known to black voters through a "grapevine" and not through the press. The latter strategy assumed that black voters would be intimidated at the polls or white voters mobilized to vote for the candidates opposing the one "tainted" by black support. The organization aimed to create a finely tuned machine that could tightly control a growing black electorate. Dobbs and his supporters wanted the league to become the undisputed voice of the black community, engendering the fear, if not the respect, of white officials.[62]

The first real test of the Civic and Political League's muscle did not come until 1938, when the city announced a school bond issue in conjunction with a multi-million dollar federally funded city-improvement plan. The school bond election was the first since 1935. Then black Atlantans threw their lot in with white officials and supported a school bond that barely recognized black schools, gaining some recognition and sewers for the black community. Since that election, black leaders had regretted their acquiescence; to date, the Board of Education had not spent even the measly amount that had been slated for black schools. Although black Atlantans protested this inaction through petitions and personal appeals, they received only polite recognition, giving ample proof that new, more militant tactics had to be employed.

In 1938, the league intended the outcome would be different. The Civic and Political League, in cooperation with the NAACP and the Atlanta Urban

League, put together all that the black leadership had learned since the debacle of 1935 in an effort to test the black electorate's muscle. Like then, black schools were grossly underrepresented in the bond proposal, but unlike 1935, the black community now had a "clearing house" electoral organization of its own which could openly confront the white political machine supporting the bond.[63]

When the bond was announced, the Civic and Political League jumped on it as the first important opportunity to test its power and established a systematic strategy for opposing the issue. The league formed a fact-finding committee in conjunction with the Atlanta Urban League to determine the exact nature of the inequality of black schools. The committee outlined the classroom deficit resulting in double sessions, the high student-teacher ratio that placed some pupils in classes of fifty or sixty, and the lack of auditoria, cafeterias, and gymnasia in black schools. This fact-finding mission published a pamphlet meant for white voters that outlined the deficits of black schools in terms of their contribution to juvenile delinquency and crime, terms becoming familiar to white Atlantans in touch with the social-work rhetoric of New Deal Atlanta. The pamphlet "Does Atlanta Know and Approve of These Conditions?," was a political innovation and a sign of the growing independence of the black elite. Instead of making dubious back-room bargains with white officials at election time, black reform leaders were now vocal in their opposition. They voiced it to the white public, using publicity that exposed white-imposed "deficits" in the black community through dispassionate statistics and the language of reform.[64]

The Civic League's main efforts focused on black Atlantans, in an attempt to get them to register for the vote in large numbers. It used black churches with activist pastors who would encourage their congregations to register to mobilize potential voters. It proposed to open seven "registration centers" at churches around the city where people could gather for citizenship training and transportation to the courthouse to register. League Leaders saw the church as the "bulwark" of the black community's "assemblage" and believed that it would provide them with the "mass contact" they needed to achieve widespread voter registration. The ADW applauded this move, which reminded its editors of a bygone era, "when our citizenship was in flower," and when the "church was a potent factor in affairs touching our political well being." Once again the church "stands in its old place as the beacon for the struggling, the troubled, and those seeking readjustments in their civic and political lives."[65] In this new era of activist ministry, the Civic League held out great hope for the church as a mobilizing tool to achieve secular aims. Interestingly, its leaders claimed no connection to the "masses" themselves and looked to another agency, the church, to do their mobilizing for them.

When election day came and went, the bond issue was defeated, but not because of the black vote. Rather, both black and white voters stayed away from the polls. In order for the bond to pass, a majority of registered voters had to cast a ballot. In fact, only 830 votes were cast against the ballot. At best, fewer than half the black voters registered when the Civic and Political League's bond election campaign began actually voted in the election or voted with the league against the issue.[66]

Clearly, the Civic League had not achieved its mission of mass mobilization in the black community. The cumulative poll tax may have been the reason, making it too onerous for many black Atlantans to register, although in this election women who had never registered were able to do so by only paying the current year's levy. A major reason for the poor showing of the black community seems to be related to the Civic and Political League's continuing elitism. Despite its desire to find 10,000 African Americans willing to register and vote, it still aimed its message primarily at the higher echelons of black society. The 10,000 voters league leaders envisioned, about 10 percent of Atlanta's African American population, was still the "talented tenth." The group's goals represented this bias; although it worked for better schools and hospitals which would benefit the whole community, its other campaigns for higher teachers' salaries, the admittance of black physicians to Grady Hospital, and black police for black neighborhoods, would benefit most directly these high-status groups.[67] Although it believed that black teachers, physicians, and police, like black bureaucrats, would ultimately provide the greatest good to the black community, it did not attack those economic issues that would most directly improve the lives of most black Atlantans. In order to reach this goal, it would have to broaden its appeal.

Despite the Civic League's failure in the 1938 campaign, it did set the groundwork for future electoral battles in its strategy and methods. Sophisticated publicity aimed at whites outlining publicly imposed black disadvantages would become an increasingly important weapon in the ongoing campaigns for better schools and teachers' salaries and black police. The voter recruitment strategies it employed would form the basis of future attempts to mobilize potential black voters. Yet it recognized that relying on churches and their ministers, no matter how militant, to get out the vote was not enough. It needed to canvas and organize black neighborhoods itself. Moreover, its ability to act as the clearinghouse and the mouthpiece of black Atlanta in presenting a united front to white officials would become an important ingredient in future electoral successes. All it needed now was a constituency to back up its authority and boost the power of the black community, or its surrogate, the Civic and Political League.

The mass constituency that eluded the AUL, the NAACP, and the Civic and Political League throughout the 1930s continued to be tapped by the Communists during the same decade. Black reform agencies were not completely hostile to the Communist Party—the NAACP, for example, on several occasions handled the complaints of party faithful Clarence Weaver over discrimination against black painters on federal works sites. Mainstream black leaders continued to voice their opposition to the party, however, partly as a rhetorical ploy to limit persistent white red-baiting of the AUL and NAACP, but also because it worked on issues so removed from the reform mandate that they hoped to achieve.[68]

The Communists persisted as a presence in black Atlanta throughout the 1930s. The police continued raiding meetings in black neighborhoods, forcing the party underground. But in 1938 the Communists resurfaced, under the banner of the Workers' Alliance, a national union for WPA workers. The alliance, which had separate black and white locals, never found much support among whites in Atlanta. Its African American organization, the only all-black unit in the South, boasted at least three hundred loyal members. It worked staunchly with them to defend and protest against discrimination on federal projects and to end regional wage differentials for southern workers on work relief.[69]

The alliance's black local addressed issues of importance to African American WPA workers, and especially the vast majority assigned to unskilled labor. It complained when the agency laid off black workers, replacing them with white. These race-based local layoffs, as well as more general ones directed from Washington, D.C., always affected black workers disproportionately. The alliance made special appeals for WPA relief for black women, the largest group of unemployed workers in the city. It also protested the placement of black women in heavy outdoor labor, like those employed at Washington Park, and sought to get them reassigned to less strenuous indoor labor. These were the issues that most directly affected black workers in Atlanta, and they were at the forefront of the alliance's mandate. The union considered these concerns to be "mass" issues affecting the majority of the black community. By contrast, the NAACP considered these same complaints to be secondary, isolated cases, of less importance than its program to obtain higher teachers' salaries or enroll African Americans in citizenship training.[70]

The Alliance's tactics were vastly different from those of Atlanta's black reform organizations. While acting as a broker organization for its constituency of WPA workers, it also directly involved its supporters in its activist strategy, relying on confrontational techniques, such as public demonstrations and strikes. For example, the WPA finally reassigned the black women workers delegated to Washington Park when they refused to dig a ditch and instead went to the alliance's office. They threatened to remain there until Gay Shepperson granted them a conference. They only returned to work when federal officials said they would no longer be assigned to such work. On other occasions, hundreds of workers organized by the alliance, many or mostly black, marched on the Fulton County Commission, WPA headquarters, and city hall. They demanded more money for direct relief for the thousands who were unemployed and ineligible for local direct relief or federal work relief, and they agitated for more jobs from the WPA. WPA officials and even Gay Shepperson herself met with delegations of demonstrators. Federal administrators did not meet the alliance's demands in the waning days of New Deal work relief when the WPA was laying off thousands of workers. Nevertheless, the alliance strategy had mobilized hundreds of black workers by addressing the issues that most directly affected them, and by employing a strategy of direct action in which, unlike voting, black workers could actively participate.[71]

Despite the limited success of the Workers' Alliance, it did demonstrate that black activism could take a different path from the one outlined out by elite black reformers. First, the alliance recognized the primacy of the issues most important to black WPA workers, and consequently to the majority of black Atlantans. It worked to extinguish the economic and work-place disparities that affected all black workers, not just black professionals. Second, it involved black workers in open and confrontational activism, which, because of the backing of a national organization, was recognized positively by white local and federal officials. This militant strategy, which had never before had such success in Atlanta without a heavy-handed police crackdown, only bolstered black support for the alliance, which allowed its members to voice their complaints openly. The alliance knew that it had to involve its members to run a successful social movement.

By contrast, mainstream black reformers complained of the apathy of black Atlantans unwilling to hand over their money or unconditional support to an elite leadership. But these reformers neglected to invite any but the most accomplished onto their executive committees, and defined a mass movement as one in which the "talented tenth" knew what was best for the black community, controlling the other 90 percent.

Finally, the Workers' Alliance had something that none of the black reform groups had—a mass constituency. The social, economic, and political incorporation wrought by the New Deal for African Americans meant that WPA workers formed an ideal group for mobilization. The Communists had never had such success before the New Deal in attracting black supporters dispersed across the city in domestic work or common labor. With the WPA, they had a group of workers with the same pay, working conditions, and grievances, whose single employer, the federal government, did not share the virulent antiunionism of private employers in the South. Whether or not they were directly influenced by the Workers' Alliance example, black reformers would begin to recognize the potential power of such federally organized constituencies in their continuing move from elite-led reform to elite-led political activism.

III

The New Deal & Local Politics in Black and White

7

A Jungle World
Breeding Jungle Life

*The White Campaign for
Slum Clearance and Public Housing*

In 1939 the Public Works Administration (PWA) memorialized a proud achievement, its pioneering slum-clearance and public-housing program, in the agency's final report, *America Builds*. In celebrating this "low-income" program, the agency highlighted Atlanta, home to two of the PWA's first housing projects, and, paradoxically, the benefits one of them accrued to the city's wealthiest white residents. Before slum clearance in 1934, the authors noted that "a trip downtown for the young ladies of Peachtree Street, Atlanta, had one discouraging aspect." In order for these women to get from their homes in tony North Atlanta to fashionable downtown shops "they had to pass a slum." This area, with its "gray, dilapidated shanties, with back yards full of trash, lay adjacent to the campus of the Georgia Institute of Technology, at the doorway of downtown Atlanta."

According to the PWA, this slum was the site of a plethora of social evils; it was a "notorious area," and "Atlanta's Problem Area Number I" for social workers, police, firefighters, and public-health workers, costing the city far more than it contributed. In short, it was a "blight on the city," and importantly to the authors, "the blight was not static—it was moving glacierlike toward high-priced business property, carrying depression of values along with it steadily and surely." The PWA's slum-clearance and public-housing program resolved this crisis. By 1936, "the young ladies of Peachtree Street could have rubbed their eyes in amazement to see what had happened to Atlanta's prize slum. The shacks and swampy yards had vanished, giving way to trim brick apartment buildings and group houses with clean-cut lines, set amid pleasant green lawns."[1]

This celebration of the PWA's low-income housing program in terms of its benefits to elite whites perfectly represented the impetus and interests driving its success in Atlanta. The city's pioneering role in the federal housing program was largely a product of intense lobbying by representatives of big business and local government hoping to protect white Atlanta's middle-class residential neighborhoods from black encroachment and the central business district from the blight of black neighborhoods that surrounded it.[2]

Elite white interests used the PWA and the subsequent prewar programs of the U.S. Housing Authority (USHA) to initiate slum clearance in four black neighborhoods in the northern and central sectors of the city, replacing them with public housing for whites, thus forcing thousands of African Americans to join a migration of black Atlantans to the west side of the city, where city officials hoped to contain the black population. On the west side, the federal government demolished rundown black neighborhoods, replacing them with public housing for black residents as a further inducement for the westward movement of African Americans. In eight Roosevelt-era slum-clearance projects, the PWA, and then the Atlanta Housing Authority (AHA) displaced only a handful of white families but more than five thousand black citizens, uprooting them from their homes and leaving them to fend for themselves in the city's notoriously tight black housing market.[3]

The story of Atlanta's New Deal housing program follows the broad contours of a pattern repeated in cities around the country, a template for racialized urban development that would endure for decades to come. The federal government's policies literally remade the face of American cities by infusing massive amounts of funding for redevelopment projects, first for low-income housing, then for highways and urban renewal. Nationwide, business leaders, seizing on millions of federal slum-clearance and low-cost-housing dollars, pursued their own vision of community development. Seeking to protect and expand their cities' downtowns as central business districts, they used public authority and federal funds to remove the working class, and particularly poor people of color, from the long-established neighborhoods that encroached on city centers. While they couched their program in terms of the economic and public-welfare benefits that would accrue through the demolition of decrepit "slums," their program represented the beginning of a massive twentieth-century public-

Map 2. Atlanta's Prewar Slum Clearance and Low-Income-Housing Projects. (Adapted from map in Atlanta Housing Authority, *Rebuilding Atlanta: Second Annual Report*, 1940, Charles Forrest Palmer Collection, Special Collections Department, Robert W. Woodruff Library, Emory University)

works program that would reconfigure the racial geography of American cities.

Federal programs and policies that grew out of the New Deal would create the "second ghetto" of public housing in the postwar era, and would play a crucial role in marginalizing minority city dwellers economically and politically in the second half of the twentieth century.[4] As George Lipsitz has pointed out, New Deal urban redevelopment and housing programs represented the beginning of America's "racialized social democ-racy"[5] through which powerful new forms of structural, and putatively race-blind, discrimination emerged to replace the overt white supremacy of Jim Crow segregation. Atlanta was at the forefront of this transforma-tion. In fact, it had one of the nation's most ambitious New Deal housing programs—so ambitious in fact, that by the end of the Second World War the city had more public housing per capita than any other American city, the prelude to a decades-long orgy of urban renewal that would eventually uproot one-fifth of black Atlantans from their homes.[6]

Such a major reshaping of Atlanta's racial landscape did not happen overnight. In fact, the city's housing reformers had to coax white support for this costly program that would involve the government for the first time in the private real estate market. Furthermore, slum clearance and pub-lic housing were a difficult sell in a city where whites had tolerated, with little or no complaint, overcrowded and greatly dilapidated black neigh-borhoods, some in the shadows of the city's most important white insti-tutions, including the State Capitol building. The squalid living conditions with which most black Atlantans had to contend were virtually invisible to white Atlantans who considered African Americans to dwell beyond the margins of civic life, if they considered them at all. Further, thousands of middle-class white Atlantans perpetuated the "slum" conditions of black neighborhoods as landlords in these communities. A modest investment in leaky and sewerless shotgun shacks guaranteed high returns for the owners of black rental property.[7]

In response to white indifference or opposition, housing advocates preyed on white Atlantans' fears of black contamination and sold the gov-ernment housing program as a way to eliminate the "threat" black people and their neighborhoods posed to white Atlanta. Before the New Deal ushered in the era of state activism, whites could not imagine govern-ment at any level having the will or the authority to transform the racial geography of the city, thus making black housing conditions an accepted and seemingly organic part of city life. Toleration of black slums was the price the white community paid for profiting from the exploitation of black labor. White anxiety about the social cost of black slums, then, was spurred by the knowledge that the federal government could and would remove them. The "ladies of Peachtree Street" who had once considered dilapi-dated black neighborhoods a natural part of the city's landscape, with no apparent connection to their lives, now wondered if and how the squalor might rub off on them, and readily joined the bandwagon for slum clear-ance and low-income housing.[8]

Consequently, inclusion in the federal slum clearance and low-income-housing program had pernicious implications for poor African Americans, previously largely invisible to white eyes, as they came under close scrutiny by the white community and government officials. This scrutiny resulted in the razing of entire black neighborhoods, thus deepening the social, economic, and political marginality of thousands of black Atlantans.

The racialized nature of the slum-clearance and low-income-housing program emerged out of how local officials nationwide applied federal policy and not out of Washington itself. The most significant element in this regard was the PWA's fateful decision to concentrate on slum clearance and new building rather than on the refurbishment of low-income neighborhoods when it initiated the New Deal's public-housing program in 1933. White business elites and their political allies throughout urban America embraced the clearance-to-rebuild model for reasons quite divorced from the modernist community-building visions of the PWA's Housing Division. They saw in this interventionist initiative an opportunity to develop a new kind of urban planning that circumvented the parochial interests of municipal politics and minimal taxation powers of local government in order to reshape cities according to their economic and infrastructure needs.[9]

In Atlanta, these possibilities first caught the imagination of Charles Palmer, a major downtown real estate investor and president of the National Association of Building Owners and Managers, who was said to own more office space than any other landlord in the South.[10] He quickly recognized the potential of the federal slum-clearance and public-housing program that began with the creation of the PWA, whose mandate was to build socially beneficial public works and provide jobs for the nation's thousands of unemployed construction workers. In 1933 the PWA's Housing Division began to accept applications for slum-clearance and housing projects from municipalities lured by the promise of government loans for 85 percent of the projects at 4 percent interest amortized over thirty years.[11] Across the United States, local governments, chambers of commerce, and real estate investors like Palmer started submitting their plans to eradicate unwanted neighborhoods and to provide work for the unemployed.

Palmer's interest in the government's housing program stemmed from his desire to eradicate the rundown residential area known as Tanyard Bottom, or Tech Flats, which bordered the southern flank of the white Georgia Institute of Technology. This largely black neighborhood blocked Georgia Tech from downtown, and its spread threatened the value of Palmer's real estate investments and limited the development of the central business district, key to Palmer's long-term plan for the city. Shortly after the PWA announced its program in 1933, Palmer applied for money for slum clearance and a low-income-housing project for white tenants in Tanyard Bottom. Palmer's enthusiasm quickly expanded beyond the demolition of Tech Flats, however; he soon saw potential in the government housing program to change the face of Atlanta permanently, at federal expense. Palmer was the quintessential New Deal businessman who understood how government investment could serve his needs. He distinguished himself, however, through his curious mixture of Progressive reform instinct and relentless self-promotion, which led him to fashion himself into a prominent housing expert. He visited Europe (including Fascist Rome and Communist Moscow) to meet public-housing bureaucrats and to view housing projects, organized junkets of European housing experts to visit the United States, and paraded his newfound interest before the Roosevelt administration whenever he could. He drew national attention to Atlanta as a pioneering city in public housing, and his reward came in 1941 when Roosevelt appointed him the national defense housing coordinator.[12]

Like other New Dealers, Palmer expressed both his sympathy for the poor and his desire to ameliorate their wretched living standards, but he wished to achieve his reforms without fundamentally challenging the economic structures that created those conditions. He believed that because of the region's low-wage economy, Atlanta's poor could not move out of their rundown neighborhoods into better housing. Local "slumlords" could not improve the condition of their properties because, at such low rents, to do so would be unprofitable. Atlanta's poor, in other words, could not be both "economically" and "decently" housed by private real estate, given their abysmally low earnings. Palmer believed therefore, that in order to eradicate slums, public nonprofit housing would have to be built after slum clearance, or else slums would reemerge. He turned to the federal government to modernize the city's housing for its poor, thus leaving the city's wage structure intact and relieving private real estate from any responsibility for the problem. As he told the Atlanta Association of Building Owners and Managers about the government's role in the eradication of slum housing: "No other agency has the resources to undertake it, or the authority and obligation to proceed. It cannot any longer be left to laissez-faire."[13]

Palmer's self-proclaimed spirit of "enlightened capitalism" had much support among the white business elite in Atlanta. For example, the

Atlanta Chamber of Commerce, of which Palmer became president in 1939, had been active in city planning since the 1920s, and had been devising its own redevelopment scheme to protect property values when Palmer unveiled his scheme. The chamber abandoned its designs after Palmer's announcement and backed him enthusiastically, lobbying for the federal housing legislation that would put his project into effect. The federal government's plan was irresistible to big business and the largest real estate developers in Atlanta, since its provision of millions of dollars in loans allowed these groups to realize for the first time their vision for the major redevelopment and modernization of the city.[14]

Big business also supported federal intervention into housing because this outside aid helped it to resist the opposition of smaller business and real estate interests that had stymied its plans in the past. Residential real estate organizations launched a vigorous campaign against Palmer's scheme because it would demolish their black properties and hit them hard in an already flooded white rental market. The Tech Flats slum-clearance scheme, for example, displaced hundreds of black families, while the Techwood housing project built over Tanyard Bottom opened 600 new housing units for whites. Palmer's plan went through, nonetheless, backed by millions of dollars in federal money, the promise of hundreds of jobs for a construction industry devastated by the Depression, and the support of the city's business, media, and political elites.

After his initial success, Palmer became a relentless promoter of slum clearance and public housing in Atlanta and launched an energetic public-relations campaign on behalf of the movement. He sold his idea for slum clearance and public housing to prominent white Atlantans, including the president of Georgia Tech and the editor of the *Atlanta Constitution*. His public-relations campaign resulted in Mayor James Key's blessing when he established a limited-dividend corporation for the clearance of the Tech Flats slum and the erection of a public-housing project for white Atlantans. At the same time, Palmer became an advocate and lobbyist for another limited-dividend corporation initiated by Atlanta University's John Hope for a similar project to house African Americans in the university neighborhood. In 1934, the city government caught Palmer's slum-clearance fever and established a Municipal Housing Authority which planned to administer, through a municipally funded corporation, an ambitious and widespread federally funded scheme to eradicate all "blighted areas" in the city. Local officials scrapped these plans in April 1934, when the federal government took control of the limited-dividend schemes because of concerns over the sources of local financing and the failure of the Georgia legislature to approve the city's Municipal Housing Authority.[15]

How did Palmer and his supporters sell their schemes? Their first task was to change the white public's impressions of black neighborhoods, whose deplorable housing conditions had always been accepted as an unchangeable part of the city's fabric. In short, they had to transform Atlanta's black working-class neighborhoods into "slums" that needed to be eradicated. Charles Palmer and members of the Municipal Housing Authority promoted their early efforts to the white public by pointing out the extent and public cost of Atlanta's working-class black neighborhoods. Palmer constantly talked of Atlanta's "deficit districts" where municipally funded police, fire, and social services far outran tax payments. Similarly, Raymond Torras, secretary of the Municipal Housing Authority and the City Planning Commission, published a series of spot maps which he distributed to influential white Atlantans and newspapers. These maps pointed out the convergence of "slum" conditions with concentrations of adult crime, juvenile delinquency, tuberculosis, infant mortality, alley housing, and, most ominous, African American population.

In his study, Torras identified in a "somewhat arbitrary" fashion Atlanta's "blighted areas," which housed approximately 44,000 of Atlanta's 270,000 residents. Torras showed in his study that these areas contributed almost a third of juvenile and adult crimes in the city, despite representing only about 5 percent of the city's area and 17 percent of its population. Annual police costs in these areas were twice that of the city at large. Similarly, he showed that of 830 tuberculosis deaths between 1931 and 1933, almost 294 originated in the slums, contributing again to a drain on the city's resources.[16]

While Palmer and Torras's rhetoric always had a rational, business-minded tone which emphasized the economic costs of maintaining these areas, its subtext preyed upon the racial fears of the city's white inhabitants. Torras included a map in his report showing the convergence of African American population with "slums," crime, and disease, claiming that 66 percent of slum dwellers were black and 34 percent white, almost the reverse proportions of Atlanta's population as a whole. These statistics, equating slum dwellers with Atlanta's black citizens, swelled white Atlantans' deeply felt fear of the city's black population living in its shadow city of bottoms and alleys.

While white Atlantans sought to preserve the social conditions that per-

petuated black poverty, they also feared the implications of black destitution. Therefore, they supported New Deal investment in sewers, recreation, and school building programs in black districts in order to control
black disease, crime, and delinquency and prevent it from reaching into
white neighborhoods. Nowhere was the rhetoric capitalizing on these fears
more powerful and successful than in creating public support for the slum-
clearance project that preceded the building of public-housing projects in
Atlanta, and indeed in cities across the United States.[17]

White Atlantans most dreaded being contaminated by African Americans through disease. Contagious diseases such as tuberculosis continued
to pose serious threats to black and white Atlantans in the 1930s. It was
not lost on whites, therefore, that tuberculosis and African Americans met
on Raymond Torras's map in Atlanta's "deficit districts." Black Atlantans
suffered disproportionately from the disease, both in their rate of infection
and the incidence of death, and white Atlantans feared that epidemics in
the black community could spread to white neighborhoods. This fear was
so powerful that black reformers used it in a common and effective ploy to
force the white public to recognize black concerns and local government
to act on them. Black reformers pointed out that white Atlantans, as employers of black domestic workers, were not as isolated as they might think
from the "unsanitary tenements" housing black Atlantans. They used the
threat of an epidemic spreading from black neighborhoods to white homes
through the conduit of these servants as a ploy to force local government
and social agencies to act to improve conditions in black neighborhoods.
"Disease for the goose is disease for the gander," proclaimed the ADW in
1935. "Our white friends cannot hope to be free from disease germs under
a set-up whereby our people must come in contact with them,"[18] the editorial continued, as it urged white support for a bond issue that would bring
sewers and mosquito control to black areas. The Neighborhood Union, in
its 1931 petition to City Council for $500 in emergency relief, warned that
the health of black children must be preserved, "for should an epidemic
break out among them, no child in the city of Atlanta would be safe."[19] This
kind of talk had tremendous rhetorical power among white Atlantans, as
it preyed on their gravest fears of contamination by blacks.

While white Atlantans feared black disease, they also dreaded black contamination of more metaphorical kinds; for example, many felt that mythic
black criminality and lawlessness endangered their neighborhoods. Slum-
clearance advocates played up this threat by publicizing the racial and
social makeup of "slum" areas. This alarm stemmed partly from black

neighborhoods' invisibility in the eyes of whites. Black Atlantans lived in neighborhoods virtually unknown to white Atlantans, particularly the middle class. Many black workers lived far from the center of civic life, tucked away in industrial areas or near railroad tracks or in bottomland rarely traversed by anyone outside the community. Even more threatening, many of the poorest African Americans did not live on public streets but on hidden alleys, sometimes behind the homes of their white employers, but more often in black neighborhoods.[20]

Whites feared that in these "invisible" neighborhoods anarchy prevailed and could easily spread to other sections of the city. In a promotional film documenting Atlanta's public-housing program, filmmakers preyed on white Atlantans' fear of black lawlessness. A narrator accompanied a scene showing two black boys loitering around an abandoned house with the following: "It's a jungle world breeding jungle life, where many children learn to steal, to fight civil authority, to forage like little jungle animals and often take what they want wherever and whenever they can find it." Changing to a scene of a black family outside their alley house, the commentary continued: "So these areas breed a group from which we cannot expect much toward the upbuilding of the city or the nation. A group that obviously has a degrading influence on the body politic, the community standards of life and the very physical standards of the race itself." Cutting to an image of a laundry worker stirring a tub on top of a fire outside her squalid hut, the narrator proceeded: "Like a bad apple in the barrel, the slum must drag down the level of the whole community to its primitive level. A slum like any other blight must be treated as a disease of the body politic, must be wiped from the face of this earth for it's a condition not to be tolerated by a humane and civilized people."[21]

As this example demonstrates, when the fear of disease extended to a fear of the black population in general, disease became a metaphor for the "slum" areas themselves. Depressed neighborhoods became a "cancer" that had to be excised from the city in order to preserve property values and social order. When the Techwood housing project was first announced in 1933, the Atlanta Woman's Club opposed the scheme, arguing that the entire Tech Flats neighborhood should be razed for a park, lest a new black slum rise from the rubble. Club leaders feared that it was "of no avail to cut out the source of a cancer and expect to cure the disease by substituting new tissue, for the roots of the evil surrounding the new section soon will make the whole area cancerous again."[22]

The disease metaphor for poor black neighborhoods became a truism for white Atlantans. They shared a consensus that these neighborhoods were irredeemable and needed to be excised from the city. White liberals such as Arthur Raper, president of the Georgia branch of the CIC, believed that "areas that are sick should be broken into," and that these neighborhoods "should be cleaned out even if the Municipal Authorities [have] to use the power of eminent domain."[23] He wished to shut down the slumlords in these areas. Business leaders like Charles Palmer, however, had a different justification to rehouse slum dwellers. He believed that these areas were a drain on city resources like police and fire protection and that "as long as they menace the health of the community because of the spread of disease and vice that comes from their condition, the community is economically justified in housing them better to protect itself from the contamination of that cancerous area."[24]

This metaphorical elucidation of white fears fed the support of the city's first slum-clearance projects and low-income-housing projects, Techwood for whites and University Homes for blacks. The disease imagery continued to be effective after these two projects were built, particularly when Palmer moved to create a Housing Authority for Atlanta in 1938 in order to undertake a widespread, municipally sponsored slum-clearance program. This time, however, he had a concrete foundation on which to base his rhetoric. On the night of March 27, 1938, a fire began in a factory in the semi-industrial area adjacent to Grady Hospital, the city's largest hospital. The fire quickly spread to the wood-frame houses next to the factory and raged on to ignite the roof of Grady's boiler room, burning embers from which threatened a nurses' residence, the venereal disease clinic, and the main hospital itself.[25]

Fire played an important part in the city's collective psyche and historical memory. It was fire that destroyed Atlanta during Sherman's March in the Civil War, after which white Atlantans were proud to remember that their city "rose from the ashes like a phoenix." But more immediate to the direct experience of residents in the 1930s was the fire of 1917 that leveled seventy-three square blocks of the city and displaced 10,000 people. The 1938 fire, though much smaller, shared two important similarities to the conflagration of 1917; both were thought to have begun in the same working-class black neighborhood, and both spread to white-controlled institutions and residences.[26]

These two facts helped Palmer immeasurably in his campaign for a local housing authority. Suddenly the cancer metaphor became concrete as white Atlantans saw how the slums posed an immediate threat to white

sections. The white public came to see as problematic the physical proximity of slum areas to important public institutions such as Grady Hospital
and the State Capitol. White housing reformers no longer talked of rehous-
ing slum dwellers but of protecting public institutions. Aerial photographs
in newspapers showed the slums "that encircle the main business section
of Atlanta in a ring of squalor."[27] A fire in this ring, Palmer warned, "could
very easily result in a conflagration in the downtown district that would do
millions of dollars worth of damage and cost dozens of lives."[28] New Deal
slum-clearance and housing projects would create fireproof buffers that
would protect these institutions from fire and from poor black residents.

The fire, and the resulting public-relations campaign on behalf of slum
clearance, prompted a once-reluctant Mayor Hartsfield and the city council to support the creation of the Atlanta Housing Authority. It soon secured
loans from the U.S. Housing Authority for seven new slum-clearance and
housing projects, two white and five black. Not surprisingly, four of the
new projects were adjacent to public edifices, including Grady Hospital
and the State Capitol, and Georgia Tech and the Atlanta University Center
in extensions of University and Techwood Homes.

Clearly, the white rhetoric surrounding the housing program had repressive implications for poor African Americans in Atlanta. White officials showed new awareness of black Atlantans' living situation, scrutiniz-
ing and criticizing the abysmal conditions of working-class neighborhoods.
But while these investigations cast some much-needed attention on the
"slums" in which black Atlantans were forced to dwell by virtue of poverty
and segregation, white officials' talk turned quickly from action against
the "slums" to action against poor black "slum dwellers." For now that the
words were backed up by millions of federal dollars, Atlanta's white elite
could control the African American population in ways never dreamt of
before the age of state intervention.

The location of Techwood and University Homes reflected white worries
about the city's black poor. Primary among the concerns of white elites
in this period was the protection of the central business district. But the
problem was not just that a "blight" surrounded the city's core; rather, the
problem was that now the city was inhabited by poor, disfranchised black
Atlantans, who resided outside the boundaries of the political, commercial, and social mainstream of civic life.

In the 1930s, Mayor William Hartsfield and other progressives in city
government began a push to annex the suburbs to which white homeowners had fled, leaving their neighborhoods to poor blacks and whites.

Capitol Homes, one of the housing projects for whites, which "protected"
Atlanta's important white neighborhoods and institutions by replacing the black
"slums" that threatened them. (Charles Forrest Palmer Collection, Special
Collections Department, Robert W. Woodruff Library, Emory University)

Hartsfield hoped to extend Atlanta's borders in order to keep his middle-class constituency, and their taxes, within the city's limits. His rhetoric demonstrated the popular middle-class perception of what the inner city had become: "Atlanta's citizenship is being undermined by the constant migration of its home-owning citizens. Pretty soon only city employees, relief rollers and persons who rent property will be left in town. It is important for the city to retain on its voters' lists those conservative home owners who believe in clean government."[29]

Atlanta's population was not only becoming poorer, it was becoming blacker (see Appendix, Table 1). White leaders responded to this demographic shift by moving to control the city's black population in a number of ways. Hartsfield's move to annex the suburbs was one such political response, but he failed to garner enough support from Fulton County suburbanites to achieve this goal until after the war. City leaders found more success in 1937 when they redrew the city's political boundaries, reducing the number of wards from 13 to 6, thus eliminating two majority-black wards and ensuring that African Americans remained a safe political minority around the city. Hartsfield was very aware of the political threat black voters presented in special elections and was prescient in anticipating the end of the white primary.

While political maneuvers kept the black electorate in check, white leaders faced the more daunting task of controlling black residential growth in the city in order to protect their economic and social interests. In some ways city leaders were resigned to letting African Americans remain in the center of the city, and perhaps even wanted to keep them there to protect their labor supply and the new "white" suburbs. Charles Palmer, for example, did not advocate removing the poor entirely from the center of the city. In fact he believed that these families should remain within Atlanta's center "rather than . . . move . . . away from their work to more speculative border areas, where the expense of utilities, transportation and other facilities will be an added tax burden."[30] So all but one of the housing projects was built well within the city's limits.

While powerful whites acquiesced to a black presence in the city's core, they had very specific ideas about where black Atlantans would reside and where their neighborhoods would spread. With the slum-clearance and housing program, those neighborhoods encroaching too closely on important public institutions such as the State Capitol or Grady Hospital could be demolished and a housing project built in their stead. The Atlanta Housing Authority's first annual report described how difficult it was to decide on "suitable areas for slum clearance." Having "limited the risks in every way," the authority never picked sites "completely surrounded by substandard houses," claiming that then "the good would . . . be lost in the bad." Rather, it contended that it was "compelled" to "start at the edge of a slum district and anchor [the] projects so as to receive the protection of public institutions or other improvements of a permanent character."[31] In truth, the authority reversed this formula in choosing slum-clearance areas; it cleared slums in areas next to these institutions to protect these important public and white-controlled spaces from the further threat of the "slums'" encroachment.

Further, slum-clearance areas were chosen according to important racial considerations. Beginning in the 1920s blacks began moving out of the southeastern and northwestern quadrants of the city into the southwest, in a move that was sanctioned and facilitated by the city's white political and business magnates. The first clearance projects helped consolidate this racial shift by demolishing two black neighborhoods. The Tech Flats neighborhood was the last large black neighborhood in the white, middle-class north side of the city. Its demolition and the white housing project built in its stead removed the threat of black residential spread in this section of the city and retarded white flight to the suburbs. Similarly, the clearing of Beaver Slide for University Homes opened attractive, modern housing to black Atlantans, drawing even more of them to the west side. This program to redirect and control Atlanta's racial geography intensified with the more ambitious program of the Housing Authority. It located three out of four of the new prewar housing projects for African Americans on the city's west side and the two new white projects displaced blacks from threatening a white neighborhood and the State Capitol, respectively.

The successful reconfiguration of the city's racial geography required political finesse. While virtually all white Atlantans supported Jim Crow, many groups were invested in retaining the city's existing racial geography, and opposed the white elite's particular segregationist vision. The city's white working class, in particular, many of whose members lived in or nearby the areas now being chosen for black relocation, vigorously opposed the forced exodus of black Atlantans from east to west. They struggled to quash the housing program, but the white elite's alliance with the federal government allowed Palmer's plans to prevail, backed as it was by millions of dollars in federal money and the promise of hundreds of jobs for a construction industry devastated by the Depression. Throughout the first half of the twentieth century, African Americans moving onto the frontier of westward expansion risked the firebombing of their homes by white vigilante groups. Not a few families were forced to abandon their new homes after the Ku Klux Klan and other vigilantes made their intentions clear to recalcitrant black pioneers by bombing their porches, stoning their children, or flogging them after abducting them from their homes in the dark of night.

Just such vigilantism occurred when the AHA announced its decision in the spring of 1939 to build the 1,200-unit John Eagan Homes in an area just south of Booker T. Washington High School on Westview Drive. Westview Drive at that time formed the west side's unofficial border between blacks and whites. The white community, known as the West End, on which the city's west-side black community shared this contested border, was made up of working-class and lower-middle-class whites, including many members of the city's police force and fire department, with whom the city's African Americans had a turbulent relationship.[32]

On the night of 9 May 1939, shortly after the John Eagan project was announced and one day after a white woman was allegedly assaulted by an African American in the West End neighborhood, white vigilantes seized the janitor from the woman's apartment building. They took Ed Harper and his roommate to a deserted country road where the gang placed nooses around the two men's necks, questioned them, stripped them, and finally flogged them. After deciding they had sufficiently frightened and humiliated the two men, the vigilantes left Harper and his friend stranded, warning them not to return to Atlanta. After walking the miles back to Atlanta, the roommate did leave the city, whereas Harper returned to his room and his job after laying low in another part of town for a few days.[33]

While the ostensible reason for this attack was the standard white southern story of black, male sexual predation of a white woman, it was widely perceived by blacks and liberal whites as the first stage in an intimidation campaign to stop the housing project from being built.[34] The campaign soon moved to a more legitimate strategy that brought thousands of white West Enders to oppose the project vocally, including the West End Woman's Club, West End Businessmen's Association, Civic Club of West End, the local post of the Veterans of Foreign Wars, and various white parent-teacher associations. Opponents to the scheme, numbering 3,800, signed petitions to city council and began writing their congressmen and the president to tell them, in the words of black sociologist Walter Chivers, that the "civic organizations of West End . . . decided the Negroes have come as far as they want them to go."[35]

The Housing Authority altered its plans for Eagan Homes, proposing an awkward solution that would buttress the existing racial boundary. In the new scheme the project would house fewer families and would be divided into a white section facing West Side Drive and a black section facing Hunter Street, separated by a wide, fenced-in "No Man's Land." Otherwise, the authority voted unanimously to continue with the project. Both vigilante actions against blacks and community pressure against local and federal politicians continued, however, and the authority finally caved in to white pressure. It moved the now all-black project north to Connally Park, an area of abandoned land once intended for a black park but actually used as an unofficial garbage dump.[36]

The John Eagan Homes controversy marked a real watershed in Atlanta's political development. It represented the beginning of the end for non-elite whites to use their political clout to alter the racial geography of Atlanta. Mayor Hartsfield, first elected in 1936, represented the city's business elite, including representatives like Charles Palmer or Robert Woodruff of Coca-Cola, and the city's white professional class. These constituencies had long advocated, or at least supported, African American migration to the west side of Atlanta, at least partly because this drift would protect their northern and eastern neighborhoods from black encroachment. Hartsfield spent much of his time in office in the 1930s and 1940s trying to bolster these constituencies through measures like annexation. While he was thwarted in that campaign, he succeeded in proposing at-large elections for city council members. This political reform disempowered working-class whites, who had been used to wielding great influence in city politics through their councilmen. In 1938, West End whites faced the reality that in the next city council elections their votes would be diluted and their interests would compete with many others in the political calculations of their municipal representatives.[37]

But while West End whites worried about their dwindling influence in municipal politics, they feared the Atlanta Housing Authority even more. As new autonomous and nondemocratic governing body introduced nationwide by the New Deal, housing authorities allowed powerful interests to immunize themselves against white working-class influence by creating an independent institution free from local political manipulation.[38] While Atlanta City Council established the housing authority, local officials had no power over it once it was in place. Roy Callaway, the only councilman to oppose the creation of the authority, accused Hartsfield of having "sacrificed his birthright by appointing an authority over which council has no control."[39] However, the body was very much in Hartsfield's interests because it facilitated the development goals of his elite constituency while sidestepping the political mudslinging of city council. Thus control of federal funding allowed the city's white elite to wield unprecedented jurisdiction over city affairs and to impose their race and class vision on Atlanta.[40]

White liberals supported the work of the housing authority and of the housing program in general because it provided essential protection to black Atlantans against the opposition of working-class whites. The Fulton-DeKalb Committee of the cic, for example, contemplated action against the west-side floggings and was asked by Mayor Hartsfield to help diffuse the John Eagan Homes situation. The committee members despaired over effecting any change at the local level, since little white support existed for the black project, and they knew from past experience the difficulty in getting white Atlantans more than mildly disturbed about white vigilantism against blacks, even when it resulted in death. One committee member concluded that the only effective pressure could come from outside: "The only hope the Negro has in Georgia is with the Federal Government. The pressure that is effective is the pressure from Washington and the groups which have voices in Washington." By extension, given white community opposition to black projects, it was unlikely that without an independent, federally funded Atlanta Housing Authority, the Eagan Homes would have been built anywhere, or that one thousand more black units than white would have been built in the authority's prewar projects.[41]

The real victims in the city's low-income-housing program were those whose neighborhoods were razed to make way for housing projects. Slum clearance for Techwood and University Homes displaced hundreds of black families, none of whom found housing in the projects built on top of their old neighborhoods. Housing officials made no provision for these refugees, who had to find new housing in Atlanta's notoriously tight black housing market. The Atlanta Housing Authority addressed this problem by creating a bureau to find new homes for the more than 2,500 black families displaced in prewar slum clearance. However, gross inequities continued to be embedded in Atlanta's housing program. Very few ex-residents were chosen to live in the new housing projects, only black neighborhoods were destroyed, and the thousands of African Americans who lost their homes to make way for the Capitol and Clark Howell projects were barred from residency in these all-white projects.[42]

White housing rhetoric demonized the neighborhoods set for slum clearance as the vilest, basest, most anarchic areas of the city. But who exactly were the people who lost their homes through slum clearance? One of the clearest pictures of this group comes from W. E. B. Du Bois, who, solicited by John Hope, authored a survey of Beaver Slide, the community housed in the area slated for University Homes. In preparing the report, Du Bois and his Atlanta University sociology students discovered a group of people quite unlike those portrayed by slum-clearance advocates. Du Bois's study portrayed a stable, black working-class neighborhood, not terribly different from many around the city. It had a few prosperous residents, including a physician, but the overwhelming majority of the inhabitants eked out their living through the mainstays of black occupational life, domestic work, and unskilled labor. The neighborhood had been devastated by the Depression, with most men out of work, women picking up jobs doing laundry and casual domestic work where they could, and many depending on meager city relief to tide them over. Du Bois showed that most families had been living in the area for five years or more, and that they cared for their modest homes, landscaping them with flowers and shrubbery. In short, he called Beaver Slide "a slum area because of poverty, and not by reason of vice and crime."[43]

While inhabitants of Beaver Slide were not the demonized "jungle dwellers" of the housing reformers' rhetoric, they were nevertheless marginal figures in city life. They knew very little about the housing project that was to replace their homes because no one had bothered to inform them about it. They knew only that they had to get out. Most did not want to live in the project even if they could because they believed the homes would be the squalid and immoral places that black Atlantans associated by experience and reputation with apartment living. At the same time, they did not know where they would go after the demolition of their homes, and indeed most of them disappeared into some other black neighborhood once slum clearance began.

Another indication of the marginality of Beaver Slide and its residents was the way in which the PWA carried out the evictions in that area. The agency contracted the task of purchasing the properties in the slum-clearance area to the Atlanta Real Estate Board, which assigned appraisers from local companies who already had dealings in the areas slated for demolition. These companies foresaw little difficulty in obtaining the properties in Beaver Slide, most of which had become unprofitable rental properties for their absentee owners, or were owned by struggling black residents whose mortgages were on the brink of foreclosure.[44] Entering into this buyers' market, the real estate appraisers for Beaver Slide interpreted federal instructions to offer to purchase the homes at a price that a "willing seller could get from a willing buyer for cash" as a carte blanche to intimidate the sellers into accepting basement prices for their investments. These forced sales were a particular problem in Beaver Slide because, according to Charles Palmer, "the Techwood project had higher class real estate men working on theirs, [and] . . . men [who] were chosen to make the University Housing appraisals . . . had had experience in dealing with Negro tenants and were really . . . mainly rent collectors."[45] In other words, the appraisers had experience exploiting black tenants and mortgage holders, and they continued to do so in their new role as government agents. Their strong-arm tactics were so effective that the initial government purchases in Beaver Slide came in $85,000 below the estimated cost.

The excessively low prices offered for Beaver Slide properties also reflected the peculiar racial factors affecting real estate values in Atlanta. Black homeowners in Beaver Slide had likely paid much more for their properties than their actual worth. Limits on black residential growth enforced by residential segregation meant an extremely tight housing market for blacks and one in which sellers always dominated buyers. The government never offered black owners a price near to the overvalued one they had paid to purchase their houses. Second, although Tanyard Bottom had been a black area, Techwood Homes would be white, resulting in an immediate appreciation in property values in the area when the housing project was announced.[46]

Atlanta University's advisory committee for University Homes fought these practices and sought to protect Beaver Slide's homeowners as best it could. Members complained to the PWA, meeting with them and local real estate interests. The real estate board altered its appraisal procedure for Beaver Slide, bringing it up to the standards of ordinary appraisals, and offering to value the property at about 50 percent more than its first appraisals. Homeowners continued to resist the forced sale of their houses, however. In response, the federal government instituted condemnation proceedings against recalcitrant owners of 200 buildings and 134 parcels of land in the area.[47]

Condemnation, which according to the *Constitution* had the ". . . endorsement of leading citizens of the city," meant that twenty days after institution, government officials could take possession of the buildings and tear them down whether the owner had sold his or her property to the government or not. In a clearly disingenuous statement, Harold Ickes of the PWA told Atlantans that they "should not consider the institution of condemnation proceedings as a threat or a reflection on the property owners."[48] But clearly this supreme exercise of the federal government's right of eminent domain was a threat, and particularly to poor black land-owners, most of whom had struggled for years to own their own homes.[49]

In many ways this episode in the slum-clearance program had a famil-iar ring to black Atlantans. After all, they were used to being exploited and bullied by the impersonal forces of the real estate market and the individual tactics of its agents. Yet it also had ominous new overtones. The slum-clearance project represented the first federal presence inside the marginal, working-class black neighborhoods of Atlanta. This presence was an entirely repressive one that allowed local white real estate, busi-ness, and political interests to make an aggressive and ambitious move on behalf of their development goals for the city entirely at the expense of the city's poorest residents. So while most white and many black Atlantans perceived the housing program as the most visible and positive program of the federal government on behalf of poor Atlantans, for many of the poor themselves the federal government was a negative force powerful enough to literally destroy their neighborhood entirely at their expense.

8

A Laboratory
for Citizenship

*The Black Campaign for
Slum Clearance and Public Housing*

On Easter Sunday 1938, Atlanta University ad-
ministrators and faculty, leaders of the city's black social-welfare agencies, and prosperous members of the west-side community gathered in
the playground of University Homes, Atlanta's first public-housing project
for African Americans, and one of the first of such projects in the United
States. They joined the tenants in a commemoration of the first anniversary of the PWA-funded development. After tearing down a prop paste-
board house, meant to represent Beaver Slide, the "slum" cleared to make
way for the project, tenants put on a pageant written by Atlanta School of
Social Work students. Entitled "Thy Neighbor as Thyself," the Neighborhood Union's motto, it attributed the inspiration for University Homes to
the NU's settlement-house work, and traced the private welfare activities
that preceded the announcement of the project and the role that AU played
in its fruition. The pageant ascribed the success of the project to local black
leaders, not the federal government; and, of the dozen figures portrayed
in the pageant, Harold Ickes, national administrator of the PWA, was the
sole New Deal representative.[1]

It is unsurprising that black reformers celebrated University Homes and
claimed ownership of it. The housing program was undoubtedly racialized
as whites like Charles Palmer conceived it. However, black housing reformers embraced the program because, like white businessmen, they felt it
allowed them to reshape the city, or at least the black community, according to their vision. In particular, they enthusiastically joined Palmer and

his cronies in lobbying the federal government to redevelop Atlanta's black west-side neighborhoods, starting with the area around Atlanta University. Further, they applauded the federal government's housing policy, and especially its emphasis on slum clearance, its highly selective tenant eligibility standards, and its community-building vision because it permitted them to both reshape the black community and further their citizenship efforts for the respectable. In short, while the "outer wheel," represented by the federal government and white housing officials, controlled the housing program, black reformers actively participated in this effort because it so well matched their intentions for the "inner wheel" of the black community.

In turn, white federal and local housing officials, needing the support of black reformers in order to achieve slum clearance and public housing's controversial aims, and recognizing their kindred goals, made black reformers junior partners in Atlanta's housing program. Such recognition from powerful whites legitimated black reformers as never before and would mark the beginning of their ever-growing participation in the city's development politics. Furthermore, by becoming active participants in the low-income housing program, black reformers could finally put their ideological convictions into action, with material consequences for the entire black community.

Black reformers' victory bolstered their power as brokers for African Americans and reinforced their tendency to conflate their own group interests with the interests of the black community at large. Such conflation masked the housing program's impact of deeply dividing Atlanta's black community according to the contradictions of the politics of respectability. For a select few chosen to live in the housing projects, the program had genuinely democratic consequences in uplifting them from their marginal and parochial existence at the fringes of civic life and preparing them to take their rightful place in the political and economic mainstream. Reformers used the projects as laboratories for citizenship, where black leaders could finally develop a constituency for their aspirations for racial uplift, insulated from the environment of immorality, parochialism, and apathy that they believed had impeded past efforts.

For these reasons, the black reform elite enthusiastically supported the program, even though it ushered in a decades-long orgy of urban renewal which cut huge swathes out of working-class black neighborhoods and uprooted thousands of black Atlantans.[2] Thus, while public housing became one of the most important sites of black activism in Atlanta, the black elite–sanctioned federal slum-clearance and housing program actually victimized legions of poor black Atlantans and deepened their marginalization instead of helping them into the mainstream. The ideological motivations that guided black reformers' active cooperation with this program highlight the paradoxes and limits of their inclusion in Atlanta's New Deal order, and the long-term consequences of their choices. Indeed, the housing program demonstrated how the federal government privileged proponents of racial uplift by allowing them to put their ideas into practice, with lasting and divisive consequences for Atlanta's black community. This dynamic suggests that crucial decisions among an influential group of African Americans about how best to deal with American society's racialist order shaped the impact of the New Deal social democracy on the black community in Atlanta.

When the first negotiations began in 1933 for slum clearance in Atlanta, AU's president, John Hope, saw an opportunity to achieve his long-held dream of transforming the neighborhood around the university into a respectable, middle-class enclave, a neighborhood befitting the best black schools in the United States. This neighborhood would be filled with ambitious and law-abiding people. In turn, residents would be rewarded by modern housing, a full complement of city services, and the prestige and protection that went along with association with the university community.

Hope's desires represented the pent-up aspirations of the black elite and the upwardly mobile African Americans in Atlanta to overcome the containment of residential segregation that forced all black people, no matter their status, to live cheek by jowl. Such ghettoization was a particularly galling feature of Jim Crow for the black elite and its aspirants because it prevented them from achieving a hallmark of American bourgeois life — spatial segregation from the poor. Moreover, all black Atlantans lived on or near sewerless, lightless, garbage-strewn, and unpaved streets, a daily reminder of their shared exclusion from the public life of the city.[3]

The Atlanta University neighborhood represented the implications of ghettoization most dramatically. Despite efforts stretching back to the nineteenth century to control residential development around the campuses, AU and Spelman and Morehouse Colleges, along with the homes of faculty members and the columned mansions of the city's wealthiest African Americans sat on hills overlooking the shacks that crowded the flood-prone "bottom" called Beaver Slide.[4] This neighborhood was never black Atlanta's worst district in terms of physical conditions or crime, and indeed

Beaver Slide prior to slum clearance. Atlanta University loomed above the neighborhood. (Charles Forrest Palmer Collection, Special Collections Department, Robert W. Woodruff Library, Emory University)

a report authored by W. E. B. Du Bois on the area emphasized that it was a "slum area because of poverty, and not by reason of vice or crime," pointing out that the only illicit behavior he found was "some playing of numbers and some gambling and drinking,"[5] activities found all over Atlanta.

Nevertheless, university leaders perceived Beaver Slide as a decided threat to the enclave of respectability and black citizenship that they were trying to establish around the colleges. According to one black reformer, the "poverty-stricken" life of Beaver Slide created a "marginal minded"[6] people, totally unsuited to the university community. Even more ominous, the "immorality" of some of Beaver Slide's residents concerned AU leaders worried about the continued respectability of the colleges. In 1925 the university and the Neighborhood Union formed a "Beaver Slide" committee with white police and law officials to control the area by cracking down on criminal activities. Florence Read, president of Spelman College, expressed the urgency of the university's struggle to control the neighborhood when she stated at a meeting that for thirty years only "combined moral force has kept Beaver Slide in confines."[7]

Such fears echoed white Atlantans' fear about the "cancer" of black

neighborhoods in general, and reflected black reformers' desire to redevelop the west side as an enclave of respectability. Since the 1920s, black
Atlantans with the will and the means had moved westward to separate
themselves physically from the overcrowded, poverty-stricken, and sometimes vice-ridden east side. By contrast, the west-side suburbs, with their
newer housing, empty land ripe for residential development, and proximity to the Atlanta University Center and Booker T. Washington High
School, represented an opportunity to join a burgeoning black community
in the gaze of solid black institutions, far from the madding crowd of the
east side.[8] Beginning during the acute black-housing shortage that immediately followed the First World War, real estate developers and agents, starting with the pioneering African American developer Heman Perry, realized the potential market for African American housing on the west side.
Working with the approval of the city's white officials, these entrepreneurs
and their customers risked the violent wrath of white west-siders by buying and building houses for the African American market at the frontier
of black expansion on Ashby Street. White elites had determined that the
west side would be conceded to African Americans and in fact, in the 1920s,
located Booker T. Washington High School at the center of the area of most
contention. Black Atlantans jumped at the opportunity this community expansion represented. By 1940, 40 percent of black Atlantans lived on the
west side.[9]

Westward migration intensified during the 1930s. Black developers such
as W. H. Aiken and white builders like attorney Edgar Craighead sold modern single-family homes on relatively large lots in housing developments
with paved streets, electricity, and sewers. These bungalows and two-story
homes set back from the street with their suburban yards could not have
been more different from other black housing in Atlanta. The growing
black middle class, of "ministers, doctors, dentists, teachers, government
workers, and outstanding citizens from the other walks of life," as the *ADW*
put it, long without the opportunity to live in "modern middle-class surroundings,"[10] rushed to purchase these new homes. "Step by step," W. H.
Aiken boasted, "I have set out to provide housing for these people."[11] His
campaign meant that by the end of the 1930s, the west side had become
synonymous with respectability, and the east side with the disreputable
"masses" left behind.

These neighborhoods were not middle class in the white sense. While
proportionately more white-collar and professional people lived in these
areas than Atlanta's other black districts, the area also became the destina-

tion of choice for many members of the striving working class of construction craftsmen and semiskilled workers and better-paid service and domestic workers who wished to escape the east side and live in respectable
surroundings as homeowners. For example, Ruby Blackburn, who worked
as a maid in the public schools, and her husband, Andrew, who worked as
a laborer, porter, and foundry coremaker during the 1930s, owned a home
on Simpson Street that they purchased in the early 1930s. W. H. Aiken
facilitated home ownership for workers such as the Blackburns by lobbying
the Federal Housing Administration to lower its building and loan requirements in its low-interest loan program, and to allow both husband and wife
to sign for payments. Thus he helped bring a large group of African Americans into the federal mortgage pool, which helped millions of Americans
achieve the dream of homeownership. Craighead encouraged this dream
privately in his Hunter Hills development by allowing purchasers to buy
$150 to $350 lots for "five dollars down, five dollars per month" and then,
once a certain percentage of the lot had been paid for, building homes for
low monthly payments.[12]

For many black Atlantans, the move to the west side was a great step
forward in their personal crusade for full citizenship and respectability. As
the *ADW* rather floridly described it, the new residents of Hunter Hills, "[a]
people 'Up From Slavery'" and "treading the wine press alone," had "so
impressed capital" with their "thrift, industry and effort to make genuine
American citizens," that developers had invested "thousands of dollars . . .
for better homes, street improvements, lights and sewerage for the comfort of deserving souls."[13] However, this idealized portrayal of the west
side was challenged by the reality of life there. While the district was less
crowded and had more decent housing than the east side, its residents still
contended with the white-imposed conditions that defined Jim Crow. Further, the area still contained pockets, including Beaver Slide, that belied
the progress trumpeted by the *ADW*'s editors. Unlike the white middle class,
AU elites and the west-side migrants could not ignore these sections because they were forced to live among them, a bitter reminder of their caste
position in relation to white Atlanta.

Unable to escape their poor and unrespectable neighbors, black reformers sought to uplift them. The Neighborhood Union emerged just out
of this impulse. According to longtime member and AU librarian Hallie
Brooks, "Dr. and Mrs Hope . . . bemoaned the fact that here were educational institutions surrounded by a slum, ghetto-type of community and
environment, and so she . . . started the Neighborhood Union to really

educate the people in . . . citizenship, sanitation, plus having a purpose of easing their lives."[14] These activists shared an environmentalist interpretation of respectability and social mobility, believing that the marginal position and condition of most black neighborhoods bred a "poverty complex"[15] in their residents that made them politically apathetic and satisfied with broken-down, overcrowded, and dirty living conditions. John Hope echoed his sentiment, remarking that Beaver Slide was "a condition of character, an economic condition, an educational and health condition." In short, for Hope, Beaver Slide was a "state of mind."[16] These commentators considered the sewerless, garbage-strewn, and shack-lined streets of black Atlanta to contribute directly to immoral and even criminal behavior, for example, linking the lack of "wholesome" public recreation in black neighborhoods and the surfeit of juke joints and pool halls to juvenile delinquency. Reformers also worried about the implications for sexual morals when families lived five or six to a bedroom, mixing parents with adolescent and young children. "What chance have young people to preserve any modesty," asked an instructor at the Atlanta School of Social Work, "amid such degrading home conditions?"[17]

In response, for decades elite black reformers had engaged in private rescue efforts to make black communities tidy, clean, and moral. One of the most venerable of these efforts was the annual Negro Health Week. Originated in 1915 by Booker T. Washington, every April black social-service agencies brought health-education and clean-up campaigns to black communities nationwide. In Atlanta, the black division of the Atlanta Tuberculosis Association usually coordinated the campaign with help from the Neighborhood Union and the ASSW. While Negro Health Week in Atlanta always included some kind of clinic or inoculation effort, its most visible focus was cleaning up black neighborhoods and black people. Organizers led efforts to pick up trash in alleys and vacant lots, to paint houses, and to beautify neighborhoods through the planting of flowers, trees, and vegetable gardens. Volunteers also organized parades and programs for children to instill in them the value of personal cleanliness and were vigilant against all forms of filth in the neighborhoods. For instance, during the 1934 Negro Health Week, chairperson Sudie Howard reported that her North-East Committee of the ATA "found a number of untidy boys on the streets and had taken them to the barber shop where they were given free hair cuts and warm baths."[18]

Other campaigns sought to improve the condition of black neighborhoods. Ruby Blackburn, for instance, the public school maid who had moved to the west side, was president of the TIC (To Improve Conditions)

Club, which initiated and supported many campaigns during the 1930s to modernize and beautify the black community. She lobbied local leaders to remove a public dump from the west side. She promoted a plan shared by white clubwomen to plant dogwood trees and crepe myrtle bushes in order to beautify the city. She and her members worked with local utilities to bring electricity, sewers, paved streets, and public transportation to the new black neighborhoods, and they lobbied the Board of Education to reopen a previously white school for black students in order to ease classroom overcrowding on the west side. The TIC Club's letterhead illustrated Blackburn's dream: one side featured a "before" image of a broken-down shack and its downcast residents, representing marginal black neighborhoods, while the other presented an "after" drawing of an idealized suburban home and its forward-looking owners.[19]

These private efforts to improve existing African American neighborhoods were all part of an effort to demonstrate black citizenship through respectability in face of white-imposed conditions that denied that possibility. It was a Sisyphean struggle, however, and in fact demonstrated black reformers' powerlessness. No section of the black community could be truly respectable when the city refused to recognize its residents' citizenship by collecting their garbage. But with the announcement of the slum-clearance program for the neighborhood surrounding Atlanta University, black reformers could overcome these roadblocks to their goals. The federal government would sidestep the city's indifference by building a black neighborhood with a full complement of modern city services where only the most respectable black Atlantans would live.

Thus, two deeply entwined impulses motivated Atlanta's black housing reformers. One was to redevelop the Atlanta University neighborhood into an enclave of respectability and prosperity, distant from the degrading influence of "slums" and their inhabitants. The other was to rehabilitate the environment of black neighborhoods in an effort to uplift their residents into full citizenship. While the first impulse necessarily led to the development of the second during the "nadir" of Jim Crow, the New Deal housing program made manifest the latent contradiction between these two goals, the first of which sought to distance Atlanta's respectable few from the "masses" who imperiled the university community, and the second of which sought to uplift poor black Atlantans through their contact with the university and its leadership. The limits of the slum-clearance and low-income-housing program, and the unavoidable triage that resulted in choosing who would benefit from it, established the primacy of the first goal and almost entirely sacrificed the second. However, black reformers'

T. I. C.

To Improve Conditions

Office of the President
1102 Simpson Road, N. W.
Atlanta, Georgia

BEFORE

AFTER

OFFICERS:

MRS. RUBY BLACKBURN,
PRES.

MRS. LUDIE·SMITH,
VICE·PRES.

MRS. JUANITA HARRIS,
RECORDING SECRETARY

B. E. HILL,
CORR. SECRETARY

MRS. LUM HARDEMAN,
TREASURER

MRS. FRANCIS FOUCH,
REPORTER

MRS. PEARL REESE,
BUSINESS MANAGER

The TIC club was organized by Mrs. Ruby Blackburn
and a group of seven women. This small group of
people with the determination to improve conditions
in the community in which they lived named the club TIC
meaning to improve conditions. The club has been exceedingly suc
successful in its program it has secured the removal of
an unsightly and unhealthy dump, given scholorships to
worothy students, completed a beautification project
in planting crepemurtles and dogwoods on Atlanta sidewalks
donated to worothy organizations. The club also secured
a school in the Pine acre section and has been working for
bus service for the westside for a number of years
but has not been successful yet. The club has been
instrumental in getting another city school namely the
Davis St. school, which was to be ready by the first of
the year but will be used now to house the junior high school
students that were ousted by the fire at booker T. Washington
high school Friday. The club is now working to establish
a day nursery for the children of working mothers. The
membership of this club has grown into the hundreds.
The theme song of this club is Trees the colors are red
and white- the motto is "Be ashamed to die until you
have done something for humanity."

The TIC Club's letterhead reflected black Atlantans' linking of good housing with citizenship and respectability. (Ruby Blackburn Collection, Auburn Avenue Research Library) elitism and the opportunities the projects presented for black uplift meant that they accepted and applauded federal policy with few reservations and in fact participated actively in implementing it.

In order to understand black reformers' accomplishment in using the federal housing program to their own ends, we need first to place it within the context of the federal and local development politics that shaped the program in its early years. Much confusion surrounds the beginnings of public housing in the New Deal. Despite its explicit connection today to be a shelter of last resort for the utterly destitute, public housing in the 1930s was intended to provide employment to a devastated construction industry, build citizenship and community, and provide low-cost shelter for Americans who could use it as a stepping stone to home ownership. In other words, it was not a poverty program. As Lawrence Friedman pointed out in the 1960s, American low-income housing policy has always been driven by two competing aims. Primarily and most popularly, it has been propelled by fears of slums' social cost, or the idea that these areas presented threats to health, social order, and the body politic that extended far from the neighborhoods themselves. This was the notion that Charles Palmer so skillfully used in selling the low-income-housing program to white Atlantans. The second impulse was the social-welfare benefit that would accrue to the poor were they provided with low-cost and decent housing. This idea was always a harder sell because only the poor—a group even in the Depression largely perceived as "undeserving"—would benefit from such a program. The idea of housing as welfare only succeeded during the 1930s when a large proportion of "deserving" middle-class and upwardly mobile Americans had lost their footing, and many their houses, and would take any help they could in reestablishing themselves. Given these political realities, the first public-housing projects were aimed explicitly at the "middle third" of the American housing market, not at the bottom, and very rarely rehoused the people they displaced through slum clearance.[20]

A policy to raze the social menace of the slums while providing housing to the submerged or potential middle class exactly fit the aims of Atlanta University's leaders, who first initiated the housing program in 1933. The university project, like Techwood, originated as part of the PWA's short-lived, limited-dividend-corporation housing program in which local groups created slum-clearance and low-income-housing corporations and then applied for housing loans and grants from the federal government. In

1933, engineer O. I. Freeman and architect W. J. Sayward submitted a proposal to John Hope for the redevelopment of Beaver Slide. Hope was extremely enthusiastic and worked with AU's trustees and benefactors to put the structures in place to take advantage of the program. In 1934 he created a biracial board of trustees whose white members were all prominent liberals, including Florence Read; Will W. Alexander of the Commission of Interracial Cooperation (CIC); Kendall Weisiger, assistant to the president of Southern Bell Telegraph and Telephone Company; and Dean Sage, New York philanthropist and chair of AU's board of trustees. The black group was a conservative one, comprised of prominent business people and professionals including A. T. Walden, attorney and president of the local NAACP, who was later replaced by funeral director David T. Howard; L. D. Milton, co-owner of Yates and Milton Pharmacy, vice president of the Citizen's Trust Company, and chair of AU's Business and Economics department; E. M. Martin, secretary of Atlanta Life Insurance Company; and S. W. Walker, vice president of the Pilgrim Life Insurance Company.[21]

AU's plan was not the only one for African Americans to emerge at this time; a competing scheme sponsored by white real estate interests submitted an alternative proposal to raze "Dark Town," arguably the city's poorest and most rundown black neighborhood, wedged between the central business district and the State Capitol on the city's near east side. Due to a strenuous lobbying effort by the AU committee, the PWA never considered this option seriously, even given its more obvious suitability for "slum" clearance than the university neighborhood.[22]

As this example demonstrates, like white elites, AU used the federal government as a tool to achieve its goals for the black community against other interests. The university's victory also demonstrates how its leaders' role as brokers for and manager of the black community was transferred from the local to the federal realm during the New Deal. John Hope had chosen shrewdly in including the CIC's Will Alexander for the housing committee. Alexander, a white liberal, had the ear of Clark Foreman, the ex-Atlantan who was the Interior Department's, and consequently the PWA's, adviser on Negro affairs. Alexander promoted the university project on the basis of the role AU could play in the project's success. As Alexander wrote Foreman, "The fact that the university sponsors the project gives it a chance of permanent direction." He continued that those "who are sponsoring the AU project have, for a generation, been known for their interest in Negro welfare in this city, and they have no political or real estate connections."[23]

Secretary of the Interior Harold Ickes addresses the crowd at the 1934 inauguration of slum clearance in Beaver Slide while Atlanta University president John Hope (third from right) looks on. (*Atlanta University Bulletin*, July 1936, p. 10, Robert W. Woodruff Library, Atlanta University Center)

In fact, Alexander's intercession demonstrated that the AU *did* have political connections—to the New Deal administration. These links strengthened when the PWA took over control of the limited-dividend scheme soon after the agency approved the university project. Even though local white officials had great latitude in choosing the location for slum clearance and the new housing, once the projects were approved they were under the firm control of the agency's Housing Division and, ultimately, the iron fist of the PWA's head, Harold Ickes. While everyone from national housing visionaries to local white political leaders complained about Ickes's dictatorial ways, African American reformers did not. They liked the fact that the federal government, and particularly the liberal Ickes, exerted such control because it provided them with a powerful ally to protect and promote their interests in their battles against local whites who would exclude or exploit them. Thus, under Ickes's leadership, more than one-third of PWA project units nationwide were earmarked for black families.

The PWA's support for black housing extended beyond earmarking units for African Americans to ideological commitments shared by AU's housing reformers about the projects' potential importance for racial uplift. The PWA Housing Division's commitment to help the "deserving" poor was a fundamental aspect of this partnership, as was its community-building aims. In its early days, the Housing Division conducted an extensive national public-relations campaign promoting the then-novel idea of building housing in complexes that would comprise "complete neighborhoods"[24] rather than erecting individual apartment buildings or houses. Not only were such schemes more economical than traditional building patterns, the PWA maintained, but also they would promote and strengthen community and citizenship along with providing decent shelter. These community-building goals are what lay behind the clearance-to-rebuild model implemented by the PWA's modernist housing visionaries. Such thinking had particular appeal for African Americans who, nationwide, suffered ghettoization's overcrowded and overpriced housing conditions. Nonprofit public housing would erase this exploitation.

More specific to black Atlantans, Harold Ickes and his Negro Affairs advisers, first Foreman, then the black economist Robert Weaver, recognized the AU committee as an ally and used University Homes as a national showcase for the housing program as an instrument of economic and social incorporation for deserving African Americans. Thus, working with the AU advisory committee and the local Urban League, the PWA initiated one of the federal government's first antidiscrimination programs, which compelled building contractors, first in Atlanta and then elsewhere in the nation, to employ black skilled and unskilled construction workers for both black and white projects in numbers commensurate with African Americans' participation in the local job market. Further, after much anxiety and wrangling with local officials, the AU leveraged its influence with the PWA to ensure the project's management was placed in black hands handpicked by the university committee. In 1937, Alonzo Moron, a prominent social worker from the U.S. Virgin Islands with connections to Lugenia Burns Hope, Robert Weaver, and Eleanor Roosevelt led University Homes' management staff of a dozen black professionals.[25]

The local white elite also proved to be a valuable ally in the housing program, even though black reformers were at first understandably chary of Charles Palmer and his cronies, given these white boosters' racialist promotion of slum clearance and low-income housing. However, Charles Palmer and his group wanted black housing development on the west side just as the AU committee did, and his vigorous support of the university scheme led to the beginning of an unprecedented partnership between black and white elites. After the Atlanta Housing Authority was formed, the alliance strengthened, providing powerful and politically invulnerable support for black expansion on the west side against white working-class opposition. This cooperation meant that even with the AHA's creation, its white administration consulted black housing leaders about project location on the west side, and African American staff ran the black projects and chose their tenants.[26]

With powerful allies in place, university leaders could dare to be ambitious about their vision for the renewal of their community as it related to the development of the university. For Atlanta University, the housing project represented not so much a chance to rehouse the poor residents of Beaver Slide as an opportunity to remove them and their neighborhood in order to elevate the AU community. In other words, they subscribed to the social-cost concept for slum clearance and low-income housing. John Hope saw the federal program as a chance to achieve his long-held dream of transforming the neighborhood around the university into a respectable, middle-class enclave, a neighborhood befitting the best black schools in the United States. This vision was an extension of his plan to create a consortium of all the city's postsecondary institutions on the west side. In Hope's conception, the neighborhood would be filled with ambitious and law-abiding people free from the ghettoization's exploitation and unshackled to realize their ambitions for a better life. Hope envisioned residents living in a project that would be "straight and clean and full of light,"[27] with a full complement of city services and the prestige and protection that went along with association with the university community. For Hope and the University Homes committee, a housing project would create a protective federal umbrella in the neighborhood under which Atlanta's most respectable black residents could find shelter from Jim Crow and the immorality they believed it spawned.

Before this vision could be realized, the threatening "slum" had to be excised and "slum dwellers" extradited. In promoting the area around the university for slum clearance to the PWA, Hope elucidated his dream:

It seems to me that for present advantage and for guaranteed future advantage no Negro neighborhood in America is quite so promising for a Negro housing project as the one in the neighborhood of Atlanta University. So far as helping to relieve the slums is concerned, there is a wretched slums condition within the bounds of the University Housing Project which is not only bad in itself but threatens one of the best Negro neighborhoods in the South. . . . Where you have such a remarkable association of slums and higher advantages, it does occur to me that here is the place to get rid of the slums and give one Negro neighborhood in this city opportunity for untrammeled development.[28]

In other words, he wanted to create the first black neighborhood in the city that represented the citizenship of its respectable residents.

In order to achieve this goal, university leaders were especially concerned about the type of people who would inhabit the project. The advisory committee talked openly about Beaver Slide's demolition as resulting in a "better University community,"[29] according to Florence Read. They meant not only that slum clearance would eliminate a run-down neighborhood, but also that the project would be out of the reach of all but the highest echelons of black Atlanta. In fact, federal officials criticized AU's first proposed plan as "grandiose" because "it did not bring the housing accommodations within the reach of the people who needed them,"[30] even within the federal government's limited notion of eligibility.

Alternatively, university reformers wished to house only those black workers whom they believed could appreciate the benefits of housing and who would bring credit to the neighborhood. The housing committee outlined its objectives in the minutes of one of its early meetings: "[The] University wishes to serve [the] wage earning class who have sufficient ambition, character and skill to have steady employment under anything like normal conditions," the minutes recorded. "Select on the basis of their desire to live in the neighborhood of the University both because they appreciate the general atmosphere and will contribute something."[31] Engineers Sayward and Freeman thought the fact that federal rental rates would still keep the housing out of the hands of all but "the frugal, industrious, and deserving" was a decidedly good thing because "a [housing] development for their benefit would render a real service in reward for effort, encourage advancement, and prove economically sound."[32]

In addition, the housing advocates wanted "the highest class" of African Americans to be represented in the projects. According to Read, the university committee believed that "a sprinkling" of black professionals "would help to do what we desire in the community"[33] by setting an example for which humbler residents could strive. At one point early in negotiations, the committee responded favorably to Freeman and Sayward's suggestion that the apartments built immediately adjacent to the colleges be "of a more attractive type than the general development," and presumably of a higher rent, thereby serving "as a protection to the University Campus."[34]

While AU leaders envisioned the University Homes' slum-clearance and public-housing project as eliminating slum dwellers from the university's midst, many members of Atlanta's burgeoning black social-work community had a decidedly different vision for the program. This group whole-heartedly supported locating the project near AU, not to remove Beaver Slide and its residents but to rehouse them or people like them and to expose them to the edifying moral influence of the university community. While their rhetoric was full of the same definitions of black respectability as those of AU leaders, black social workers' community-building vision for the project was explicitly more wide reaching and transformative, even radical. They hoped that the resources and services of the federal government and the university would redeem the poorest black Atlantans by removing and protecting them from the racial and class exploitation which kept them from respectability, and hence, from full citizenship.

Unlike the university group whose members wished to use the project to protect AU, members of this group wished to use the university to protect project residents; social workers' descriptions of the project frequently wrote of it being "bounded," or "surrounded," by the Atlanta University Center institutions, thereby shielding it from the encroachment of slums and from any distractions that might keep tenants from participating in their own uplift. This was a crucial, if fine, distinction. It eluded the closely linked members of the AU advisory committee and leaders of Atlanta's social work community who worked as if they believed their aims were in concert. For many others in these groups it remained an unresolved contradiction in their own minds, with one impulse dominating the other but without excluding either. Nevertheless, the social workers' dominant perspective represented their continuing belief in the uplift possibilities of public housing as an instrument of social welfare.

This vision for the project was the embodiment of the long tradition of racial uplift through social rehabilitation in the Atlanta University neighborhood. For social workers, the housing project seemed to be the culmination of their efforts. In fact, Neighborhood Union members believed the housing project was "a God send to them in that it was a realization of one of their pet schemes"[35] to improve the university neighborhood. The NU's members rejoiced because the housing program solved black social workers' persistent dilemma of finding a willing constituency for their efforts by bringing at least some black Atlantans out of the shadows of the narrow streets and alleys of their "slums" into black-managed public-housing projects, where they could become a captive audience to the edifying efforts of black reformers. In praising the housing program, the editors of the black *Atlanta Daily World* (*ADW*) explained that in the past the "group pulling heavy on our average was almost wholly out of our reach." With most black Atlantans living "clustered in alleys, poorly numbered as kept, with no system for social activity or control," it claimed that "much of our possibility has been allowed to go to the wind." By contrast, housing projects would "bring in the open the great task before us" and allow the "social, political, and religious worker to tackle in daylight the problems confronting the group."[36]

No wonder, then, that black housing reformers embraced the Housing Division's intention to build the projects as "long term investments with wise and kindly management and not as speculative developments whose sponsors care only for quick sale and getting out from under."[37] For them, it was not enough merely to give tenants better living conditions. Slum dwellers who were conditioned to accept, according to black sociologist Walter Chivers, "overcrowded sleeping, the immodesty of community toilets, the lack of modern bathing facilities, et cetera," would "tend to reduce any kind of housing project or higher standard neighborhood to a slum"[38] unless they were supervised to live up to their new environment. Consequently, the project's management should represent, in the words of the Atlanta Urban League, "a corporate fatherly body to direct the entire project and give it a program of community and social service planning,"[39] which would bring tenants into full citizenship. For example, Frankie Adams, the "group work" specialist on the faculty of ASSW, argued for supervised recreation for the projects: "You have heard it [said] here that leadership supervision is important; you have heard it [said] too that [recreation] can build good citizenship. Just [to] plan [for] providing space for people to play in and nobody there to see how they play— it certainly doesn't [develop] citizenship."[40] These visions for the housing project point to the pent-up aspirations of black reformers in Atlanta, aspirations unleashed by the federal government's announcement that it would spend undreamed-of millions in the black community. Like Atlanta University's leaders, black social workers in Atlanta saw the project as their own, not as the federal government's or white elites'. For them, it was as an extraordinary opportunity to fulfill long-held goals for the development of black Atlanta's neighborhoods and, importantly, their residents.

W. E. B. Du Bois, recently returned to Atlanta University in 1934 as chair-person of AU's sociology department and mentor to NU leaders and many black social workers, most clearly articulated this vision of the project as an instrument of community uplift when University Homes was still in its planning phases. He compared the sociological survey he made of Beaver Slide to the pioneering Atlanta University Conferences for the Study of the Negro Problem he spearheaded during his first tenure at AU at the turn of the century. Some of the first sociological studies of African American life emerged out of these meetings, and according to Du Bois these efforts had prompted "a great interest among Atlanta Negroes in social work," leading to the formation of the Neighborhood Union and other voluntary efforts in the city, and ultimately to the creation of the School of Social Work. Simi-larly, his survey of Beaver Slide would guide social-work activism in the project. By making "a study of the people living in the area before it was cleared," he and his students had ascertained "the exact type of commu-nity which the cleared area represented, their income and expenditures" and, most important, "their demands in the matter of housing and other facilities."[41]

Du Bois believed that Beaver Slide's families could benefit enormously from public housing and the potential social services that would accom-pany it. He envisioned the project as an all-black enclave where tenants would be uplifted by services previously denied to them. For example, he called for a cinema in University Homes because he saw film as an emerg-ing "source of education both for children and adults." Du Bois did not want African Americans to miss this opportunity, and so he hoped that a "light, beautiful and airy" project theater could replace the "old, dirty, and unsanitary" black movie houses that promoted the "worst aspects of commercial control of moving pictures." Private cinemas in African Ameri-can neighborhoods, he wrote, kept all but "the worst and most salacious pictures" from their patrons.[42]

Du Bois's desire to shield project inhabitants from the capitalist exploita-tion they had suffered in their old neighborhoods extended to his elaborate scheme for consumer cooperatives in the project. He envisioned Fulton County's black farmers providing food for the tenants, laundry-worker ten-ants doing all the washing for the homes, and communal food preparation eliminating the expense of restaurant meals for the tenants.[43] He believed that this kind of cooperative black economy marked a positive step toward economic development and "independent action" on the part of African Americans against "race prejudice" made worse by the crisis of the Depres-sion. He believed that blacks should see cooperatives as "a new method

for protecting themselves by the very segregation of which they are victims; that they concentrate . . . consuming power for mass buying. . . . I
believe it has clear possibilities of success . . . if it eliminates the private
profit motive."[44]

The prospect of creating a self-sufficient and self-sustained black community at University Homes excited Du Bois because it gave him the opportunity to see one of his most cherished schemes come to fruition. Portrayed most often as the consummate integrationist, in the 1920s and 1930s
Du Bois began calling with growing urgency for the creation of a separate black economy. Du Bois believed this path to be the only pragmatic
option for African Americans, who had seen their opportunities dwindle,
rather than expand, in the decades after Emancipation. Along with eliminating racial exploitation, the parallel black economy envisioned by Du
Bois would also eradicate capitalist profiteering at the expense of black
workers. In Du Bois's black economy, the welfare of the cooperative's producers and consumers, and not individual profit, motivated and guided
production. Hence, cooperative members as producers could exercise their
vocational aspirations unimpeded by Jim Crow and as consumers could
avoid the usurious prices and shoddy merchandise of unscrupulous retail-
ers. By shielding African Americans from white supremacy through a separate economy, and by reorganizing that economy to eliminate capitalist
abuses, Du Bois believed he had found the key to racial uplift.

University Homes represented this separatist cooperative vision on a
small scale. Du Bois's scheme found enthusiastic support among other
housing reformers in Atlanta and Washington, D.C. His vision represented
the broad ideological aims of the progressives who founded the Housing
Division with the aim of building self-contained communities. Some of
these bureaucrats concurred with Du Bois's vision for University Homes
and proposed an "economically self-contained"[45] project where tenants
would barter goods and services among themselves and where many tenants would not go out to work but, rather, would serve the good of the
community as doctors and laundry workers, teachers and cooks. Other
visions for the project were less ambitious but nonetheless stressed that
cooperation and communal living would benefit black workers. Robert
Weaver wanted laundry facilities in the project to be large enough so that
home laundry workers (who comprised a full fifth of black Atlanta's female
labor force) could do their work outside of their apartments, thus improving the "cleanliness and comfort in the laundresses' homes." More important, he believed that such an arrangement would "allay the prejudice"

against home laundries that commercial laundries, in a successful bid for the laundresses' white clientele, had labeled as unclean. Thus he would modernize the work of home laundry workers to the level of commercial establishments while at the same time protecting these workers from the new types of racial discrimination emerging from the industrial order. Similarly, Weaver envisioned a sewing room and carpentry shop that, in addition to allowing tenants to economize, would introduce workers to modern machines and techniques, making their products competitive with factory-made clothing and furniture.[46]

This radical vision for University Homes contrasted sharply with the AU committee, whose members more pragmatically sought the redemption of a deserving few through public housing, rather than a transformation of the polity. For Du Bois, respectability and full citizenship could only come to African Americans with a second Reconstruction in which the black "masses" were not only included as full participants in society, but indeed were at its center. And while his vision still saw the black elite as guiding and directing the uplift that was to result, the main beneficiaries would be the poorest members of the black community, who had suffered the most from capitalist and racial exploitation. Thus, for Du Bois, inclusion in University Homes did not represent the salvation of the redeemable few from the degradation of the "slums." Rather, it represented a fundamental democratizing shift in American society that would finally allow all African Americans to achieve racial uplift.

Atlanta's black social workers found support for their schemes among the vocal left wing of the American housing-reform community. Theirs was a distinctly African American version of the redemptive objectives of national organizations such as the National Public Housing Conference (NPHC), also dominated by social and settlement workers, which lobbied for a massive government public-housing program to rehouse America's very poorest city dwellers and to eliminate slums.[47] Despite support from some PWA Housing Division and Interior Department officials, this vision was always the less politically tenable one, and became even more unlikely as the housing program came to fruition. When the PWA first formulated its national slum-clearance and low-income-housing program, it intended that the rents from the new developments pay back only 55 percent of the building costs amortized over sixty years. The federal government would pay the other 45 percent as a grant. In this way, some federal housing officials believed they could house some tenants with very low incomes and provide them with various facilities and social services. In February of

1936, however, the comptroller general of the United States ruled that such grants were illegal and that all project costs would have to be recouped by the rents.[48]

Legislation also constrained the possibilities for social services in the projects. The Wagner-Steagall Act of 1937 decentralized the housing program to local housing authorities which received yearly grants from the newly created U.S. Housing Authority (USHA), thus removing the influence of the visionary housing reformers who worked for the PWA. In addition, the act strengthened the policy that rents had to meet the projects' operating costs. The legislation's features had two other important implications. First, the rent policy restricted tenancy to those who could afford it and indeed barred the unemployed completely. Consequently, those displaced by slum clearance were hardly ever eligible to find housing at the site of their old homes. Second, local housing authorities, including Atlanta's, had great leverage over the administration of their housing, including using the federally set maximum tenant income as their minimum, thus reserving housing for a very narrow slice of the populace.[49]

These policies had serious ramifications for University Homes. It meant that the economic motives superseded all others in the minds of government officials, who almost immediately scrapped all of the visionary plans for the projects. Atlanta's social-work community had no recourse, even at the local level, since AU did not invite a social-work advocate to join the advisory committee, which was dominated by conservative business leaders most interested in protecting the university through neighborhood redevelopment.

This exclusion, and the cementing of federal policy, had most direct implications for the Neighborhood Union. In fact, the University Homes project was directly responsible for the demise of the agency as an effective and independent social-welfare agency.[50] When the University Homes project was announced, the NU assumed its advocacy role and began lobbying the federal government to include social rehabilitation programs in its plans for the project. Even though slum clearance would destroy the union's headquarters, members were reassured by the PWA's promise that it would build them a new Neighborhood House in the project and rent to them for a nominal fee. They hoped this new setup would allow them to expand their program, envisioning a center large enough to contain an auditorium, gymnasium, and perhaps even a swimming pool available to the entire black community. However, with cost-cutting federal legislation, social-welfare schemes for proposed projects were eliminated. The Neighborhood Union's community house was scrapped from plans for Univer-

sity Homes. Lugenia Hope attempted to resurrect the center through direct appeals to federal "black cabinet" leader Mary McLeod Bethune and
to Eleanor Roosevelt, but it was never built. Instead, the Neighborhood
Union purchased another house west of University Homes and revived its
activities. The union, however, never became more than a shadow of its
former self. Although it continued its clinic, the Neighborhood Union became more of a social club than a social-welfare agency, raising money for
various causes but never again spearheading activities as it once had.[51]

The Neighborhood Union's demise marked the end of an era and of a
vision. The building of University Homes, the fulfillment of Neighborhood
Union's agitation for government responsibility for black citizens, had the
ironic result of making the union redundant. Its mission and activities
were assumed by government welfare agencies. Moreover, the community
house debacle at University Homes demonstrated what was lost with the
shifting of welfare responsibility from the autonomous black control of private agencies and charities like the Neighborhood Union to public agencies
with their competing constituencies and interests.[52]

Yet even before regulations required that PWA projects be self-
liquidating, indeed from the planning stages of the project, the Housing
Division intended for University Homes to be out of reach of the majority of
black Atlantans. Government officials wanted to whittle the tenant population down to those who had a "reputation as desirable neighbors." As
one PWA official told an Atlanta newspaper: "We propose to humanize our
methods of selecting tenants and get into those buildings persons who deserve to live there." He elaborated by saying that the government built the
projects to "provide homes for that element of the population who deserve
and appreciate good homes and good surroundings but cannot afford to
pay the prices of privately-owned apartments or homes."[53]

This policy, while shared by the AU advisory group, was not a consensus position in the national public-housing community at the time. In a
scathing critique, the NPHC condemned the PWA Housing Division for barring from Techwood Homes, by income, those who had once lived in the
Tech Flats slum. The NPHC believed that the Housing Division should make
as its first priority the housing of former residents. Without such a policy,
it believed, "the net result will be the creation of new substandard areas
by the economic needs of former residents dispossessed by clearance and
construction."[54] Eleanor Roosevelt, too, in a surprise visit to the University
Homes site, praised the project but criticized it for not providing housing
at sufficiently low rent for average black families.[55]

Official rhetoric and press reports, both black and white, downplayed these criticisms and the elitism of the housing program in Atlanta. They portrayed those chosen to live in the projects as generic "slum dwellers," those Atlantans who most needed to be rehoused. They never mentioned that none of the ex-residents of the slum-clearance areas found housing in the projects. Black reformers, no matter their convictions, were loathe to criticize a program that they all agreed recognized Atlanta's black community like no other, especially at the insecure time when responsibility for public housing was about to devolve from the federal government to a local authority. Therefore, they almost never publicly challenged the evasions about the program, but when they did, the heated exchanges that resulted exposed the divisions in black reformers' expectations of what the projects should become.

Forrester B. Washington, president of ASSW, was one of those to dispute the rhetoric. In a 1938 speech at Morehouse College where he acknowledged that he was "treading on delicate ground," Washington criticized government and university committee claims about the project's achievements and "ridiculed to the point of sarcasm" the idea that the project had in any way helped poor black Atlantans. In fact, he felt that the housing program had made their living situations even more precarious by evicting them from their homes and tightening the housing market even further. He contended that "[l]awyers, doctors, preachers and teachers were the professions well represented" in black housing projects around the country, including in Atlanta, because the poor could not afford any apartments except the smallest ones, and that their large families usually disqualified them from those. Washington believed that the government should subsidize public housing even further so that the poor who really needed the housing could be accommodated. He pointed to European government housing as an alternative model, and proposed a similar scheme for the United States. Wealthier African Americans, he continued, should be housed by the private sector.[56]

Alonzo Moron, manager of University Homes, attended Washington's talk. His response to Washington's criticisms, both on the night of the speech and later in a front-page article in the ADW, unveiled the meaning behind the Atlanta University committee's rhetoric. Moron did not deny that University Homes housed black professionals instead of the poorest black Atlantans. But he contended that "the members of the professions" housed in the project were "not by any means in the high income group," reminding Washington of the teachers' ongoing fight for equal salaries, so that they could finally earn a "living wage."[57] And Moron cited Du Bois's report on the University Homes slum-clearance area to show that not only the poorest black Atlantans lived in that "slum." Using Du Bois's statistic that Beaver Slide families earned from less than two dollars to over fifty dollars a week, with an average of around ten dollars a week, Moron sought to show that black neighborhoods did not only house the poor, but a diversity of income groups. "Perhaps this is an exceptional case," he wrote, "but select any slum area of equal size and see for yourself if all the people residing in this area are on the same social or economic level."[58]

Moron admonished Washington for not acknowledging the good that the projects had done for the black community as a whole and told him that the question of the project's value should be answered by the tenants and all other black Atlantans who had and would benefit from it. He told Washington to ask the "hundreds" of black construction workers who found work building the project in the depths of the Depression, and the additional hundreds of white- and blue-collar workers who, he predicted, would find jobs running University Homes "at a time when new fields of employment are needed to absorb our college graduates, our mechanics, and our unemployed laborers."[59]

Moron's answer to Washington exposed the raison d'être of University Homes. Local government officials and the AU committee never intended the project to help lift the poorest black Atlantans out of the depths of their poverty; instead, they intended it to serve respectable members of the black community through housing and jobs. The poor meant to be housed were those upwardly mobile black workers and professionals who, had they been white, would have been middle class, but, because of occupational, residential, and educational segregation, had been barred from the jobs, equal salaries, and housing commensurate with their social position. Further, the projects would give employment to this same group, "our college graduates, our mechanics, and our unemployed laborers," in an all-black enclave that would allow a chosen group of African Americans to achieve their full potential. Such motivations for the program suggest that the New Deal's social democracy was not simply racialized; rather, it began the process, so evident today, of dividing the black community into those who were deserving of full inclusion into the polity, including the enormous expansion of political and economic rights in the decades following the New Deal, and those who continued to be consigned to the margins of civil society. In the 1930s, however, the relative poverty and substandard living conditions of all African Americans obscured these divisions within the black community. In comparison to white Atlantans, the city's black residents were all poor slum dwellers. Thus Forrester B. Washington bit his tongue after his debate with Moron, effectively ending the debate on the issue among Atlanta's black reformers. After all, most black reformers reasoned pragmatically that in a Jim Crow city even a very limited public-housing program would provide enormous benefit to its black tenants, no matter who they were.

The social workers' acceptance of this reality also pointed out the contradictions of the politics of respectability. While they subscribed to Du Bois's vision for the project as an ideal, they also often accepted individual behavioral explanations for the reasons for black marginality. Sociologist Walter Chivers's rhetoric reflected this paradox. A Morehouse sociology professor and a key adviser to the Neighborhood Union, he offered astute Du Boisian analyses of the social and economic structures that kept African Americans in their place at the bottom of the economy. He fought throughout his career to open black occupational opportunities, particularly for those in the most "servile" positions like domestic workers. However, he also worked on the 1920s committee to crack down on crime in Beaver Slide, and believed that African Americans had not "attained maturity" or the "American 'way of life'" because they were a "marginal-minded racial group" that needed to be "taught to want adequate living."[60] Given such an understanding of African Americans' plight and the limits of the housing program, black social workers accepted that those black Atlantans most amenable to the politics of respectability should have first dibs at public housing and the redemptive possibilities it represented.

These ideological paradoxes silenced black reformers from responding to federal and local policies for the housing program that had enormous implications for Atlanta's black community. The defeat of the social workers' vision for the project meant that thousands of black Atlantans were further marginalized by slum clearance while another group favored by inclusion in the housing program found themselves on the road to fuller citizenship. Slum clearance for Techwood and University Homes displaced hundreds of black families, none of whom found housing in the projects built on top of their old neighborhoods. Although both federal officials and the University Committee had suggested at various points that some provision be made to help the displaced to relocate, this group's wellbeing was never a priority, and no provision or compensation was ever instituted. Instead, as the *ADW* editorialized, residents of Beaver Slide "quietly 'folded their tents like the Arabs'" with the announcement of slum clearance. "Out of those hundreds of poor souls whose shoes carried the mud from Beaver Slide wherever they went," it continued, "none returned when the housing unit was completed for residence as far as we can learn."[61] Nor did anyone bother to track their relocation.

The Atlanta Housing Authority addressed this public-relations problem by creating a bureau to find new homes for the more than 2,500 black families displaced by its prewar slum-clearance projects. However, gross inequities continued to be embedded in Atlanta's housing program. Black AHA staffers only chose a handful of ex-residents to live in the new black housing projects, only black neighborhoods were destroyed in the slum-clearance program, and the thousands of African Americans who lost their homes to make way for the AHA's Clark Howell and Capitol Homes were barred entirely from residency in these all-white projects.[62]

Further, the PWA's national income policies for public housing also discriminated against poor black Atlantans. For the purposes of the housing program, the government defined "low income" families as those earning less than between $1,000 and $1,500, depending on their size. However, this definition was grossly off-target for African Americans in Atlanta, and indeed throughout the South. In Atlanta, black families earning $1,000 were an exception. A 1937 study of family income sponsored by the U.S. Labor Department determined that fully four-fifths of black families earned less than $1,000 in the city, and that half of black families in Atlanta earned $550 per year or less. Furthermore, W. E. B. Du Bois showed in his study of the University Homes slum-clearance area that of 235 families reporting, forty-one had incomes of less than $5 per week, and that sixty-nine had no income at all and depended on relief, thereby shutting them out of public housing altogether.[63]

Despite the very low income of black families in Atlanta, the PWA accepted applicants for University Homes who earned up to $1,800 a year. And while the project's management constantly boasted that the project housed families with annual incomes as low as $416, when the project was three-quarters full, 60 percent of the tenants had a family income of between $572 and $780, thus exceeding the income of most of Atlanta's black families. At least one tenant family earned $1,924 a year, exceeding even PWA income limits. Overall, tenant incomes were even higher, with the average for 1937 at $990 per year, and the average for tenants renting the cheapest two-room units at $742. Even with these relatively high tenant incomes, most were technically too low for the project; the cheapest two-room apartment in University Homes rented for $16 a month, and required a monthly income of five times that—$80 a month or $960 per year. Perhaps the most telling statistic regarding the inaccessibility of University Homes to the majority of black families was that, despite the acute housing shortage for black Atlantans of all incomes, forty-five of the largest apartments of four and five rooms remained empty six months after the project was opened. These apartments rented for around $30 a month, and thus required a monthly income of $120 or a yearly income of $1,440.[64]

In 1938, this situation improved somewhat when the U.S. Housing Authority authorized a rent decrease in its public-housing projects. Charles Palmer claimed that the rent reduction meant that all but 13 percent of black families in Atlanta could afford a unit in University Homes. Yet despite this improved accessibility, project managers permitted those tenants who now earned too much for their apartments to move into larger apartments or to remain in their units if they continued to pay the initial rent, instead of vacating them for poorer families. This policy contrasted markedly to the one which forced University Home tenants hurt by the economic recession of the winter of 1938 to move out of their apartments less than a year after moving in because of their reduced or lost income. By 1939, the average tenant family's annual income had only dropped to $952, barring far more than 13 percent of Atlanta's black families from better housing.[65]

Despite the high rent at University Homes, on first glance the tenants chosen to live in the project seemed to represent, as Alonzo Moron claimed, a broad cross-section of Atlanta's African American community, including "teachers, preachers, laborers, insurance agents, clerks, maids, hotel workers, domestics and the various classes of railway employees."[66] Indeed, the largest number of tenants comprised unskilled laborers and domestic workers, making up 80 percent of the first 450 lessees. But while this statistic seemed to belie criticisms of exclusion and elitism, in fact most members of these occupational groups were shut out from the project.[67]

The majority of black workers in Atlanta toiled in domestic service or unskilled labor. But while these jobs were considered menial occupations, that did not mean that there were no hierarchies within them. For example, income and status divided domestic workers, who comprised over 80 percent of the black female work force in Atlanta in 1930. Cooks earned more than did maids. Those with steady, daily employment in one home generally earned more than did those working on a casual basis. Maids working in department stores, factories and mills and, like Ruby Blackburn, in the public schools, earned more than most of their sisters working in private service.

According to city-directory data, the workers who moved into University Homes belonged to the higher echelons of the bulwarks of black employment. They had steady employment, often outside of private homes or with prominent white Atlantans, while those who had lived in Beaver Slide generally had no regular employer. For example, of 267 residents in the slum-clearance area who indicated their occupations to the city directory in 1934, the largest number were 79 unskilled laborers who comprised 30 percent of the total reporting. In University Homes in 1938, only 34 of 563 men were laborers, while the largest group of 114 men, or 20 percent, worked as porters, a steadier and better-paying form of employment.

Furthermore, University Homes residents represented the full complement of occupations that working-class African Americans could fill, including industrial jobs in factories, commercial laundries, and bakeries, which black reformers had been encouraging black workers to take when they could. In University Homes these workers comprised 12 percent of all residents, representing twelve occupations, while in Beaver Slide, only 6 percent of residents worked in laundries, bakeries, factories, or machine shops, or as warehousemen, candy makers, or pressers. But perhaps the greatest evidence that University Homes workers had more "modern" occupations than the slum dwellers they replaced is that University Homes housed no home laundry workers, while in Beaver Slide 17 percent of all those employed were laundresses and, in Atlanta as a whole, one-fifth of employed black women earned their living this way. Home laundry work was a dying occupation in the 1930s, with more and more consumers favoring commercial laundries as more convenient and supposedly more sanitary. Furthermore, this low-paying and irregular work, where black women worked in the slums in which they lived, did not produce the income or an example of modern black life that black housing reformers required of the projects' residents.[68]

These statistics point to the more intangible variables that went into tenant selection at University Homes. Black housing officials chose the "deserving poor" to live in the homes. Black managers interviewed applicants in their homes to discover how they kept house. Project staff questioned applicants' neighbors as to their neighborliness and their reputation. They carefully checked the incomes and credit histories of all prospective tenants.

This scrutiny kept out all but the most respectable black Atlantans, a process that those chosen seemed to appreciate. One successful applicant, Lula Daugherty, pointed out that technically anyone could qualify for a unit who could pay the rent. "But," she continued, "if you was . . . what would you call it? . . . [T]hey called it an alley. They didn't let them kind of people come in here. . . . [E]ven you had to tell them what church you belonged. We did when we were moving in. And how long we had belonged there, and how much rent we was paying." She did not object to the process, then or in retrospect, reasoning that the management "was just trying to make it nice. They was trying to get us out of the gutter. . . . they was trying to show you how decent people lived. But some of us don't want that."[69] In other words, housing officials were lifting the respectable poor "out of the gutter" and into decent living, removing them from the alleys, and more important, from alley dwellers. They completed this rescue from the slums when the tenants moved into their apartments. As each new family arrived, their belongings were washed with disinfectant and sprayed with pesticide to ensure that they did not bring any of the "slums" into the project with them. Only then were they prepared to be uplifted and trained for citizenship.[70]

When the 675 resident families chosen to live in University Homes started moving into their new apartments in April 1937, many of them entered an unfamiliar world of running water, refrigerators, and responsible landlords. Living in University Homes had great meaning for these residents. Even middle-class tenants had had to contend with abysmal housing conditions given the chronic housing shortage for blacks in Atlanta. The project units' amenities—their modern facades, indoor bathrooms, and electric appliances—were virtually unknown to all but the wealthiest black Atlantans. These amenities meant that bathing was merely a matter of turning on the hot-water faucet, rather than of hauling water from an outside pump or spigot, heating it up in a kettle on top of a wood- or coal-burning stove, and pouring it into a metal tub.[71]

But the modernizing influences of University Homes went beyond its physical features. Slum clearance destroyed not only a warren of narrow streets and alleys lined with small wood-frame houses but also a neighborhood of people bound together in a community. The project, with its strict geometry and severe architecture, introduced a new kind of living to the tenants, for whom apartment living was alien.[72] They came from all over the city, from close-knit communities such as Summerhill, Pittsburgh, or the Old Fourth Ward, where neighbors were bound together by history, churches, and the social obligations of kinship and fictive kin, to live among strangers in the project. And while these new neighbors might try to forge new community ties in University Homes, they might not, instead preferring the anonymity of apartment living. Lula Daugherty, commented on the differences between her old neighborhood, Pittsburgh, and University Homes: "Well, everybody was strangers. . . . And some of them was

This aerial photograph of University Homes deliberately highlights the project's strict geometry and distinction from surrounding neighborhoods. (Charles Forrest Palmer Collection, Special Collections Department, Robert W. Woodruff Library, Emory University)

neighborly, and some of them weren't. Because . . . it just made a change. People just changed after they got able to get in a place where they could live kind of decent."[73]

The projects, with their links to the federal government and high public visibility, also allowed tenants to experience living in neighborhoods that local authorities recognized as legitimate. City sanitation workers always collected the trash of Atlanta's public-housing projects promptly and regularly. More telling, the housing projects protected residents from the regular police harassment that plagued other black neighborhoods. The projects had their own security force to guard and regulate the project, answerable to the housing manager. Only in times of real trouble did he call the city police for backup. Some tenants believed that a bargain between the federal government and local officials shielded them from the police. The projects' low arrest rates made it entirely probable that the projects' high visibility and their federal connections made the police gun-shy within their confines[74]

Freedom from the Atlanta police meant that the project had to be self-policing, and so it was. Alonzo Moron monitored his residents' behavior with benevolent paternalism. Born in the U.S. Virgin Islands and educated at Hampton Institute, Brown University, and in social work at the University of Pittsburgh, Moron was the quintessential black housing manager. He had worked as the first social worker hired by the Baltimore Emergency Relief Commission and had been the public welfare commissioner in the U.S. Virgin Islands, where he had consulted with Lugenia Hope to organize communities according to the strategies of the Neighborhood Union. He had also attended a management training course cosponsored by the National Association of Housing Officials and the PWA. He was handpicked to lead University Homes by AU's Advisory Housing Committee for his professional qualifications and his sympathy to the aims of the black reform elite.[75]

Moron worked hard to achieve the incorporative goals of black reformers in Atlanta despite federal restrictions on social-service programs in housing projects. His mission was to take the tenants, uprooted from the parochialism of their old neighborhoods, and mold them into respectable and progressive citizens. He exerted moral authority over the projects as a "symbolic father" and exercised "strict influence" over tenants' lives. Under his watch, tenants were obliged to keep their apartments and communal yards clean and tidy. They were to keep their children off the streets after a certain hour. He was vigilant in ensuring that the project continued to be island of respectability, even going "undercover" as a laborer in order to entrap a small-time bootlegger living in the project.[76]

After adapting to their respectable new surroundings, Moron encouraged tenants to participate in programs initiated by the project's management and other black reformers. Every citizenship-training, public-health, or voter-registration reformer in black Atlanta went first to University Homes with his or her campaigns, sure to find an active and interested constituency there. University Homes' residents formed a tenants' association with hotly contested yearly elections, and organized themselves into Men's and Women's Clubs, Boy Scouts, and Girls and Boys Reserves. Moron also encouraged tenants' upward mobility. He was particularly concerned with helping tenants move out of the project and into home ownership by encouraging them to save their money and even giving them breaks on their rent to that end. For many residents, tenure at University Homes became a stepping stone to a house in one of the new black suburbs. Finally, University Homes fulfilled the goals of black housing visionaries by becoming a center of black activism and the black economy. The project's audito-

Pioneers In Housing Personnel Management

Seated (L to R) - Mrs. Walter Mae Hamilton (Deceased) Rent-Clerk, Cashier, Management Aide, Housing Manager of Alonzo Herndon Homes.
    Alonzo Moron - first Negro Housing Manager in the U. S. A. Present Position - Now Assistant to the Regional Administration Housing and Home Finance Agency, Virgin Islands.
    Mrs. Cordelia Hill, Secretary to Housing Manager - Present Position Secretary to President Benjamin F. Mays, Morehouse College, Atlanta, Ga.
    Standing (L to R) - Mrs. Maggie Carter, our Management Aide - 12 years Present Position - Management Aide, Carver Community Housing Development.
    Julius Alexander, Superintendent of Maintenance - Present Position: Building Contractor, Montgomery,

University Homes manager Alonzo Moron (seated, second from left) surrounded by the project staff. The photo's caption reveals that this employment proved a stepping stone to upward mobility for these professional and white-collar workers. (*University Homes, Atlanta, Georgia: Twenty-Fifth Anniversary Edition*, 1962, Charles Forrest Palmer Collection, Special Collections Department, Robert W. Woodruff Library, Emory University)

rium, the only one strictly for African Americans in Atlanta, became the venue for community-wide public forums, voter-registration drives, and citizenship-training programs. The NAACP and the AUL lobbied hard for the shops built into the project to be filled with black businesses, and although one was taken by an A&P grocery with an all-white staff, another was rented by Atlanta's first black-owned self-service market. Thus University Homes became the oasis of respectability and uplift envisioned by its earliest proponents.

In University Homes and the other public-housing projects that were to follow during the 1940s, black reformers like Alonzo Moron finally found a constituency on which they could experiment. No other New Deal program, despite the vigorous efforts of the reform elite both within and outside government, established such a reliable constituency on which reformers could work their schemes for uplift. As the New Deal era proceeded, black reformers shifted their strategies from elite reform to mass activism requiring a large base of support. In the public-housing projects, tenants who were chosen for their amenability to the reformers' vision would become the vanguard of this mobilization.

Black reformers saw University Homes and the black public-housing project that followed it in the 1940s as furthering their goals of bringing African Americans out of the shadows and alleys of their overcrowded neighborhoods. But the projects that replaced "slum" areas did not house the former residents of the demolished areas. Instead, they were peopled by the "striving" poor who were hand-picked by black housing managers as being the most suitable candidates to be brought into the economic, political, and cultural mainstream. State incorporation thus divided the black community physically and politically into those chosen to move into full-fledged citizenship and those who were consigned to remain at the margins of civic life.

IV

Wartime Atlanta
& the Struggle
for Inclusion

9

The Inner Wheel
Breaks Out

*Wartime Atlanta and
the Urban League*

In 1943, the *Atlanta Daily World* published an edi-
torial cartoon distributed by the Associated Negro Press. Entitled "This Is
Your Responsibility," it presented a tableau of African American society. In
the cartoon a dissolute couple, shown slouching and loitering at the corner
of "Slum Boulevard" and "Any Street," with a factory in the distance, are
encountered by a group representing the black elite, including a minister,
a lawyer, and a "society woman," who look at the couple as if seeing them
for the first time. In the lower right-hand corner a white man addresses
the elite group, admonishing its members, "Better try to lift them! You can
go no higher than *they!*"

At first viewing, the elitism represented by this cartoon confirms the
age-old anxieties of black reformers. Their disdain and fear of the "unrespectable" black poor, their distance from the "masses," and their belief
in the importance of racial uplift all come together in the montage. Yet
the cartoon's explicit linking of the black elite and the "masses" marks a
vital shift in reformers' perceptions of the black community growing out of
their Depression-era experiences and the new social and political context
of wartime Atlanta. The New Deal had strengthened elite black reformers'
legitimacy and allowed them to attract and nurture the beginnings of a
mass constituency by including black reformers in its administration and
allowing them unprecedented access to the black community through programs like public housing. This following, and the lessons learned through
their fruitless battles in local politics, prompted the black reform elite to

Editorial cartoon, *Atlanta Daily World*, 17 October 1943.

imagine new, more democratic solutions to their struggles for full citizenship—solutions which, by necessity, included all black Atlantans.

By reshaping their strategies for citizenship, Atlanta's black reformers
became part of the broad national wartime push for southern democracy,
participating in the politically ecumenical movement which struggled valiantly to turn the era's democratic promise into reality. Representatives of
local, regional, and national organizations as diverse as the NAACP, the
Congress of Industrial Organizations, and the Southern Conference on
Human Welfare shared a common goal in this period to seize the unprecedented opportunities created by the era's urbanization, industrialization,
and evolving Democratic Party liberalism, to lift the veil of Jim Crow, and
to remove the barriers that excluded African Americans from the mainstream of the South's economic and political life. The linchpin of this effort
was the South's black-defense work force and its struggle for inclusion in
the region's industrializing wartime economy. This southern democracy
movement embraced these workers' struggles and employed their nascent

autonomy and growing public visibility to further its struggles for economic and political equality.[1]

Atlanta's black reform elite participated as a full partner in this apparently egalitarian movement, marking a turning point in its members' struggles for black citizenship. Their willingness to participate in this worker-centered movement marked their partial emancipation from a decades-long tradition of racial uplift ideology. In the evolving movement toward southern democracy, they understood, as the cartoon suggests, that their progress toward full citizenship was tied directly to that of the majority of the black community. But, as the cartoon also suggests, elitism and mistrust of the black working class continued to mark these reformers' vision of the path to full black citizenship.

Wartime industrialization was crucial to the democracy movement in the South. By modernizing the southern economy, it completed the process begun by New Deal programs, releasing hundreds of thousands of black southerners from the paternalism and dependency of traditional "Negro work." Escaping farm tenancy or domestic service, these African Americans became vital members of the wartime work force, migrating to southern cities, more than ready to seize on or to push for work opportunities beyond the veil of segregation in war industries and the larger wartime economy. This economic "emancipation" was a crucial prelude to the postwar civil rights movement, creating a sizable autonomous and publicly visible African American industrial work force, freed from the grossest forms of isolation, exploitation, and white scrutiny which marked their prewar employment, and ready to be mobilized as the postwar civil rights constituency.

Despite fighting for wartime industrial opportunity in order to create these emancipatory possibilities, the black reform elite also sought to control it according to its old ideological preoccupations. This group's members worried about the increasing visibility of the black working class and its growing participation in public life. They feared that by becoming visible before being uplifted, the black "masses" would imperil the struggle for democracy and black citizenship by demonstrating African Americans' unsuitability or unpreparedness for such progress. Although they understood that the modernization of the South was crucial to their goals for full citizenship, black reformers feared that the veil was lifting too quickly for the unready black "masses." In particular, they feared that black workers were joining urban, industrial society before they had been prepared, with grave consequences for the entire black community and black citizenship.

Therefore, while the black reform elite worked for full democracy, its mobilization efforts focused on those African Americans who could or would share its notions of citizenship and behavior while excluding those who did not. In fact, black reformers refused to countenance, and even condemned, those citizenship struggles of the black working class that did not conform to their notions of respectability, citizenship, or democracy.

At the forefront of organized wartime black activism in Atlanta was the Atlanta Urban League (AUL), whose leaders recognized the enormous potential opportunities presented by industrial employment and sought to maximize black participation in war production. The AUL worked indefatigably to force open the doors of defense training and industry to black workers. Its efforts made it the most important wartime broker between the black community and government and private industry, ultimately resulting in it becoming an essential partner in war manpower coordination in the city, and giving it the power to choose those black workers who would receive the limited number of jobs available for black workers in defense plants. The AUL's influence, both with government agencies and the black community, marked its debut as an important partner in Atlanta's ruling coalition.

Despite its growing power, the AUL could not obtain assembly-line defense jobs for more than a small minority of Atlanta's black workers. The AUL's triage in determining which workers would receive these jobs had enormous implications for the future of Atlanta's black community. The agency made its decisions on the basis of its leaders' continuing conservative definitions of black citizenship. These hand-picked workers became the critical core of postwar civil rights mobilization by the AUL, whose leaders from the beginning of the war had explicitly linked black incorporation into the South's modernizing society and economy to the attainment of civil rights. Those who were not chosen found themselves excluded from the upward mobility afforded by industrial employment and their concerns unrepresented by the emerging, narrowly defined movement for racial equality.

In 1944, white liberal and Georgia Tech lecturer Glenn Rainey wrote to his friend, the ex-Atlantan and young historian C. Vann Woodward, about the trials of being a new father. Chief among them was the unwelcome novelty of having to deal with his infant son's dirty diapers. "Since the emancipation of the Negro is now consummated," he wrote, "we are largely doing our own work, with the blessed help of the Lullaby Diaper Service, though we find that ninety diapers a week are not more than a challenge to his excretory powers."[2]

Rainey's offhand remark suggests the fundamental changes experienced by Atlanta's black community in wartime and the challenges these changes presented to the city's Jim Crow racial order. His assumption that under normal conditions, even his always insecure and insubstantial income as an adjunct lecturer at Georgia Tech could support a maid or a home laundry worker, and his equation of "the Negro" with domestic work was highly emblematic of prewar Atlanta's paternalistic racial order and black Atlantans' dependent position within it. Moreover, his observation that black workers had experienced a second emancipation highlights the changes for African Americans wrought in wartime Atlanta.

Black Atlantans' new emancipation was fundamental, but its importance has sometimes been obscured by whites' successful efforts to limit its scope. Both government officials and defense employers in the South collaborated in an effort to graft traditional Southern labor practices onto the South's mushrooming industrial sector. Despite the massive war-induced labor demands and federal antidiscrimination policies, they continued to treat black workers as a separate caste, a "special and exogenous phenomenon,"[3] as historian Bruce Nelson put it, unwelcome on the assembly lines of the region's new economic sector. So important to whites was the exclusion of black workers from defense industries that the War Manpower Commission (WMC) created artificial labor shortages by ignoring black workers, resulting both in the importation of white workers to southern defense centers, and the disruptive and dangerous overcrowding that plagued virtually all southern cities during the war.[4]

Atlanta was no exception to the pattern. Black workers were grossly underrepresented in industrial and government defense work during the war. Despite making up more than 40 percent of Atlanta's population and work force, African Americans never accounted for more than 30 percent of government workers and 15 percent of industrial workers. The employment they did find consisted of a replication of traditional "Negro work" translated to the industrial setting. At the Bell Aircraft plant in Marietta, the Atlanta region's largest defense employer and the largest industrial employer of black workers between 1942 and 1945, only 2,500 black Atlantans found positions out of a total work force that reached nearly 30,000. Unsurprisingly, the work black Atlantans obtained at Bell was overwhelmingly in menial positions. Only 800 black employees worked on the line, while the remainder were consigned to work as "industrial maids," janitors, or cafeteria workers.[5]

This exclusionary pattern is testament to whites' anxiety over the implications of industrialization for the future of white supremacy, and particularly whites' inability to prevent wartime industrialization from disrupting traditional racialized labor patterns. Even black workers' limited participation in the economic and social modernization implicit in wartime industrialization threatened the foundations of the Jim Crow regime. In the massive, impersonal munitions factories, bomber plants, and shipyards of the wartime South, ex-sharecroppers and domestic workers could escape the exploitative paternalism and dependency on whites that defined traditional "Negro work."

The first thing that the war offered black Atlantans was mobility. Ever since the Great Migration of the First World War, southern African Americans had seized upon industrial opportunities to free themselves from the paternalistic anachronisms and gross exploitation that had trapped them for generations. Until the 1940s, this movement took them out of the South and its kitchens and cotton fields, but, as the region industrialized and modernized with the Second World War, such freedom could also be created within the South. After an initial exodus of black workers in 1940 and 1941 in which more than 14,000 African Americans left the city, Atlanta's black community mushroomed. By 1950 Atlanta's African American population had reached 121,416, representing a 16 percent increase over 1940 figures, or twice the rate of growth for the white population (see Appendix, Table 1).[6]

These new Atlantans were drawn to a burgeoning and diversifying economy. Along with the defense plants, including Bell Aircraft's Marietta operation and a Firestone rubber factory, virtually every industrial concern in the city converted to war production. More than 8,000 black Atlantans found work in these "essential" defense establishments. In addition, government employment exploded with the opening of several military installations, including an army air base and ordnance depot and Lawson General Hospital for military personnel. By 1945, fully 25,000 black and white Atlantans worked for the federal government, including civilians employed by the military, compared to only 7,000 in 1940. Opportunities also exploded for black Atlantans outside defense industries, especially in the service sector. Just as much of Atlanta's work force left for military units or defense installations, demand multiplied for restaurant meals, hotel rooms, and commercial leisure with the influx of war workers, soldiers, and military officials into the city. Black women, for example, became waiters in the dining rooms of Atlanta's most exclusive hotels for the first time during the war, moving into this relatively lucrative work when the regular staff was drafted or sought defense work.[7]

Such a panoply of employment choices was unprecedented for black workers. For decades, black men's job options had steadily declined in the city, especially when white men had turned such "black" work as brick-masonry or bellhopping into exclusively "white" occupations. The erosion of black-male employment opportunities left black women to fill the breach through domestic work, the only job option open to most of them. In 1940, about as many black women as men worked in Atlanta, and almost 70 percent of black female workers toiled in domestic service, earning a pittance for a seventy-hour work week. The caste system that underlay African Americans' position in the labor market effectively perpetuated Jim Crow by marginalizing black workers through exclusion and subjecting them to white control through poverty and economic dependency.

The war broke open this situation. For the first time, many black workers could pick and choose among employers and a variety of jobs. Although most did not find places on the assembly lines, their positions as waiters, janitors, or production helpers in Atlanta's new defense economy represented a crucial shift in their work lives. Even the move from being a maid or cook in a private home to a factory cleaner or cafeteria worker represented a real step up from traditional "Negro work." Not only did these new jobs provide shorter and more regular hours, and higher, even sometimes union-protected, wages, but they also largely freed workers from the paternalistic and dependent relationships that white domestic employers and planters had tried to impose on their black "help."

Black workers seized on the emancipatory possibilities of the tight wartime labor market. They shopped around for jobs, constantly seeking the kind of work and the employer offering the best conditions and pay, consequently yielding enormously high turnover rates for defense contractors. More fundamental, they left the most demeaning of their prewar work sites in droves, often for good. By 1950, only about half of Atlanta's black female work force toiled in domestic labor, a precipitous and permanent decline in this bulwark of black employment. "Negro women," wrote black sociologist Walter Chivers, "were so soured on the 'romance' of domestic service and so thoroughly disillusioned by the fickleness of the loyalty of 'their white folks,' whom they had served so 'loyally,' that they were ready for the . . . 'good money' dangling before their eyes as a reward."[8] Now Atlanta's Glenn Raineys would have to change diapers themselves.

As wartime wages eased their Herculean efforts merely to scrape by, black workers used their unprecedented economic security to distance themselves from workplace exploitation. Some black women, for example, retreated from the labor market during the war and remained at home with their children, a luxury made possible by spouses' defense-industry wages or servicemen's allotments high enough to cover all family expenses. One study found that most families who chose this option actually suffered some drop in income, suggesting their pent-up aspirations for family life denied when both parents had to work long hours.[9]

By offering black workers jobs in the new war plants, and breaking the bonds of persistent paternalism, industrialization brought black workers much greater public visibility. While the types of work they performed may not have changed, the workplace had. Again, the experience of ex-domestic workers provides the most dramatic example. These women and men no longer scattered through the city to toil in obscurity in white neighborhoods and homes. Rather, they joined a mass, biracial wartime work force in Atlanta's most modern industrial settings or they found work in government installations, office buildings, hotels, and restaurants, often in the city's central business district, bringing them to the geographic and economic centers of the wartime city.

The new visibility of black workers and their centrality to the new wartime work force meant the forging of new relationships with white employers and workers. For example, wartime industrialization forced the city's white union establishment to acknowledge and include black workers after decades of ignoring or deliberately excluding them. Black workers became an important constituency when the cio initiated an organizing drive in Atlanta to correspond with the wartime industrialization of the local economy, and culminating with an organizing victory at Bell Aircraft in 1943. Its success can be attributed, at least in part, to the union's willingness to organize and recognize black defense workers. The Atlanta Federation of Trades, representing Atlanta's afl-affiliated trade-union establishment, was caught off guard by the cio's campaign. Although the cio in Atlanta did little for black members once they were organized, it had a better record than the afl's national and local pattern of racism and exclusion. Scrambling to maintain its preeminence among Atlanta's workers, the aft began courting black workers openly in its contest with the cio. But given that the Machinists' Union, one of Atlanta's most openly racist, led the aft's organizing drive at Bell, black workers gave little credibility to this abrupt about-face, which reflected more a survival instinct than a desire to serve black workers.[10]

The cio's victory at Bell showed the aft the importance of black workers in Atlanta's new labor order. Consequently, the aft's wartime effort at self-preservation, in conjunction with black workers' new economic position, achieved the greatest unionization victory to date for the city's black workers with the 1943 organization of commercial laundry workers. Prior to unionization the city's 3,000, mostly female, black laundry workers were among the city's poorest, sometimes earning less than three hundred dollars a year. The AFT supported the laundry workers in an eight-week strike in 1943 in which they defied the War Labor Board and the AFL's wartime no-strike promise. Through the WLB's intervention, the laundry workers won a fifty-hour week, paid vacations, and overtime pay, with their base wages set at between thirty and fifty cents an hour. Although two segregated locals won the strike, in 1945 they merged into one organization led and dominated by black members. Such recognition pointed to the fundamental changes experienced by black workers during the war. Not only did black women, like Glenn Rainey's imagined "Negro," leave home-laundry work in droves, but also, as they joined the commercial or industrial work force, like the Lullaby Diaper Service, their new visibility and autonomy allowed them to assert their rights as workers successfully. They continued to toil at tasks similar to those required by their prewar employment, but their changing work-force position produced fundamental improvements in their work lives.[11]

Other black Atlantans also used their newfound autonomy and visibility to push their rights as citizens and workers. With growing assertiveness, they fought the arbitrary limits placed on their economic and vocational opportunities. A rash of shop-floor incidents erupted during the war when black industrial workers defied their caste position and white supremacy by attempting to use machinery forbidden to them or refusing to assume the subservient mien or behavior demanded by their position, then fighting back courageously when incensed white workers attacked them violently for their challenge to Jim Crow.[12]

Similarly, if less dramatically, black defense workers used the visibility granted to them by federal government and labor-movement recognition to assert their rights as workers and citizens. In droves, they used the complaint mechanisms opened to them by the Fair Employment Practices Commission, allowing them for the first time to record officially their dissent to the discrimination they had always faced at work. The FEPC was the wartime agency established to investigate employment discrimination in defense industries. Franklin Roosevelt had banned such discrimination in 1941 through Presidential Order 8802 after black union organizer A. Philip Randolph had threatened a mass "March on Washington" by African American workers from around the country. Taking advantage of this hard-fought victory, which forced the federal government for the first time to acknowledge the existence of racial discrimination, hundreds of Atlanta's black defense workers registered their experiences with the new federal agency. They carefully described hostile working environments where white supervisors, intent on limiting black workers' visibility and ensuring their subordination, established a myriad of roadblocks to hamper black success at defense plants. Among other complaints, these workers charged that their supervisors regularly barred them from the training that would allow them skilled work, demoted them from semi-skilled positions to janitorial work without justification, forced them to work seven-night shifts every week, required them to obtain passes to use the toilet while white employees went to the restroom at will, and issued them demerits that sometimes led to dismissal for coming back from breaks or the toilet a few minutes later than arbitrarily deemed necessary. While such complaints almost never resulted in sanctions against the offending employer, their number and scope reveal black workers' pent-up frustrations and their sense of entitlement to equal opportunity and treatment at the workplace. Their growing autonomy, along with the federal government's implicit recognition of their citizenship, allowed them finally to protest their treatment openly.[13]

Black Atlantans' increasing activism as workers also had important implications for their freedom struggle outside of the workplace, allowing them to fight against white constraints on their citizenship more openly and assertively. With increasing fearlessness they claimed public space and defied segregation. As in Birmingham, the most dramatic of these struggles in Atlanta occurred on public transportation.[14] Given extreme wartime crowding on streetcars, black and white riders encountered each other more often than ever before as they made their way to the same defense workplaces. Many used this situation to play out the racial tension emerging out of African Americans' greater wartime mobility, visibility, and autonomy. In fact, the Federal Bureau of Investigation, in its "Survey of Racial Conditions in the United States," singled out public transportation as the most important stage for resentful blacks and whites to act on their mutual animosity. The survey's authors reported that African Americans chafed against Jim Crow segregation laws that "resulted in a scarcity of rapid and available transportation for Negroes. This scarcity, coupled with the reported change in attitude of Negroes in the South, is said to be the cause of numerous minor clashes and fights between Negroes and whites throughout the South."[15]

Certainly whites' day-to-day defense of the Jim Crow order became more violent during the war as they protected their traditional claims on increasingly limited public space. White passengers, who by custom had always entered streetcars before black riders, now asserted this right by shoving or assaulting blacks who dared enter before them, even when this occurred by accident. Streetcar drivers and passengers regularly cursed, beat, and sometimes killed black passengers who contravened racial etiquette by refusing to relinquish their seats when extra white passengers forced back the fluid line separating white and black. Streetcar motormen (who had police powers in Atlanta) frequently armed themselves with guns or used the "streetcarman's best weapon,"[16] the switch steering stick, to beat black passengers.[17]

Black Atlantans did not take this abuse sitting down, however. They often fought back or even "provoked" violence from white drivers and passengers by defiantly entering streetcars before whites, sitting in the white section of the streetcars, or answering white passengers and drivers' abuse with curses and threats. As Robin Kelley has theorized, streetcars, being moving enclosed space, were places where African Americans could openly resist white authority. Even if whites brutally punished them for this behavior, as they often did, defiant black passengers had a captive white audience forced to witness their actions and acknowledge their presence in an important segment of the city's public space. Moreover, if black passengers constituted a majority of passengers on a streetcar, they could tip the balance of power for the time of their trip and, for a change, force whites to cower in their presence. In a terse digest of the "Racial Situation" in Atlanta, the War Department reported the following Atlanta streetcar incidents during a three-week period in 1945. On the twelfth of January, "Three young Negroes slashed at whites on a street car after a white man reprimanded one for cursing. Some of the 60 other Negroes aboard pulled the trolley pole and others hung out windows stopping passing trolleys." On the twenty-third, "Negroes argued with a driver and one pulled the trolley pole." On the first of February, "A Negro girl threatened to cut a white girl after they fought on a streetcar when the Negro pushed the white," and on the second, "Twelve months on public works was the sentence for a Negro who cut a white man in a bus fight."[18]

Both black and white participants in these incidents realized that they were engaged in a hand-to-hand racial battle, a violent contest in which the very foundations of Jim Crow were at stake. As the war progressed, black passengers increasingly made explicit the connections between their defiant behavior and their entitlement to full citizenship. For example, in 1945 a police report detailed one incident in which a streetcar motorman was "victimized" by a black passenger supposedly "in a drunken condition" who called the motorman an "S.O.B." upon being ejected from the car. After beating the black man with the streetcar's control handle, the motorman found himself on the other end of the stick as the passenger returned the favor, ultimately leaving the "victim" with broken glasses, a badly cut ear, and a swollen left temple.[19]

This fight began when the black passenger told the insulting white motorman that he was "a man just like him," a common refrain during the war, when black Atlantans fought rhetorically as well as physically for recognition of their citizenship. On the streetcars, these protests often took the form of an angry "Greek chorus" commenting from the rear on specific incidents of discrimination as they occurred. In one incident, an elderly man who had to stand at the front of a very crowded streetcar asked the driver if he could exit by the front, rather than fighting the crowd to get to the rear door where African Americans usually had to exit. When the driver refused, black passengers protested vocally. As the streetcar left downtown and became less crowded, the driver roughly told black passengers standing in the front to get to the back where they belonged. An unidentified black man responded by retorting, "You don't have to talk to us like we were dogs." The incensed driver then demanded that the man behind the voice identify himself, which he did. The driver then drew his pistol and ordered the man to leave the car. Exemplifying the defiance and increased fearlessness of blacks during wartime, the man demanded his fare back from the driver, who was still aiming his gun. He got his token and coolly left the streetcar by the rear exit with the driver's gun pointed at his back.[20]

Thus, working-class black Atlantans protested Jim Crow at the workplace and on the streets. As the streetcar examples attest, these black Atlantans became more and more willing to assert their rights openly and militantly as workers and citizens. The war sparked their actions. They battled the deep contradictions implicit in the fight against Hitlerism in Europe while they continued to face Jim Crow at home. But what permitted their fight was the economic emancipation that wartime industrialization brought to Atlanta's black community. Black Atlantans no longer would submit to the rules of deference and enforced inequality, and their newfound mobility, autonomy, and visibility meant they no longer had to.

Like Atlanta's black working class, the city's reform elite also seized upon the opportunities wartime industrialization presented. For years, this group of social workers, academics, and journalists had been working for the inclusion of African Americans into the mainstream of Atlanta's economic and political life, but to little avail. They understood such changes would require a fundamental transformation of the South's economic traditions of black exclusion and exploitation. They believed in the transformative potential of Atlanta's wartime industrialization to achieve their ends and intended that black Atlantans would play an integral role in modernizing the South's economy and society. Yet instead of interpreting black workers' wartime mobility, visibility, and activism as essential to their goals, they often viewed these developments as detrimental to their dreams of full citizenship for African Americans. Understanding the challenges confronting the black reform elite's leadership and ideology during the war can partially explain this apparent paradox.

Since the Communist upsurge of the early 1930s, black reformers had faced few challenges to uplift ideology. Poverty, illiteracy, and dependency kept most African Americans invisible and immobile, thus allowing the black elite to claim legitimacy as the natural leaders and saviors of the black community. Yet when wartime industrialization freed many black workers from their fixed status as farm tenants or servants, and when black workers' acts of resistance and group assertion became publicly visible, the black elite felt their self-proclaimed leadership challenged. Many of the most profound wartime changes for black Atlantans occurred without elite intervention. Black workers' migration to the city, employment in defense industry, higher living standards, and increasing public visibility were all largely a product of the war and the labor demands of war industries, not elite reform campaigns. Furthermore, the most dramatic of these changes wrought by industrialization occurred among poor, working-class African Americans, whose agency and interests had heretofore been ignored by the reform elite, which had as much difficulty as whites in seeing their strivings, if for very different reasons.

As their New Deal campaigns demonstrated, black reformers always envisioned the "masses'" progress toward full economic and political citizenship as a gradual, elite-led process. In fact, a key component of uplift ideology emphasized that the "pathologies" of black urban life stemmed from African Americans' supposed unpreparedness for the shift from "peasant" to modern city dweller. In a 1940 passage which echoed uplift rhetoric since the beginnings of the mass exodus of African Americans from the countryside, Forrester B. Washington of the black Atlanta University

School of Social Work outlined what he considered black migrants' fundamental difficulties in adjusting to city life and urban employment. Migrants had "little conception . . . of the urban requirements of unskilled labor, such as prompt appointments, attitudes in applying for work, and ability to understand simple specifications of job analysis." "Moreover," he continued, "there is a minimum of personal appearance required on unskilled jobs in the city. . . . Neither the male nor the female ex-agricultural laborer can toil half-clad or semi-nude in the city as they could in the country."[21]

As such rhetoric suggests, the black reform elite did not accept that uneducated African Americans could engage in their own freedom struggle, believing they lacked even a basic understanding of modern life or elementary political consciousness. In fact, reformers based their claims to leadership of the black community on these beliefs. Before the war, they could sustain this myth, given black workers' marginality. But with events like the commercial laundry workers' unionization drive, or the escalating tension on public transportation, they had to reconfigure their ideology by adapting it to black workers' public activism on their own behalf.

The black reform elite reasserted their leadership's legitimacy by interpreting the wartime activism of African American workers as evidence of social pathologies and unpreparedness for civic citizenship and membership in the industrial order. Thus the black passenger who asserted his manhood to the streetcar motorman was not making a legitimate claim for citizenship. His drinking, his swearing, and his violent retaliation disqualified him from respectability and, hence, citizenship. Proponents of uplift interpreted black Atlantans' street and workplace struggles as signs of their ignorance, laziness, and lack of self-respect and responsibility, instead of as a different quest for citizenship. This interpretation invalidated the importance of working-class black Atlantans' efforts to fight on their own behalf and blinded black reformers from seeing or acknowledging the war-era struggles of many black workers.

Black reformers blamed black Atlantans' misbehavior on the war's dislocations and the "social disorganization" which they felt resulted when poor African Americans left their traditional social moorings without adequate supervision or support. For example, Helen Whiting, supervisor of teaching practice in Atlanta University's education department, lectured a group of Georgia's black teachers in 1943 about how the "high degree of mobility, vertical and horizontal," within the black community had created "severe stresses and strains" and an "intense crisis," which imperiled her goals for black citizenship "in a world of peace after the war."[22]

What exactly did Whiting and her fellow teachers mean by a "crisis"? For them, wartime mobility had broken down traditional kin and community ties, leaving children and youth adrift, just at the time when African Americans were moving into the "mainstream," through their expanded vocational opportunities. Luckily, in Whiting's view, black teachers could step into the breach by becoming parental surrogates to their students, guiding them to make "proper adjustments" to these enormous changes, and specifically, according to Spelman College history instructor Margaret Curry, "educating for democratic citizenship."[23] Black school teachers saw themselves on the frontlines of this effort, being the "Senior Technical Craftsmen" on "Freedom's Assembly Line,"[24] as the patriotic yearbook editors at Booker T. Washington High School put it.

While the citizenship training Whiting and the other teachers conceived included the kinds of universal-rights rhetoric explicit in the South's wartime democracy movement, it also sought, in the spirit of uplift ideology, to teach black students a behavioral code of citizenship, hoping to prepare them for public visibility and participation in the mainstream. Spelman College English instructor Henrietta Herod's instructions to high school English teachers engaged in citizenship education concentrated almost completely on teaching students civility and the social niceties of bourgeois America. She wrote that the teacher "will endeavor to train his [sic] pupils so that they are able to converse graciously and intelligently with others, to agree or disagree with courtesy, and to carry on relationships with regard for social amenities." The teacher of English, "will know that he [sic] must send out students who are able to use the English language with proper regard for those literacies of expression approved by cultivated men and women." For Herod, such skills were imperative to and inseparable from citizenship.[25]

While Herod sought to instill the civil behavior of good citizenship in black Atlantans through a campaign of positive change, many other reformers worked to change attitudes and behavior through criticism and condemnation of working-class black actions and attitudes. Such negative messages betrayed the black reform elite's impotence to control black workers' behavior. While teachers could intervene directly in the lives and behavior of young people through the schools, no comparable institution could guide adults. One of the most overt displays of this attitude of shame and mistrust of the black working class appeared in a series of editorial cartoons published between 1943 and 1945 in the *ADW*. Distributed by Continental Features, a black news service, and drawn by an artist with the pseudonym "Stann Pat," these cartoons, taken together, comprised a series of do's and don'ts—but mostly don'ts—for black behavior in wartime. The drawings portrayed graphically a series of situations in which black workers found themselves every day. They demonstrated the black elite's fear that the increased visibility of the black working class might jeopardize claims for full citizenship.

One of the most prominent themes of this series focused on proper street and public transportation behavior. Stann Pat depicted ordinary black people as uncouth boors, shoving others to get onto streetcars, eating and drinking on the street, and deliberately taking up more than their share of space. A caption condemning the ignorance, selfishness, and immorality of the action, and warning of its danger for the entire black community, accompanied each image. All the captions explicitly linked such behavior to the black freedom struggle, demonstrating the reform elite's awareness of the opportunities presented by wartime visibility for black citizenship and their terror that this same visibility might destroy this chance for black uplift. "Shoving others about in public conveyances for some slight satisfaction or convenience is selfish and small," complained one caption. "We fight jimcrow on trolley cars, trains and subways because we are human and deserve better treatment." Thus the cartoon implicitly invalidated working-class assertions against Jim Crow by condemning African Americans for undermining the elite's uplift program when they fought whites for their share of space on public transportation. "[All] forms of eating on the street are contrary to good conduct and taste," exhorted another cartoon. "You and I will have to learn these things, lest our protest for full citizenship be in vain." Thus Pat condemned black people for a practice that was nearly unavoidable during the war, thus demeaning black workers' struggles and the social realities of southern cities in wartime.

Although the reform elite knew that its objectives could be achieved only through the increased visibility of African Americans, these cartoons demonstrated its members' fear of this visibility and their impulse to control it. Increasingly, reformers used their growing authority with whites to mobilize a constituency of the respectable poor and middle class to achieve their goals for the black community. Soon the visible organization of these groups, presented by black leaders as an example of virtuous and lawful black citizenship, would have an enormous impact on the future of the city and the black community.

Atlanta's black reform elite worried so obsessively about the behavior of the black working class because its members understood the importance

"Do's and Don'ts"

WE ALL PAID OUR FARE

A fellow who exercises his sporting instincts in a game where he exchanges blow for blow, wouldn't do this. Shoving others about in public conveyances for some slight satisfaction or convenience is selfish and small. We fight jimcrow on trolley cars, trains and subways because we are human and deserve better treatment.

Editorial cartoon, *Atlanta Daily World*, 22 September 1943.

"Of course you may not go this far, but all forms of eating on the street are contrary to good conduct and taste. There are just some things that people don't do. You and I will have to learn these things, lest our protest for full citizenship be in vain. Better stop kidding yourself.

Editorial cartoon, *Atlanta Daily World*, 21 April 1944.

of wartime industrialization to the future of the black community. They knew that the period's circumstances gave black Atlantans a window of opportunity to break into industrial work and that this opportunity could have enormous implications for their struggles to destroy Jim Crow. Because the stakes were so high and the industrial opportunities so limited, black reformers fought to control the black defense work force so that it would represent and advance, not jeopardize, their goals for black citizenship. Thus, while their goal was economic and political democracy for the South, limited industrial opportunity along with uplift ideology produced a fundamentally elitist strategy to achieve this egalitarian end.

The Bell Aircraft plant was the most important symbol of the potential latent in Atlanta's wartime modernization. For Atlanta's leaders, both black and white, it represented a modern future for the city, the South, and its citizens. Atlanta, not a major manufacturing center, had never seen an industrial concern on the scale of this plant, built in Marietta, just outside the city. By luring Bell to the Atlanta area, city boosters hoped to make a great leap forward in modernizing the local economy. In the 1940s, no manufacturer could compete with the prestige of the aviation industry, which symbolized the pinnacle of American technological and industrial achievement. Local officials hoped the Bell plant's success would prove to the rest of the country that southern workers, traditionally perceived as too uneducated, inexperienced, and unskilled for industrial work, could manufacture bombers as efficiently as any group elsewhere. Bell officials often referred to their pioneering effort in Georgia. In 1944, company president Larry Bell called the Marietta plant "a great trade school" that would "prove of great value to Georgia in the difficult post-war days . . . when the industrial skills available here will be of great importance to this community and to the South as a whole."[26]

Not merely looming large in the city's imagination, the Marietta plant literally towered over any industrial concern the city had ever seen. With its main assembly bay "large enough to house the nation's total annual cotton crop," the plant's size tested the descriptive powers of one WMC official: "To look at the plant from a distance is to experience an emotional shock. . . . It is as though one had suddenly come across the architecture of a people from another and larger planet—people used to doing things on a scale that dwarfs the familiar buildings and dwellings of mere earth-men."[27] Appropriate to such an enormous and utterly modern industrial plant, Bell officials described the movement of the tens of thousands of workers inside the plant in language evoking machinery. "The flow of workers will be controlled with precision," one Bell news release explained. "They will enter the plant through tunnels into the basement containing locker rooms, showers and cafeterias. A network of stairways will enable each to go to his particular job area by the most direct route."[28]

This image contrasted sharply with stereotypes of a lazy, premodern South, with its personalized and paternalistic labor relations and its workers' supposed indifference to time discipline. Atlanta's black reform elite also interpreted the Bell Plant's opening as the dawn of a bright modern future for the city's black community. Its members envisioned black workers' inclusion in the clean, technologically sophisticated aircraft industry as hammering the first nail into the coffin of Jim Crow and its traditions of black exclusion and exploitation. They believed that the Bell plant represented the potential modernization of the southern economy and society, and they intended that black Atlantans would play an integral role in this transformation.[29]

For this reason, the AUL spent the war years devoting its efforts to opening up black opportunities for skilled defense work, particularly at Bell Aircraft. Inclusion of black workers in war industry depended almost entirely on protracted grassroots struggles to force defense industries and federal manpower agencies to comply with federal antidiscrimination legislation. The weak authority of the FEPC did not ensure compliance. The agency did not have enforcement power; instead, it could only investigate, expose, and recommend executive action that FDR was loathe to take. Still the presidential order had crucial importance in recognizing the citizenship of racial minorities and their entitlement to full participation in the war effort. The AUL and other black reformers across the South used this moral authority to shift the status quo in the region. No longer did African Americans have to justify the benefits and utility of black employment in industry by proving the citizenship of African Americans. Instead, they could put local, state, and federal officials on the defensive by forcing them to justify the exclusion of African Americans from employment by federally funded defense contractors.[30]

In Atlanta, these efforts for inclusion began in 1942, after federal authorities granted $200,000 for aircraft manufacture training to local officials who excluded African Americans from their instruction programs, despite directives that these funds be distributed without discrimination. The black reform elite realized that if black Atlantans were to join the industrial mainstream it would be crucial that they be included in the skilled labor pool for Bell's potential work force of 40,000. Bell made it clear that only qualified workers would be hired for aircraft assembly, yet none of the federally funded training equipment intended to establish fifteen aircraft assembly instruction centers in and around Atlanta was made available to black Atlantans.[31]

Understanding the devastating implications of this exclusion, the AUL founded the Council for Defense Training (CDT) to work on creating courses for black workers to match the white program for Bell. Composed of luminaries of the reform elite, including AUL secretary William Bell, public-housing manager and AUL industrial secretary Jacob Henderson, and *ADW* editor C. A. Scott, the CDT worked tirelessly throughout 1942 to achieve its goals, battling against the plots and subterfuges of white officials who sought to prevent the launching of a black training program. Borrowing their strategy from the March on Washington Movement, the CDT mobilized black Atlanta to protest its exclusion from the program. It undertook a registration drive of all African Americans in Atlanta who wished to participate in the Bell training program. Prompted by the slogan "Could you use $35 a week?" (through a skilled job at Bell), black Atlantans responded to the council's appeal in droves. While the council set 2,000 registrants as its original goal, between 5,000 and 10,000 black Atlantans, or perhaps as much as 10 percent of Atlanta's black community, participated in the ten-day drive.[32]

The CDT's registration effort represented a strategic turning point for Atlanta's black reform elite, built on the groundwork of activism it had established in the 1930s. This campaign's success led the reformers to abandon their decades-old strategy of back-room negotiation for an opposite strategy of making the black community as visible as possible, and demonstrating its leadership of the black "masses" to government officials and Bell's management. Federal manpower agencies like FEPC or WMC also compelled this shift. The reactive policy of these agencies meant that the federal bureaucracy acted on black workers' behalf only when they themselves complained of their treatment or demonstrated their availability for defense work.

The CDT's effort forced federal officials to acknowledge black Atlantans as a significant segment of the local labor force, something that local manpower bureaucrats had refused to recognize. The council's registration drive deliberately paralleled that of the U.S. Employment Service (USES), the agency responsible for registering and referring all potential candidates for federal defense-training programs. The USES, like other branches of the WMC, ignored black workers as potential defense workers. The resounding quantifiable success of the council's registration drive compelled government officials to consider African Americans as part of the mainstream labor pool. Although that acknowledgment did not ensure defense training, it did force recalcitrant federal and state agencies to justify excluding of African Americans from training.[33]

The CDT used its registration campaign and federal policy to maneuver local officials into an increasingly defensive position. Using Washington contacts made in the 1930s, the CDT's members complained constantly to the FEPC, WMC, and USES officials about the misuse of federal funds in Atlanta, bringing increasing pressure for including black Atlantans in the defense-training program. Their campaign's effectiveness and their shrewd use of a national network of bureaucrats and activists meant that Atlanta became a crucial test site for federal antidiscrimination legislation and policy. Impressed by the CDT's campaign, the National Urban League chose to make the Atlanta situation the focus of its campaign to force Washington officials to redress the dismal state of defense training for blacks in the South and to end the unlawful practice of "earmarking" programs for African Americans by only offering black workers training in skills they had traditionally practiced.[34] Ultimately, this pressure and the strength of the case led to victory when the CDT filed a discrimination complaint against Atlanta and Georgia's defense-training officials after being chosen for representation at regional FEPC hearings in Birmingham in June 1942. The commission ordered Atlanta authorities to establish an aircraft assembly instruction program for African Americans. In November 1942, a center, the "first training program ever opened in the deep South for prospective [black] aircraft workers,"[35] opened with much fanfare at Booker T. Washington High School (BTWHS), Atlanta's only black secondary school.[36]

Through these extraordinary efforts, the AUL became the most powerful black agency in Atlanta. While the CDT's registration efforts were initially designed to protest and publicize the discrimination of local officials, and to publicize the availability of black workers, white officials eyed the council and the AUL as potential allies in managing the local defense labor force. The AUL's actions demonstrated its access to black Atlantans, who were badly needed as unskilled workers in defense industries. Even USES officials grudgingly praised the efforts of the council in "stimulating the recruitment of . . . potential Negro trainees, and the proper registering of these trainees with the Atlanta office." Although the local USES office obstructed the aspirations of skilled black workers throughout the war, it did face pressure from above to register available black workers for unskilled positions. The registration drive demonstrated that the AUL could deliver these workers. One Washington administrator for the WMC, of which the USES was a part, suggested to the National Urban League that "comparable cooperative programs" to Atlanta's "be worked out between [the USES] and the National Urban League in other strategic defense centers." And the work of the CDT also brought representatives of the labor-strapped southern shipbuilding industry to the AUL in search of black workers willing to migrate to Brunswick, Georgia, or Mobile, Alabama, for defense jobs.[37]

This recognition enormously increased the AUL's prestige and legitimacy with white officials. It became an important adjunct to federal manpower agencies in the city, emerging as a vital referral agency for black workers for the USES, Bell Aircraft, and the Civil Service Commission. In fact, these agencies often only dealt with black workers if they had been referred by the AUL, which registered and selected those black workers who attended the BTWHS defense school. The AUL also became an important buffer agency for black workers, steering them to the proper wartime agencies and preparing them for the hostility and bureaucratic hoops that they would be required to hurdle.

After the success of the CDT's drive, the AUL continued to employ its new strategy of mass mobilization. It coordinated FEPC complaint campaigns among black workers against USES discrimination in job placement, and the lily-white policies at Atlanta's Firestone Rubber factory and in the UAW local at a nearby Chevrolet plant to undergird its protest to government and union officials in Washington and Detroit. However, these campaigns originated with the AUL, not with workers, none of whom filed an independent FEPC complaint about Firestone's exclusionary practices. Rather, those workers who cooperated with the AUL sought to benefit from the agency's growing influence over black defense employment by supporting its programs.[38]

Not all workers could afford to support the AUL, nor did the AUL's wartime programs represent the majority of black Atlantans' wartime interests. The defense-training program that resulted from the CDT's registration campaign achieved virtually nothing for most black workers. The course, held during the day and for no pay, faced logistical and financial roadblocks that barred most working-class black Atlantans from participating. Other potential students were stymied by educational prerequisites that required a sixth-grade education. Further, given the history of black exclusion from industry, ordinary black workers recognized that there was no guarantee that they would be employed in skilled jobs at Bell or any

Defense trainees, Booker T. Washington High School, 1943. (Atlanta Public Schools Archives Department)

other defense plant in Atlanta even with qualifications. Only those able to afford three weeks without wages could seek better-paying jobs in defense industries through training.

In fact, most black workers did not make the sacrifice the training program required, preferring instead to take the relatively well-paying unskilled jobs that became available in Atlanta in 1942–43 as military installations opened or expanded their operations and the draft tightened the local labor market. Further, many black Atlantans left the city before 1943 to work in southern shipbuilding centers where they could earn almost double the wages local employers offered. The AUL had to make constant appeals to rectify the severe underenrollment at the BTWHS day course, and even the night program which began in June 1943 suffered from small enrollments. Thus, while the AUL's campaigns sought to improve the situation of black workers, and increasingly used mass-mobilization strategies, they did not necessarily benefit Atlanta's black workers or represent their most immediate wartime interests. Instead, the league's strategies represented both its own goals for the black community and its response to the bureaucratic demands of wartime agencies like the FEPC, which required official complaints to be filed by individuals in order to act on the AUL's behalf.[39]

Comprehending these differences of interest and goals between black workers and the AUL is crucial to understanding the achievements and limits of the reform elite's fight to obtain assembly-line work for black Atlantans at Bell. In order for the defense-training drive to amount to anything concrete, the company had to make an unprecedented move by training and hiring skilled black workers. Through defense training, the AUL wanted to make it as difficult as possible for the company to exclude black workers from its Marietta production labor force. Although Bell repeatedly promised federal and local officials that it would exhaust the area's labor supply before looking elsewhere for workers, president Larry Bell also reassured local whites before coming to Atlanta that "there are certain traditions sacred to the South and we expect to abide by them."[40] Interpreting the contradiction in Bell's public rhetoric as an indication that Bell could be persuaded to hire black Atlantans in large numbers to operate machinery, the AUL exerted its new influence as power broker for the black community, attempting to wield as much influence as it could over company policy regarding black workers.

Repeating the effort of the registration drive, the AUL became the unofficial referral agency for black Atlantans desiring work at Bell, thus once again deliberately "supplementing the work of the United States Employment Service."[41] After all, the USES might work with company officials to underrepresent blacks when reporting the available work force and to keep blacks out of the plant in all but the most menial, nonmechanical positions.

Delegations from the AUL also met regularly with Bell officials long before the Marietta plant opened to discuss ways in which they could work together "to increase understanding of the factors which influence the successful utilization and well-being of Negro workers."[42] Through these negotiations, AUL representatives like Jacob Henderson convinced company officials to hire African Americans for white-collar positions in the Marietta plant's personnel department. The AUL thus buttressed its efforts by positioning its agents within the company for the hiring of skilled African Americans. Bell conceded to this demand shortly after the plant opened, when it appointed two men hand-picked by the AUL—Milton White, principal of Atlanta's D. T. Howard Night School for black students, and Joel Smith, ADW reporter—respectively as employment interviewer and personnel counselor for Bell's black workers.[43]

Only through these efforts did Bell employ any black assembly-line workers. When the company opened its Marietta plant in late 1942, all the African Americans it hired were janitors and maids, no matter their previous work or training experience. Even those who had completed aircraft training at BTWHS were offered only menial positions at the plant. Bell did not engage black workers for skilled positions until 1944. This step derived from protracted back-room talks with AUL officials, after which the company took over the training program at BTWHS, upgraded its equipment and standards for training through intelligence tests, and began to pay sixty-five cents an hour to trainees, who, having completed the three-week program, were guaranteed skilled work.[44]

It soon became apparent that Bell's unprecedented offer of skilled work to black Atlantans would be extremely limited. Of the average of 2,500 Bell positions held by African Americans during the war, 800 were skilled. While this number represented nearly one-third of all black workers at Bell, it only comprised a tiny proportion of the total work force at the Marietta plant, which employed 18,000 to 28,000 workers between 1943 and 1945. Furthermore, the skilled blacks hired by Bell represented only those who had managed to be selected by the AUL for the company training program before the unofficial quota of 800 was rapidly reached. After that point, Bell refused to assign any African Americans to skilled positions, no matter the experience of the applicants and its often-acute assembly-line labor shortages.[45] The skilled workers Bell did take on were segregated into all-black work units at the Marietta plant or an entirely separate facility on Roswell Road.[46]

The AUL remained silent regarding Bell's refusal to expand assembly-line work to other eligible black Atlantans once its initial quota had been reached. Jacob Henderson remembered quietly encouraging qualified workers, whom Bell refused to consider for skilled work, to lodge complaints with the FEPC. Yet these clandestine efforts paled in comparison to the AUL's open campaign of mass mobilization against discrimination in defense training. The reform elite feared rocking the boat with Bell officials, lest they jeopardize the opportunity to challenge Jim Crow labor practices even with limited employment of African Americans at Bell. This outlook, however, sometimes placed the AUL and its agents in compromising positions. For example, black FEPC complainants often named the black personnel officers at Bell as the company officials who informed them that advertised assembly-line positions were for whites only, thus implicating the two men with the company's discriminatory policy.[47]

This collaborationist approach, stemming from black Atlantans' insecure foothold on industrial work, shaped the AUL's attitude toward and treatment of Bell's black workers. As Atlanta's preeminent racial broker, and the quasi-official employment agency for the city's black defense workers, the AUL had enormous influence over the composition and assignment of Bell's black assembly-line work force. Given the limited opportunities for skilled work, the AUL was forced to perform triage, selecting those who, in its opinion, would make the most of the available assembly-line positions, aiding in the goal to protect and expand black opportunity in industry. Its new prestige in the eyes of white officials intensified the AUL's tendency to exclude all but a very narrow segment of the black community from the focus of its reform efforts.

While they lobbied hard for black workers at Bell, black reformers also expressed their long-held concern that these same men and women, in their minds as much products of southern economic and social custom as whites, could not handle the demands of the modern, industrial workplace. Therefore, in the AUL leadership's view, the future of black industrial employment rested not only on Bell's black pioneers' immediate adjustment to their new working conditions, but also on their quick transformation into paragons of the industrial work force. With Bell's opening, the reform elite's perennial concern that working African Americans prove themselves efficient and indispensable took on new urgency. Although even unskilled work at Bell was unionized, well paid, and regulated by modern industrial labor-relations practices, the AUL worried that black wartime workers, many of whom were recent migrants to Atlanta, would not prove themselves on the job. While it began its wartime campaign and gained legitimacy from white officials by mobilizing the "masses," the reform elite's ideological convictions and black Atlantans' tenuous hold on industrial jobs prompted the AUL to retreat to its familiar elitist strategy in its approach to Bell.

Given their ideological fears and the demand for skilled work attested to by the CDT's defense-training registration campaign, AUL leaders unsurprisingly referred to Bell many workers whose social and economic profile did not match that of average black Atlantans. In one study of Bell workers' wartime experience (in which 100 skilled black Bell workers were chosen at random), 44 had belonged to the elite ranks of the black community, either having been students, or professional, white-collar, and skilled workers before being selected for training. The wages of Bell riveters, assemblers, or drill press operators, which far exceeded what they had been earning as teachers, insurance salesmen, or mechanics' helpers clearly attracted these black Atlantans. The impeccable qualifications (indeed over-qualifications) of the skilled black work force at Bell not only demonstrated worker demand for high-paying jobs. The AUL, having screened all applicants for skilled work at Bell, ensured that the company personnel office met only those whom the agency judged as the most educated, respectable, and responsible of Atlanta's black labor force.[48]

Whereas the AUL could provide Bell a skilled work force, which it had hand-picked, it had little or no influence over the unskilled workers who comprised the majority of the company's black employees. The AUL dismissed these workers and their problems at Bell because their behavior did not set the example of black citizenship the agency advocated. Anxious about its inability to direct these African Americans, the AUL held a 1944 series of workshops for Bell employees entitled "Hold Your Job." These meetings, intended to help "new employees to become adjusted to working conditions in a large industrial establishment," covered such topics as absenteeism and the "problems growing out of supervisor-employee relations," but the sessions were very poorly attended. Jacob Henderson, remarking on the virtual absence of unskilled laborers "in the Janitorial and Cafeteria Departments, and men employed as Common Laborers and Productive Helpers," complained that these workers were precisely the ones "who need expert advice on techniques of 'holding their jobs.'"[49]

Those who did attend found little empathy or understanding of their position as mudsills of the industrial work force, plagued by "low pay and little or no chance to be upgraded."[50] At one typical "Hold Your Job" meeting, Ira DeA. Reid, a black economist and consultant to the Social Security Board, placed much of the burden of the future of black industrial employment on the shoulders of African American workers. Reid warned Bell workers "that if Negroes are to keep their present jobs after the war, they must throw out personal feeling and do their work efficiently. 'Don't carry a grudge out on the job,' he said." Reid also advised the workers to use the personnel services of the company and to work "through the regular channels" when dealing with any grievances, if they wanted to retain their jobs.[51] Such directives merely reinforced a message constantly reiterated implicitly and explicitly by the city's black reform elite, living up to its members' tacit bargain with Bell's management that in return for assembly-line jobs they would discipline the company's black work force.[52]

Black workers at Bell knew from experience the absurdity of Reid's directives. Bell's personnel department ignored their complaints of discrimination, even when they worked through the "regular channels" for

Thumbigg your nose at the boss, whether by sulking when asked to do something, by being late because you know he can't get help or just plain dumbness, will bring about that dreadful day of retribution, that sign you have seen so often, "white only."

Editorial cartoon, *Atlanta Daily World*, 8 December 1943.

making grievances and when they enlisted the help of the FEPC.[53] As dozens of FEPC complaints attest, shop-floor discrimination ran rampant at Bell, especially for unskilled workers who, unlike their skilled counterparts in their all-black unit, labored alongside or beneath white employees. Whether the AUL would even support these workers was unclear, given the agency's emphasis on respectable and efficient worker behavior and its unwillingness to push Bell once the company hired black assembly-line workers. However, the FEPC's Atlanta reports indicate that none of the complainants had anything but the most sophisticated understanding of the nature of industrial work, belying the AUL's and Bell management's characterization of their troubles. Still, their complaints indicate that white supervisors used racial stereotypes of black laziness or inefficiency to keep black workers subordinate or to exclude them from the Bell work force altogether.[54]

Ira DeA. Reid's emphasis on workers using the "regular channels" to resolve their complaints of discrimination reflected the reform elite's concern that the interracial battles raging on Atlanta's wartime streets and shop floors would jeopardize its back-room strategy for black industrial employment. The AUL wished to avoid the very real threat of the kind of racial violence surrounding jobs and housing that erupted in defense centers like Detroit and Mobile during the Second World War. They worried that such disturbances in Atlanta, fomented by black workers' own internecine and organized wartime activism, would imperil the limited opportunities in private industry that they had so carefully negotiated. "We must recognize in Atlanta . . . the great impact these riots have . . . on local thinking," the ADW editorialized in June 1943, after racial violence in Detroit and Beaumont, Texas, captured the nation's attention. "Intelligent Negroes and whites of Atlanta know the psychological effects of riots. . . . They do not wish to see the harmonious and peaceful relations upset here. . . . Neither do they wish to have production, so vital to our war stopped."[55]

The black reform elite feared the newly emancipated black "masses" during the war and sought to channel worker discontent through official and quasi-official complaint mechanisms, like the FEPC and the AUL, staffed by members of the reform elite or its white allies. Although actions such as the CDT's defense-training petition drive appeared to represent the "masses'" interests, later developments showed that the black reform elite was pushed into this strategy by the bureaucratic exigencies of federal agencies such as the FEPC or USES. In fact, none of the reform elite's wartime campaigns originated with black workers themselves. Rather, those black workers, like the hand-picked defense trainees and assembly-line workers who saw the benefits of supporting the AUL's wartime campaigns, supported them.

These professional proxies for black workers and black citizens dealt with individual and general issues of discrimination through private negotiations with government and defense-industry officials. The AUL's wartime victories owed much to the cautious pragmatism and conservatism of this approach, but it ignored many of the very real issues facing most black workers, such as white violence on the streets and streetcars, shop-floor harassment and discrimination at work, and economic and educational barriers to training and upward mobility. Thus the AUL leaders' concern for community interest, as they defined it, superseded concern for the struggles of the majority of Bell's black employees, and the social justice issues they confronted at the workplace during the war. Constrained by the continuing realities of Jim Crow and their ideological priorities, the black reform elite chose to concentrate their efforts on the "respectable" skilled workers they could control, help, and lead, while ignoring, and sometimes even condemning, the majority they could not.

Epilogue The Politics of Inclusion

On 12 February 1946, only six weeks before the Supreme Court struck down the white primary in Georgia, Atlanta voters went to the polls to elect a successor to their longtime U.S. congressman, Robert Ramspeck. This "special" election in which black Atlantans were permitted to vote represented a crucial test of African American electoral power for a reform elite that had been mobilizing black Atlantans for voter registration for more than twenty years. When the ballots were finally counted, Helen Mankin, an underdog candidate supported by black electoral organizations, won an upset victory over Ramspeck's hand-picked successor, Thomas Camp. Mankin owed her success to the support of the black electorate, which had swelled from 3,000 to close to 7,000 in a voter-registration campaign leading up to the election.

The success of the postwar voter-registration effort was something of a surprise to the black reform elite, whose prewar registration efforts rarely garnered more than 1,000 black voters, or less than 1 percent of the black population. Even after the repeal of Georgia's cumulative poll tax in 1945, this group had only been able to convince 3,000 black Atlantans to register that year, despite the destruction of this pillar of white supremacy. Buoyed by their success in the congressional election, black reformers decided to launch an unprecedented effort to reach all potential black voters in Atlanta and to urge them to register for the 1946 gubernatorial primary. This would be the first such opportunity for black Atlantans since 1899 due to the repeal of Georgia's white primary.

Drawing from their prewar experience coordinating private black relief efforts and the struggle for defense training, Atlanta Urban League (AUL) leaders Grace Towns Hamilton, Jacob Henderson, and Robert Thompson, and Atlanta University (AU) historian Clarence Bacote organized the All-Citizens Registration Committee, including representatives from all black reform organizations, to run an intensive and extensive registration campaign. Dividing the city into the 1,162 blocks on which African American citizens lived, committee leaders recruited 870 volunteers to reach black

Atlantans of voting age around the city. The AUL printed and distributed 50,000 handbills to prospective voters. The committee enlisted ministers like Martin Luther King Sr. and William Holmes Borders to urge their congregations to vote and arranged carpools to deliver their members to the courthouse. This registration blitz garnered extraordinary results. In the fifty-one days of the campaign before the registration books were closed, nearly 18,000 new black names were added to the rolls, yielding a total of more than 24,000 eligible voters. Thus marked the spectacular debut of African Americans as a political force in the city.[1]

The 1946 registration campaign marked a new political era in Atlanta. Although the oppressive strictures of Jim Crow did not come tumbling down, African Americans could no longer be ignored in the public life of the city. William Hartsfield, recognizing the power of the black vote, actively began to court African American voters in the late 1940s. He appointed eight black police officers in 1948, a step for which black reformers had been working for over fifty years. He cracked down on the Ku Klux Klan and other white vigilante organizations. And he consulted with black leaders on the ever-explosive issues of housing and urban development. Ultimately, Atlanta's black reform elite, backed by the significant voting bloc it controlled, was included in the inner circle of business, political, and community leaders that decided the city's future.[2]

Clarence Bacote was the first historian to write in detail about the events leading to postwar black political involvement in Atlanta. Despite being one of the key participants in the voting and registration activities of 1944 to 1946, Bacote's 1955 *Phylon* article, "The Negro in Atlanta Politics," rather modestly and narrowly framed the black community's emergence as an influential player in the city's public life in terms of national and state political developments and legal decisions. While he admitted that "the spirit of the New Deal as well as World War II had their impact" in bringing black Atlantans to the registrar and to the polls, he saw liberal governor Ellis Arnall's election in 1943 and the subsequent repeal of the poll tax and nullification of the state's white primary as being most significant in ushering in "a new era in Georgia politics and the beginning of the period of Negro participation in Atlanta politics."[3] Certainly the destruction of these barriers to black political participation had an enormous and immediate impact on black voter registration and participation all over the South. They marked a racial opening in the political life of Atlanta and other cities in the South. Postwar black political activism prompted by these reforms would help make southern cities the crucible of the civil rights movement.

Nevertheless Bacote, director of the NAACP's citizenship training program in the early 1930s, underplayed the impact of the black community's decades-long "striving towards self-realization," as W. E. B. Du Bois put it. Thus the story of the recognition and inclusion of African Americans in the city's public life should be seen as the culmination of black reformers' Roosevelt era strategies to move black Atlantans from their marginal and parochial existence at the fringes of civil society and to prepare them to take their rightful place in the political and social mainstream. The shape that inclusion took also bore the black reform elite's imprimatur.

In some ways black Atlantans' turn to politics after the war represented the failure of wartime and postwar efforts to expand the economic rights of African Americans. Although Atlanta did not match the history of black labor organization and radicalism of cities such as Memphis and Birmingham, reform organizations like the AUL did devote most of their energies during the war to expanding black Atlantans' vocational opportunities only to see most progress nullified with reconversion. The AUL was so frustrated in its postwar efforts for black workers that it abandoned its traditional mandate by dissolving its industrial department in 1946 and refocused on the more attainable goals of black voter registration and housing.[4]

AUL leaders had reason to feel frustrated. Peacetime reconversion was a difficult and tension-filled process in Atlanta, with blacks bearing the brunt of the resulting racial conflicts. Returning veterans encountered hostility and ingratitude, coming home to a boomtown that had just gone bust for black workers. Although wartime migrants did not leave the city after the war, the jobs that had attracted them to Atlanta in the first place did. Bell Aircraft and Firestone shut down their plants as the city's military installations began to close up or scale down their operations in preparation for peace. These closings, accompanied by the return of black veterans with military experience in technical, clerical, or mechanical work, flooded the local labor market with skilled black workers. As elsewhere, they had no comparable place in the postwar economy. Many African Americans, living off what they had saved from defense work or servicemen's allotments, stayed unemployed as long as they could before returning to the unskilled work to which they were again consigned and for which they were often vastly overqualified. Many veterans expressed vocational aspirations by taking advantage of the training and educational opportunities offered by the GI Bill. Sadly, they most often found that the high school, college, and apprenticeship training they received could not be put to practice in Atlanta or the South.[5]

While tight housing markets and vocational limits were nothing new to black Atlantans, postwar inequities were particularly severe and difficult to endure after blacks' relatively diverse and well-paying wartime job opportunities and the patriotic contribution of black soldiers. The same was true of the active and hostile campaign waged by thousands of whites to reassert white supremacy and control of black workers. Between November 1945 and October 1946, four black men were shot on Atlanta's buses and streetcars, three of them by motormen exercising their police powers. Three died, two of them veterans. The police killed one and shot two other veterans in 1945 and 1946, beating countless others in incidents where officers were "provoked" by the veterans' perceived wealth or "uppity" behavior. The police were officially sanctioned to arrest black men at will, after Mayor Hartsfield ordered that they round up and arrest any "idlers" on vagrancy charges in order to provide unskilled workers for the labor-strapped construction industry. Clearly, the white establishment in Atlanta wanted to reestablish prewar race relations as quickly as possible by hastening black workers' return to subordinate dependence on white employers.[6]

The officially sanctioned antiblack violence of the motormen and police was accompanied by the reemergence of white vigilantism in Atlanta. The Ku Klux Klan enjoyed a brief postwar resurgence in the city after a hiatus of almost twenty years. Among its members were dozens of police officers and local politicians, the same groups that had swelled the organization's ranks at its peak in the 1920s. More threatening, however, were the Columbians, a new white supremacist organization aimed at stopping the movement of African Americans to west-side white neighborhoods. Dominated by white veterans, the Columbians' tactics intensified the vigilantism that had plagued black migrants to the west side since the 1920s.

They began their campaign in September 1946 in the area surrounding Sells Avenue, a modest historically white working-class neighborhood of tenant-occupied frame houses. Vigilantes dynamited porches and stoned black residents and their homes, and angry mobs confronted black tenants and homeowners. In 1946, the intensity, violence, and organization of the protests increased markedly from earlier decades. Both blacks and whites suffered from a housing shortage after the war, although for African Americans the situation was much more dire. When white homes were sold for top dollar to black homeowners or when owners evicted longtime white tenants for black citizens willing to pay much higher rents, the reaction was swift and violent. On Sells Avenue, Columbians roughed up and threatened black residents in front of the police, who did nothing but to tell black residents to abandon their new homes now that they had received "fair warning" from the vigilantes. White mobs drove residents from their homes, not even letting them gather their belongings. Unidentified gunmen shot at black-occupied houses and at an Atlanta Life Insurance agent making his rounds of west-side policy holders. In October, the protests spread to other streets threatened with black incursion, where white tenants and home owners placed "White Only" signs in the front yards of houses for sale. The Columbians also began patrolling the west side for black "loiterers" whom they detained for the police or "arrested," exacting their own justice through beatings and threats.[7]

These depressingly familiar incidents gave rise to a feeling among local progressives that the war had changed nothing. Yet in fact, the intensity and brutality of the white crackdown on blacks testified to how much change had taken place in the city during the Roosevelt era. One Sells Avenue demonstrator told a newspaper reporter that his protest was not an effort to reclaim housing for whites, but rather a means to help "straighten out the South" by reasserting his supremacy over black residents. He expressed the fear shared by the Columbians, the Klan, the police, and streetcar motormen that only a violent backlash against African Americans could reverse the trends which threatened the racial status quo.[8]

The most basic change that occurred in Atlanta during the 1930s and 1940s was a dramatic increase in the black population. Over 30,000 more African Atlantans lived in Atlanta in 1950 than in 1930, continuing an upward trend, beginning in 1920, of the proportion of African Americans in the city's population. This would result in a majority black city by 1970. By their sheer numbers, then, African Americans were becoming a more visible and important group in civic life.

White officials recognized this fact. Mayor Hartsfield continued to push the annexation of Atlanta's white northern suburbs throughout the war, hoping to counterbalance the growing black population in the innercity. In a letter to white north-side residents in 1943 urging the passage of his plan to expand the city limits, he wrote:

The most important thing to remember, cannot be publicized in the press or made the subject of public speeches.

Our negro [sic] population is growing by leaps and bounds. They stay right in the city limits and grow by taking more white territory inside Atlanta. Our migration is good white, home owning citizens.

With the Federal government insisting on political recognition of negroes [sic] in local affairs, the time is not far distant when they will become a potent political force in Atlanta if our white citizens are just going to move out and give it to them.

This is not intended to stir race prejudice because all of us want to deal fairly with them, but do you want to hand them political control of Atlanta, either as a majority or a powerful minority vote?[9]

Despite his dire predictions, annexation did not happen until 1952. Consequently Hartsfield, the consummate politician, chose to deal with Atlanta's large and growing black voting bloc. His recognition of demographic trends in the city kept him in power; he won the support of black voters by capitulating to some some of black reformers' longest-held wishes for the black community, including the appointment of the first black police.[10]

Other changes in the black community were less visible and tangible, but no less important. While African Americans continued to be relegated to the lowest-paid and most menial work in the city, a significant minority achieved upward mobility within the ranks of the city's unskilled workers during the Roosevelt era. The most important changes occurred in domestic work. The proportion of black workers employed in household labor was almost halved between 1930 and 1950, from 40 percent to 22 percent. This decline was most dramatic for black women, almost half of whom found employment outside whites' homes in 1950, as compared to under one quarter two decades before. Most striking for male workers was their increased opportunity to work in the wartime and postwar economy. By 1950, they comprised 58 percent of the city's African American work force, an almost 10 percent increase over 1930, suggesting an easing of the chronic unemployment and underemployment that had plagued black men since the end of Reconstruction after the Civil War (see Appendix, Tables 2 and 3).

African Americans continued to be relegated to the lowest-paid and most menial work in the city. Female ex-domestic workers moved in greatest numbers to service work, while men became unskilled laborers. However, for most of these black Atlantans, such occupational shifts represented significant upward mobility within the ranks of the city's unskilled workers. For many of these "deserters," there was no looking back. Maids became cleaners in commercial and industrial establishments, porters became production helpers, and previously unemployed men became laborers in Atlanta's postwar industries.[11]

While the new duties of these ex-domestic workers may have been very similar to their former positions, the new employment was very different. By leaving white households, black Atlantans left the paternalism and dependency on whites that defined domestic work. Although black workers continued to be beholden to their white employers, the terms of this subordination were much less oppressive and personalistic than in domestic work. Most postwar black employment continued to be hot, dirty, and poorly paid. But usually the hours were set, Sundays were free, and the wages were hourly—and in cash, not in kind. The jobs might even be unionized, as in the case of commercial laundry work.

These workplace changes had important implications for reformers' aspirations to mobilize them for full citizenship. As the tenant-selection process for public housing demonstrated, the black elite saw personal service workers such as porters, janitors, industrial maids, and truck drivers to be much better candidates for full citizenship than domestic servants or laundresses. Reformers believed that these workers' higher wages prompted them to want more for their families and communities. Their relative autonomy from whites also gave them more freedom to work openly for racial uplift. More practical, these workers had more time for reform efforts than their brothers and sisters in domestic service, who often worked twelve hours or more a day with only Thursday afternoon off. Freed from household work, these black Atlantans were also less isolated from civic life and from other black workers, making them more accessible for reformers to contact and to organize. Thus changes in black employment made it easier for reformers to mobilize the African American community politically.[12]

Black reformers could work with this group of striving black workers after the war because it was only then that they could effectively reach them. Ironically, only after the federal government had acknowledged the citizenship of black Atlantans by including them in New Deal and wartime programs could Atlanta's black reform elite unite the black community to further its citizenship goals for black Atlantans. Before the New Deal, Atlanta's black reform elite only had the haziest and sometimes prejudiced notions of the city's black neighborhoods. Its members often wrote with frustration of the apparent impenetrability of neighborhoods like Summer Hill or Dark Town. Yet these neighborhoods did not lack respectable residents interested in racial betterment through vocational, economic, and political opportunity. Rather, black reformers, despite their best efforts, lacked the resources and authority to engage these communities and make their residents appreciate the economic and political benefits of joining their crusade. Generally, it was impossible for them to unite sympathetic black Atlantans from the city's disparate black neighborhoods for a common cause.

Federal programs helped close the gap between black reformers and Atlanta's black community writ large. For one, the New Deal, through the WPA's white-collar relief projects, surveyed and enumerated black Atlantans more exhaustively than they ever had been before. Often led by social scientists from AU, government surveyors, clerks, and statisticians compiled dozens of demographic studies detailing the vital statistics of Atlanta's black community. This research detailed the exact nature and extent of the inequalities of black schools; it established average income, rate of unemployment, and educational attainment by census tract; and it charted the occurrence of communicable diseases like tuberculosis and syphilis in the black community.

This information became an indispensable tool to black reformers in their various citizenship and community improvement campaigns. During the war, the AUL used statistics first garnered during the New Deal to gain white support for the equalization of black and white schools and teachers' salaries, and to work toward the hiring of black police. However, the greater importance of these numbers was in educating black reformers themselves about the black community. In 1946, Robert Thompson, who had worked on the WPA's Real Property Survey of Atlanta, used his experience with that project, which had exhaustively compiled the housing conditions on every block in every census tract of the city, to organize the 1946 voter registration drive. Because of the survey, he knew where virtually every black person in Atlanta lived, and in what kind of housing, and could therefore pinpoint the areas of most potential for the voter registration drive. Through his New Deal experience he had also obtained a model for efficiently and systematically ensuring that campaign volunteers covered every section of the city. He developed a hierarchical organizing strategy in which campaign leaders were each assigned a census tract which they in turn divided into blocks assigned to volunteers who were responsible for visiting every home in their assigned area, until the whole area was covered. While in the past the Neighborhood Union (NU) had organized its work in a similar way, it had been years since black leaders had attempted such a systematic organizing campaign. Its success was largely due to black reformers' use of New Deal demographic projects to gain a better understanding of the city's black community.[13]

While black reformers' sophisticated postwar understanding of the demographics of black Atlanta finally gave them the knowledge they needed to organize an effective voter registration campaign, they could not be assured that black Atlantans would finally register and vote. So they placed special emphasis on the constituency they had already developed through the New Deal—the five thousand or so potential voters living in Atlanta's five prewar public-housing projects for African Americans, along with the hundreds of others who had "graduated" from public housing into private home ownership during the war. These citizens had been training for years to be at the vanguard of any assertion of black citizenship, thanks to the efforts of their black managers. Indeed, these upwardly mobile black Atlantans would become the core of the constituency that black reformers mobilized in the mass tactics of the postwar period.

In preparation for this mobilization Jacob Henderson, when he was not working for the AUL in its defense training and voter registration efforts, organized a variety of citizenship training campaigns for his tenants at John Eagan Homes, beginning when he assumed the project's management in 1941. He held elaborate annual campaigns to elect the tenants' advisory council, like those for U.S. president and congress, including conventions, primaries, and inaugural balls. After the war, the AUL organized an "informal veterans council" in all housing projects in which members were informed of their rights as ex-GIs and urged to register to vote. And Henderson, along with other project managers, worked with the Civic and Political League and the Alpha Phi Alpha fraternity, to which he belonged, in registering tenants in the myriad of voter drives preceding 1946, providing the bulk of new voters in these modestly successful efforts. By 1946, his tenants were ready to exercise their electoral muscle when he and other black leaders threw their weight behind Helen Mankin. Over 750 John Eagan tenants, or residents of the vast majority of the 548 units, voted in the election that put Mankin in office. In fact, the returns from the electoral district in which the project was located provided Mankin with the boost that put her over the top on election night.[14]

Black reformers' ability to mobilize this constituency was facilitated primarily by the housing program and their role in it. By assuming the authority to choose those black Atlantans who would find shelter under the protective umbrella of the federally funded projects, the black reform elite was able to use the projects as laboratories to build a constituency of "respectable" black Atlantans who shared their ideology and their goals for uplift and citizenship. Although they had attempted such schemes through the voluntary efforts of the NU or the NAACP, they had little or no success in building a mass constituency for their program through private means. Only through the federal government, with its resources and authority, could they build such a base. By delivering on its implicit promise of better housing and a "respectable" community free from police harassment and the underground economy, housing officials brought upwardly mobile black Atlantans together under one roof and in one self-contained community where they could work together toward common goals for citizenship and racial uplift. Thus the inclusion of black Atlantans in the housing program made them accessible to black reformers, who then manipulated the program to take full advantage of the opportunities it presented. This incorporative process comprised an indispensable prelude to the events of 1946 and later civil rights activism.

While the inclusion of black Atlantans in state programs such as public housing helped the black reform elite to create a constituency that it could then better organize for first-class citizenship, state involvement of a more basic kind also brought about grassroots mobilization among black Atlantans, largely without the intervention of the reform elite. After the war, black veterans in Atlanta became a militant and autonomous force in the African American community from which emerged a leadership group somewhat separate from the black reform elite. The largest of the black veterans groups was the Georgia Veterans' League. Closely allied with the AUL and with the voter registration effort, the league was nonetheless an independent organization working to educate veterans of their rights and benefits and to protest discrimination against veterans. Vocal and militant Veterans' League president Charles Milton was a west-side barber who spent almost two years in the Pacific theater. After his discharge, he considered moving out of the South, to a region where "the rope of discrimination and prejudice are not so binding." Instead, as he told an *Atlanta Daily World* (*ADW*) reporter, he decided to return and to "fight it out with the forces of hate"[15] by organizing black veterans into a powerful voting bloc. Milton was embraced by black reformers as an important part of the voter registration coalition, even though he was not part of Atlanta's black elite. His constituency of ex-servicemen was too important to ignore. Milton's inclusion in the registration effort marked black reformers' long-overdue recognition that they needed to open up their ranks if they were to achieve mass mobilization.[16]

Another black veterans group had a less sanguine relationship with the reform elite. In March 1946, the United Negro Veterans and its Women's Auxiliary organized a demonstration on city hall demanding black police. The protest, which was carried off without incident, attracted up to one thousand peaceful marchers and opened the eyes of many white Atlantans to the issue of black police and the black community's support for such a move. Despite the demonstration's success, black elites launched a smear campaign against the protest, which the United Negro Veterans organized without the knowledge, input, or cooperation of the reform establishment. An *ADW* editorial claimed that the demonstration made "a sorry mess of all that responsible Negro leaders and civic organizations are doing to achieve Negro police or any other important achievement in Atlanta."[17]

Public demonstrations had always been anathema to Atlanta's black reformers who decried any protest that threatened racial peace in the city or that could possibly contravene the code of public respectability on which they rested their claims for African American citizenship. But while they had never actively supported or initiated such activism, they had not always condemned it outright. Communist demonstrations and the March on Washington Movement had won tacit approval or at least serious consideration throughout the 1930s and early 1940s, when black reformers were still outsiders in the city trying to figure out how to gain entry to its public life. By 1946, however, black leaders believed the key to that door was black voting, and were not going to permit an alternative strategy of "ill-advised and inopportune"[18] mass protest to spoil their chances. They knew that their influence in city affairs rested on the black vote and their ability to control and channel black protest within the tight confines of electorally and legally based civil rights activism.

Much has been written about the ruling coalition between black Atlantans and wealthy north-side whites that developed after the entry of black voters in the city's electorate. This literature has usually focused on what the black community won and lost by allying itself with the city's ruling white elite. However the white business and political leaders who ruled Atlanta also derived a great deal from this relationship. The regime that governed Atlanta depended on maintaining a civic image of racial peace. As William Hartsfield liked to proclaim, the city was simply "too busy to hate." However, middle- and working-class whites, like those who joined the Columbians, did not share Hartsfield's civic aspirations. They were the whites most affected by Roosevelt-era changes in the city's racially defined geography, economy, and politics, and therefore the ones with the most to lose. They were willing to fight to maintain their supremacy over blacks and to "straighten out the South." Therefore the black vote became very important in keeping Atlanta safe from the forces of racial demagoguery that swept the state in 1946 with the return of Eugene Talmadge to the governor's office. The black vote was yet another measure used by white elites in Atlanta, like redrawing the city's ward system or annexation, to neutralize the impact of non-elite whites on the city's political affairs. However, this mutually beneficial alliance would never have been conceivable to white leaders if there had not been black leaders in Atlanta whom they could trust and with whom they could identify.[19]

It is not surprising, then, that the AUL led and controlled the mobilization campaign of the All Citizens Registration Committee. While the NAACP and various other civic groups contributed greatly to the effort, the Urban League board members put together the strategy for the registration campaign, and the organization's employees put the plan into practice. The league's leadership in this program was in some sense a matter of practicality; in 1946, it was the only black civic organization in Atlanta with the resources to put over such an ambitious campaign. That year, its $17,223 income put it many times ahead of the NAACP in terms of budget size. What is more significant, however, was that in 1946, 85 percent of the AUL's budget came from the Community Chest, an organization dominated by the city's conservative business and charitable white elite. As we have seen in the case of the NU and the Commission of Interracial Cooperation, chest leaders always scrutinized the activities of its member agencies very carefully and were ready to purge any organization deemed to be working contrary to its mission. In other words, the registration campaign that marked black Atlantans' debut as a significant force in the city's public life took place with the tacit approval of some of the most powerful white people in the city.[20]

White approval of the AUL's leadership role in the registration campaign simply marked the extension of the organization's Roosevelt-era activities. It easily assumed its postwar role as a "central connector in the city's governing coalition,"[21] as political scientist Clarence Stone defined it, given its crucial role as a powerbroker between federal agencies and the black community in the 1930s and 1940s. The AUL's wartime campaigns for defense training and skilled work had demonstrated its ability both to represent and control the black community. Its back-room maneuvering between government agencies and defense contractors had demonstrated a shrewd ability to manipulate competing bureaucracies to its own ends and a sophisticated understanding of the power of compromise. Perhaps most important, its tactics were moderate and nonconfrontational, aimed always at reducing the chances of racial violence. It would never call for mass public demonstrations to achieve its goals as the Communists, Columbians, and United Negro Veterans had done. Instead, it created committees and task forces to study the "problems" of the black community, lobbied city government and "civic-minded" white citizens for support, and worked behind closed doors with all levels of government and business to achieve its goals. The AUL's tactics represented a synthesis of modern southern liberalism and black politics, emphasizing interracial cooperation and electoral tradeoffs. But only when this strategy was combined with public demonstrations, as Atlantan Martin Luther King Jr. successfully accomplished in Montgomery and elsewhere, would segregation be destroyed.[22]

The black reform elite's participation in Atlanta's ruling coalition had an enormous influence on the future of African Americans in the city. Most obviously, the influence of black leaders grew greatly in the postwar period. No major decision in city politics or planning was made without consulting the black community's representatives in civic and political organizations. In 1953 Rufus Clement, AU's president, was elected with a ten-thousand-vote plurality to represent the majority black Third Ward on the Board of Education. In the same year A. T. Walden and Dr. Miles Amos (another reform leader), were elected to the City Democratic Executive Committee. These elections only marked the beginning of African American political representation in city politics by members of the reform elite, culminating finally in 1973 with the election of John Wesley Dobbs's grandson, Maynard Jackson Jr., as Atlanta's first black mayor.

While the inclusion of black reformers in the city's governing coalition allowed black voters to influence local policy, it also had a limiting effect on black activism. As in the case of the United Negro Veterans, black civic leaders in Atlanta became less and less willing to countenance activism conducted outside the realm of electoral politics or outside of their control. In 1949, black reformers created the Negro Voters' League, a nonpartisan voting organization that sought to strengthen the power of the black vote by getting all black voters to support a single slate in local elections.

Even more important, inclusion in the governing coalition altered the focus of the reform elite's goals for the black community in significant ways. For example, the AUL's abandonment of labor issues to concentrate on housing and urban development marked its acknowledgment that the latter issue would likely bear more fruit with the agency's new allies in local government. In 1946, in the wake of the postwar housing crunch and the Columbian protests, the AUL created the Temporary Coordinating

Committee on Housing to negotiate with local officials for "outlet areas for Negro expansion" and to encourage and coordinate private efforts to build housing for blacks in these areas. This black postwar housing effort coincided with an intensified push by white business for urban renewal and for the removal of African Americans from the center of Atlanta. The Urban League and its role in housing became an influential part of city's extensive postwar urban-renewal projects.[23]

The AUL's housing efforts garnered impressive results. Robert Thompson, the AUL's industrial-turned-housing secretary, estimated that between 1945 and 1956, some 3,450 single-family homes, 3,100 private apartments, and 1,990 public-housing units were built for blacks in the negotiated expansion areas on the city's west and south sides. Most of this real estate development was undertaken by black contractors and real estate brokers such as W. H. Aiken and T. M. Alexander, represented by the black Empire Real Estate Board, who emerged as some of the wealthiest and most influential black business people in the city. These real estate developments finally met the pent-up demand for good housing of Atlanta's upwardly mobile black working and middle classes. They could now live in neighborhoods befitting respectable people, fulfilling the decades-old dream of Ruby Blackburn, John and Lugenia Hope, and countless others. Finally, highway urban-renewal projects in central Atlanta and the negotiated expansion areas completed the shift of the city's black population to the west side. The concentration of Atlanta's black population in one area was highly desirable to the reform elite since it strengthened the power of the black vote and black influence in local affairs.[24]

However these achievements came at a cost. In return for the expansion of black housing areas, African American leaders had to accept urban renewal in central Atlanta and the massive dislocation of residents of some of the most established black neighborhoods in the city. Vine City, Buttermilk Bottom, and the Auburn Avenue neighborhood were either greatly diminished or totally destroyed in federally and locally financed renewal programs from the 1950s to the 1970s. At least 10,000 families, most of them extremely poor, were dislocated between 1958 and 1963. Black developers, politicians, and reformers were all deeply complicit in this dislocation, the scope of which makes New Deal slum clearance pale in comparison.[25]

Scholars writing about the participation of black leaders in urban renewal reason that the postwar inclusion of African Americans in the city's ruling coalition marked the divergence of interests of the black ruling elite and ordinary black Atlantans. They see the inclusion of black reformers in the city's ruling coalition as compromising their commitment to work for the good of the black community. They point out, for example, that black contractors and realtors had much to gain from cooperating with the urban renewal program and supporting the displacement of thousands of families who needed to find new homes. They also point to the postwar and post–civil rights era as the beginning of "class splits" in the black community which led to middle-class blacks wanting to distance themselves from their poorer brothers and sisters. As this study has shown, however, the solution to this race and class conundrum is more complicated and has deeper roots than these studies reveal.[26]

As the prewar slum clearance and public housing program demonstrate, the reform elite's uplift efforts were always aimed at working for full citizenship for those black Atlantans most receptive and most able to conform to the politics of respectability. Black reformers limited their efforts and appeal in this way largely because of the ways in which Jim Crow circumscribed their authority and resources. Ideologically linking respectability and citizenship, they had always centered their reform efforts at the top, and from there extended downward both geographically and demographically, as far as they could. By the end of 1946, owing to their Roosevelt-era efforts and the structural forces which improved the lot of many black Atlantans, they had reached farther than ever before, managing to register about 21,000 black voters or just over one-quarter of the potential black electorate as part of their constituency. But what of the other almost three-quarters of the black voting-age population?[27]

This group remained essentially untouched by the citizenship efforts of black reformers and outside the postwar constituency on which they based their influence. Always perceived as marginal by whites, this majority of black Atlantans became even less perceptible to black leaders after the war when they accomplished their goal of full citizenship for the respectable and to their minds, deserving segment of the black population. It became easier and easier for African American leaders to ignore the poorest black Atlantans as they gained political power and influence representing their respectable and growing postwar constituency. The reform elite thus split the black community into those whom it determined to be deserving of the fruits of inclusion into the polity and those who were shut out of the upward mobility afforded by wartime industrialization and political mobilization and consigned to remain at the margins of civic life.

Today, the legacy of the Roosevelt-era efforts of Atlanta's black reform elite can still be felt. Governed by a black mayor since Maynard Jackson's victory in 1973, Atlanta continues to be a national center of black education, business, and culture. It boasts one of the most prosperous middle-class African American communities in the country. These black Atlantans owe their success largely to the path paved by their peers fifty years ago. But Atlanta also contains some of the largest pockets of urban poverty in the United States.[28] Members of the city's so-called underclass can trace their continued exclusion from the public life of the city back to the enormous social, economic, and political barriers to African American progress during the Jim Crow era, which black reformers were most often unable and sometimes unwilling to lift for the poorest members of the black community. Offering only the most tentative challenges to Jim Crow, the New Deal served as an imperfect catalyst for African American liberation, not least for members of the black reform elite, whose experience of exclusion and discrimination inexorably limited both their ability to achieve racial uplift for all black Atlantans and their vision of African American freedom.

Appendix Tables

Table 1. Atlanta's Black Population, 1900–1980

Year	Total Population	Total Black Population	Percent Black Population
1900	89,872	35,727	39.7
1910	154,893	51,902	33.5
1920	200,616	62,796	31.2
1930	270,366	90,075	33.3
1940	302,288	104,533	34.6
1950	331,314	121,416	36.6
1960	487,455	186,820	38.3
1970	496,973	255,051	51.3
1980	425,022	283,158	66.6

Source: Ronald Bayor, *Race and the Shaping of Twentieth-Century Atlanta* (Chapel Hill: University of North Carolina Press, 1996), 7.

Table 2. Atlanta's Black Work Force, 1930

Occupations[a]	Men	Women	Total
Professional and technical workers	746	799	1,545
	(3%)	(3%)	(3%)
Managers, officials, and proprietors	499	256	755
	(2%)	(1%)	(2%)
Clerical workers	438	175	613
	(2%)	(1%)	(1%)
Sales workers	726	158	884
	(3%)	(1%)	(2%)
Craftspeople and industrial operatives	4,764	861	5,625
	(21%)	(4%)	(12%)
Household workers	1,620	19,124	20,744
	(7%)	(79%)	(44%)
Service workers	5,967	2,538	8,505
	(26%)	(10%)	(18%)
Laborers	7,121	221	7,342
	(31%)	(1%)	(16%)
Occupations not recorded	1,014	140	1,154
	(4%)	(1%)	(2%)
Total	22,895	24,272	47,167
	(100%)	(100%)	(100%)

Source: Bureau of the Census, *Fifteenth Census of the United States: 1930*, vol. 4 (Washington, D.C.: Government Printing Office, 1933), 391–93.

[a]Occupational categories are taken from Bureau of the Census, *Census of Population, Seventeenth Census of the United States: 1950*, vol. 2, pt. 11 (Washington, D.C.: Government Printing Office, 1952), 297–99.

Table 3. Atlanta's Black Work Force, 1950

	Men	Women	Total
Professional and technical workers	895	1,394	2,289
	(2%)	(5%)	(3%)
Managers, officials, and proprietors	835	299	1,134
	(2%)	(1%)	(2%)
Clerical workers	1,523	670	2,193
	(4%)	(2%)	(3%)
Sales workers	547	286	833
	(1%)	(1%)	(1%)
Craftspeople	3,986	131	4,117
	(10%)	(0%)	(6%)
Industrial operatives	9,382	3,999	13,381
	(24%)	(14%)	(20%)
Household workers	598	14,780	15,378
	(2%)	(51%)	(22%)
Service workers	9,169	6,771	15,940
	(23%)	(23%)	(23%)
Laborers	11,982	408	12,390
	(30%)	(1%)	(18%)
Occupations not recorded	501	281	782
	(1%)	(1%)	(1%)
Total	39,418	29,019	68,437
	(100%)	(100%)	(100%)

Source: Census of Population, Seventeenth Census of the United States: 1950, vol. 2, pt. 11 (Washington, D.C.: Government Printing Office, 1952), 297–98.

Table 4. Black Voter Registration, 1918–1977

	Number	Percent of Total Registered Voters	Percent of Estimated Black Population[a]
1918	715	5.2	1.1
1919	1,723	11.0	2.7
1926	1,198	8.0	1.3
1935	958	6.0	1.0
1945	3,000	4.0	2.5
1946 (Feb.)	6,876	8.3	5.7
1946 (May)	21,244	27.2	17.5
1953	17,300	18.0	14.3
1956	23,440	27.0	12.6
1957	28,604	22.1	15.3
1961	41,469	28.6	22.2
1965		34.7	
1966	64,285	35.8	25.2
1969		40.7	
1973	101,091	49.0	39.6
1975		51.8	
1977		53.5	

Source: Ronald Bayor, *Race and the Shaping of Twentieth-Century Atlanta* (Chapel Hill: University of North Carolina Press, 1996), 7, 18.
[a] Calculated from total population figures from nearest decennial census.

Notes

Abbreviations

AARL	Auburn Avenue Research Library, Atlanta
ADW	*Atlanta Daily World*
AHC	Atlanta History Center Library/Archives, Atlanta
AU	Special Collections, Robert W. Woodruff Library, Clark-Atlanta University, Atlanta
AUL	Atlanta Urban League
CAR	City of Atlanta Records, Atlanta History Center Library/Archives, Atlanta
CIC	*Commission on Interracial Cooperation Papers, 1919–1944* (Ann Arbor, Mich.: University Microfilms International, 1984)
ER Papers	Eleanor Roosevelt Papers, Franklin and Eleanor Roosevelt Library, Hyde Park, New York
EU	Special Collections Department, Robert W. Woodruff Library, Emory University, Atlanta
FDR Library	Franklin and Eleanor Roosevelt Library, Hyde Park, New York
FDR Papers	Franklin Delano Roosevelt Papers, Franklin and Eleanor Roosevelt Library, Hyde Park, New York
FEPC	Committee on Fair Employment Practices Records, RG 228, Region 7, National Archives Regional Office, East Point, Georgia
GA	Georgia Department of Archives and History, Atlanta
Hope Papers	*Papers of John and Lugenia Burns Hope* (Frederick, Md.: University Publications of America, 1984)
LA	Living Atlanta Collection, Atlanta History Center Library/Archives, Atlanta
NU	Neighborhood Union Collection, Special Collections, Robert W. Woodruff Library, Clark-Atlanta University, Atlanta
NYA	National Youth Administration Records, RG 119, Region 2, National Archives Regional Office, East Point, Georgia
OF	Official Correspondence File
SPA	*Socialist Party of America Papers* (Glen Rock, N.J.: Microfilming Corporation of America, 1975)

SRC   *Southern Regional Council Papers* (Ann Arbor, Mich.: University Microfilms International, 1984)

WMC   U.S. War Manpower Commission Records, RG 211, Region 7, National Archives Regional Office, East Point, Georgia

Introduction

1. McNeil, *Groundwork*, 84–85.
2. Earlier scholarship on this group emphasized its symbolic importance, noting that its members had little influence over the administration of New Deal programs. See Weiss, *Farewell to the Party of Lincoln*, 136–56; Kirby, *Black Americans in the Roosevelt Era*; Sitkoff, *A New Deal for Blacks*, 77–79. I would argue that while Roosevelt and his cabinet members saw black appointees this way, the "black cabinet" members used their positions as an opening wedge in influencing federal policy. Patricia Sullivan confirms this view in *Days of Hope*, 46–56. As this study shows, black professionals working on the local level to put social-welfare programs into effect were even more important in terms of concrete influence.
3. Logan, *The Negro in American Life and Thought.* For details of legal efforts to subjugate black Atlantans, see Bacote, "The Negro in Atlanta Politics," 342. Often these laws only reinforced racial custom. Rabinowitz, *Race Relations in the Urban South*, 329–39. The actions of antiblack white vigilantes during the "nadir" resulted in a bloody race riot in 1906 that left at least twenty-five blacks and one white killed. During the resurgence of the Ku Klux Klan in the 1920s, the organization located its national headquarters in Atlanta. Jackson, *Ku Klux Klan in the City*, 29–44; Dittmer, *Black Georgia in the Progressive Era*, 123–31.
4. Jacqueline Moore skillfully outlines the development of the "lifting as we climb" ethos among post-Reconstruction black elites in *Leading the Race.*
5. Adolph Reed Jr., *Stirrings in the Jug*, 18–23.
6. James, *Transcending the Talented Tenth*, 17.
7. Higginbotham, *Righteous Discontent*, 188. See also Gilmore, *Gender and Jim Crow*, xix.
8. Gaines, *Uplifting the Race*, 2.
9. Cohen, *Making a New Deal.*
10. For examples of the challenges faced by black elites in the North (Cleveland) and the South (Birmingham), see Phillips, *Alabama North*, 190–225; and Kelley, *Hammer and Hoe*, 108–16.
11. Lester Granger quoted in Sullivan, *Days of Hope*, 49.
12. George Streator, "On to Asbury Park!," *The Crisis* 41 (May 1934): 133. See also, Leon P. Miller, "A Greater N.A.A.C.P.," *The Crisis* 43 (July 1936): 213.
13. W. E. B. Du Bois, "Postscript," *The Crisis* 41 (March 1934): 86.

14. The NUL, the NAACP, and their local chapters changed their tactics during the 1930s to reflect this new spirit. See Sullivan, *Days of Hope*, 84–93; McNeil, *Groundwork*, 120, 131–55; Earl Lewis, *In Their Own Interests*, 143–66; and Fairclough, *Race and Democracy*, 46–73.

15. W. E. B. Du Bois, "Forum of Fact and Opinion," *Pittsburgh Courier*, 19 June 1937; Du Bois, *Black Reconstruction in America*.

16. Du Bois, "Federal Action Programs and Community Action in the South," 376.

17. Lipsitz, *The Possessive Investment in Whiteness*, 5. See also Brodkin, *How Jews Became White Folks*.

18. A. J. Allen, "Selling Out the Workers," *The Crisis* 45 (March 1938): 80.

19. Lewis, *In Their Own Interests*, 135.

20. Lester Granger, "Step-Children of the Depression," *Opportunity*, July 1934, 219.

21. Bettie E. Parham, "What of the Negro Bourgeoisie?" *The Crisis* 43 (July 1936): 215.

22. W. E. B. Du Bois, "Postscript," *The Crisis* 38 (September 1931): 314.

23. Atlanta's black reform elite shared this perspective with other "vanguard" leaders of twentieth-century political movements worldwide. James C. Scott has made an important point about the elitism of progressive and revolutionary leaders in their use of the terms "mass" and "masses." As he notes, "Nothing better conveys the impression of mere quantity and number without order than the word 'masses.' Once the rank and file are so labeled, it is clear that what they chiefly add to the revolutionary process are their weight in numbers and the kind of brute force they can represent if firmly directed. The impression conveyed is of a huge, formless, milling crowd without any cohesion— without a history, without ideas, without a plan of action." Thus for these elites, the "bourgeois intelligentsia" is not only "essential to the tactical cohesion of the masses but also must literally do their thinking for them." Scott, *Seeing like a State*, 150.

Chapter One

1. "A Tribute of Love and Appreciation to Lugenia Hope, Honoring Her on the Twenty-Fifth Anniversary of the Founding of the 'Neighborhood Union,'" [1933], Box 3, NU.

2. L. D. Shivery, "Suggestions for the Pageant," typescript, [1933], Box 3, NU.

3. "A Tribute to Lugenia Hope."

4. Hunter, *To 'Joy My Freedom*, 99.

5. Dittmer, *Black Georgia in the Progressive Era*, 127.

6. Ibid., 123–31; Hunter, *To 'Joy My Freedom*, 126–27; Rouse, *Lugenia Burns Hope*, 42.

7. Blackwelder, "Women in the Work Force," 337.

8. U.S. Bureau of the Census, *Fifteenth Census of the United States*, 4:393.

9. Painter, *The Narrative of Hosea Hudson*, 62–65.

10. Phyllis Wheatley Branch, YWCA, "Domestic and Personal Servants in Atlanta —A Study with the Aim of Program Development through the Industrial Dept of the YWCA," 1939, pamphlet, Reel 48, *CIC*; Anderson and Bowman, "The Vanishing Servant," 219–23; Blackwelder, "Women in the Work Force," 341; Kytle, *Willie Mae*, 119.

11. Dittmer, *Black Georgia in the Progressive Era*, 97–104; Pierce, *The Atlanta Negro*, 51; Estelle Clemmons interview, Box 36, LA.

12. The police employed an equal-opportunity policy in their harassment of black Atlantans. Forrester B. Washington, president of the black Atlanta School of Social Work, told the Fulton-DeKalb Interracial Committee in 1940 that police were "roughing up" pool-room patrons, "terrorizing" domestic workers coming home late from work without an identifying letter from their employers, and taunting teachers returning home from a fraternity dance by asking them, "What're you nigger women doing out here, want us to take you to jail?" "Called Meeting, Fulton-DeKalb Committee," 22 April 1940, Reel 48, *CIC*.

13. Hunter, *To 'Joy My Freedom*, 128; Rouse, *Lugenia Burns Hope*, 44–45.

14. Lewis, *In Their Own Interests*, 91–92.

15. Hunter, *To 'Joy My Freedom*, 136–38.

16. Montgomery, "Some Social Aspects of the Reed Street Baptist Church," 6. For a rich account of the culture of mutuality and interdependence created by poor African Americans in another city, see Borchert, *Alley Life in Washington*, 57–217. See also Earl Lewis on the importance of street life for African American urban culture. Lewis, *In Their Own Interests*, 95.

17. Stokes, "The Root Doctor in Atlanta," 19, 24, 29; DeCosta, "A Study for the Atlanta Urban League," 20; Clark-Lewis, *Living In, Living Out*, 77–81; Painter, *The Narrative of Hosea Hudson*, 66, 232, 236; Kytle, *Willie Mae*, 161.

18. Kuhn, Joye, and West, *Living Atlanta*, 95–108.

19. Thompson, Lewis, and McEntire, "Atlanta and Birmingham," 20; Will W. Alexander to Clark Foreman, 6 February 1934, Reel 9, *CIC*; "Fire Razes Auburn Section; 90 Homeless," *ADW*, 27 October 1937; "Citizens Appear to Ask Closing of Auburn Avenue Wine Shop," *ADW*, 1 September 1944; Horace Sinclair interview, Box 39, LA.

20. Crimmins, "Bungalow Suburbs," 90–91; Preston, *Automobile Age Atlanta*, 109.

21. Estelle Clemmons quoted in Kuhn, Joye, and West, *Living Atlanta*, 42.

22. Du Bois, *The Souls of Black Folk*, 63.

23. Hallie Brooks interview, Box 35, LA.

24. Byrne and White, "Atlanta University's 'Northeast Lot,'" 157–58; Crimmins, "Bungalow Suburbs," 92; Preston, *Automobile Age Atlanta*, 111. For a detailed history of John Hope's efforts to consolidate the colleges, the completion of which happened when Clark University moved from south Atlanta to the Atlanta University Center in 1941, see Bacote, *The Story of Atlanta University*, 256–72, 308–11, 328–30, 332–35.

25. Kuhn, Joye, and West, *Living Atlanta*, 44, 158; Leroy Davis, *A Clashing of the Soul*, 313–14.

26. William H. Crogman quoted in Dittmer, *Black Georgia in the Progressive Era*, 127–28.

27. Dorsey, "Cemetery as Historical Artifact."

28. On the professionalization of the NU, see Hunter, *To 'Joy My Freedom*, 140–41.

29. Gatewood, *Aristocrats of Color*, 92.

30. W. H. Aiken was the football coach at Clark University from 1930 to 1933, while the others were long-time faculty members in the economics department at Atlanta University. "Walter Aiken," n.d., Box 7, Long-Rucker-Aiken Family Papers, AHC; Bacote, *The Story of Atlanta University*, 285–86.

31. E. C. P. to Lizzie, 28 April 1941, Box 1, Elizabeth and Irvin McDuffie Collection, AU.

32. Pearlie Dove interview, Georgia Government Documentation Project, Special Collections, Georgia State University. For other examples of this social distance, see Hallie Brooks interview; L. D. Milton interview, Box 38, LA; Homer Nash interview, Box 38, LA; Alice Holmes Washington interview, Georgia Government Documentation Project; and Suzette Crank interview, Georgia Government Documentation Project.

33. Pearlie Dove interview.

34. For an examination of the black elite's dilemma in the Jim Crow era and its evolving response to it, see Jacqueline M. Moore, *Leading the Race.*

35. Montgomery, "Some Social Aspects of the Reed Street Baptist Church," 6, 8, 9, 38.

36. Forrester B. Washington, [questionnaire], 30 October 1939, Reel 49, *CIC*; "Atlantan Nominated for Vice Presidency," *ADW*, 5 June 1936.

37. [Reginald A. Johnson], "Report of Executive Secretary to Board of Directors, Atlanta Urban League," January 1933, Box 1931–32–33, John Hope Administration Papers, AU; "Eleventh Annual Report of the AUL," 1932, Box 1931–32–33, Hope Administration Papers; Madeline V. White to John Hope, 5 July 1932, Box A–Pu, Hope Administration Papers.

38. "Thirteenth Annual Report of the Atlanta Urban League, 1934," *The Urban League Mirror*, 20 January 1935, Box 5, NU; Pradd, "A Study of the Neighborhood Clubs," 15; "Report of Executive Secretary to Board of Directors, Atlanta Urban League," March 1933, Box 1931–32–33, Hope Administration Papers. Social work and politics were interconnected for black reformers nationwide. Gordon, *Pitied but Not Entitled*, 132–35.

39. "'31 League Report Is Released," *ADW*, 16 March 1932; "Thirteenth Annual Report of the Atlanta Urban League, 1934"; Jesse O. Thomas, "Urban League," *Atlanta Constitution*, 20 May 1935; "42 Janitors to Receive Awards," *ADW*, 31 May 1938; Jesse O. Thomas, "Urban League," *Atlanta Constitution*, 5 June 1938 (hereinafter cited as *Constitution*).

40. Pradd, "A Study of the Neighborhood Clubs," 45. On black social workers'

efforts to instill better work habits in their clients, see Crocker, *Social Work and Social Order*, 75–78.

41. Kuhn, Joye, and West, *Living Atlanta*, 138–39.

42. J. B. Blayton to John Hope, [May 1929], Box A–Pu, Hope Administration Papers; "Atlanta Executive Committee," 30 September 1930, Reel 46, *CIC*; "Reasons for Employing Negro Police," [1933], Reel 51, *CIC*; Jessie Daniel Ames to Rev. John Moore Walker, 10 October 1933, Reel 51, *CIC*.

43. "Minutes: Annual Meeting, Georgia Commission on Interracial Cooperation," 15 January 1930, Reel 45, *CIC*.

44. For a description of the Neighborhood Union's clashes with the Community Chest, see chapter 3. The black community was involved in the chest's annual fund-raising campaign, but it rarely raised even a fraction of the amount donated by whites, both because of the poverty of most African Americans and because of understandable black hesitancy to place money in the controlling hands of whites. Lowe, "A Study of the Opinions of 50 Negro Contributors and 50 Non-Contributors to the Atlanta Community Fund," 20–21, 25. This disparity placed even more burden on black chest agencies to prove their "worth" to white charitable leaders. At the Atlanta School of Social Work, students and faculty set aside their studies during the chest campaign, devoting half of their time to the chest's fund-raising effort. Forrester B. Washington to John Hope, 4 October 1934, Reel 11, *Hope Papers*.

45. Atlanta School of Social Work, "Situations like This Do Affect You," pamphlet, n.d., Reel 11, *Hope Papers*.

Chapter Two

1. A pseudonym.

2. Anonymous interview by Bernard West, Box 35, LA.

3. Ibid.

4. As historian Jacqueline Jones has shown, Beale's story of occupational displacement, migration for jobs, and family separation has been a typical one throughout the twentieth century for poor people both trying to make ends meet or to achieve and maintain some measure of upward mobility. Jones, *The Dispossessed*, 5, 205–32.

5. Jesse O. Thomas to Frank Miller, 3 October 1931, Box 1931–32–33, John Hope Administration Papers, AU; "Report of the Executive Secretary from May 15–31" [ca. 1932 or 1933], Reel 19, *Hope Papers*; "Negro Bricklayers Form Organization," *ADW*, 12 June 1932.

6. "Room for 20 Families on Farm," *ADW*, 14 September 1932; "People Back on Farm Happy," *ADW*, 27 October 1932; "To Ed. Constitution from R. C. Stevens" *Constitution*, 29 October 1933; Fleming, "Atlanta, the Depression, and the New Deal," 112.

7. John Hammond Moore, "Communists and Fascists," 443–45; "Police Raid Ends in Death," *ADW*, 25 April 1932; "Stray Shot Kills Lad Sunday," *ADW*, 25 April 1932; J. Raymond Henderson, "Pastor Asks $5000 Defense Fund," *ADW*, 28 April 1932; "Woman Hit, Fined for Not Moving on Car," *ADW*, 25 April 1932. The killing that most concerned the reform elite was of one of their own. In July 1930 white vigilantes gunned down Dennis Hubert, a fifteen-year-old Morehouse College sophomore and son of a prominent minister, for allegedly insulting a white woman. Leroy Davis, *A Clashing of the Soul*, 313–14.

8. "Memorandum of Conversation of Mrs. John Hope with Mr. Nix of Relief Center," 22 December 1931, Reel 19, *Hope Papers*.

9. Rouse, *Lugenia Burns Hope*, 48, 83–85; Walter Chivers to Mrs. John Hope, 9 March 1931, Box 3, NU; "Mrs. John Hope's Report," 31 March 1931, Box 3, NU; Shivery, "A Brief Summary of the High Points of Achievement of the Unemployment Committee," 1932, Box 3, NU; Thomas Jefferson Flanagan, "Neighborhood Union Honors Mrs. Ludie Andrews, R.N.," *ADW*, 9 February 1938.

10. "Minutes of Executive Board of Neighborhood Union," typescript, 11 January 1932, Box 3, NU; Thomas Jesse Jones to John Hope, 9 July 1926, Reel 12, *Hope Papers*; "Neighborhood Union Financial Report for 1927," Reel 19, *Hope Papers*.

11. "Neighborhood Union," [ca. 1933], Reel 19, *Hope Papers*.

12. "20,000 Atlantans to be Without Aid from Relief Body," *Constitution*, 17 June 1932.

13. Students of Atlanta School of Social Work, "Negro Families in Need," 1933, Box 3, NU.

14. Ibid.; "Minutes, Meeting of the Board of Directors of the AUL," 6 January 1933, Box 1931–32–33, Hope Administration Papers; Wilma Van Dusseldorp interview, Box 36, LA.

15. "'31 League Report Is Released," *ADW*, 16 March 1932; Louie Delphia Davis Shivery, "The History of Organized Social Work among Atlanta Negroes." Linda Gordon contends that during the Depression social work agencies led by men, such as the Urban League, began for the first time to challenge women's organizations, such as the Neighborhood Union, for "visibility," and "leadership on welfare issues." The AUL's success in becoming the preeminent black social work agency in Atlanta while the Neighborhood Union fell into decline also had much to do with the former agency's employment of professional social workers, an essential marker of legitimacy in the social welfare community during the 1930s. Gordon, *Pitied but Not Entitled*, 112.

16. L. D. Shivery, "How the Union Handled the Unemployment Crisis," n.d., Box A–Y, Hope Administration Papers; "Partial Report of Activities of the West Side Unemployment Committee of the Neighborhood Union," [1931], Box 3, NU; "The West Side Unemployment Relief Committee Issues Its Annual Report, February 1931 to March 1, 1932," [1932], Box 3, NU.

17. "Mrs. John Hope's Report."

18. "Partial Report of Activities of the West Side Unemployment Committee of the Neighborhood Union."

19. Charles Martin, *The Angelo Herndon Case*, 19–20.

20. The Communists approached black plasterers organized in an auxiliary to the white plasterers' union local. Atlanta Federation of Trade's president A. Steve Nance testified about this "infiltration" in November 1930 to a congressional committee led by Hamilton Fish Jr. to investigate Communist activities across the country. U.S. Congress, *Hearings before a Special Committee to Investigate Communist Activities*, 240–42; John Hammond Moore, "Communists and Fascists," 439; Charles Martin, *The Angelo Herndon Case*, 19–23.

21. The CP in Atlanta, as in other southern cities, always attracted more blacks than whites, and almost all of the party's meetings in Atlanta were held in the black community. White workers had difficulty overcoming the cultural force of white supremacy and accepting an interracial working-class movement into their communities. In fact, the Black Shirt movement has been interpreted as a white reaction to Communist infiltration in Atlanta. "Bar Negroes from Relief Meeting," *ADW*, 30 June 1932; U.S. Congress, *Hearings before a Special Committee to Investigate Communist Activities*, 203–6; John Hammond Moore, "Communists and Fascists," 444–47; Charles Martin, *The Angelo Herndon Case*, 5–7.

22. William Patterson quoted in Solomon, *The Cry Was Unity*, 201.

23. Ibid., 191–206; Carter, *Scottsboro*, 322–324.

24. Charles Martin, *The Angelo Herndon Case*, 12.

25. Solomon, *The Cry Was Liberty*, 195.

26. Ibid., 165–66, 194–201.

27. "Bar Negroes from Relief Meeting"; "Red Lawyer Here for Trial," *ADW*, 30 August 1932.

28. Painter, *The Narrative of Hosea Hudson*, 226. For an elite description of People's Town, see Haynes, "Ecological Distribution of Negro Population in Atlanta," 30–31, 36.

29. "No Race Prejudice," n.d., Communist Party pamphlet reproduced in U.S. Congress, *Hearings before a Special Committee to Investigate Communist Activities*, 224.

30. R. C. Miller quoted in ibid., 220.

31. Edith Washburn to M. H. Barnes, 20 July 1929, Reel 12, *SPA*.

32. Ibid.

33. Kelley, *Hammer and Hoe*, 113–14.

34. Ibid., 108–10.

35. Painter, *The Narrative of Hosea Hudson*, 224–25.

36. Frank Marshall Davis, "Another Crisis," *ADW*, 8 August 1932.

37. W. E. B. Du Bois, "Postscript," *The Crisis* 41 (March 1934): 86.

38. See, for example, W. E. B. Du Bois's "Postscript" in *The Crisis* 35 (May 1928):

170; 40 (April 1933): 93; and 41 (April 1934): 116. Du Bois's call for a separate black economy was insupportable by the NAACP's integrationist leadership. It led to his resignation from the editorship of the organization's mouthpiece *The Crisis* in 1934, and the very public airing of his ideological and personal disagreements with the NAACP's executive secretary, Walter White.

39. Janken, *Rayford W. Logan*, 106–10.

40. J. Raymond Henderson, "Rev. Henderson Is with Socialists," *ADW*, 7 November 1932.

41. J. Raymond Henderson, "Pastor Asks $5000 Defense Fund," *ADW*, 28 April 1932. For an account of Davis's extraordinary life, see Benjamin J. Davis Jr., *Communist Councilman from Harlem*.

42. Benjamin Davis Jr. to W. W. Alexander, 9 September 1933, Reel 7, *CIC*; Solomon, *The Cry Was Unity*, 221.

43. "Emory Senior Takes Police 'Rap' When KKK Pickets Negro Rally," *Constitution*, 11 December 1933.

44. Rev. J. Raymond Henderson, "Close Range versus Long Range Interest," *ADW*, 23 July 1935.

45. "U.S. Will Come to Communism, Du Bois Tells Conference," *Baltimore Afro-American*, 20 May 1933.

46. "Attack on NAACP by ILD Here Bars Herndon Group from Church," *Constitution*, 26 March 1934; Janken, *Rayford W. Logan*, 107.

47. Will Alexander to Roger Baldwin, 24 January 1933, Reel 7, *CIC*.

48. Will Alexander in particular fought the ILD and attempted to influence the tactical direction of Herndon's defense through his contact with Roger Baldwin of the American Civil Liberties Union, which worked closely with the ILD on the Herndon case. The ACLU, like the CIC, wished to try the case purely as a "free-speech" case. Like the Scottsboro trial, where the national NAACP opposed ILD tactics, the ILD prevailed in its strategy. Charles Martin, *The Angelo Herndon Case*, 71–80.

49. See chapter 3 for details of this crackdown.

50. "One Cotton Mill in Operation Here," *Constitution*, 6 September 1934; "Mill Strike Here Quiet, Peaceful," *Constitution*, 9 September 1934; Hall et al., *Like a Family*, 329, 333–35.

51. Charles Martin, *The Angelo Herndon Case*, 128–29; Painter, *The Narrative of Hosea Hudson*, 230–31.

52. "Communist Applications Disguised, Boykin Says," *Constitution*, 18 October 1934; "Bond Is Refused, 4 Held as Reds," *Constitution*, 20 October 1934; "Boykin Urges South to Join 'Red' Fight," *Constitution*, 26 October 1934; Painter, *The Narrative of Hosea Hudson*, 229–30; Charles Martin, *The Angelo Herndon Case*, 128, 130.

53. "Presentments of Fulton Co. Grand Jury, September–October Term, 1934," *Constitution*, 3 November 1934.

54. *Kourier* 10 (November 1934): 3, quoted in Charles Martin, *The Angelo Herndon Case,* 130 (n. 22).

55. "Minutes of NAACP, 1934," [1935], Box 7, NU.

56. "Dr. Cox Pleads for Free Speech, Hits Communism," *Constitution,* 28 October 1934. Henderson noted later that this missive was the only letter that the *Constitution* published out of the many he had written over the years. He believed that the editors printed it only because it repudiated Communism. Rev. J. Raymond Henderson to the Editor, *ADW,* 2 October 1937.

57. John C. Wright and H. S. Murphy to Fellow Citizen, 15 November 1934, Reel 11, Hope Collection; "Minutes of NAACP, 1934," Box 7, NU.

58. Hosea Hudson found that he could not speak openly about Communism among black workers by the mid-1930s, largely because "they was regular hunting communists there in Atlanta then." Painter, *The Narrative of Hosea Hudson,* 237.

Chapter Three

1. The phrase is Linda Gordon's. Gordon, *Pitied but Not Entitled,* 190.

2. Georgia Department of Public Welfare with Works Progress Administration of Georgia, *A Report of the Social Security Survey in Georgia,* 56; Katz, *In the Shadow of the Poorhouse,* 215–16.

3. The following account of the details of the political and administrative history leading up to the "federalizing" of New Deal relief programs in Georgia is based in part on Holmes, *The New Deal in Georgia,* 15–59, 83–85. References to sources other than Holmes's book are cited by notes in the text.

4. Allen Johnstone to Harry L. Hopkins, 18 September 1933, Box 1, Gay Bolling Shepperson Papers, AHC.

5. "Minutes, Meeting of the Board of Directors of the Atlanta Urban League," 6 January 1933, Box 1931-32-33, John Hope Administration Papers, AU.

6. Gay Shepperson to Frank Bane, 10 April 1933, Box 1, Gay Shepperson Papers. See also Rhoda Kaufman, "Paper for G.C.S.W.—Columbus," 4 April 1935, Box 2, Rhoda Kaufman Papers, GA.

7. For the life path of Shepperson's contemporaries in a national context, see Linda Gordon, *Pitied but Not Entitled,* 67–110. While Gordon emphasizes the predominantly northern roots of the American social work leadership, my research suggests a parallel and overlapping southern network of white social workers. "Miss Shepperson's Success Story Recalls Woman's Rise to Executive," *Constitution,* 26 December 1937; League of Women Voters of Georgia, "Let's Talk about Public Welfare in Georgia," Publication No. 15, May 1951, Folder 1, Box 1, Rhoda Kaufman Papers.

8. Rhoda Kaufman, "Paper for G.C.S.W."; Van Dusseldorp interview.

9. Johnstone to Hopkins.

10. Gay Shepperson to Harry L. Hopkins, 5 June 1933, Box 1, Shepperson Papers.

11. Ibid.

12. Johnstone to Hopkins.

13. F. D. R. to Harry L. Hopkins, 19 August 1935, Box 1, Shepperson Papers; Gay B. Shepperson to Harry L. Hopkins, 5 September 1935, Box 1, Shepperson Papers.

14. "Talmadge Attack Not to Bar Relief, Says Roosevelt, President Declares US Relief Program in Georgia Will Not Be Curtailed by Political Fights," *Constitution*, 20 April 1935.

15. Funded by his own Georgia supporters and northern Republicans, Talmadge made his presidential bid in 1936, hoping to split southern Democrats from the national party with a platform that linked blacks to the New Deal and bitterly opposed the progress of both. Anderson, *The Wild Man from Sugar Creek*, 114–40; Howard N. Mead, "Russell vs. Talmadge," 39–40.

16. Van Dusseldorp interview.

17. Rhoda Kaufman, "An Address on Public Welfare," Supplement to *Public Welfare* 3:6 (March 1929), n.p., Box 1, Kaufman Papers; Kaufman, "Paper for G.C.S.W."; Van Dusseldorp interview.

18. Kaufman, "An Address on Public Welfare."

19. For a scathing critique of this ideology, see Mills, "The Professional Ideology of Social Pathologists."

20. "Relief Must Be Individual, Social Workers Are Told," press clipping [*Macon Telegraph?*], [ca. 17 April 1934], Box 2, Kaufman Papers.

21. "'Pick Cotton or Get Off Relief Roll,'" *ADW*, 15 August 1935.

22. "University to Open Class in Social Work," *Constitution*, 26 September 1934. An Atlanta school for white social work was not envisioned until 1947, when the city's white social work community began to lobby Emory University to establish such a program. R. L. Foreman Jr., "The Atlanta Letter: Helping to Build a City Is Helping to Build the World," 15 March 1948, Box 3, Kaufman Papers.

23. Atlanta School of Social Work, "Bulletin 1934–35, Announcements, 1935–36," [1935], Box 4, NU; Bacote, *The Story of Atlanta University*, 329.

24. Many teachers found work with FERA as adult or vocational education teachers. Additionally, FERA reopened public schools throughout the state that had been closed in the Depression crisis and, in an unprecedented move, paid black and white teachers equally. Jesse O. Thomas, "Weekly Bulletin of the Urban League," *Constitution*, 11 September 1933; Will W. Alexander to Howard Odum, 13 October 1934, Reel 9, *CIC*.

25. Both black Republicans and Democrats had historically benefited from their party activism. Although there were vastly more of the former in Atlanta and the South in general by the Hoover Administration, the days of Republican patronage "largesse" toward the southern black party faithful were long over. W. A. Murphy to President F. D. Roosevelt, 30 April 1933, Box 1, OF

93, FDR Papers; "Republicans Name Delegates," *ADW*, 26 April 1936; Judge Elbert P. Tuttle interview, transcript, Georgia Government Documentation Project, Special Collections, Georgia State University.

26. Alexander, along with Edwin Embree, president of the Julius Rosenwald Fund, was instrumental in obtaining Foreman's appointment. Ellis, "'Uncle Sam Is My Shepherd,'" 48–49.

27. Will W. Alexander to George Foster Peabody, 16 May 1933, Reel 15, *CIC*; For another case of "new-style" influence peddling, see Dr. J. A. Somerville to John Hope, 29 June 1934, Reel 11, Hope Papers.

28. Thomas's memoir outlines his battles for equitable education, municipal services, and recreational facilities for African Americans during his twenty-two years in Atlanta. Jesse O. Thomas, *My Story in Black and White*, 96–124.

29. Will W. Alexander to Aubrey Williams, 25 January 1934, Reel 9, *CIC*.

30. Will W. Alexander to Aubrey Williams, 16 January 1934, Reel 9, *CIC*.

31. Alexander to Williams, 25 January 1934; Ellis, "'Uncle Sam Is My Shepherd,'" 49.

32. Benjamin Davis [Sr.], "Ben Davis Talks of GOPs," *ADW*, 24 June 1936.

33. Sullivan, *Days of Hope*, 47–48. There continued to be some "old-style" black patronage appointments after FDR's victory, although they diminished in relation to the number of functionaries hired by the administration, especially in Atlanta.

34. Atlanta University, "Leadership, the Heart of the Race Problem," 1931, Box A-Atlanta's, Florence M. Read Administration Papers, AU.

35. Stephanie Shaw shows how many black social workers were used by local New Deal agencies to control the black community during the Great Depression. Shaw, *What a Woman Ought to Be and to Do*, 188–90.

36. Margaret MacDougall interview, Box 38, LA. See also Augusta Dunbar interview, Box 36, LA; and Josephine Heyman interview, Box 37, LA.

37. Black and white social workers did not interact only in their work for federal agencies but also increasingly in professional organizations. "Program, Tenth Annual Georgia Conference on Social Work," 4–17 April 1935, Box 2, Kaufman Papers; Augusta Dunbar interview; MacDougall interview; Van Dusseldorp interview; Heyman interview; Eliza Paschall interview, Box 38, LA.

38. "South Barefoot, Frances Perkins," *Constitution*, 23 May 1933.

39. "Perkins Confused on Shoes Figures: Atlanta Executive Attacks Labor Secretary's Statements," *Constitution*, 25 May 1933.

40. R. C. Stevens to Editor, *Constitution*, 29 October 1933.

41. Mrs. Beaufort Mathews Williams to Franklin D. Roosevelt, 27 November 1933, Box 1, OF 93, FDR Papers. See also R. C. Stevens to Editor, *Constitution*.

42. "Talmadge Named Election Winner," *Constitution*, 9 September 1934. While Talmadge's anti–New Deal rhetoric eventually consigned him for a time in the political wilderness, his antiblack pronouncements were always popular with Georgia's white voters and ultimately brought him back to power.

43. "Assembly Fights 'Carpetbag' Rule," *Constitution*, 16 February 1935.

44. "Carpetbagger Relief Rules Charged in House Attacks," *Atlanta Journal*, 14 February 1935 (hereinafter cited as *Journal*).

45. "Assembly Fights 'Carpetbag' Rule."

46. Ibid.; "Group Protests Attacks on GERA," *Constitution*, 18 February 1935.

47. "Shepperson Denies Races Work Together," *Constitution*, 8 August 1935.

48. Will W. Alexander to Howard Odum; "Fined $12 Because He 'Did Duty,' Youth Relates Story," *ADW*, 27 May 1936; "WPA Places 8 'Fired' Workers," *ADW*, 23 January 1937.

49. Julian V. Boehm to Arthur Raper, 27 November 1935, Reel 46, *CIC*.

50. Executive Committee to Sponsors, n.d., Box 10, Mary Cornelia Barker Papers, EU; "Institute Director Denies Red Charges," *Constitution*, 6 May 1935; Jesse O. Thomas, "Urban League Weekly Bulletin," *Constitution*, 5 June 1935; "Atlanta Public Forum, Project Report," 1 February–30 June 1937, Box 2, Jane Van De Vrede Papers, GA.

51. This timidity persisted throughout the 1930s. "Meeting of the Executive Committee, Fulton-DeKalb Committee," 13 May 1938, Reel 48, *CIC*; "NAACP Body to Investigate WPA Discrimination," *ADW*, 10 June 1936. When liberals did engage in activities previously unnoticed by the white community, such as a 1937 interracial meeting of white Agnes Scott College students and black college students in Atlanta, the Americanism Committee was quick to respond and forced liberals underground once again. See, for example, William L. Van Dyke to Dr. J. R. McCain, 24 May 1937, Reel 46, *CIC*.

Chapter Four

1. Jacob Henderson interview, Georgia Government Documentation Project, Special Collections, Georgia State University; "History," [1937,] Box A-Atlanta's, Florence Read Administration Papers, AU; "Alumni Notes," *AU Bulletin*, July 1941 10–11.

2. Shaw, *What a Woman Ought to Be and to Do*, 5.

3. J. A. Martin, "Meets on Vote are Fruitful," *ADW*, 26 April 1932.

4. Henderson interview; "Eagan Homes Democrats Also Win by a Landslide," *ADW*, 21 November 1944; "Plan Housing Project Registration Contest," *ADW*, 30 November 1945. For details of Mankin's 1946 victory and Henderson's tenants' role in it see Epilogue.

5. Works Progress Administration, *Urban Workers On Relief* 110.

6. J. Jerome Robinson, Alton M. Childs II, J. Garfield Dashiell, Lawrence Jr., "A Comparative Study of Teachers Salary Differentials in Georgia, Tennessee, and North Carolina," n.d., unpublished manuscript, Reel 41, *CIC*; Gay Shepperson to Dr. M. D. Collins, 20 November 1934, Reel 9, *CIC*; Walter R. Chivers, "Effects of the Present War upon the Status of Negro Women," *Southern Frontier*, 4 (December 1943): n.p., Reel 30, *CIC*.

7. Augusta Dunbar interview, Box 36, LA.

8. Atlanta School of Social Work, "Bulletin 1934–35, Announcements 1935–36," [1935], Box 4, NUC.

9. Neighborhood Union to Gay Shepperson, 16 July 1935, Box CR to YMCA, John Hope Administration Papers, AU.

10. "How the FERA, PWA and WPA Change Affects Us," *ADW*, 14 September 1935; Robert Ratcliffe, "WPA Strike May Affect Many Here," *ADW*, 8 November 1935; R. M. Ratcliffe, "Death of FERA to Speed Gloom to Many White Collar Workers," *ADW*, 9 November 1935; "NAACP Joins League in WPA Tilt," *ADW*, 10 November 1935; Fleming, "Atlanta, the Depression, and the New Deal," 225–29.

11. Evan M. Hurley to His Excellency, Franklin D. Roosevelt, [ca. 1935], Box 7, Personal Papers File 21A, FDR Papers.

12. Neighborhood Union to Gay Shepperson, 16 July 1935, Box CR to YMCA, Hope Administration Papers, AU.

13. [Minutes of the Neighborhood Union], 19 July 1935, Box 4, NUC. Other organizations like the Georgia Colored Parents and Teachers Association and the Georgia Teachers and Education Association (a black teachers' group) made similar appeals for white-collar personnel throughout the state. F. S. Horne and Alva Tabor to Gay Shepperson, 20 July 1935, Box 3, Georgia Department of Education, Division of Negro Education, Director of Negro Education Subject files, GA.

14. "Memorandum for Dr. Tugwell," 12 July 1935, Box 1, Good Neighbor League Papers, FDR Library. Adolph Reed points out that such explicitly class-based appeals were exceptional; most often the individual gains of educated African Americans were and are presented as corporate "race" accomplishments. Adolph Reed Jr., *Stirrings in the Jug*, 31.

15. Will W. Alexander to Lucy Randolph Mason, 6 September 1933, Reel 9, *CIC*.

16. George Foster Peabody to Gay Shepperson, 22 July 1935, Box 1, Gay Bolling Shepperson Papers, AHC; Ellis, "'Uncle Sam Is My Shepherd,'" 48.

17. Gay B. Shepperson to George Foster Peabody, 26 July 1935, Box 1, Shepperson Papers.

18. Black staff served African American relief clients nationwide. Phyllis Palmer, *Domesticity and Dirt*, 102.

19. Harvey, "Changing Opportunities in Social Work for Negroes," 2–15.

20. NYA, "Meeting of Negro Leaders," 8 August 1935, Reel 3, *New Deal Agencies and Black America*.

21. Daniel and Miller, "The Participation of the Negro in the National Youth Administration Program," 359.

22. "Annual Report of the Division of Negro Affairs," [1936–1937], Reel 1, *New Deal Agencies and Black America*; "Confidential Report on the Negro Program," Reel 2, *New Deal Agencies and Black America*. For a description of the NYA's achievements, see Cook, *Eleanor Roosevelt*, 269–72.

23. D. B. Lasseter to Garth Akridge, 28 February 1938, Entry 336, Box 1, NYA.

24. NYA, Division of Negro Affairs, "Final Report of the NYA Division of Negro Affairs," 1943, Reel 3, *New Deal Agencies and Black America.*

25. R. W. Bullock, "A Brief Statement Concerning the Services and Benefits Extended to Negro Youth under the National Youth Administration Program in the State of Georgia for the Academic Year 1935–1936," 1 June 1936, Reel 46, *CIC*; "NYA Project at YMCA Is Impressive," *ADW*, 12 December 1937; D. B. Lasseter to Garth Akridge.

26. "Start Work on 'Youth Center,'" *ADW*, 26 January 1936; Bullock, "A Brief Statement."

27. "Conference of Negro State Administrative Assistants and Members of State Advisory Committees: The National Youth Administration. Findings and Recommendations as Adopted February 13 1937," Reel 1, *New Deal Agencies and Black America.*

28. "NYA Showing Fine Record of Placement in US," *ADW*, 13 September 1936; Lamar Q. Ball, "Twofold Purpose Is Accomplished by NYA Sewing School for Girls," *Constitution*, 9 August 1936; National Youth Administration of Georgia, *Report on the National Youth Administration of Georgia*, 5; Pete Daniel, "Going among Strangers," 889.

29. NYA of Georgia, *Report on the National Youth Administration of Georgia*, 4.

30. Bullock, "A Brief Statement."

31. NYA of Georgia, *Report on the National Youth Administration of Georgia*, 1.

32. "Start Work on 'Youth Center,'" *ADW*, 26 January 1936. On the South Atlanta Center, see also "Atlanta School of Social Work Youth Center Gives Jobs to 19 Workers," *ADW*, 19 March 1936.

33. Bullock, "A Brief Statement"; Rufus E. Clement, "Report of the President for the Academic Year 1937–1938," Atlanta University, 1938; "Report Shows NYA Aided Total of 9,000 Youths in Georgia," *ADW* 14 July 1940.

34. Arthur Raper interview, Box 39, LA.

35. John P. Davis, "Let Us Build a National Negro Congress," October 1935.

36. "Minutes of Meeting of NYA Officials at Butler Street YMCA," 21 August 1937, Reel 4, *New Deal Agencies and Black America.*

37. R. W. Bullock, "A Brief Statement"; Gladstone Williams, "$970 or Less Was Annual Income of Half Atlanta Families in '35–'36," *Constitution*, 24 October 1937.

38. "Minutes of Meeting of NYA Officials at Butler Street YMCA."

39. "Atlanta University School of Social Work . . . Re: Special Negro Fund Allotment," 27 August 1939, Reel 2, *New Deal Agencies and Black America.*

40. United States Department of the Interior, Office of Education, "Choosing Our Way: A Study of America's Forums," Bulletin 1937, Misc. No. 1, 1–7, Box 4, Emily Woodward Papers, EU.

41. Daniel J. Walkowitz has commented on the social distance of black social workers from their clients. Walkowitz, *Working with Class*, 240–42.

42. "Atlanta Public Forum, Project Report," 1 February–30 June 1937, Box 2, Jane Van De Vrede Papers, GA.

43. "Atlanta Public Forum, Project Report"; "Logan, Scott This Week's Two Speakers," *ADW*, 2 May 1937; "Dr. Logan Again Forum Speaker This Evening," *ADW*, 9 March 1937; "Slade, Logan Again Forum Lecture Duo," *ADW*, 23 May 1937.

44. "Dobbs to Lead Forum in New Project Center," *ADW*, 18 December 1938; "J. B. Blayton, J. W. Dobbs in Closing Public Forums," *ADW*, 27 February 1939.

45. Atlanta Public Forum, "Project Report." In New York City, the program was terminated in 1939 because of local backlash against black-run forums on controversial or "unpatriotic" subjects. Morgan, "Finding a Way Out," 19.

46. "Big Forum at Project Tonight," *ADW*, 28 November 1938; "Dobbs to Lead Forum in New Project Center," *ADW*, 18 December 1938.

47. Atlanta Public Forum, "Project Report."

48. For details of FERA's Workers' Education program, see chapter 5. For the Urban League's unionization efforts and the Workers Alliance's activities, see chapter 6. For the laundry workers' efforts, see chapter 9.

49. "Big Forum at Project Tonight"; "Dobbs to Lead Forum in New Project Center."

50. Ibid.

51. Parran, "No Defense for Any of Us," 251. Along with the Atlanta program detailed here, Parran's good intentions would result in the infamous Tuskegee syphilis experiment in which black public health workers were even more deeply complicit. James H. Jones, *Bad Blood*, 57–60.

52. See chapter 5 for more details of the antisyphilis campaign in Atlanta.

53. "Compulsory Syphilis Exam Unnecessary," *ADW*, 7 November 1939; "Attacks Whole Race in Social Disease Article," *ADW*, 2 November 1940.

54. "Leonard Street Orphans' Home," *Public Welfare* 11 (March 1936): 3–4; "Dr. H. E. Nash to Lecture Tonight," *ADW*, 1 April 1937; "City-Wide Mass Meet at Ebenezer Tonight," *ADW*, 1 May 19. The Wasserman test, which was almost the only syphilis test used in Georgia, is notoriously unreliable, with some experts claiming that it produces false positives 25 percent of the time. Brandt, *No Magic Bullet*, 152. State officials claimed that 86 percent of 990 food handlers given mandatory syphilis tests between July and November 1940 came out positive, a figure so high that it is not credible. Edna Ruth Reid, "A Study of Free Treatment Facilities Available to Negroes," 7.

55. Parran, "No Defense for Any of Us," 201.

56. Jesse O. Thomas quoting Dr. Herman Nash, "Urban League," *Constitution*, 12 June 1938.

57. J. C. McMorries, "Free Venereal Disease Control Clinic Merits Public Support," *ADW*, 1 June 1939; James C. McMorries, "News of Atlanta's Negro Community," *Journal*, 4 June 1939; Reid, "A Study of Free Treatment Facilities Available to Negroes," 22–25.

58. NYA Atlanta, "Report of Health Examinations of Colored Females Working in the Sewing Rooms," April 1937, Box 7, Atlanta Lung Association Collection, AHC; Reid, "A Study of Free Treatment Facilities Available to Negroes," 26.

59. NYA Atlanta, "Report of Health Examinations of Colored Males Employed on a Work Project, Fulton County, GA," April 1937, Box 7, Atlanta Lung Association Collection; NYA Atlanta, "Report of Health Examinations of White Females Working in the Sewing Rooms," May 1937, Box 7, Atlanta Lung Association Collection.

60. "Discuss Move to Examine Domestics," *ADW*, 19 March 1937; "Resolution Adopted by the Health Committee of the Atlanta Chamber of Commerce," 21 April 1937, Chamber of Commerce Minute Books, Atlanta Chamber of Commerce.

Chapter Five

1. Lucy B. McIntire, "The Confused Worker," Box 1, Jane Van De Vrede Collection, GA.

2. "Minutes of Meeting, Colored Branch Atlanta Tuberculosis Association," 15 March 1934, Box 3, Atlanta Lung Association Collection, AHC.

3. Wilma Van Dusseldorp interview, Box 36, LA.

4. Ibid.

5. Ibid.

6. Alexander, "The NRA and the Southern Negro."

7. Jane Van De Vrede, "A History of the Georgia Civil Works Administration 1933–1934," [1935?], Box 1, Van De Vrede Collection.

8. [Rhoda Kaufman], "A Community Program for Child Welfare," Summer 1928, Box 2, Rhoda Kaufman Papers, GA.

9. "Relief Roster in Atlanta Analyzed by Occupations," *Constitution*, 24 April 1935; Blackwelder, "Women in the Work Force," 341.

10. Jane Van De Vrede, "Talk Made at WSB Broadcast of Recreation Project Program," 15 May 1937, Box 1, Van De Vrede Collection. For a discussion of the national scope of the conservative ideology and considerations underlying New Deal work relief for women, see Phyllis Palmer, *Domesticity and Dirt*, 100–102.

11. Kytle, *Willie Mae*, 174.

12. Ibid.

13. "Minutes of the Third Training Conference," 6–8 October 1938, Box 1, Van De Vrede Collection.

14. "WPA Sewing Room Group Denied Edgewood Site," *ADW*, 29 January 1938.

15. Complaints that African Americans refused private employment because they could receive more money for less work on relief continued throughout the

New Deal. Frank Drake, "Some of Workers in County Scored for Arrogance," unidentified newspaper clipping, [ca. 29 October 1939], Box 10, Atlanta Lung Association Collection; Van Dusseldorp interview; Nell Blackshear interview, Box 35, LA.

16. "Minutes of the Third Training Conference." After hundreds of women were laid off from the WPA in 1936, Forrester B. Washington spoke of 700 or 800 black women "starving because of faulty handling of government relief funds" and advocated "pressure groups" politics in the form of a letter-writing campaign to Washington to secure redress. "Political League Work Is Laid Firmly," *ADW*, 25 March 1936. Earl Lewis describes similar layoffs of black sewing-room workers in Norfolk, Virginia. Lewis, *In Their Own Interests*, 154.

17. Kytle, *Willie Mae* 174.

18. Black women were hardly touched by the other Social Security program, Aid to Dependent Children, for which African American women were putatively eligible. Widespread white notions that African Americans could take care of their own for less meant that black women were underserved by the precursor to the late-twentieth-century's preeminent "welfare" program, Aid to Families with Dependent Children (AFDC), despite the fact that one-third of black families in Atlanta were headed by women. Georgia Department of Public Welfare with Works Progress Administration of Georgia, *A Report of the Social Security Survey in Georgia*, 74.

19. "Functioning through Committee," n.d., Box 2, Van De Vrede Collection.

20. "Talk Made at WSB Broadcast of Recreation Project Program"; "Servant Problem Aid Given in WPA Schools," *Constitution*, 21 October 1935; [William Huck], "Fulton County Board of Public Welfare, Annual Report of Director"; "Information Concerning WPA Assistance and the WPA Training Unit at Grady Hospital," [1941?], unpublished manuscript, Box 2, Van De Vrede Collection.

21. Col. Joseph Hyde Pratt, "Summary of Weekly Report for Week Ending January 23 [1935] of Col. Joseph Hyde Pratt—Southeastern States," Box 57, Harry L. Hopkins Papers, FDR Library.

22. "Talk made at WSB Broadcast of Recreation Project Program."

23. See, for example, Pratt, "Summary of Weekly Report for Week Ending January 23 [1935]."

24. Mary Morton interview, Box 38, LA.

25. "Meeting of the Executive Committee, Fulton-DeKalb Committee," 13 May 1938, Reel 48, *CIC*.

26. "Servant Problem Aid Given in WPA Schools."

27. Lorena Hickok to Harry L. Hopkins, 1 November 1934, Box 57, Hopkins Papers. Hickok, a great friend of Eleanor Roosevelt's, was one of several individuals hired by Harry Hopkins to report on the federal relief program at the local level. She traveled through the South in the winter and spring of 1934. The unselfconscious racism of her reports reveals the prejudices of even liberal

white New Dealers. Lowitt and Beaseley, *One Third of a Nation: Lorena Hickok Reports on the Great Depression*, xxx–xxxiii.

28. Emma D. Hawthorne, "Additional Lecture on Behavior and Working Relationships," n.d., Box 2, Van De Vrede Collection.

29. A pseudonym.

30. Anonymous, interview, Box 35, LA.

31. "Minutes and Record of Fifth of Series of Training Conferences Held with Area Supervisors, Assistant Area Supervisors, Field and Technical Supervisors of Sewing, Field Supervisors of Women's and Professional Projects Division," 19–20 January 1939, Box 1, Van De Vrede Collection; "Minutes and Record of Sixth of Series of Training Conferences Held with Area Supervisors, Assistant Area Supervisors and Field Supervisors of Professional and Service Projects," 28–30 March 1939, Box 1, Van De Vrede Collection.

32. For an excellent account of the social and cultural history of African Americans and syphilis, see James H. Jones, *Bad Blood*, 16–29.

33. The American Social Hygiene Association, "A Synopsis of the Report of a Social Hygiene Study of the City of Atlanta," [1927?], pamphlet, Box 1, Kaufman Papers, GA.

34. "Syphilis Tests Given [to] 120,000 in State in '37," *Constitution*, 6 February 1938.

35. "Syphilis Tests Given 120,000 in State in '37"; J. C. McMorries, "Start Campaign against Disease, Unselfish Physicians Helping," *ADW*, 13 December 1938.

36. One study of 250 employers estimated that by 1939, 50 percent required a physical examination of their domestic workers. May, "Employment of Women in Domestic and Personal Service," 31; "Discuss Move to Examine Domestics," *ADW*, 19 March 1937; "Resolution Adopted by the Health Committee of the Atlanta Chamber of Commerce," 21 April 1937, Chamber of Commerce Minute Books, Atlanta Chamber of Commerce.

37. In her compelling book about domestic workers in emancipation-era Rio de Janeiro, Sarah Lauderdale Graham demonstrates that apparently benevolent and progressive social work and public health measures were often motivated by a desire for social control on the part of the public officials instituting them. In reference to a free examination program for wet nurses, Graham writes that it had as much to do with white anxiety over a newly free black domestic work force as with charitable concern with the women's health. Through measures like the medical examinations, ex-masters hoped to "yoke public power to private purpose" in "shor[ing] up the customary authority of the household," much of which had been eroded with emancipation. Similarly in Atlanta, white householders anxious about their increasingly independent and mobile domestic employees used New Deal programs to control their maids and cooks. Graham, *House and Street*, 126.

38. Kornbluh, *A New Deal for Workers' Education*, 3–5.

39. Federal Emergency Relief Administration, "Memorandum to Guide the Organization and Instruction of Workers Education Classes under Point 3 of the Federal Emergency Relief for Unemployed Teachers as Authorized September 26, 1933," Box 8, Mary Cornelia Barker Papers, EU.

40. Tom Tippett, "Atlanta Project, Affiliated Summer School Report," 1934, Box 8, Barker Papers.

41. "Urban League Weekly Bulletin," *Constitution*, 23 April 1934; Tippett, "Atlanta Project, Affiliated Summer School Report."

42. Hilton E. Hanna, "Atlanta Project, Affiliated Schools for Workers," [ca. 1934], Box 8, Barker Papers; Tippett, "Atlanta Project, Affiliated Summer School Report."

43. "The Affiliated Summer School for Workers, Staff Meeting, Atlanta Workers' Educational Project," 18 May 1934, Box 8, Barker Papers.

44. "The Affiliated Summer School for Workers . . . ," 4 May 1934, Box 8, ibid.; "The Affiliated Summer School for Workers . . . ," 18 May 1934.

45. "The Affiliated Summer School for Workers . . . ," 25 May 1934, Box 8, ibid.

46. "The Affiliated Summer School for Workers . . . ," 18 May 1934.

47. Tippett, "Atlanta Project, Affiliated Summer School Report"; "The Affiliated Summer School for Workers . . . ," 4 May 1934.

48. "The Affiliated Summer School for Workers . . . ," 18 May 1934. See also "Workers' Educational Project, Staff Meeting," 12 May 1934, Box 8, Barker Papers.

49. "The Affiliated Summer School for Workers . . . ," 18 May 1934.

50. "The Affiliated Summer School for Workers . . . ," 4 May 1934. Some teachers got around this problem by setting labor songs to the tune of well-known spirituals. "The Affiliated Summer School for Workers . . . ," 18 May 1934.

51. "The Affiliated Summer School for Workers . . . ," 4 May 1934.

52. "Workers' Educational Project, Staff Meeting," 12 May 1934.

53. "The Affiliated Summer School for Workers . . . ," 4 May 1934.

54. Tippett, "Atlanta Project, Affiliated Schools for Workers."

55. The WPA project, which ran from 1937 to 1940, only had one black teacher, whose work was "confined entirely to community organizations where controversial subjects were less likely to be injected." Works Projects Administration of Georgia, "Report of the Statewide Conference Workers' Service Project," 12–18 February, [1940?], Box 3, Van De Vrede Papers.

56. Mary Barker to Mr. Tippett, 7 July 1934, Box 8, Barker Papers; Tom Tippett to Miss Barker, 27 June 1934, ibid.

Chapter Six

1. "All Atlanta Backing Parade to Show City NRA Support," *Constitution*, 30 September 1933.

2. The southern laundry code wage of 14 cents per hour was half that set for the North. NRA officials believed that if it was set any higher, commercial laundries would go out of business, competing with home laundry workers who worked for abysmally low wages, unregulated by federal codes. Allen Johnstone to Harry L. Hopkins, 18 September 1933, Box 1, Gay Bolling Shepperson Papers, AHC; Raper, "The Southern Negro and the NRA," 139–41.
3. "Support of NRA Plan Pledged by Negroes," *Constitution*, 24 August 1933.
4. "Big CWA Program Will Start Today to Benefit 60,000," *Constitution*, 20 November 1933.
5. Rev. J. Raymond Henderson, "Close Range versus Long Range Interest," *ADW*, 23 July 1935.
6. Jesse O. Thomas, "The Negro Citizens Look at the Proposed Bond Issue," *ADW*, 17 July 1935.
7. Reginald Johnson to James L. Key, 13 August 1935, Box 4, NU.
8. "NAACP Meet Tonight Is Important," *ADW*, 24 July 1935; "City Federation Has Important Meet Today," *ADW*, 18 August 1935.
9. "Registration Booths Will Help Voters," *ADW*, 1 September 1935; "Bond Issue Rally Is Planned," *ADW*, 13 September 1935; James L. Key, "A Message from the Mayor," *ADW*, 14 September 1935.
10. "Rooting for Bonds," *ADW*, 9 September 1935.
11. Jesse O. Thomas, "Bond Issue Urged by Urban League," *Constitution*, 17 September 1935.
12. Although the poll tax was a barrier to many in 1935, women who had never voted were not required to pay a cumulative tax if they had not previously registered, nor were men and women who had reached the age of twenty-one since the last election. See "Bond Issue Rally Is Sunday," *ADW*, 14 September 1935; "Over 1,000 Citizens to Vote," *ADW*, 16 September 1935.
13. Jesse O. Thomas, "All Things Being Equal," *ADW*, 18 May 1935.
14. W. E. B. Du Bois to Mr. [Barry C.] Smith, 13 April 1935, in Aptheker ed., *The Correspondence of W. E. B. Du Bois*, 61–64; "Colored Farmers' Markets Open Here Now," *ADW*, 5 June 1936; Jesse B. Blayton to Franklin D. Roosevelt, 28 June 1936, Box 1, OF 2246, FDR Papers.
15. "Baptists to Boost City Bond Drive," *ADW*, 11 September 1935.
16. "Civic, Political League Meeting Interests City," *ADW*, 30 March 1937.
17. "Baptists to Boost City Bond Drive," *ADW*, 11 September 1935; "AME Ministers to Assist NAACP in Making Study of Recent Killing," *ADW*, 6 August 1937; "A.M.E. Ministers Petition Board for Teacher Pay Raise," *ADW*, 5 August 1938. Black ministers were often hesitant to speak out because of a patronage system in which prominent white figures and businesses contributed to church funding. This money was particularly crucial during the Depression, when many churches faced mortgage foreclosure or bankruptcy. William Holmes Borders, for example, who would become one of the most militant pastors in the city,

refused the presidency of the local NAACP chapter in 1938 because at that time he was accepting financial aid from the Southern Bell Telephone Company to get Wheat Street Baptist Church out of the red and to launch an ambitious expansion program. He also supported another school bond issue in 1938 on the urging of Southern Bell and against the antibond campaign launched by black leaders. Forrester B. Washington to Walter [White], 21 January 1939, Reel 11/20, *Papers of the NAACP*.

18. Taschereau Arnold, "Ministers' Council Is Organized Here," *ADW*, 6 April 1939.

19. Rev. Taschereau Arnold, "Ministers' Council Stirred by Speeches of Paschal, Wright," *ADW*, 13 April 1939.

20. "Claim Three Clerks in Attack," *ADW*, 17 November 1935; "A & P Theft Denied by Redwine," *ADW*, 19 November 1935; "A & P Store Fight Kept Alive," *ADW*, 20 November 1935; Jones, "Trade Boycotts"; Pierce, *Negro Business and Business Education*, 26–27. For details of the prewar boycott movement, see Meier and Rudwick, *Along the Color Line*, 314–32.

21. "Ku Klux Klansmen Ride through Auburn Ave.," *ADW*, 10 November 1937.

22. Phillips, *Alabama North*, 190–225. See also Kelley, *Hammer and Hoe*, 108–16.

23. "A & P Store Fight Kept Alive."

24. T. Arnold Hill, "A Plea for Organized Action," *Opportunity*, August 1934, 250.

25. T. Arnold Hill, "The Urban League and Negro Labor," *Opportunity*, November 1935, 340, 342.

26. Edith M. Washburn to M. H. Barnes, 20 July 1929, Reel 12, *SPA*; "The Affiliated Summer School for Workers, Staff Meeting, Atlanta Workers' Educational Project," 4 May 1934, Box 8, Mary Cornelia Barker Papers, EU; Charles Martin, *The Angelo Herndon Case*, 128–29.

27. "Thirteenth Annual Report of the Atlanta Urban League 1934," 20 January 1935, Box 5, NU; Reginald A. Johnson, "The Urban League and the A.F. of L.," *Opportunity*, August 1935, 247; "Painters Get into Union," *ADW*, 22 January 1937.

28. T. Arnold Hill, "Workers to Lead the Way Out," *Opportunity*, June 1934, 183.

29. Lester B. Granger, "The Negro—Friend or Foe of Organized Labor," *Opportunity*, May 1935, 144.

30. Lester B. Granger, "Leaders Wanted—1934 Model," *Opportunity*, October 1934, 311.

31. "Thirteenth Annual Report of the Atlanta Urban League 1934," *Urban League Mirror*, 20 January 1935, Box 5, NU.

32. "The Affiliated Summer School for Workers . . . ," 25 May 1934, Box 8, Barker Papers.

33. "Minutes, NAACP, March 7, 1933, Appendix," 7 March 1933, Box 7, NU; R. M. Cosby, "Minutes of the NAACP 1934—Appendix," 1 January 1935, Box 7, NU. For details of Walden's conservative leadership, see Janken, *Rayford W. Logan*, 107–8.

34. J. Raymond Henderson to Walter White, 20 October 1932, Series A, Reel 10, *Papers of the NAACP*. See also E. M. Martin to Walter White, 11 March 1936, Series A, Reel 10, *Papers of the NAACP.*

35. Roy Wilkins to A. T. Walden, 27 April 1932, Series A, Reel 10, *Papers of the NAACP*; Roy Wilkins to Walter White, 23 January 1936, Series A, Reel 10, *Papers of the NAACP.*

36. "NAACP Body to Investigate WPA Discrimination," *ADW*, 10 June 1936; Charles B. Washington, "We Are Defenseless against Police Brutality, Public Opinion Must Help Us," *ADW*, 29 September 1936; "NAACP Body to Investigate WPA Discrimination," *ADW*, 19 June 1936.

37. Atlanta Negro Chamber of Commerce, "Atlanta—You Ought to Know Your Own!—1937 Directory and Souvenir Program of the National Negro Business League Convention," 1937, 29.

38. "NAACP Plans Action for Family," *ADW*, 10 March 1937; "'Gross Misconduct' Charged Officers," *ADW*, 13 March 1937; Police Committee of Council, "Regular Meeting," 2 April 1937, Police Committee Minute Book, 12 January 1933–17 June 1938, CAR; "NAACP Votes Aid in King Action," *ADW*, 14 April 1937.

39. "NAACP Opens Herndon Building Office Today," *ADW*, 14 November 1936.

40. Charles Hamilton Houston quoted in McNeil, *Groundwork*, 77, 84. For the ILD's influence on his thinking, see ibid., 119–21.

41. "Atlanta NAACP Urged to Make Fight against Fundamental Problems," *ADW*, 9 October 1937.

42. For the broadening of other chapters' leadership, see Fairclough, *Race and Democracy*, 57–60; Nelson, "Organized Labor and the Struggle for Black Equality"; and Lewis, *In Their Own Intersts*, 148.

43. "NAACP Outgrows Present Quarters; In New Location," *ADW*, 12 October 1936; "Atlanta NAACP Urged to Make Fight"; "Executive Committee of NAACP Increased in Size: Young Blood Balances Ranks," *ADW* 16 December 1937.

44. "Minutes of NAACP 1934," [1935], Box 7, NU; "Teachers' Salary Equalization Issue Results in Spirited, Promising NAACP Meet," *ADW*, 24 November 1937; "NAACP Maps Wage Fight for Tutors," *ADW*, 11 May 1938; Robert Ratcliffe, "NAACP Legal Aid Offered in Equal Salary Fight Here," *ADW*, 22 May 1940.

45. "Minutes of NAACP 1934."

46. William A. Folkes, "Seeing and Saying," *ADW*, 21 May 1940. See also "Atlanta NAACP Urged to Make Fight against Fundamental Problems," *ADW*, 9 October 1937.

47. "Citizenship Course," n.d., [1932–33], Box A through Pu, John Hope Administration Papers, AU.

48. "Minutes of NAACP 1934;" See also Janken, *Rayford W. Logan*, 103–4.

49. "Citizenship Course."

50. "Conservative Party Wins in Close Race for President of Howard Evening School; Smith Chosen," *ADW*, 13 December 1936.

51. "Y Boy Group to Broadcast at 8 Tonight," *ADW*, 19 July 1935. See also "BW Political Campaign On," *ADW*, 1 October 1936; "Washington Hi Officers to Take Oath on Monday," *ADW*, 29 October 1939.

52. "Minutes of NAACP 1934." Although Clarence Bacote writes of the NAACP citizenship schools lasting until at least 1938, there is no publicity for them in the *ADW* after 1934. Bacote, "The Negro in Atlanta Politics," 342.

53. Often in their ignorance about the black community, whites could be convinced that black organizations were more powerful than they really were, especially if they did not have to demonstrate mass support from the black community. For example, T. M. Alexander, a prominent black realtor, claimed that while the Negro Chamber of Commerce, founded in 1932, had a very small membership, its officers "never advertised that fact and few people questioned our potency regarding Black business affairs." Alexander, *Beyond the Timberline*, 68.

54. J. W. Dobbs, "A Call to Duty: An Open Letter to the Public," *ADW*, 7 February 1936.

55. "Dobbs Calls Civic Meet," *ADW*, 1 March 1937; Gamewell Valentine, "Full Citizenship for Colored Race Urged by Jackson," *ADW*, 4 June 1937; Robert M. Ratcliffe, "Dr. Powell Fires Atlanta Audience," *ADW*, 15 February 1940.

56. "Political League Work Is Laid Firmly," *ADW*, 25 March 1936.

57. "Robinson Is Militant in Talk," *ADW*, 15 April 1936.

58. "Political League to Convene," *ADW*, 14 April 1936.

59. "Line Up, Colored Citizens," *ADW*, 17 September 1936. Because of this selectivity, the league did not enjoy mass appeal. Its membership was estimated only to be around 1,000, and active participation in the organization was limited to only a handful of members. Bunche, *The Political Status of the Negro*, 488.

60. "League Puts Pep in City Vote Drive," *ADW*, 15 October, 1941; "Clip Sheet," Series IV—No. 3, 15 October, 1944, *CIC*; Spike Washington, "Hundreds Qualify to Become Voters," *ADW*, 4 May 1944.

61. "Atlanta—You Ought to Know Your Own!," 31.

62. Robert M. Ratcliffe, "League Elects Officers, Maps Future Plans," *ADW*, 3 March 1937; "Group Seeks 12,000 Registered Voters," *ADW*, 6 March 1937; "League to Notify Members of Approved Candidate for Sheriff by 'Grapevine,'" *ADW*, 23 February 1938.

63. "A Challenge to Adult Citizenship," *ADW*, 13 May 1937.

64. Atlanta Civic and Political League, "Does Atlanta Know and Approve of These Conditions?," 2 August 1938, pamphlet, Reel 49, *CIC*; Bunche, *Political Status of the Negro*, 491.

65. "The Church a Vital Factor in Our Civic and Political Life," *ADW*, 29 October 1938.

66. "Bond Issue Defeated," *ADW*, 3 November 1938.

67. In most African American urban communities, black police ranked as profes-

sionals, "almost on a level with teachers and social workers," in the words of Horace Cayton and St. Clair Drake. Not only was their pay good, but also as public officials black officers had authority over black citizens, if not white. When Atlanta finally appointed eight black policemen in 1948, all had at least some college education, a situation that was not unique around the South and in the nation. By contrast, college or even high-school graduates were a rare exception among white members of the police force. Cayton and Drake, *Black Metropolis*, 511; W. Marvin Dulaney, *Black Police in America*, 54; Rosenzweig, "The Issue of Employing Black Policemen in Atlanta," 68.

68. "NAACP Body to Investigate WPA Discrimination," *ADW*, 10 June 1936; James B. LaFourche, "White Group Fails in Attempt to Brand NAACP 'Red,'" *ADW*, 24 April 1937; "Beware of Communism," *ADW*, 6 April 1938.

69. "WPA Labor Seeks Pay Increase," *ADW*, 12 August 1938; "Workers' Alliance Is Given Charter," *ADW*, 4 September 1938; "Alliance President Promises Decent Wages to Followers," *ADW*, 9 May 1939.

70. James H. Boykin, "Ask Race Supervisors, Foreman on the WPA," *ADW*, 18 December 1938; "Workers Alliance to Hold State-Wide Meeting July 22," *ADW*, 2 July 1939; "More Jobs to Be Topic as Reliefers Meet at City Hall," *ADW*, 2 November 1939.

71. "WPA Workers Ask More Relief Funds," *Constitution*, 4 March 1938; "18 Women Workers Protest," *ADW*, 25 August 1938; "WPA Local Seeks 25c Rate Pay," *ADW*, 25 October 1938; "WPA Job Hunters Parade in Front of Courthouse," *ADW*, 4 January 1938; "WPA Workers in Conference with Miss Shepperson," *ADW*, 23 January 1939.

Chapter Seven

1. Public Works Administration, *America Builds*, 207–8.
2. "How Slum Clearance Project Here Reduced Fire Hazard," *Georgian*, 22 April 1938.
3. Walter Paschall, "N.B.C. Broadcasting," July 1947, Box 25, Charles Palmer Papers.
4. See Hirsch, *Making the Second Ghetto*; Sugrue, *The Origins of the Urban Crisis*, 33–88; Jackson, *Crabgrass Frontier*, 219–30; Bauman, *Public Housing, Race, and Renewal*; and Mohl, "Making the Second Ghetto in Metropolitan Miami."
5. Lipsitz, *The Possessive Investment in Whiteness*, 1–23.
6. Paschall, "N.B.C. Broadcasting."
7. Individual white ownership of black rental property was extremely widespread in Atlanta, as it was throughout the South and border states. Such investments were profitable and cheap enough to be accessible to most white homeowners. Even the wife of Atlanta mayor James Key invested in this way. As his daughter recalled: "my mother had a kind of a hobby of buying little colored houses, and . . . she'd save up money and buy a little house and let the

rent pay for it. . . . I couldn't tell you how many she bought, all over town." Mrs. E. Graham McDonald interview, Box 38, LA; Borchert, *Alley Life in Washington*, 35–36.

8. In her study of nineteenth-century Rio de Janeiro, Sarah Lauderdale Graham shows that public programs for the poor, and especially slum clearance, were compelled by similar white fears of real and metaphorical contamination by the city's black population. While Graham sees these state-sponsored efforts as motivated specifically by white desire to reassert control over black workers in the post-emancipation period, I argue that white anxiety in Atlanta and around the United States was spurred by the federal housing program. Graham, *House and Street*, 113–20. For a general discussion of how concerns about the social costs of slums spurred American housing reform, see Friedman, *Government and Slum Housing*, 4.

9. Radford, *Modern Housing for America*, 86–95; Jackson, *Crabgrass Frontier*, 195–218.

10. Fleming, "Atlanta, the Depression, and the New Deal," 25.

11. PWA Housing Division, *Urban Housing*, 28–29.

12. For details of Palmer's career, see his memoir, *Adventures of a Slum Fighter*.

13. Ibid., 8, 14; "Palmer Sees Huge Expenditure for Slum Clearance in Atlanta," *Constitution*, 13 December 1936.

14. [Municipal Housing Authority Minutes], 10 July 1934, Box 9, Bureau of Planning, CAR.

15. Charles F. Palmer, *Adventures of a Slum Fighter*, 14–17. Torras, "Atlanta," *Housing Officials' Year Book, 1935*, n.p.; PWA Housing Division, *Urban Housing*, 30, 82–83.

16. Municipal Housing Authority, "Tentative Report of Housing Conditions, Atlanta, Georgia," 1934, Box 24, Palmer Papers; Torras, "Atlanta."

17. See, for example, Argersinger, *Toward a New Deal in Baltimore*, 94.

18. "Rooting for Bonds," *ADW*, 9 September 1935.

19. "To the Mayor and General Council of the City of Atlanta from the Neighborhood Union," 23 May 1932, Reel 19, Hope Papers. For the history of whites' association of African Americans with tuberculosis, see Tera Hunter, *To 'Joy My Freedom*, 187–213.

20. Torras, "Atlanta." Concern about the "hidden communities" of Atlanta's alleys and "in-rear" housing came late to Atlanta. In other cities, most notably Washington, D.C., a movement to eradicate the "menace" of alley dwellings had been brewing since the late nineteenth century. Borchert, *Alley Life in Washington*, 45–54.

21. Atlanta Housing Authority, ". . . and the pursuit of happiness," film, [ca. 1940s], Palmer Papers.

22. "Committee Says Techwood Area Is 'Unfit' for Homes," *Journal*, 23 November 1933.

23. [Municipal Housing Authority Minutes], 10 July 1934, Box 9, Bureau of Planning, CAR.

24. [Charles F. Palmer], "The World War against Slums," [ca. 10–13 June 1935], speech text, Box 154, Palmer Papers.

25. "Vast Fire Perils Grady, Razes 25 Homes; Motor Freight Building Is Destroyed," *Constitution*, 28 March 1938.

26. For a description of the 1917 fire, see Kuhn, Joye, and West, *Living Atlanta*, 20–28.

27. "How Slum Clearance Project Here Reduced Fire Hazard," *Georgian*, 22 April 1938.

28. "15 Million to Clear Slums Sought for City," *Georgian*, 22 April 1938.

29. "Hartsfield Urges Annexation Plan," *Constitution*, 2 April 1938. See also Harold Martin, *William Berry Hartsfield*, 25–26.

30. "Urges Real Estate to Aid Slum Poor," *New York Times*, 24 June 1937.

31. Housing Authority of the City of Atlanta, "Rebuilding Atlanta: First Annual Report," 30 June 1939, 19–20, Box 24, Palmer Papers.

32. "John Eagan Homes Project Halted," *ADW*, 9 May 1939. As Nancy MacLean has shown, it was "middling" whites, like those living in the West End, who had formed the core of the Ku Klux Klan's membership in the 1920s. MacLean, *Behind the Mask of Chivalry*, 52–74.

33. R. B. Eleazer, "Report on Alleged Abduction and Beating of Negroes in West End, Tuesday Night, May 9 1939," [May 1939], Reel 48, *CIC*. Floggings became the tactic of choice among white vigilantes in Atlanta's suburbs during the 1930s. Local police ignored or actively participated in such outlaw activity until a white barber, Ike Gaston, was flogged to death in 1940 and federal officials were sent in to investigate. "Federal Justice Takes a Hand," *Journal*, 12 March 1940.

34. Nat G. Long to Glenn Rainey, 15 May 1939, Box 2, Glenn Weddington Rainey Papers, EU; Nat G. Long to Julian V. Boehm, 18 May 1939, Reel 48, *CIC*.

35. Walter Chivers quoted in "Fulton-DeKalb Committee," 12 May 1939, Reel 48, *CIC*; "West End Housing Project Is Rapped," *Constitution*, 10 May 1939.

36. "West Enders to Seek Legal Means to Prevent Eagan Homes Project," *Constitution*, 31 May 1939; "Two New Projects Will Complete Housing Plans," *Journal*, 3 March 1940.

37. "West Enders to Seek Legal Means to Prevent Eagan Homes Project." In 1937, Atlanta's city wards were reduced from thirteen to six. This move has most often been interpreted as an attempt by whites to dilute black voting power, but it more obviously weakened the political clout of the white working class, whose interests were inimical to Hartsfield's white business and middle-class constituency. Haynes, "The Ecological Distribution of Negro Population in Atlanta in 1939," 13–15.

38. "Apartment Owners to Fight 'Tech Flats' Project," *Constitution*, 19 October

1933; "West Enders to Seek Legal Means to Prevent Eagan Homes Project." On the autonomous power of public authorities in Atlanta and elsewhere see Stone, *Regime Politics*, 13–22; and Caro, *The Power Broker*, 623–31.

39. Roy Callaway quoted in "West Enders to Seek Legal Means to Prevent Eagan Homes Project."

40. Clarence Stone has written extensively about the ways in which Atlanta's non-elected ruling "regime" of white elites created institutions like the Atlanta Housing Authority to exercise their power. Stone, *Regime Politics*, 13–22.

41. Glenn Rainey quoted in "Fulton-DeKalb Committee," 12 May 1939, Reel 48, *CIC*.

42. "Building a Greater Atlanta: Report of the Atlanta Housing Authority for the Years 1943 and 1944," [1944], Box 24, Palmer Papers; "Housing Project Bid Passed On," [unidentified clipping], 20 September 1939, Charles Forrest Palmer Scrapbook, 1938–40, Palmer Papers; "Slum Razing Work at Stalemate; Can't Find Homes for Inhabitants," *ADW*, 7 October 1939; "Progress Reported in Housing Placements," *ADW*, 15 October 1939.

43. W. E. B. Du Bois, "A Study of the Atlanta University Federal Housing Area," May 1934, Box G–Lan, Read Administration Papers.

44. "Housing Project Appraisals to Be Raised," n.t., n.d., unidentified newspaper clipping, Charles Forrest Palmer Scrapbook, 1933–37, Palmer Papers; Florence M. Read to John Hope, 24 March 1934, Box G–Lan, Read Administration Papers.

45. Florence M. Read to John Hope, 24 March 1934.

46. Florence Read to John Hope, 24 March 1934; L. D. Milton interview, Box 38, LA.

47. Florence Read to John Hope, 24 March 1934; John Hope to Dean Sage, 21 December 1933, Box G–Lan, Read Administration Papers; "Housing Project Appraisals to Be Raised."

48. "US to Condemn Area of Atlanta University to Expedite Huge Slum Clearance Project," *Constitution*, 15 April 1934. Palmer wrote about the government's difficulty in obtaining the properties from homeowners but added that "as soon as they realized the Government had the power of condemnation and would use it they became more reasonable." C. F. Palmer to John Page Jones, 3 December 1934, Box 38, Palmer Papers.

49. "Legal Way Opened for Start of 2 Housing Projects Here," *Constitution*, 4 July 1934.

Chapter Eight

1. "Hundreds Attend First Anniversary Program of Federal Homes," *ADW*, 18 April 1938; "The Tenants of University Homes Invite You to the Celebration of Their First Anniversary," 17 April 1938, Reel 11, *Hope Papers*.

2. In the 1980s, several scholars published ground-breaking work unveiling the important story of the myriad ways in which white officials destroyed black communities through federal and state housing, resulting in the creation of the "second ghetto." Their pioneering work largely ignored black support of slum clearance and public housing. See Hirsch, *Making the Second Ghetto*; Fusfeld and Bates, *The Political Economy of the Urban*; Bauman, *Public Housing, Race, and Renewal*; Mohl, "Making the Second Ghetto in Metropolitan Miami." More recent scholarship shows how black leaders became advocates of urban renewal after the Second World War as they became part of the ruling elite in American cities, and thus participated in the stratification of their own communities. Thomas Sugrue's work on Detroit is a sterling example of this work. Sugrue, *The Origins of the Urban Crisis*, 181–208. By contrast, scholarship on Southern cities tends not to address the reasons behind black complicity in the demolition of black neighborhoods, black people's vision of their own communities, and black agency in relation to urban development before the advent of African-American electoral power. Bayor, *Race and the Shaping of Twentieth-Century Atlanta*; Silver and Moeser, *The Separate City*; Clarence Stone, *Regime Politics*, 40–41.

3. Norman Fainstein and Susan Nesbitt make the point that prosperous African Americans have always attempted to distance themselves from the poor, resulting in black ghettos that were "highly stratified despite being geographically compact." Fainstein and Nesbitt, "Did the Black Ghetto Have a Golden Age?," 7. Thomas Sugrue also notes this impulse in Detroit; however, in that city, elite African Americans sought to maintain the exclusivity of their neighborhood (Conant Gardens) by opposing the construction of public housing there, likely because it had no extant "slums" its residents wished razed. Sugrue, *The Origins of the Urban Crisis*, 41.

4. Thompson, Lewis, and McEntire, "Atlanta and Birmingham," 20; Byrne and White, "Atlanta University's 'Northeast Lot,'" 157–58.

5. W. E. B. Du Bois, "A Study of the Atlanta University Federal Housing Area," May 1934, Box G–Lan, Florence M. Read Administration Papers, AU.

6. Walter Chivers, "Do Our People Possess a Poverty-Stricken Complex," *ADW*, 2 June 1940.

7. Florence M. Read, [Meeting notes of Advisory Committee on University Housing], 28 October 1933, Box G–Lan, Read Administration Papers; Anon interview, Box 35, LA.

8. Kuhn, Joye, and West, *Living Atlanta*, 37–41; Crimmins, "Bungalow Suburb," 90–91; Thompson, Lewis, and McEntire, "Atlanta and Birmingham," 20.

9. N.a., n.t., n.d., [W. H. Aiken Biography,] Box 7, Long-Rucker-Aiken Family Papers, AHC; Haynes, "The Ecological Distribution of Negro Population," 19–21; Thompson, Lewis, and McEntire, "Atlanta and Birmingham," 19–21; Kuhn, Joye, and West, *Living Atlanta*, 40–45; White, "The Black Sides of Atlanta," 216,

218. Thomas Sugrue outlines the development of "black enclaves" in Detroit for African Americans with the will and the means to move away from the inner city. Sugrue, *Origins of the Urban Crisis*, 37–41.

10. "Hunter Hills Show Place of Atlanta," *ADW*, 16 October 1938.

11. [W. H. Aiken Biography]; "Amazing Development in Hunter Terrace," *ADW*, 14 August 1938. See also Walter Chivers, "Case of the Negro Masses," *ADW*, 25 August 1940; Haynes, "The Ecological Distribution of Negro Population," 25; Thompson, Lewis, and McEntire, "Atlanta and Birmingham," 20; and "Teacher's Idea Resulted in 300 New Homes for Atlanta," *ADW*, 4 June 1944.

12. [W. H. Aiken Biography]; Indenture [Warranty Deed?], 13 August 1935, Box 9, Ruby Blackburn Collection, AARL; Atlanta *City Directory*, 1933–40; "Over 60 Homes Have Been Built in Hunter Hills," *ADW*, 14 November 1939; "The Ecological Distribution of Negro Population," 25; Crimmins, "Bungalow Suburbs," 92.

13. "Glories of Hunter Hills Are Described by Writer," *ADW*, 29 April 1940.

14. Hallie Brooks interview, Box 35, LA.

15. Walter R. Chivers, "Sanitation as It Relates to Negroes in Fulton and DeKalb Counties, Georgia," 12 February 1938, Reel 48, *CIC*.

16. John Hope quoted in Leroy Davis, *A Clashing of the Soul*, 330.

17. [Sarah Ginsberg,] "Housing in Atlanta," [1931], Reel 6, *CIC*.

18. "Minutes of Meeting, Colored Branch Atlanta Tuberculosis Association," 17 May 1934, Box 3, Atlanta Lung Association Collection, AHC.

19. N.a., n.d., typed ms. on TIC Club stationary, Box 4, Blackburn Collection; "A. G. Moron, Housing Project Chief, in Talk to TIC Club," *ADW*, 22 December 1936; "T.I.C. Club to Present Mass Meeting Sunday in Drive to Secure Regular Bus Service to West Side Section," *ADW*, 4 November 1937; Mrs. W. A. Scott Sr., "Noted White Speakers on Animated TIC Program Sunday Afternoon," *ADW*, 9 November 1937.

20. Lawrence M. Friedman, *Government and Slum Housing*, 4–22. See also Radford, *Modern Housing for America*, 95–98, 108.

21. Ruechel, "New Deal Public Housing, Urban Poverty, and Jim Crow," 922–23.

22. Leroy Davis, *A Clashing of the Soul*, 324–25.

23. Will W. Alexander to Clark Foreman, 6 February 1934, Reel 9, *CIC*; John Hope to Charles E. Pynchon, 6 February 1934, Box G-Lan, Read Administration Papers; Harold Ickes to P. C. McDuffie, 24 May 1934, ibid.

24. Michael Straus and Talbot Wegg quoted in Radford, *Modern Housing for America*, 95.

25. Robert C. Weaver, "An Experiment in Negro Labor," *Opportunity*, October 1936, 295–98; Mrs. John Hope to Mrs. Franklin Delano Roosevelt, 2 May 1934, Box 2685, Eleanor Roosevelt Papers; Alonzo G. Moron to Mrs. John Hope, 8 October 1935, Reel 11, *Hope Papers*; "Open Atlanta University Housing Project Registration Monday; Moron Taking Charge," *ADW*, 18 October 1936.

26. This partnership represented the beginning of the biracial ruling regime that continues to control Atlanta to this day. See Stone, *Regime Politics*.

27. John Hope quoted in Charles F. Palmer, *Adventures of a Slum Fighter*, 17.

28. John Hope to Charles E. Pynchon. See also Lofton, "The Atlanta Laboratories," 36.

29. Florence M. Read, "University Housing," 4 December 1933, Box G–Lan, Read Administration Papers.

30. Florence M. Read to Trevor Arnett, 16 October 1933, Box G–Lan, Read Administration Papers.

31. Read, "University Housing." Black businessman L. D. Milton, who was on the advisory committee for University Homes, echoed these sentiments even more explicitly in an interview in the 1970s. Asked about the criteria for the first slum-clearance and housing project, he replied, "Oh, that section of the city which was most likely to attract Negroes and attract not poor Negroes, but Negroes with their minds uplifted and wanting to advance themselves and the race generally. And we considered an area close to the University system. And don't forget, Fair Street ran right down straight through the university system of Atlanta. And so we logically built our minds up on that potentially valuable real estate. And that real estate has [been] considered to be valuable . . . to this day." L. D. Milton interview, Box 38, LA.

32. W. J. Sayward and O. I. Freeman to Board of Trustees, 4 December 1933, AU Archives, Box G–Lan, Read Administration Papers.

33. Read, "University Housing."

34. Sayward and Freeman to Board of Trustees.

35. [Minutes of the Executive Committee of the Neighborhood Union,] 11 May 1934, Box 4, NU.

36. "Apartment Life Comes South," *ADW*, 3 March 1940.

37. Michael Straus and Talbot Wegg quoted in Radford, *Modern Housing for America*, 95.

38. Walter R. Chivers, "Sanitation as It Relates to Negroes in Fulton and DeKalb Counties, Georgia."

39. "Urban League Weekly Bulletin," *Constitution*, 15 October 1934.

40. "Annual Meeting, Fulton-DeKalb Interracial Committee," 5 December 1939, Reel 48, CIC.

41. W. E. B. Du Bois to Mr. [Barry C.] Smith, 13 April 1935, *The Correspondence of W. E. B. Du Bois*, 63–64. The conferences, held almost yearly between 1896 and 1917, resulted in *The Atlanta University Publications*, a treasure trove of sociological information about African Americans and the uplift ideology that informed black sociologists and social workers' perspective during the Progressive era.

42. W. E. B. Du Bois to Will W. Alexander, 5 May 1934, Reel 9, CIC.

43. Ibid.; W. E. B. Du Bois to [George] Streator, 17 April 1935, *The Correspondence of W. E. B. Du Bois*, 87; Du Bois to Mr. Smith.

44. W. E. B. Du Bois to [George] Streator, 24 April 1935, *The Correspondence of W. E. B. Du Bois*, 91.

45. N.a., "Visit to Atlanta," typed ms., 24–26 February 1936, Box G–Lan, Read Administration Papers.

46. Robert C. Weaver with Dr. Foreman, "Report to Housing Bureau on Slum Clearance Projects, Re: Atlanta, Georgia," January 1934, Box G–Lan, Read Administration Papers.

47. On the NPHC, see Radford, *Modern Housing for America*, 89, 185.

48. Florence M. Read, "President's Report," 25 April 1936, Box 4, John Hope Administration Papers; "No Low Rents for Housing Projects!" *ADW*, 10 February 1936.

49. Radford, *Modern Housing for America*, 102–4, 167, 189.

50. Rouse, *Lugenia Burns Hope*, 73; Hallie Brooks interview, Box 35, LA.

51. Harold Ickes to Eleanor Roosevelt, 20 October 1936, Reel 11, *Hope Papers*; Mrs. John Hope to Mrs. Franklin Delano Roosevelt, 25 September 1936, Reel 11, *Hope Papers*; Mary McLeod Bethune to Mrs. John Hope, 30 September 1936, Reel 11, *Hope Papers*; Brooks interview, 4–5; Neighborhood Union Executive Committee to John Hope, 18 July 1934, Box CR to YMCA, Hope Administration Papers; [Neighborhood Union Board Meeting Minutes,] 18 January 1935, Box 4, NU.

52. Harold Ickes to Eleanor Roosevelt, 27 August 1936, Reel 11, *Hope Papers*. See also "Visit to Atlanta."

53. "Techwood to Be Ready for Tenants Next Summer, PWA Chief Says," *Constitution*, 1 December 1935.

54. "Tenant Policy Threatens Housing Program," *Public Housing Progress*, 15 April 1935, 2, Box 49, Palmer Papers.

55. "First Lady Pays Techwood Return Visit," *Journal*, 6 March 1937.

56. Gamewell Valentine, "U.S. Housing Projects Ridiculed by Social School Executive," *ADW*, 30 November 1937. For other critiques of the Public Housing program by Washington, see Forrester B. Washington, "Alice Maree," *ADW*, 2 October 1937; and Washington, "Economic Problems of Rural Negro Migrants in Atlanta," *Georgia Observer*, supplement, August 1940, Reel 49, *CIC*.

57. Alonzo Moron, "Housing Project Serving Purpose, Moron Declares," *ADW*, 1 December 1937.

58. Ibid.

59. Ibid.

60. Chivers, "Do Our People Possess a Poverty-Stricken Complex?"; see also W. R. Chivers to John Hope, 25 February 1925, Reel 12, Hope Collection; Atlanta Negro Chamber of Commerce, "Atlanta—You Ought to Know Your Own!," 28; and Colored Division, National Youth Administration of Georgia, "Narrative Report on N.Y.A. Work Program—Negro," April 1937, Box 1, NYA.

61. "The Transfer of the Slums," *ADW*, 4 December 1937. See also John Hope to

Dean Sage, 21 December 1933, Box G–Lan, Florence M. Read Papers,; and J. H. Brown to M. D. Carrel, 5 April 1934, Box 23, U.S. Public Housing Administration Project Files, RG 196, NA.

62. "Building a Greater Atlanta: Report of the Atlanta Housing Authority for the Years 1943 and 1944," Box 24, Palmer Papers; "Housing Project Bid Passed On," 20 September 1939, n.t., Charles Forrest Palmer Scrapbook, 1938–40, Palmer Papers; "Slum Razing Work at Stalemate; Can't Find Homes for Inhabitants," *ADW*, 7 October 1939; "Progress Reported in Housing Placements," *ADW*, 15 October 1939.

63. Public housing was denied to relief recipients. Gladstone Williams, "$970 or Less Was Annual Income of Half Atlanta Families in '35–'36," *Constitution*, 24 October 1937; Du Bois, "A Study of the Atlanta University Federal Housing Area."

64. Alan L. Ritter, "Annual Family and Occupational Earnings of the Residents of Two Negro Housing Projects in Atlanta, 1937–1944," [1945?], Box 50, Palmer Papers; "Last 44 Homes of Project Set," *ADW*, 6 June 1937; "Federal Housing Open to Tenants," *Constitution*, 6 June 1936; "University Project Is Now 93% Rented," *ADW*, 26 September 1937; Robert M. Ratcliffe, "Project's Lower Rent Creates New Problems," *ADW*, 15 July 1938; Weaver, "The First Anniversary of University Homes," 17 April 1938, Box 11, Records of the Intergroup Relations Branch, U.S. Public Housing Administration Project Files, RG 196, NA.

65. "Lower Rent for Local Project," *ADW*, 19 June 1938; John Lear, "Uncle Sam Uses Atlanta as His Housing Laboratory," 28 August 1938, Charles Forrest Palmer Scrapbook, 1938–40, Palmer Papers; Robert M. Ratcliffe, "Project's Lower Rent Creates New Problems"; Waters, "The Ex-Residents of University Homes," 30.

66. "University Homes Ready for Occupancy Saturday, April 17," *ADW*, 11 April 1937.

67. "Last 44 Homes of Project Set."

68. Atlanta, *City Directory*, 1934, 1938; Tera Hunter shows that home laundry work was on the decline by the 1930s. Tera Hunter, *To 'Joy My Freedom*, 207–8. Such exclusion of laundry workers and lower-paid domestics in public housing was typical of public housing in other cities as well. Argersinger, *Toward a New Deal in Baltimore*, 96.

69. Lula Daugherty interview, Box 36, LA. See also Clara Render interview, Box 39, LA; Kytle, *Willie Mae*, 180–82.

70. Daugherty interview.

71. Render interview; Daugherty interview; Rev. Jimmy Collier interview, Box 2, Sweet Auburn Neighborhood Project, AARL; Kytle, *Willie Mae*, 185–86.

72. A. C. Shire, "Report on Techwood Housing Project, Atlanta, Georgia," 22 December 1933, Box 28, Project Files, 1933–37, RG 196, NA.

73. Daugherty interview.
74. Render interview; Daugherty interview; "The University Homes Neighborhood: A Survey of Changes Associated with Re-Housing," n.d., Box 72, Palmer Papers; Alonzo Moron to Robert R. Weaver, 11 April 1938, Reel 1, Robert Clifton Weaver Papers, Manuscripts Department, Schomburg Center for Research in Black Culture, New York.
75. Florence M. Read to H. A. Gray, 2 October 1936, Box G–Lan, Read Administration Papers; "Open Atlanta University Housing Project Registration Monday; Moron Taking Charge," *ADW*, 18 October 1936; Mrs. John Hope to Mrs. Franklin Delano Roosevelt, 2 May 1934, Reel 11, *Hope Papers*; Alonzo G. Moron to Mrs. John Hope, 8 October 1935, Reel 11, *Hope Papers*; Read, *The Story of Spelman College*, 291.
76. "University Homes, Atlanta, Georgia, 25th Anniversary Edition," 1962, [printed yearbook], Box 38, Palmer Papers.

Chapter Nine

1. The most complete work dealing with this wartime movement for southern democracy is Patricia Sullivan's *Days of Hope*. Her book builds on the work of labor historians who have examined the impact of wartime industrialization on black workers and southern society. See, for example, Korstad and Lichtenstein, "Opportunities Found and Lost"; Nelson, "Organized Labor and the Struggle for Black Equality"; and Honey, *Southern Labor and Black Civil Rights*.
2. [Glenn Rainey] to [C.] Vann [Woodward], 25 April 1944, Box 3, Glenn Weddington Rainey Papers, EU.
3. Nelson, "Organized Labor and the Struggle for Black Equality," 957.
4. Ibid., 955–58; Pete Daniel, "Going among Strangers," 898–901. For evidence of the WMC's policy in Atlanta, see [WMC], "Preliminary Statement on the Atlanta and Marietta Labor Market," 10 December 1942, Box 1, Series 12, WMC; "Estimate of In-Migration into the Atlanta, Georgia, Labor Market Area during the Six Months Beginning November 1, 1943," 27 November 1943, Box 1, Series 12, WMC; War Manpower Commission, Division of Reports and Analysis, Region VII, "Estimate of In-Migration into the Atlanta, Georgia, Labor Market Area during the Six Months Beginning January 1, 1945," 28 December 1944, Box 1, Series 12, WMC.
5. Atlanta Urban League, "Timeless: The Task of Preventive Social Work among the Most Under Privileged," [1942], Box 5, Grace Towns Hamilton Papers, AHC; War Manpower Commission, "Labor Market Developments Report," 15 April 1943, Box 7, Series 12, WMC; [WMC], "Labor Market Developments Report," 15 June 1943, Box 7, Series 12, WMC; War Manpower Commission, "Proposed Manpower Program for the Atlanta Area," 20 August 1943, Box 20,

Series 11, WMC; [WMC], "Labor Developments Report for Atlanta, Georgia," 28 December 1943, Box 7, Series 12, WMC; War Manpower Commission, "Summary of ES-270 Reports," September 1944, Reel 124, *SRC*.

6. In the same period, Atlanta's white population increased by only 8.5 percent — from 193,393 in 1940 to 209,898 in 1950. Charles S. Johnson and Clifton R. Jones, "Memorandum on Negro Internal Migration, 1940–1943: An Estimate by the Department of Social Sciences, Fisk University," 16 August 1943, Box 4, OF 4245g, FDR Papers.

7. "Reports on War Production Centers, WPB Region 4, Atlanta-Marietta, Georgia Area," 14 February 1944, Box 17, Series 12, WMC; Kuhn, Joye, and West, *Living Atlanta*, 364.

8. Walter R. Chivers, "Effects of the Present War upon the Status of Negro Women," *Southern Frontier*, 4:12, December 1943, Reel 30, *CIC*; Willie Mae Jackson interview, Box 37, LA; [War Manpower Commission], "Labor Market Developments Report," 30 August 1943, Box 7, Series 12, WMC; Atlanta Urban League, "Timeless: The Task of Preventive Social Work."

9. Alan L. Ritter, "Annual Family and Occupational Earnings of the Residents of Two Negro Housing Projects in Atlanta, 1937–1944," n.d., Box 50, Charles Forrest Palmer Papers, EU; Pete Daniel, "Going among Strangers," 895.

10. Minutes, 4 February 1943 and 11 February 1943, Box 139, Machinists Lodge #1 Records, Southern Labor Archive, Georgia State University; "Federation in All-Out Drive to Organize Bell Bomber Plant," *Journal of Labor*, 14 May 1943; "Organization Drive at Bell Bomber Plant Gaining Momentum," *Journal of Labor*, 5 November 1943; Pete Daniel, "Going among Strangers," 898.

11. Willie A. Allen, "A Study of the Negro Members of the Laundry Workers' International Union," 3–10, 25.

12. Minutes, 19 February, 17 September, 9 July 1942, Box 138, Machinists Lodge #1 Records.

13. For Atlanta area FEPC complaints, see Closed Cases Boxes 2–7, FEPC.

14. Robin Kelley, " 'We Are Not What We Seem,' " 103–10.

15. Hill, ed., *The FBI's RACON*, 254; Kelley, " 'We Are Not What We Seem,' " 103–10.

16. Sanders Ivey interview, Box 37, LA.

17. "Atlanta NAACP Plans Appeal of $27 Fine Given in Trolley Case," *ADW*, 2 October 1941; [Minutes, Annual Meeting, Fulton-DeKalb Interracial Committee,] 20 October 1942, Reel 48, *CIC*; Spike Washington, "Brutality Victims Are Fined in Police Court," *ADW*, 14 January 1944; Douglas Carter and James O. Slade, "SRC, Inc., Transportation-Segregation Study, Municipal Transportation, Atlanta, Georgia," 7 August 1945, Reel 61, *SRC*.

18. War Department, Army Service Forces, Office of the Commanding General, "Racial Situation in the United States," 3 February–17 February 1945, Box 9, OF 4245g, FDR Papers. See also Police Committee of Council, "Regular Meet-

ing," 3 November 1943, Police Committee Minute Book, July 1938–January 1946, CAR; Spike Washington, "Brutality Victims Are Fined in Police Court"; Douglas Carter, "Schedule for Observation of Urban and Interurban Streetcars, Trackless Trolleys and Buses," 2 August 1945, Reel 61, *SRC*.

19. Douglas Carter, "SRC, Inc., Trans-Seg. Study-Aggravated Assault on Trolley Car," 5 June 1945, Reel 61, *SRC*.

20. [Incident report], [ca. 5 July 1945], Reel 61, *SRC*.

21. Forrester B. Washington, "Economic Problems of Rural Negro Migrants in Atlanta," *Georgia Observer*, supplement, August 1940, Reel 49, *CIC*. Washington's portrayal of black migrants matched the "distaste and condescension" marking other observers' portrayal of white rural folk flocking to southern cities during the war. Pete Daniel, "Going among Strangers," 902.

22. Office of Supervisor of Practice, Atlanta University, "Summary of High Points of Seminar on Secondary Education," 1943, Box 7, Georgia Department of Education, Division of Negro Education, Director of Negro Education Subject Files, GA. See also Rubye Weaver, "As a Woman Sees It," *ADW*, 7 October 1945.

23. "Summary of High Points."

24. Senior Class, B. T. Washington High School, "The Cornellian," Atlanta, 1944, Samuel Howard Archer Papers, AARL.

25. "Summary of High Points."

26. Larry Bell quoted in "Progress Report," n.d., *Bell Bomber Source*, Box 2, Series 17, WMC.

27. Bell Aircraft Corporation, "Press Release," 14 March 1943, Box 2, Series 17, WMC.

28. Ibid.

29. Weaver, *Negro Labor*, 109, 129–30.

30. For the most complete examination of these grassroots struggles to force compliance with federal nondiscrimination policies for defense workers, see Reed, *Seedtime for the Modern Civil Rights Movement*.

31. William Y. Bell Jr., "Defense Training for Atlanta Negroes," *Georgia Observer*, 3 (September–October 1942), Reel 49, *CIC*.

32. Sub-Committee of the Council on Defense Training for Negroes to E. A. Adams, 11 March 1942, Box 12, Series 2, WMC; "Drive for Defense Courses Continues," *ADW*, 12 March 1942; "Registration for Defense Courses Gaining Impetus," *ADW*, 13 March 1942. Although the *ADW* claimed more than 10,000 registrants resulting from the CDT's drive, the AUL only reported 5,000. "Over 10,000 File Cards in Defense Training Job," *ADW*, 23 March 1942; Atlanta Urban League, "Timeless: The Task of Preventive Social Work."

33. The USES situation in Atlanta was not unique to that city. In the first quarter of 1941, USES placed some 35,000 workers in industrial jobs nationwide, of whom only 245 were black. Fusfeld and Bates, *The Political Economy of the Urban Ghetto*, 46. Even after the CDT won its battle for defense training for

blacks, USES continued to undercount the city's black work force, demonstrating the agency's national recalcitrance in integrating black workers into assembly-line jobs during the war. Weaver, *Negro Labor*, 145–51.

34. "WPB Chief Nelson Gets Protest on Failure to Train Negroes for Bomber Plant Work," *ADW*, 2 April 1942.

35. "Defense Training Classes Started," *ADW*, 24 November 1942.

36. William Y. Bell Jr., "Defense Training for Atlanta Negroes"; Merl Reed, *Seedtime for the Modern Civil Rights Movement*, 185–91.

37. John J. Corson to Franklin O. Nichols, 4 April 1942, Box 12, Series 2, WMC; "Washington Officials OK Defense Registration Drive"; Lawrence A. Oxley to James H. McGinnis, 25 March 1942, Box 12, Series 2, WMC; Mrs. G. T. Hamilton to Mr. Cy W. Record, [ca. June 1943], Box 2, Series 18, WMC.

38. A. Bruce Hunt to Will Maslow, 3 April 1944, Closed Cases Box 4, FEPC; Amos Ryce Jr. to Bruce Hunt, 12 April 1944, RG 228, Closed Cases Box 4, FEPC; Sallie McCrary, "Complaint," 13 April 1944, Closed Cases Box 4, FEPC; Anon to A. Bruce Hunt, n.d., [ca. July or August 1944], Closed Cases Box 4, FEPC; H. W. Sewell to A. Bruce Hunt, 5 September 1944, Closed Cases Box 4, FEPC; Atlanta Urban League, "United States of America before the President's Committee on Fair Committee on Fair Employment Practice, Complaint," 20 October 1944, Closed Cases Box 1, FEPC; [Witherspoon] Dodge, n.t., [typed memo on scrap of paper], [ca. 6 November 1944], Closed Cases Box 1, FEPC.

39. "Aircraft Grads Hear Nicholson," *ADW*, 13 January 1943; "Urge Enrollment for Bell Bomber Courses," *ADW*, 29 March 1943; Robert Thompson, "Brief Report of Vocational Department of Atlanta Urban League, Sept. 1942–April 1943," Box 19, Rainey Papers; War Manpower Commission, "Labor Market Developments Report," 15 April 1943, Box 7, Series 12, WMC; "Day Classes at Aircraft School May Be Stopped," *ADW*, 23 July 1943; "Need More Students at Aircraft School," *ADW*, 1 August 1943; [WMC], "Labor Developments Report for Atlanta, Georgia," 28 December 1943, Box 7, Series 12, WMC; "Atlantans Urged to Use Aircraft School Facilities," *ADW*, 30 June 1944.

40. "Progress Report."

41. "Urban League to Register Group for Bell Work," *ADW*, 22 January 1943.

42. "Progress Report"; Atlanta Urban League, "Timeless: The Task of Preventive Social Work"; Sub-Committee of the Council on Defense Training for Negroes to E. A. Adams, 11 March 1942, Box 12, Series 2, WMC; [War Manpower Commission], "Preliminary Statement on the Atlanta and Marietta Labor Market," 10 December 1942, Box 1, Series 12, WMC.

43. Atlanta Urban League, "Timeless: The Task of Preventive Social Work"; Joel Smith interview, Box 39, LA; Jacob Henderson interview, Georgia Government Documentation Project, Georgia State University.

44. A. Bruce Hunt to Frank Constangy, 8 January 1944, Closed Cases Box 2, FEPC; Turner, "A Study of One Hundred Skilled Negro Workers at Bell Aircraft Cor-

poration," 2; William Shell to Dillard B. Lasseter, 30 June 1945, Box 1, Series 20, WMC.

45. Bell Aircraft advertised constantly for assembly-line workers in Atlanta's white newspapers throughout 1944 and 1945, and even offered training to unskilled workers to fill these positions. African Americans were excluded entirely from these jobs and training opportunities. See Bell Aircraft FEPC complaints in Closed Cases Boxes 2, 6, and 7, FEPC.

46. "Occupational Classification of Negro Workers at Bell Aircraft during World War II," Box 1, Housing Center Files, 1933–49, Atlanta Urban League Collection [unprocessed], AU; Turner, "A Study of One Hundred Skilled Negro Workers at Bell Aircraft," 2. Bell did such a good job at segregating skilled black workers from the rest of the Marietta work force that many white workers were not even aware that the company hired blacks in skilled positions. Catherine Cohen interview, Box 36, LA.

47. See, for example, Minnie Harvey, "Complaint," 7 February 1944, Closed Cases Box 2, FEPC; Corria L. Durden, "Complaint," 26 June 1944, Closed Cases Box 2, FEPC; Lureline Thomas, "United States of America before the President's Committee on Fair Employment Practice, Complaint," 20 January 1945, Closed Cases Box 2, FEPC.

48. Turner, "A Study of One Hundred Skilled Negro Workers at Bell Aircraft," 11; Nelson C. Jackson to Lester B. Granger, 27 April 1947, Box 1, Housing Center Files, 1933–49, Atlanta Urban League Collection.

49. "Workers' Education to Be Topic for Bell Employees," *ADW*, 27 April 1944.

50. William H. Shell to Dillard B. Lasseter, 31 July 1945, Box 1, Series 20, WMC. See also Pete Daniel, "Going among Strangers," 902.

51. "War Workers Warned to Work On and Off Job for Security," *ADW*, 31 October 1944.

52. In this way, black reformers acted very much like wartime and postwar union leaders who, in their new partnership with corporate leaders, took over "much of the company's personnel work" and became "the disciplining agent of the rank and file." Mills, *The New Men of Power*, 224.

53. All FEPC complainants protesting on-the-job discrimination at Bell told of white personnel officials dismissing their charges or, in the case of workers protesting discriminatory suspension, threatening them with permanent dismissal if they made an official grievance. See Bell files in Closed Cases Box 2, FEPC.

54. Annette Devine Giddings, "Complaint," 15 February 1944, Closed Cases Box 2, FEPC; Annie Mae Hightower, "Complaint," 16 February 1944, Closed Cases Box 2, FEPC; Lamar Ross, "Complaint," 3 March 1944, Closed Cases Box 2, FEPC; Spicey Simmons, "United States of America Before the President's Committee on Fair Employment Practice, Complaint," 19 February 1944, Closed Cases Box 2, FEPC; Dora Smith, "United States of America before the Presi-

dent's Committee on Fair Employment Practice, Complaint," 19 February 1944, Closed Cases Box 2, FEPC; "Report by Flournoy on Cases No. 197–198," 30 May 1944, Closed Cases Box 2, FEPC; Sarah Madison, "United States of America before the President's Committee on Fair Employment Practice, Complaint," 1 May 1944, Closed Cases Box 2, FEPC.

55. "Don't Let It Happen Here," *ADW*, 27 June 1943.

Epilogue

1. Clarence Bacote, "The Negro in Atlanta Politics," 344; Bayor, *Race and the Shaping of Twentieth-Century Atlanta*, 20.

2. Bacote, "The Negro in Atlanta Politics," 349; Stone, *Regime Politics*, 29. For an excellent account of the struggle for black police in Atlanta, see Dulaney, *Black Police in America*, 38–44.

3. Bacote, "The Negro in Atlanta Politics," 343–44.

4. Spritzer and Bergmark, *Grace Towns Hamilton*, 90–91.

5. Evans, "A Study of Twenty-Five Negro Veterans Who Are 'On-the-Job' Training," 20, 25; Turner, "A Study of One Hundred Skilled Negro Workers," 45; Sandy Gregg Reid, "A Study of the Social Problems of Fifty Veterans," 10–12, 14, 21.

6. "Brutality Charged State Police at Capitol and Soldier's Homes," *ADW*, 3 July 1945; "Deplore Treatment of Negro Veterans by Atlanta Police," *ADW*, 27 November 1945; "Murder on Bus Evokes Grave Concern Here," *ADW*, 30 November 1945; "Coroner's Jury Frees Two Policemen in Arrest-Slaying," *ADW*, 14 December 1945; "Vets to Discuss Police Brutality," *ADW*, 16 December 1945; "Motorman Slays Youth at Door of Trolley," *ADW*, 11 April 1946; "Streetcar Conductor Freed for Shooting," *ADW*, 15 May 1946; "Another Veteran Shot by Georgia Power Motorman," *ADW*, 29 September 1946.

7. W. B. Hartsfield to Chief Hornsby, 7 June 1946, Box 11, Herbert T. Jenkins Papers, AHC; "Hooded Men Stone Dixie Hills Bus," *ADW*, 28 August 1946; Ned to AF, 3 September 1946, Manuscript Collection, Box 51, Ralph Emerson McGill Papers, EU; "Police Patrol Sells Avenue after Threat," *ADW*, 11 September 1946; "Atlanta's Tension Spots," *ADW*, 17 September 1946; "Committee Seeks to Ease Housing Trouble," *ADW*, 25 September 1946; "Agent's Car Shot Up at Sells-Ashby," *ADW*, 11 October 1946; "Chestnut Street Demonstration Draws Police," *ADW*, 30 October 1946; "Mayor Orders Columbians Probe Here," *ADW*, 31 October 1946; "Police Intensify Probe of Columbians," *ADW*, 1 November 1946; "Call Columbian, Witness Claims, Rather than Cop," *ADW*, 6 November 1946; "Continue Probe of Columbians Monday," *ADW*, 17 November 1946.

8. " Police Assure Protection in Sells Ave. Housing Row," *ADW*, 15 September 1946.

9. William B. Hartsfield to Gentlemen, 7 January 1943, Box 29, William Berry Hartsfield Papers, EU.

10. Harold H. Martin, *William Berry Hartsfield*, 41–42, 85; Stone, *Regime Politics*, 27–28, 30–31.

11. Griffin, "A Study of Employment Changes," 16–19; Turner, "A Study of One Hundred Skilled Negro Workers at Bell Aircraft," 2.

12. As Elizabeth Clark-Lewis details, when domestic workers in Washington shifted from live-in to day work, often one of the first things they did was to become actively involved in church organizations from which they had earlier been prevented from contributing because of work commitments. Clark-Lewis, *Living In, Living Out*, 168–72.

13. Grace Towns Hamilton interview, Georgia Government Documentation Project, Georgia State University; Works Projects Administration of Georgia, *Report of the Real Property, Land Use, and Low Income Housing Area Survey of Metropolitan Atlanta*.

14. "Plan Housing Project Registration Contest," *ADW*, 30 November 1945; AUL, "Timeless: The Task of Preventative Social Work, 1946 Annual Report," Box 35, Austin Thomas Walden Papers, AHC; Bacote, "The Negro in Atlanta Politics," 347.

15. William A. Fowlkes, "World War II Vet Head Seeks Ballot," *ADW*, 13 July 1944.

16. "World War II Veterans Organize Georgia League; Milton, Leader," *ADW*, 9 September 1945; "Atlantans Ask 'Integration of Veterans' in Hospital Planning," *ADW*, 19 December 1945; "Veterans Call at Doors Today," *ADW*, 31 March 1946.

17. "And So They Marched," *ADW*, 8 March 1946. See also "E. J. Boddie to Organized Labor," 11 January 1946, Reel 42, *SRC*; "NAACP Not Behind Demonstration by Veterans Group," *ADW*, 28 February 1946; "Groups Not Behind Monday 'Police March,'" *ADW*, 3 March 1946; "Undoing Good Work," *ADW*, 3 March 1946; Police Committee of Council, "Regular Meeting," 14 March 1946, Police Committee Minute Book, 28 February 1946–11 June 1952, CAR; J. T. Lattimore to the World Editor, *ADW*, 24 March 1946.

18. "United Veterans in March on City Hall," *ADW*, 5 March 1946.

19. Among those who have written provocatively about the political coalition between black Atlantans and wealthy north-side whites include Clarence Stone, Michael Goldfield, and, most recently, Ronald Bayor. Stone, *Regime Politics*, 28–50; Goldfield, "Black Political Power and Public Policy in the Urban South"; Bayor, *Race and the Shaping of Twentieth-Century Atlanta*, 25–52.

20. "Table I: Source of Income, Atlanta Urban League, 1946–1949," 26 March 1958, Manuscript Collection, Box 48, McGill Papers; Robert Thompson interview, Georgia Government Documentation Project. Although many scholars place the NAACP as the instigator of the All Citizens Registration Committee, contemporary accounts show that the AUL was responsible for most if not all of

the campaign's day-to-day planning. Grace Towns Hamilton pointed this out to Lester Granger, the National Urban League's executive secretary, when she wrote him about the AUL's role in the registration effort: "We are not giving any publicity to the fact that our agency has prepared all the materials, made all the necessary analyses of population distribution, and has set up the basic 'community organization machinery' which is now being used by an Atlanta Citizens Registration Committee." Grace Towns Hamilton to Lester Granger, 15 March 1946, Box 1, Housing Center Files, 1933–49, AUL Collection [unprocessed], AU. While the AUL did not publicize its role in the campaign, it took no great pains to hide it, either. Spritzer and Bergmark, *Grace Towns Hamilton*, 111.

21. Stone, *Regime Politics*, 34.
22. Ibid., 32–34.
23. Ibid., 34; Thompson, Lewis, and McEntire, "Atlanta and Birmingham," 13–83.
24. Thompson, Lewis, and McEntire, "Atlanta and Birmingham," 35.
25. Stone, *Regime Politics*, 41.
26. Bayor, *Race and the Shaping of Twentieth-Century Atlanta*, 256; Silver and Moeser, *The Separate City*, 128–31, 136–44, 152–62; Stone, *Regime Politics*, 40–41. Generally, historians who write about urban development in Atlanta and elsewhere do an excellent job at unraveling the myriad of ways in which white officials oppressed and destroyed black communities. They also do a good job in showing how black leaders participated in the "oppression" of their own communities once they become part of the ruling elite. They are less successful in examining the reasons behind black complicity in the destruction of black neighborhoods, black people's vision of their own communities, and black agency in relation to urban development before the advent of African American electoral power.
27. Bureau of the Census, *Census of Population, Seventeenth Census of the United States: 1950*, 218. Black registration rates in Atlanta continued to be low into the 1960s. See Bayor, *Race and the Shaping of Twentieth-Century Atlanta*, 7, 18.
28. This apparent paradox is a favorite topic for journalists in Atlanta and elsewhere. Trotter, "America's Public Housing Capital"; Reddick, "Black Workers Find Tale of Two Cities"; Thomas D. Boston, "Black Middle Class Shifts over Time"; Carrie Teegarden, "Is the City a Mecca for African Americans?"

Works Cited

Manuscript Collections

Atlanta, Georgia
Atlanta Chamber of Commerce
   Atlanta Chamber of Commerce Minute Books
Atlanta History Center Library/Archives
   Atlanta Lung Association Collection
   City of Atlanta Records
   Grace Towns Hamilton Papers
   Herbert Jenkins Papers
   Long-Rucker-Aiken Family Papers
   Police Committee Minute Books
   Gay Bolling Shepperson Papers
   Austin Thomas Walden Papers
Auburn Avenue Research Library
   Samuel Howard Archer Papers
   Ruby Blackburn Collection
Georgia Department of Archives and History
   Department of Education Records
   Division of Negro Education
   Director of Negro Education Subject Files
   Rhoda Kaufman Papers
   Jane Van De Vrede Papers
Robert W. Woodruff Library, Clark-Atlanta University
   Atlanta Urban League Collection
   John Hope Administration Papers
   Elizabeth and Irvin McDuffie Papers
   Neighborhood Union Collection
   Florence M. Read Administration Papers
Robert W. Woodruff Library, Emory University
   Mary Cornelia Barker Papers
   William Berry Hartsfield Papers
   Ralph Emerson McGill Papers
   Charles Forrest Palmer Papers

Glenn Weddington Rainey Papers
Emily Woodward Papers
Southern Labor Archive, Georgia State University
    Machinists Lodge #1 [International Association of Machinists, AFL] Records

College Park, Maryland
National Archives
    Record Group 196
    U.S. Public Housing Administration Project Files

East Point, Georgia
National Archives Regional Office
    Record Group 119
    National Youth Administration Records. Region 2.
    Record Group 211
    U.S. War Manpower Commission Records. Region 7.
    Record Group 228
    Committee on Fair Employment Practices Records. Region 7.

Hyde Park, New York
Franklin Delano Roosevelt Library
    Good Neighbor League Papers
    Harry L. Hopkins Papers
    Eleanor Roosevelt Papers
    Franklin Delano Roosevelt Papers

New York, New York
Schomburg Center for Research in Black Culture
    Robert Clifton Weaver Papers

Manuscripts on Microfilm

Commission on Interracial Cooperation Papers. Glen Rock, N.J.: Microfilming Cor-
    poration of America, 1984.
New Deal Agencies and Black America. Frederick, Md.: University Publications of
    America, 1984.
Papers of John and Lugenia Burns Hope. Frederick, Md.: University Publications of
    America, 1984.
Papers of the NAACP. Frederick, Md.: University Publications of America, 1981.
Socialist Party of America Papers. Glen Rock, N.J.: Microfilming Corporation of
    America, 1975.
Southern Regional Council Papers. Glen Rock, N.J.: Microfilming Corporation of
    America, 1984.

Interviews

Georgia Government Documentation Project, Special Collections, Georgia State University Library
Crank, Suzette. Interview by Kathryn Nasstrom, 12 April 1993.
Dove, Pearlie. Interview by Kathryn Nasstrom, 9 April 1992.
Hamilton, Grace Towns. Interview by Cliff Kuhn, 26 June 1986.
Henderson, Jacob. Interview by Duane Stewart, 8 June 1989.
Thompson, Robert. Interview by Duane Stewart, 5 June 1989.
Tuttle, Elbert P. Interview by Cliff Kuhn, 21 September 1992.
Washington, Alice Holmes. Interview by Kathryn Nasstrom, 15 April 1993.

Living Atlanta Collection, Atlanta History Center Library/Archives
Anonymous. Interview by Bernard West, [ca. 1978–79].
Blackshear, Nell. Interviewed by Anonymous, [ca. 1978–79].
Brooks, Hallie. Interview by Bernard West, [ca. 1978–79].
Clemmons, Estelle. Interview by Bernard West, [ca. 1978–79].
Cohen, Catherine. Interview by Adina Back, [ca. 1978–79].
Daugherty, Lula. Interview by Bernard West, 19 October 1978.
Dunbar, Augusta. Interviewed by Cliff Kuhn, 3 August 1979.
Futch, Opal. Interview by Cliff Kuhn, [ca. 1978–79].
Heyman, Josephine. Interview by Cliff Kuhn, [ca. 1978–79].
Idlett, Arthur. Interview by Bernard West, [ca. 1978–79].
Ivey, Sanders. Interview by Cliff Kuhn, [ca. 1978–79].
Jackson, Willie Mae. Interview by Bernard West, [ca. 1978–79].
MacDougall, Margaret. Interview by Cliff Kuhn, [ca. 1978–79].
McDonald, Mrs. E. Graham. Interview by Cliff Kuhn, [ca. 1978–79].
Milton, L. D. Interview by Bernard West, [ca. 1978–79].
Morton, Mary. Interview by Bernard West, [ca. 1978–79].
Nash, Homer. Interview by Bernard West, [ca. 1978–79].
Paschall, Eliza. Interview by Cliff Kuhn, [ca. 1978–79].
Raper, Arthur. Interview by Cliff Kuhn, [ca. 1978–79].
Render, Clara. Interview by Bernard West, [ca. 1978–79].
Sinclair, Horace. Interview by Bernard West, [ca. 1978–79].
Van Dusseldorp, Wilma. Interview by Cliff Kuhn, [ca. 1978–79].

Sweet Auburn Neighborhood Project, Auburn Avenue Research Library
Collier, Rev. Jimmy. Interview by Melinda S. and Patricia W., 25 July 1978.

Newspapers and Periodicals

Atlanta City Directory
Atlanta Constitution

Atlanta Daily World
Atlanta Georgian
Atlanta Journal
Atlanta Journal of Labor
Atlanta University Bulletin
Baltimore Afro-American
The Crisis
New York Times
Opportunity
Spelman Messenger

Government Documents

Georgia Department of Public Welfare with Works Progress Administration of Georgia. *A Report of the Social Security Survey in Georgia*, by Ada M. Barker. Atlanta: Georgia State Department of Public Welfare in Cooperation with Works Progress Administration of Georgia, 1937.

National Youth Administration of Georgia. *Report on the National Youth Administration of Georgia, 1935–1938*, by Dillard B. Lasseter. Atlanta: National Youth Administration of Georgia, 1939.

Public Works Administration. *America Builds: The Record of PWA*. Washington, D.C.: Government Printing Office, 1939.

Public Works Administration Housing Division. *Urban Housing: The Story of the P.W.A. Housing Division, 1933–1936*. Washington, D.C.: Government Printing Office, 1936.

U.S. Bureau of the Census. *Fifteenth Census of the United States: 1930*. Vol. 4. Washington, D.C.: Government Printing Office, 1933.

———. *Census of Population, Seventeenth Census of the United States: 1950*. Vol. 2, part 2. Washington, D.C.: Government Printing Office, 1952.

U.S. Congress. House. *Hearings before a Special Committee to Investigate Communist Activities in the United States of the House of Representatives*. Part 6, vol. 1. 71st Cong., 2d sess. Washington, D.C.: Government Printing Office, 1930.

U.S. Department of the Interior, Office of Education. *Choosing Our Way: A Study of America's Forums*. Bulletin 1937, Misc. No. 1, 1–7. Washington, D.C.: Government Printing Office, 1937.

Works Progress Administration, Division of Social Research. *Urban Workers on Relief*. Part 2. Washington, D.C.: Government Printing Office, 1936.

Works Projects Administration of Georgia. *Report of the Real Property, Land Use, and Low Income Housing Area Survey of Metropolitan Atlanta*. Part 1. Atlanta: Housing Authority of the City of Atlanta, 1940.

Books, Articles, Dissertations, and Theses

Alexander, Theodore Martin. *Beyond the Timberline: The Trials and Triumphs of a Black Entrepreneur.* Edgewood, Md.: M. E. Duncan and Co., 1992.

Alexander, Will W. "The NRA and the Southern Negro," *The World Outlook* (December 1933): 404–8.

Allen, Willie A. "A Study of the Negro Members of the Laundry Workers' International Union, Local 218, Atlanta, Georgia." M.A. thesis, Atlanta University, 1946.

Anderson, C. Arnold, and Mary Jean Bowman, "The Vanishing Servant and the Contemporary Status System of the American South." *American Journal of Sociology* 49 (November 1953): 215–30.

Anderson, Karen Tucker. "Last Hired, First Fired: Black Women Workers during World War II." *Journal of American History* 69 (June 1982): 82–97.

Anderson, William. *The Wild Man from Sugar Creek: The Political Career of Eugene Talmadge.* Baton Rouge: Louisiana State University Press, 1975.

Aptheker, Herbert, ed. *The Correspondence of W. E. B. Du Bois.* Vol. 2. Amherst: University of Massachusetts Press, 1976.

Argersinger, Jo Ann E. *Toward a New Deal in Baltimore: People and Government in the Great Depression.* Chapel Hill: University of North Carolina Press, 1988.

The Atlanta University Publications. New York: Arno Press, 1968.

Bacote, C. A. "The Negro in Atlanta Politics." *Phylon* 16, no. 4 (1955): 333–50.

———. *The Story of Atlanta University: A Century of Service, 1865-1965.* Atlanta: Atlanta University Press, 1969.

Bauman, John F. *Public Housing, Race, and Renewal: Urban Planning in Philadelphia, 1920-1974.* Philadelphia: Temple University Press, 1987.

Bayor, Ronald. *Race and the Shaping of Twentieth-Century Atlanta.* Chapel Hill: University of North Carolina Press, 1996.

Blackwelder, Julia Kirk, "Women in the Work Force: Atlanta, New Orleans, and San Antonio, 1930 to 1940." *Journal of Urban History* 4 (May 1978): 331–58.

Borchert, James. *Alley Life in Washington: Family, Community, Religion, and Folklife in the City, 1850-1970.* Urbana: University of Illinois Press, 1980.

Boston, Thomas D. "Black Middle Class Shifts over Time." *Atlanta Journal-Constitution,* 21 May 1995.

Brandt, Allan M. *No Magic Bullet: A Social History of Venereal Disease in the United States since 1880.* New York: Oxford University Press, 1985.

Brodkin, Karen. *How Jews Became White Folks and What That Says about Race in America.* New Brunswick, N.J.: Rutgers University Press, 1998.

Bunche, Ralph J. *The Political Status of the Negro in the Age of FDR.* Chicago: University of Chicago Press, 1973.

Byrne, Ann DeRosa, and Dana F. White. "Atlanta University's 'Northeast Lot': Community Building for Black Atlanta's 'Talented Tenth.'" *Atlanta Historical Journal* 26 (Summer–Fall 1982): 155–76.

Caro, Robert. *The Power Broker: Robert Moses and the Fall of New York.* New York: Alfred A. Knopf, 1974.

Carter, Dan T. *Scottsboro: A Tragedy of the American South.* Baton Rouge: Louisiana State University Press, 1979.

Cayton, Horace, and St. Clair Drake. *Black Metropolis: A Study of Negro Life in a Northern City.* New York: Harcourt, Brace, 1945.

Clark-Lewis, Elizabeth. *Living In, Living Out: African-American Domestics in Washington, D.C., 1910–1940.* Washington: Smithsonian Institution Press, 1994.

Cohen, Lizabeth. *Making a New Deal: Industrial Workers in Chicago, 1919–1939.* New York: Cambridge University Press, 1990.

Cook, Blanche Wiesen. *Eleanor Roosevelt.* Vol. 2: *The Defining Years, 1933–1938.* New York: Penguin, 1999.

Crimmins, Timothy J. "Bungalow Suburbs: East and West." *Atlanta Historical Journal* 26 (Summer–Fall 1982): 82–94.

Crocker, Ruth. *Social Work and Social Order: The Settlement Movement in Two Industrial Cities.* Urbana: University of Illinois Press, 1992.

Daniel, Pete. "Going among Strangers: Southern Reactions to World War II." *Journal of American History* 77 (December 1990): 886–911.

Daniel, Walter G., and Carroll L. Miller. "The Participation of the Negro in the National Youth Administration Program." *Journal of Negro Education* 7 (July 1938): 357–65.

Davis, Benjamin, Jr. *Communist Councilman from Harlem: Autobiographical Notes Written in a Federal Penitentiary.* New York: International Publishers, 1969.

Davis, Leroy. *A Clashing of the Soul: John Hope and the Dilemma of African American Leadership and Black Higher Education in the Early Twentieth Century.* Athens: University of Georgia Press, 1998.

DeCosta, Beautine Hubert. "A Study for the Atlanta Urban League of the Social Conditions in a Selected Area as a Basis for Program Planning." M.A. thesis, Atlanta University, 1942.

Dittmer, John. *Black Georgia in the Progressive Era, 1900–1920.* Urbana: University of Illinois Press, 1977.

Du Bois, W. E. B. *Black Reconstruction in America.* 1935. Reprint, New York: Atheneum, 1992.

———. "Federal Action Programs and Community Action in the South." *Social Forces* 19 (March 1941): 375–80.

———. *The Souls of Black Folk.* 1903. Reprint, New York: Gramercy Press, 1994.

Dulaney, W. Marvin. *Black Police in America.* Bloomington: Indiana University Press, 1996.

Ellis, Ann Wells. "'Uncle Sam Is My Shepherd': The Commission on Interracial Cooperation and the New Deal in Georgia." *Atlanta Historical Journal* 30 (Spring 1986): 47–63.

Evans, Lillian Virginia. "A Study of Twenty-Five Negro Veterans Who Are 'On-the-

Job' Training in Ten Establishments in Atlanta, Georgia." M.A. thesis, Atlanta University, 1946.

Fainstein, Norman, and Susan Nesbitt. "Did the Black Ghetto Have a Golden Age? Class Structure and Class Segregation in New York City, 1949–1970." *Journal of Urban History* 23 (November 1996): 3–28.

Fairclough, Adam. *Race and Democracy: The Civil Rights Struggle in Louisiana, 1915–1972.* Athens: University of Georgia Press, 1995.

Fleming, Douglas Lee. "Atlanta, the Depression, and the New Deal." Ph.D. diss., Emory University, 1984.

Friedman, Lawrence M. *Government and Slum Housing: A Century of Frustration.* Chicago: Rand McNally and Co., 1968.

Fusfeld, Daniel R., and Timothy Bates. *The Political Economy of the Urban Ghetto.* Carbondale: Southern Illinois University Press, 1984.

Gaines, Kevin K. *Uplifting the Race: Black Leadership, Politics, and Culture in the Twentieth Century.* Chapel Hill: University of North Carolina Press, 1996.

Gatewood, Willard B. *Aristocrats of Color: The Black Elite, 1880–1920.* Bloomington: Indiana University Press, 1990.

Gilmore, Glenda Elizabeth. *Gender and Jim Crow: Women and the Politics of White Supremacy in North Carolina, 1896–1920.* Chapel Hill: University of North Carolina Press, 1996.

Goldfield, David R. "Black Political Power and Public Policy in the Urban South." In *Urban Policy in Twentieth-Century America*, edited by Arnold Hirsch and Raymond Mohl, 159–82. Brunswick, N.J.: Rutgers University Press, 1993.

Gordon, Linda. *Pitied but Not Entitled: Single Mothers and the History of Welfare, 1890–1935.* New York: The Free Press, 1994.

Graham, Sarah Lauderdale. *House and Street: The Domestic World of Servants and Masters in Nineteenth-Century Rio De Janeiro.* New York: Cambridge University Press, 1988.

Griffin, Twyler Wenona. "A Study of the Employment Changes since the Close of World War II and How These Changes Affect 100 Persons Seeking Services at the United States Employment Service Office in Atlanta, Georgia." M.A. thesis, Atlanta University, 1946.

Hall, Jacquelyn Dowd, James Leloudis, Robert Korstad, Mary Murphy, LuAnn Jones, and Christopher B. Daly. *Like a Family: The Making of a Southern Cotton Mill World.* New York: W. W. Norton, 1989.

Harvey, Jeanette Wynn. "Changing Opportunities in Social Work for Negroes as Shown by a Study of the Placements of the Graduates from the Atlanta University School of Social Work from June 1934 through June 1943." M.A. thesis, Atlanta University School of Social Work, 1944.

Haynes, Laroy Howard Milton. "The Ecological Distribution of Negro Population in Atlanta in 1939." M.A. thesis, Atlanta University, 1940.

Higginbotham, Evelyn Brooks. *Righteous Discontent: The Women's Movement in the*

Black Baptist Church, 1880–1920. Cambridge, Mass.: Harvard University Press, 1993.

Hill, Robert A., ed. *The FBI's RACON: Racial Conditions in the United States during World War II.* Boston: Northeastern University Press, 1995.

Hirsch, Arnold R. *Making the Second Ghetto: Race and Housing in Chicago, 1940–1960.* Cambridge: Cambridge University Press, 1983.

Holmes, Michael S. *The New Deal in Georgia: An Administrative History.* Westport, Conn.: Greenwood Press, 1975.

Honey, Michael. *Southern Labor and Black Civil Rights: Organizing Memphis Workers.* Urbana: University of Illinois Press, 1993.

Hunter, Tera W. *"To 'Joy My Freedom": Southern Black Women's Lives and Labors after the Civil War.* Cambridge, Mass.: Harvard University Press, 1997.

Jackson, Kenneth T. *The Ku Klux Klan in the City.* New York: Oxford University Press, 1967.

James, Joy. *Transcending the Talented Tenth: Black Leaders and American Intellectuals.* London: Routledge, 1997.

Janken, Kenneth Robert. *Rayford W. Logan and the Dilemma of the African-American Intellectual.* Amherst: University of Massachusetts Press, 1993.

Jones, Jacqueline. *The Dispossessed: America's Underclasses from the Civil War to the Present.* New York: Basic Books, 1992.

Jones, James H. *Bad Blood: The Tuskegee Syphilis Experiment.* New York: The Free Press, 1993.

Jones, William. "Trade Boycotts: A Brief Study of the Newest Economic Weapon Employed Successfully by Negro Groups in Their Efforts to Open Fresh Employment Opportunities." *Opportunity* 18 (August 1940): 230–41.

Katz, Michael B. *In the Shadow of the Poorhouse: A Social History of Welfare in America.* New York: Basic Books, 1996.

Kelley, Robin D. G. *Hammer and Hoe: Alabama Communists in the Great Depression.* Chapel Hill: University of North Carolina Press, 1990.

———. "'We Are Not What We Seem': Rethinking Black Working-Class Activism in the Jim Crow South." *Journal of American History* 80 (June 1993): 75–112.

Kirby, John. *Black Americans in the Roosevelt Era: Liberalism and Race.* Knoxville: University of Tennessee Press, 1980.

Kornbluh, Joyce L. *A New Deal for Workers' Education: The Workers' Service Program, 1933–1942.* Urbana: University of Illinois Press, 1987.

Korstad, Robert, and Nelson Lichtenstein. "Opportunities Found and Lost: Labor, Radicals, and the Early Civil Rights Movement." *Journal of American History* 75 (December 1988): 756–81.

Kuhn, Clifford M., Harlon E. Joye, and E. Bernard West. *Living Atlanta: An Oral History of the City, 1914–1948.* Athens: University of Georgia Press, 1990.

Kytle, Elizabeth. *Willie Mae.* New York: Alfred A. Knopf, 1958.

Lawrence, Charles Radford, Jr. "The Social Background of Negro Junior High School Pupils, Atlanta, Georgia." M.A. thesis, Atlanta University, 1938.

Lewis, Earl. *In Their Own Interests: Race, Class, and Power in Twentieth-Century Norfolk, Virginia.* Berkeley: University of California Press, 1991.

Lipsitz, George. *The Possessive Investment in Whiteness: How White People Profit from Identity Politics.* Philadelphia: Temple University Press, 1998.

Lofton, Thomas Glaston. "The Atlanta Laboratories: An Investigation to Determine the Political and Planning Processes Involved in Erecting the First Federally Funded Housing Project in the City of Atlanta." M.A. thesis, Atlanta University, 1971.

Logan, Rayford. *The Negro in American Life and Thought: The Nadir, 1877–1901.* London: Dial Press, 1954.

Lowe, Eugene Yerby. "A Study of the Opinions of 50 Negro Contributors and 50 Non-Contributors to the Atlanta Community Fund." M.A. thesis, Atlanta University School of Social Work, 1942.

Lowitt, Richard, and Maurine Beaseley, eds. *One Third of a Nation: Lorena Hickok Reports on the Great Depression.* Urbana: University of Illinois Press, 1981.

MacLean, Nancy. *Behind the Mask of Chivalry: The Making of the Second Ku Klux Klan.* New York: Oxford University Press, 1994.

Martin, Charles H. *The Angelo Herndon Case and Southern Justice.* Baton Rouge: Louisiana State University Press, 1976.

Martin, Harold H. *William Berry Hartsfield: Mayor of Atlanta,* Athens: University of Georgia Press, 1978.

May, Agnes Elizabeth. "Employment of Women in Domestic and Personal Service — With Special Reference to Negro Women in Atlanta, Georgia." M.A. thesis, Atlanta University, 1939.

McNeil, Genna Rae. *Groundwork: Charles Hamilton Houston and the Struggle for Civil Rights.* Philadelphia: University of Pennsylvania Press, 1983.

Mead, Howard N. "Russell vs. Talmadge: Southern Politics and the New Deal." *Georgia Historical Quarterly* 65 (Spring 1981): 28–45.

Meier, August, and Elliott Rudwick. *Along the Color Line: Explorations in the Black Experience.* Urbana: University of Illinois Press, 1976.

Mills, C. Wright. *The New Men of Power: America's Labor Leaders.* New York: Harcourt Brace and Co., 1948.

———. "The Professional Ideology of Social Pathologists." *American Journal of Sociology* 47, 2 (September 1943): 165–180.

Mohl, Raymond A. "Making the Second Ghetto in Metropolitan Miami, 1940–1960." In *The New African American Urban History,* edited by Kenneth W. Goings and Raymond A. Mohl, 266–98. Thousand Oaks: Sage Publications, 1996.

Montgomery, Callie Mae. "Some Social Aspects of the Reed Street Baptist Church." M.A. thesis, Atlanta University, 1937.

Moore, Jacqueline M. *Leading the Race: The Transformation of the Black Elite in the Nation's Capital, 1880–1920.* Charlottesville: University Press of Virginia, 1999.

Moore, John Hammond. "Communists and Fascists in a Southern City: Atlanta, 1930." *The South Atlantic Quarterly.* 67 (Summer 1968): 437–454.

Morgan, Charlotte T., "Finding A Way Out: Adult Education in Harlem During the Great Depression." *Afro-Americans in New York Life and History.* 8, no. 1 (1984): 17–29.

Moron, Alonzo. "Public Housing From a Community Point of View." *Social Forces.* 19 (October 1940): 73–78.

Nelson, Bruce. "Organized Labor and the Struggle for Black Equality in Mobile during World War II." *Journal of American History.* 80 (December 1993): 952–988.

Painter, Nell Irvin. *The Narrative of Hosea Hudson: The Life and Times of a Black Radical.* New York: W. W. Norton, 1994.

Palmer, Charles F. *Adventures of a Slum Fighter.* Atlanta: Tupper and Love, 1955.

Palmer, Phyllis. *Domesticity and Dirt: Housewives and Domestic Servants in the United States, 1920–1945.* Philadelphia: Temple University Press, 1989.

Parran, Thomas. "No Defense for Any of Us." *Survey Graphic.* April 1938. 197–202, 248–251.

Phillips, Kimberley L. *Alabama North: African-American Migrants, Community, and Working-Class Activism in Cleveland, 1915–1945.* Urbana: University of Illinois Press, 1999.

Pierce, Joseph A. *The Atlanta Negro: A Collection of Data on the Negro Population of Atlanta, Georgia.* Washington: American Youth Commission of the American Council on Education, 1940.

———. *Negro Business and Business Education.* New York: Harper and Brothers Publisher, 1947.

Pradd, Tommie Lenora. "A Study of the Neighborhood Clubs of the Atlanta Urban League." M.A. thesis, Atlanta University, 1939.

Preston, Howard L. *Automobile Age Atlanta: The Making of a Southern Metropolis, 1900–1935.* Athens, GA: University of Georgia Press, 1979.

Rabinowitz, Howard N. *Race Relations in the Urban South.* New York: Oxford University Press, 1978.

Radford, Gail. *Modern Housing for America: Policy Struggles in the New Deal Era.* Chicago: University of Chicago Press, 1996.

Raper, Arthur, F. "A Day at Police Court." *Phylon.* 5, no. 3 (1944): 225–232.

———. "The Southern Negro and the NRA." *Georgia Historical Quarterly.* 64, no. 2 (Summer 1980): 128–45.

Read, Florence Matilda. *The Story of Spelman College.* Princeton: Princeton University Press, 1961.

Reddick, Tracie. "Black Workers Find Tale of Two Cities." *Tampa Tribune.* 12 May, 1996.

Reed, Adolph Jr. *Stirrings in the Jug: Black Politics in the Post-Segregation Era.* Minneapolis: University of Minnesota Press, 1999.

Reed, Merl E. *Seedtime for the Modern Civil Rights Movement: The President's Committee on Fair Employment Practice.* Baton Rouge: Louisiana State University Press, 1991.

Reid, Edna Ruth. "A Study of Free Treatment Facilities Available to Negroes with Syphilis in Atlanta, Fulton County, Georgia, 1938–1940." M.A. thesis, Atlanta University, 1941.

Reid, Sandy Gregg. "A Study of the Social Problems of Fifty Veterans of World War II, Enrolled in Booker T. Washington High School, Atlanta, Georgia 1946–1947." M.A. thesis, Atlanta University, 1947.

Rosenzweig, Charles L. "The Issue of Employing Black Policemen in Atlanta," M.A. thesis, Emory University, 1980.

Rouse, Jacqueline Anne. *Lugenia Burns Hope: Black Southern Reformer.* Athens: University of Georgia Press, 1989.

Ruechel, Frank, "New Deal Public Housing, Urban Poverty, and Jim Crow: Techwood and University Homes in Atlanta," *Georgia Historical Quarterly.* 81, no. 4 (1997): 915–937.

Scott, James C. *Seeing like a State: How Certain Schemes to Improve the Human Condition Have Failed.* New Haven, Conn.: Yale University Press, 1998.

Shaw, Stephanie J. *What a Woman Ought to Be and to Do: Black Professional Women Workers during the Jim Crow Era.* Chicago: University of Chicago Press, 1996.

Shivery, Louie Delphia Davis. "The History of Organized Social Work among Atlanta Negroes." M.A. thesis, Atlanta University, 1936.

Silver, Christopher, and John V. Moeser. *The Separate City: Black Communities in the Urban South, 1940–1968.* Lexington: University Press of Kentucky, 1995.

Sitkoff, Harvard. *A New Deal for Blacks: The Emergence of Civil Rights as a National Issue.* New York: Oxford University Press, 1978.

Solomon, Mark. *The Cry Was Unity: Communists and African Americans, 1917–1936.* Jackson: University of Mississippi Press, 1998.

Spritzer, Lorraine Nelson, and Jean B. Bergmark. *Grace Towns Hamilton and the Politics of Southern Change.* Athens: University of Georgia Press, 1997.

Stokes, Lillian Frances. "The Root Doctor in Atlanta." M.A. thesis, Atlanta University, 1945.

Stone, Clarence N. *Regime Politics: Governing Atlanta, 1946–1988.* Lawrence: University Press of Kansas, 1989.

Sugrue, Thomas J. *The Origins of the Urban Crisis: Race and Inequality in Postwar Detroit.* Princeton, N.J.: Princeton University Press, 1996.

Sullivan, Patricia. *Days of Hope: Race and Democracy in the New Deal Era.* Chapel Hill: University of North Carolina Press, 1996.

Teegarden, Carrie. "Is the City a Mecca for African Americans?" *Atlanta Journal-Constitution.* 14 January, 1994.

Thomas, Jesse O. *My Story in Black and White: The Autobiography of Jesse O. Thomas.* New York: Exposition Press, 1967.

Thompson, Robert A., Hylan Lewis, and Davis McEntire. "Atlanta and Birmingham, A Comparative Study in Negro Housing." In *Studies in Housing and Minority Groups* edited by Nathan Glazer and Davis McEntire, 13–83. Berkeley: University of California Press, 1960.

Torras, Raymond. "Atlanta." *Housing Officials' Year Book 1935.* New N.p.: York: National Association of Housing Officials, 1936.

Trotter, Michael M. "America's Public Housing Capital." *Atlanta Journal-Constitution,* 20 April 1997.

Turner, Madrid Boyd. "A Study of One Hundred Skilled Negro Workers at Bell Aircraft Corporation and the Problems Encountered in Adapting to a Peacetime Economy." M.A. thesis, Atlanta University, 1946.

Walkowitz, Daniel J. *Working with Class: Social Workers and the Politics of Middle-Class Identity.* Chapel Hill: University of North Carolina Press, 1999.

Weaver, Robert C. "An Experiment in Negro Labor." *Opportunity* 14 (October 1936): 295–98.

———. *Negro Labor: A National Problem.* New York: Harcourt, Brace and Co., 1946.

Weiss, Nancy J., *Farewell to the Party of Lincoln: Black Politics in the Age of FDR.* Princeton: Princeton University Press, 1983.

White, Dana F. "The Black Sides of Atlanta: A Geography of Expansion and Containment, 1970–1980." *The Atlanta Historical Journal* 26 (Summer–Fall 1982) 199–223.

Pamphlets

Atlanta Negro Chamber of Commerce. "Atlanta—You Ought to Know Your Own!—1937 Directory and Souvenir Program of the National Negro Business League Convention." 1937.

Davis, John P. "Let Us Build a National Negro Congress." October 1935.

"Report of the President for the Academic Year 1937–1938." Atlanta University, 1938.

Unpublished Papers

Dorsey, Alison. "Cemetery as Historical Artifact: Atlanta's South-View Cemetery and the Formation of Community in Black Atlanta." Paper presented at the Black History Workshop, University of Houston, 1998 (in possession of author).

Index